THE NATURAL ORDER AND OTHER TEXTS

In *The Natural Order and Other Texts*, Peter Shield presents the first English translations of the artist Asger Jorn's three philosophical texts - *The Natural Order, Value and Economy* and *Luck and Chance*. Offering a unique insight into an artist's attempt to make sense of a contemporary world which would accommodate his practice, these texts present an important contribution to aesthetics for modern art and an attempt at philosophical reconciliation of modern science and modern art. In 1961 Jorn resigned from the Situationist International and took the ideas of thinkers in many fields and amalgamated them into 'the first complete revision of the existing philosophical system' from the point of view of an artist. He developed a theory of artistic value and the place of the creative elite and adapted his previous ideas of extreme aesthetics to fit into this 'natural order'.

Including a comprehensive introduction, Peter Shield's translations of Asger Jorn's classic texts offer invaluable new perspectives to readers crossing the boundaries of philosophy, art history and theory, and cultural studies. Peter Shield is an art historian, whose book *Comparative Vandalism* on these and other works by Jorn is also published by Ashgate.

Ashgate Translations in Philosophy, Theology and Religion

This series presents the first English language translations of many important contemporary and classic works in philosophy, theology and word religions

Other titles in the series

Philosophy and Revelation
Vittorio Possenti translated by Emanuel L. Paparella

Environmental Ethics and Policy-Making
Mikael Stenmark

The Natural Order and Other Texts

ASGER JORN

Translated by

PETER SHIELD

LONDON AND NEW YORK

First published 2001 by Ashgate Publishing

Published 2016 by Routledge
2 Park Square, Milton Park, Abingdon, Oxon OX14 4RN
711 Third Avenue, New York, NY 10017, USA

Routledge is an imprint of the Taylor & Francis Group, an informa business

Copyright © Original Text and Diagrams: The Asger Jorn Estate, 2001.
Translation: Peter Shield 2002

Published with the aid of grants from Silkeborg Kunstmuseum and Consul George
and Mrs Emma Jorcks' Foundation, Copenhagen, by Ashgate Publishing Limited
in association with Borgens Forlag.

Peter Shield hereby asserts his moral right to be identified as the author of the
Work in accordance with the Copyright, Designs and Patents Act, 1988.

All rights reserved. No part of this book may be reprinted or reproduced or
utilised in any form or by any electronic, mechanical, or other means, now
known or hereafter invented, including photocopying and recording, or in any
information storage or retrieval system, without permission in writing from the
publishers.

Notice:
Product or corporate names may be trademarks or registered trademarks, and are
used only for identification and explanation without intent to infringe.

British Library Cataloguing in Publication Data
Jorn, Asger, 1914-1973
  The natural order and other texts. - (Ashgate translations in philosophy,
  theology and religion)
  1. Jorn, Asger, 1914-1973
  I. Title
  198.9

Library of Congress Cataloging-in-Publication Data
Jorn, Asger, 1914-1973.
  [Selections. English]
  The natural order and other texts / Asger Jorn ; translated by
  Peter Shield.
    p. cm.
  Includes bibliographical references.
  ISBN 0-7546-0429-2
    1. Aesthetics, Modern. 2. Economic policy. 3. Philosophy. I. Title.

  BH221.D44 J6713 2001
  198'.9–dc21

2001041272

ISBN 13: 978-0-7546-0429-7 (hbk)

Contents

Introduction	vii

ASGER JORN: THE NATURAL ORDER AND OTHER TEXTS

The Natural Order	1
[Part 1]	9
Part 2: Expeditions to New Worlds	47
Appendix	114
Value and Economy	117
Part 1: Critique of political economy	121
Part 2: The exploitation of the unique	147
Topical additions	213
Luck and Chance	219
Notes	355

Introduction

A reconstruction of philosophy from the point of view of an artist

International recognition and economic success came to the Danish artist Asger Jorn towards the end of the fifties. Yet in 1961, at the age of 47, he cut down on his artistic activities and began what he called 'the first complete revision of the existing philosophical system'. This was not his first attempt at theoretical work. In the late forties he had spent much time putting together a comprehensive 'organic' theory of art which reconciled his materialist and monist beliefs with his spontaneous, primitive approach to art. Although this work ran to hundreds of pages of manuscript and typescript, the resultant book was not published until 1971. Jorn's polemic with the Swiss architect Max Bill about the resurrection of Bauhaus ideals in the mid-fifties also led to a series of articles collected in the book *Pour la forme* in 1957. Here the main point of contention was whether the craft ideals or those of artists like Klee and Kandinsky had been the *primus motor* of the original movement. Bill's attitude that the artists had only an instrumental role in relation to the main craft purpose of the Bauhaus particularly infuriated Jorn.

Ironically, Jorn entered into the same situation in 1957 when he become a co-founder and strong influence on the Situationniste Internationale (SI) with Guy Debord. Jorn had been attracted to the SI by its attitudes to the increasing sterility of the urban environment and the oppression of political and economic systems. At this early stage, the SI was offering techniques rather than extreme solutions, for example, various aspects of 'play', such as the *dérive*, a purposeless but intense drift through urban situations, and the *détournement*, the subversion of pre-existent aesthetic elements for propaganda purposes. The re-establishment of contact with the newer Parisian currents through Debord, who was 17 years younger, was one of Jorn's initial motives for approaching him. However, Debord could not accept Jorn's belief that the activity of the artist had its own rules and legitimacy which could not be subordinated to the demands of revolutionary theory. After some three years, about the time he usually spent with the groupings he created or joined, Jorn amicably disengaged himself from the SI.

viii The Natural Order and Other Texts

This break with the SI appears to have had two effects. Jorn turned back to some favourite Scandinavian projects and he undertook an audit of the contradictions in his life and evolved a philosophical approach to accommodate them. To provide an organization for both these activities, Jorn founded a Scandinavian Institute for Comparative Vandalism (SISV, from its Danish initials). The various strands of Jorn's life, his upbringing in a strict Protestant sect with its abhorrence of all things Catholic, the liberal Christian Scandinavianism of his years of higher education, a hyper-critical view of the Marxism to which he was initially committed, the action of the national in or against the international, the imperatives of an artistic life, the complications of his relations with women, and many other aspects, are all examined both instinctively and in the light of the incredible amount of theoretical reading Jorn got through in this short period (1961-1964). When the SISV was wound up, his library of some 1,600 books was deposited at the Silkeborg Art Museum, and there one can judge the effect of various thinkers from the amount of marginal notes and underlinings, some almost obliterating the original text.

In 1961 in Paris, Jorn had also been made a member of the College of Pataphysics, a spoof academic organization with elaborate nonsense titles for its members. Pataphysics was invented and defined by Alfred Jarry as 'the science of imaginary solutions'. Jorn, whilst thoroughly enjoying the jokes and anti-establishment pranks, realized that 'an imaginary solution' was also a definition of the art work, and the idea of a 'science' to cover this became incorporated into his thinking.

Jorn's deliberations were published in five paperback 'Reports from the Scandinavian Institute of Comparative Vandalism'. The first volume, *The Natural Order* (1962), merged insights from the Copenhagen Interpretation of the theory of complementarity and Marxian dialectical materialism into what Jorn called triolectics. In the unresolved Heraclitan flux of ideas there is nevertheless structure, a way the human brain naturally organizes thought. Jorn's attempt to uncover this 'natural order' reveals a great philosophical *image:* a chaosmos of radiant triolectic or tri-dialectical conceptual domains bursting from points upon the rays from other domains, and radiating in turn ever outwards from the centre, whilst others, losing brilliance or relevance, shrink back into points. It is a major part of Jorn's thesis that this is a particularly Scandinavian way of thinking. The second volume, *Value and Economy* (1962), utilizes for its first section an earlier critique of Marxian economics that also postulates a category of artistic value, whilst the second part outlines the necessary conditions for a 'creative elite' to take over from the current power elite. *Luck and Chance* from 1953, furnished with a new long

Introduction ix

introduction, places Jorn's ideas about 'extreme aesthetics' in this context. By 1963-64, Jorn had gathered together a large mass of material intended originally to form one more book. This was impracticable because of its size and he abstracted one volume, *Thing and Polis*, from it, dealing mainly with an attempt to define the Danish national culture. This volume is the nearest that Jorn comes to direct Situationist *détournement* in his writing, as 50% of it consists of extended quotations from Danish authors, one of them with the paragraphs drastically rearranged. He then prepared *Alpha and Omega* to proof stage from the rest. This fifth volume dealt mainly with Jorn's highly imaginative creation myth, mixing science and mythology, and a number of miscellaneous subjects. Perhaps because it also reveals his current deep misogyny and a certain exasperation, it was only published posthumously. In 1966, a German translation and revision of *The Natural Order* and *Luck and Chance* in one volume incorporated yet more material without, however, substantially altering or adding to Jorn's thought.

The greatest difficulty with all of Jorn's texts is finding a consistent line, for he was a wilful and willing transgressor of any accepted mode of thinking. He wrote as he thought, darting off into bye-ways, pausing to savour an alliteration or an irony, drawing in analogies and analyses from all sides and quoting sources appositely and arbitrarily in equal measure, before then shooting off in a completely new direction. He lectures his readers on elementary philosophical or scientific points and then leaps without explanation into the most complex speculations about esoteric subjects. He transgresses the boundaries of any discipline, seeing no reason not to use the methods of one upon the material of another. He finds logical analysis and artistic vision equally suited to his purposes and switches from one to another in mid-argument. His method is thus neither that of the scientific enquirer nor of the philosopher but of the thinker-artist. His own position on all this, 'Rather a tangled and chaotic truth than a four-square, beautiful, symmetrical and finely chiselled lie', could just as well have been applied to his approach to painting.

Why did Jorn take all this trouble to develop these theories? He himself states that they are a kind of catharsis so that he could get on with his artistic work. However, there is a strong didactic tone in much of the theorizing, and an exasperation about the lack of response, which suggests that it was as much directed externally as internally. Perhaps it was therefore an overarching project, an imaginary solution even, an attempt to create a world in which his works of art and, indeed, his life as an artist would be part of the natural order.

The Translations

To make no bones about it, Jorn is difficult to translate. The circuitous trips through his subject matter make for extraordinarily complicated sentences with many sub-clauses, in which, as he rarely revised, he occasionally loses his way. When he did revise, this more often complicated than it simplified matters. In embarking on critiques of other writers, he often adopts their manner and it is often hard to know whether he is quoting, paraphrasing or imitating. That the work of some of these writers is not in Danish sometimes gives his Danish a strange flavour which is already complicated by his use of both vernacular expressions and the classical Danish of his beloved 19th century Danish authors. In *The Natural Order*, for instance, he uses Heisenberg's manner not from the German original but from an English translation which he then transmutes to Danish. However, these strange texts are themselves a part of Jorn's attempt to come to terms with a Scandinavian culture at odds with but yet one strand of a European culture. I have therefore regarded them as works of art rather than straightforward exegeses in a single language or style and have tried to find as many equivalent voices as possible. That this produces certain awkwardnesses is undeniable. This is also true of the originals, which have been unfairly dismissed by some Scandinavian commentators otherwise sympathetic to Jorn's project as almost unreadable.

Although I have tried, it would have been impossible to find English equivalents for all these many manners. The feeling of (mis)appropriation or Situationist *détournement* and *dérive* is thus diminished to some extent, but a certain relative clarity is gained. I have kept notes to a minimum, dealing mainly with Scandinavian issues and personalities that may be unknown to non-Nordic readers and with personal associations in Jorn's life. Wherever possible, the editions of Jorn's sources quoted are those he is known to have used. However, Jorn deliberately omitted notes or bibliographies, and even a table of contents, and I have followed his example.

Only the first three Reports have been translated here. Of the two other reports, *Thing and Polis* is expressly directed at a Danish audience, and *Alpha and Omega* shows signs that Jorn's enthusiasm was running out. However, although there is much of interest in the two later texts, the meat of Jorn's arguments is in *The Natural Order, Value and Economy,* and *Luck and Chance.*

I am extremely grateful to Troels Andersen for his thorough reading of the typescripts of my translations and the many consequent suggestions for improvement.

Introduction xi

The Natural Order

Here Jorn proposes a marriage between Marxian dialectics and the wider philosophical implications of the theory of complementarity. He approaches this through a not always apparent critique of a popular English science book by Werner Heisenberg, in language that apes him to the extent that it is difficult to know whether we have Heisenberg in translation, paraphrase or Jorn's own exegesis. For the explicitly quoted passages, I have used and acknowledged the original English text (see notes).

As almost always with Jorn, the text gives the impression of having been written at great speed, with a fair amount of redundancy and overuse of particular words. My approach here has been that of a cautious copy-editor. As Danish is less rich in synonyms than English, I have used these more and thus cut down on the overuse, and I have translated the more florid '19th century' passages, which would have seemed mannered in a literal translation, into a more modern but rather academic English. Where the text is repetitious or burdened with redundancy, I have pursued meaning rather than style.

I have omitted the final chapter of *The Natural Order* (a rehash of the final chapter to the 1953 edition of *Luck and Chance*), which is mainly a critique of President Eisenhower's 1951 invitation to worldwide educational institutions to participate 'in an international investigation of the conditions for freedom of research and speech'. It adds nothing to Jorn's philosophical arguments and he omitted much of it in the 1966 German revision. The reasons for the omission of three other shorter passages can be found in the notes.

I have also added, in an appendix, some diagrams from a slighter later work which elaborate the graphic representation of the triolectic concept. Jorn also used some of them in the 1966 edited German translation of *The Natural Order* in *Gedanken eines Künstlers*.

Except for those in the appendix, all the diagrams are facsimiles of Jorn's originals.

The Natural Order was dedicated to Jorn's son Ole.

Value and Economy

This book consists of two unequal parts. The first is a concise critique of apparent contradictions in *Das Kapital* which Jorn uses to prepare the ground for a discussion of how the work of 'the creative elite' can have 'value' in any future society aligned on communist principles. This was originally published in French by the Situationniste Internationale in 1959 and is the most

xii *The Natural Order and Other Texts*

straightforward and least discursive of all Jorn's texts, probably because Guy Debord had a hand in the editing. It may therefore seem a little perverse to translate the later Danish version to English, but Jorn, in his usual manner, intervened again and made small adjustments and additions and added a new final chapter, which aligned it to the second part.

Part 2 is three times as long and goes through a long polemic against contemporaneous Russian revisionism and the failed attempt by Denmark and Britain to join the Common Market, before coming to Jorn's main proposal, an economically independent international 'creative elite' adopting typical Scandinavian institutions to realize 'artistic value' for the greater universal good. He also attempts to reconcile the unique and individual position of the 'creative elite' with his socialist principles. Here, the asides from the point of view of 'one' or 'we', when Jorn is discussing 'the intelligentsia' or 'the creative elite', seem to be unconscious switches between objective and subjective modes. In contrast to the first part, this section appears to have been written hastily and rushed into print. Rather than make a polished translation here, I have attempted to reproduce the awkward immediacy of the original.

Luck and Chance

The first edition of *Luck and Chance* was Jorn's first published book, issued privately to subscribers in 1952. It was written during his convalescence from a serious attack of tuberculosis aggravated by malnutrition and scurvy, as his encounter with the possibility of death spurred him to a reckoning with his aesthetic ideas. Later in the process, it also became intended as a doctoral dissertation. As the reader will discover, this was doomed from the start, as the text is anything but academically oriented. Nevertheless, the professor of philosophy at Copenhagen University, Bent Schultzer, received it sympathetically and with some insight. 'The book is well-written and witness to talent. Note, however, that I am using a word which it is more reasonable to use in the characterization of a work of art than in the evaluation of scientific work. You seem to me to be an artist, a splendid artist, but are you a scientist? You answer this question yourself on p. 93 of part 2 and I am afraid that I have to agree with your answer. The strength and weakness of the book is precisely that you are completely unfamiliar with (or disregard) scientific method.'* However, he was willing to forward it to the philosophy faculty if Jorn so wished, but after a friendly exchange of letters, this project was dropped.

There is an inclination towards thinking in triads, though nothing like as systematic as a decade later. Therefore, when he re-issued *Luck and Chance* as the third of his SISV reports, Jorn added a substantial new introduction and several small insertions, clearly marked in the text, but left the original text untouched, except to omit the final chapter. The introduction reconciles the discussion of extreme aesthetics in the book to an aesthetic triolectic of the beautiful, the sublime, the extreme.

During his convalescence at Silkeborg Sanatorium, Jorn had read extensively, particularly in Kierkegaard, and *Luck and Chance* is, amongst other things, a critique of this philosopher's triad of aesthetic, ethical and religious stages, and of his definition of truth. Another powerful influence appears to be present in ghostly form, for Jorn hardly mentions him. Nietzschean ideas are treated with distaste throughout the book, although the frequent passage in italics, the word-play and the exclamatory tone of some parts demonstrate a certain emulation, as do the descriptions of national characteristics (French, German, English), which are reminiscent of parts of *Beyond Good and Evil*. Perhaps the biggest gift of Kierkegaard and Nietzsche to Jorn was, however, the perception that a philosophy could be founded on aesthetic premises.

The person pursuing such a philosophy is the *æstetiker*, which can mean both aesthetician or aesthete. In common with most modern translators of Kierkegaard, I have used the former as being most appropriate to Jorn's thought process.

Although tempted to translate all the chapter-head epigraphs chosen by Jorn, I have followed his own not always consistent procedure of leaving most of the non-Scandinavian quotations in the original language. Where Jorn used a Danish translation of English sources, I have used the original. It has, however, not always been possible to locate all the short translated passages from other languages, and I have thus been forced to translate from Jorn's Danish versions. I also suspect that some of the epigraphs were taken from a book of quotations, but have searched the contemporaneous archives of Silkeborg Library in vain for this. Some of the unattributed aphorisms could be by Jorn himself, others are fairly well-known folk sayings.

Luck and Chance was dedicated to Jorn's daughter Susanne.

xiv   The Natural Order and Other Texts

Bibliography

There are two full Danish biographies of Jorn. Troels Andersen gives a sober assessment of the life in relation to the work, relying heavily upon the documentation in the Jorn archives at Silkeborg Art Museum. Ulla Andersen's more popular work reveals the racier aspects of Jorn's life, but is weak on the art historical and theoretic side. Guy Atkins's oeuvre catalogue is extremely thorough and includes biographical fragments of those aspects of his life Jorn chose to present to his English friend.

Guy Atkins, with the help of Troels Andersen, *Asger Jorn, 1: Jorn in Scandinavia,* London, Lund Humphries, 1968, *2: The crucial years 1954-1964,* London, Lund Humphries, 1977, *3: The final years 1965-1973,* Copenhagen, Borgen,1980, *4: Supplement, Paintings 1930-73,* London, Lund Humphries, 1986, *5: Recent Discoveries,* article in *CRAS* (Silkeborg), LXII, 1992, 73-89.

Troels Andersen, *Asger Jorn. En biografi, 1: Årene 1914-53,* Copenhagen, Borgen,1997, *2: Årene 1953-73,* Copenhagen, Borgen, 1998.

Ulla Andersen, *Buttadeo. En biografi om Asger Jorn,* Copenhagen, L & R. Fakta, 1998.

There are two large-scale studies of Jorn's art theories and philosophies. Graham Birtwistle trawled through many unpublished manuscripts to build up his perceptive picture of Jorn's thinking in the period 1946-1949. After the detailed work on the translations in this series, I am rather dissatisfied with parts of my own study of the theories of 1961-67, not least my curt treatment of Jorn's relationship with the SI, but the main thrust still seems to me to be sound and I therefore offer it, in the absence of other commentaries, as a guide to the development and extent of this period of Jorn's thinking.

Graham Birtwistle, *Living Art. Asger Jorn's comprehensive theory of art between Helhesten and Cobra (1946-1949),* Utrecht, Reflex, 1986.

Peter Shield, *Comparative Vandalism. Asger Jorn and the artistic attitude to life,* Aldershot, Ashgate/Copenhagen, Borgen, 1998.

The exhaustive and accurate bibliography of Jorn's published writings by the experienced librarian Per Hofman Hansen lists all works up to 1986, i.e. over a decade after Jorn's death. So much more material has been published that a supplementary bibliography is now badly needed.

Per Hofman Hansen, *Bibliografi over Asger Jorns skrifter/A bibliography of Asger Jorn's writings,* Silkeborg, Silkeborg Kunstmuseum, 1988.

ASGER JORN

THE NATURAL ORDER
De Divisione Naturae

THE SILKEBORG INTERPRETATION
versus
THE COPENHAGEN INTERPRETATION

Report no. 1 of the Scandinavian Institute of Comparative Vandalism, 1962

To Ole

Those who think otherwise

This is an attempt to create in Scandinavia a tolerance for those who think otherwise, through a deeper understanding of the preconditions for thought processes. This understanding has nothing to do with condonation. Real tolerance consists of being able to tolerate something other than one's own ideas without being knocked off course, and is a sign of superiority and strength. To be tolerant is to be comprehensive, to have the greatest evolution, and this evolution can be described as progress if it lifts understanding to a stage where earlier conflicts are dissolved.

Such a new stage was achieved with Hegel's philosophical system, which Karl Marx then turned on its head and which in this further new form reigns over the largest part of human thought processes today. This dialectical materialism is showing itself to suffer from exactly the same shortcomings as Hegelian metaphysics, only in a negative form. There is no place for such an important problem as the existential. The critique which emanated from Søren Kierkegaard has, through Sartre, taken on the same materialistic direction as Marxism, but has shown itself to be incompatible with it. A far more searching revision of the whole of philosophy has become necessary. This is what I have attempted here.

Hegel took over from Proclus the triadic image of the circle as the sum of centre, radii or rays and periphery. In *Die mathematische Denkweise*, the Swiss mathematician Andreas Speiser identified the centre with philosophy, radiation with mathematics and art with the restraining, periphery-creating activity which achieves its beauty by turning back to the centre. In my book *Golden Horn and Wheel of Fortune* I attempted to maintain this encompassing perception of art as it also logically corresponds to the perception of dialectical materialism.[*] However, inspired by discussions with Christian Dotremont during my stay at Silkeborg Sanatorium after the collapse of the Cobra movement,[*] I arrived at the interesting result that it was impossible to identify the aesthetic with anything but the radiant or radiating principle. In this book I demonstrate that radii cannot be inscribed in a circle without losing their character of radii. With this, the circle is broken and what is more remarkable, the point takes on dimension, as each circle can be perceived as just a point under certain circumstances of observation. At the same time, the encompassing, peripheric movement becomes identical with perpetual motion. I call this complementary tripartition triolectics. It permits the setting up of three complementary dialectical systems. With this the traditional theory of decadence is exploded,

4   The Natural Order and Other Texts

as one form of dynamism automatically paralyses the second and the third. This knowledge permits the abolition of the traditional blind European conflict between ways of thought by the establishment of a fruitful interplay between the three dialectical processes. This has been said and made public so that no responsible persons will be able to say that they did not know what they were in for.

If this is a critique of Niels Bohr's theory of complementarity, then it is also to just the same high degree a critique of that dialectical materialism, that I in my earliest youth took to my heart and perceived to be the only acceptable principle for thought. Archimedes maintained that he only needed a single point outside the world in order to be able to move it. My interest in Niels Bohr's theory of complementarity consisted of my finding there that point from which I could begin to manoeuvre around dialectical materialism and investigate it from new points of view. The first result of these investigations was my Critique of economic policy, *which is a critique of the 'critique of political economy' Karl Marx set out in* Das Kapital. *My points of view in this critique are even further from the capitalistic perception of economics than the perception Karl Marx worked out on the basis of his critique of the capitalist system. They are a critique of the present socialist system.*

Although I am criticizing socialist economic doctrine, I nevertheless accept its scientific foundation as a working out of an economic equivalent for the social value of industrial production, expressed in the unit of measurement of one hour's productive work in industry. *At the same time, I accept that this conclusion only has validity if one accepts that* every person has the right to everything he himself produces, *which is the foundation of the theory of exploitation upon which the whole Marxist analysis is based. The conflict which occurs today between state socialism and free communism is concentrated around this point of how far a person should voluntarily relinquish this right to society or maintain it. Should he accept this surrender and thereby determine that his successors in the future should all live without this right? At any rate, I personally have never found an acceptable argument for giving up this right, which will really reduce Marxism to a worn-out shoe that can be thrown away. Instead it seems to me enormously interesting to take this theory further in accordance with these basic principles and construct the scientific side of this theory of equivalence so that it also is given a logical validity for spiritual and artistic values, an area which was not topical to the working-class in the last century, but which today appears to be the focus of all economic considerations.*

As I had been able to utilize the theory of complementarity to move my world, in this way, then naturally I also found it interesting to see if one could do the opposite and perceive this theory as a world in itself and dialectical materialism as a point. That was my idea with this work, but the result has been something different. I am firing off guns to both sides and at the same time attempting to combine the two principles into one. Whether I am successful or not, I will let others decide.

6   The Natural Order and Other Texts

The systematized is the unartistic, and general systemization is the determination of the possibilities in a principle. This is the reason why an artist is finished as a creative factor just as soon as he has established his principles and is finished as a social topic of interest as soon as he has published the principles by which his output is then explained. My situation is this: either what I have found here is complete nonsense, in which case I preserve my artistic success intact, or the systemization is tenable, in which case I have to reckon with failing artistic popularity. When one considers that I love art and hate principles, one has to say that such a philosophical success would cost me dear, even though I have the same attitude to popularity as Fröding.* A philosophical success would for me be the most painful and ridiculous thing I could achieve. That I have attacked this philosophical problem at all is not therefore to be right, but in the conviction that all future possibilities for artistic development are conditioned by the desire to prevent there no longer being a place in modern society for artistic thought and thus to defend of my own way of thinking. As I myself have got over the dead point I have just described, I know well that it would have been more artistic to resign myself with the thought 'after me the deluge'. I would have done this if I had been able to free myself from the thought that I am myself in the middle of it. Neither economic nor social success, which are in reality the same thing, would have been able to change this feeling. Therefore (let us now be honest), this is perhaps *why I wanted to risk all, unless I am an incurable gambler, and that is also a way to manifest oneself as an artist.*

I think I have made sure of one thing – that the stakes are as high as they could be. In my book Luck and Chance, *I undertook a complementary tripartition of aesthetics into inventive, nuanced and formative aesthetics and demonstrated that renewal in Europe, Europe's beauty, in the last couple of centuries has been the result of a complementary collaboration between German invention, French initiative and English application. The neutralization of this dynamic was the synthesis that Karl Marx extracted from* German philosophy, French revolutionary socialist programmes and English economics *and called dialectical materialism. If I feel that I have gone beyond this combination, it was initially by making it clear to myself that the French perceive this dialectical materialism as an aesthetic, a programme for the future. Sartre is the most brilliant example of this attitude. The Russians perceive it as a science, whilst in the Germanic countries, this same socialism is perceived as an ethic, something real and present. The result has been that the Nordic countries began to have social policies as soon as this socialist theory appeared. This reformism has been strongly attacked by the Soviet*

Socialist Republics' camp, but there is no fundamental difference at all to be found between this principle and the assertion that international socialism can be introduced into a country and from there spread all over the world. This is also reformism. There is just a difference of dimension. One reckons with individuals, the other with nations. I have indicated the historical foundation for this meaningless difference in the following text. It is scientifically and in principle meaningless, which is to say that both in different ways come to the same result; not humanly meaningless during *the process, only* after *it.*

There is a difference in writing off one's further artistic development and putting it at risk, for in a gamble there has to be a certain minimal chance of winning. This chance is magnified, the greater the art one possesses.

The gamble I am taking is about how far it is possible to undertake the first complete revision of the present philosophical system, a revision that breaks definitively with that level which German philosophy established with Hegel's dialectic and about which philosophy has manoeuvred ever since, whether for or against. If I have lost this gamble, then I have thus rewon my artistic freedom, but what have I gained if I win? This can only be evaluated in relation to my effort, and, as this is not my art and my individuality, it must thus be what I am stuck in, Scandinavian culture. I have staked Scandinavian culture and in this affair therefore become neither loser nor winner on my own.

Albisola, September 1961

[Part 1]

The law of contradistinction

Under the name of the Copenhagen Interpretation, Niels Bohr's theory of complementarity has gradually attracted notice the world over and day by day is penetrating more and more to the centre of the complex of problems around modern thought.

This preoccupation with the theory of complementarity is so unavoidable not on scientific but on philosophical grounds, in as much as it appears to be a new philosophical principle which, to put it mildly, is like a bull in a china shop in relation to the philosophical tradition. Really it is something far more dangerous. It is a new factor that either dissolves the possibilities or demands completely new rules of the game, because the theory of complementarity appears to be a law supported by scientific experience.

The first reaction has been attempts to repudiate the scientific character and the consequent well-knit legitimacies of the hypothesis. Since the probability of getting around the problem in this way gradually appears to have diminished, a growing mood of panic has begun to spread in philosophical circles, a panic already latent during the whole modern development of science, where philosophy or the so-called humanities have been on retreat across the board. Today philosophy has shrunk to being the branch of scholarship about the history of philosophy. At a time when the perception of philosophy as a creative activity is about to be given up and where a new ahistorical form of existence is being prepared, where humanity's historical and philosophical periods have been brought to a close, Bohr's theory appears to be the first sketch for a completely new scientific philosophy, independent of everything which has hitherto been united under the name of philosophy.

If the foundation of science is the equation, that is, comparisons of uniform dimensions or quantities, and thus above all a *doctrine of resemblance*, a doctrine of symmetry, then *the doctrine of unity* can be characterized as central to philosophy, the doctrine of the unity or correlation of things, thoughts and incidents, of their adherence to rules. One could therefore correctly maintain that any *legal* conclusion is in itself unscientific, and is a piece of philosophy even if it rests upon scientific analyses.

10   *The Natural Order and Other Texts*

Law means correlation and what creates panic in philosophy is that Bohr's law is the law of the lack of correlation, a law of incompatibility, a law of *separation*, an anti-law law or, if you will, an anti-philosophical principle with philosophical consequences, and thus a new unity of opposites, a doctrine of dissymmetry.

The philosophical consequences of the Copenhagen Interpretation are as follows: either one must accept that it is no longer possible to establish a valid philosophy or one must accept the necessity of *the simultaneous presence of several complementary or mutually incompatible but equally valid philosophical systems*, principles or tendencies.

Only the latter conclusion gives philosophy new possibilities for existence. However, if one wishes to go this way on the basis of Bohr's principle, it soon becomes apparent that it leads nowhere. If one nevertheless wishes to go this way, then it can only happen by a critique of the Copenhagen Interpretation, but as the foundation of this is scientific, a purely philosophical critique can conclude nothing at all. It can only postulate certain lacks, an incompleteness, which must be logical as well as purely experiential. Niels Bohr himself and his collaborators must either clearly prove the incorrectness of the critique and the impossibility of changing or extending the Interpretation in these realms of experience, or they must also realize the possibility of such a change. The concrete demand I pose here is colossal. It is *the demand for a third interpretation of the character of light completely independent of the wave theory as well as the particle theory*, and thus a third complementary theory of light, a theory of the plastic form of light.

When I associate myself with the necessity of the development of such third theory of light, I have two reasons, a logical one which rests on the assertion that *any complementary relationship must always be at least triple* and can never be established in a purely duple system. In any two descriptions of a phenomenon, for the description to be sufficient or complete a third necessary description is always ignored, which is only to say that the three descriptions form a unit and thus become philosophically accessible. The other reason is founded purely upon my experiences of light and colour, acquired as a painter, even though I base my opinions on the investigation made by the South Jutland painter Philipp Otto Runge around 1800 and reworked by Goethe in his theory of colour.*

Goethe's demonstration that there are concrete optical characteristics in the essence of light and colour which do not form part of the descriptions of light postulated up to that time (Newton) are, in my opinion, valid to this day with regard to both the wave theory and the particle theory. I hope to be able to demonstrate that such a concrete material exists, demanding its own separate description, without again committing Goethe's error of refuting the correctness of a scientific systemization on an amateur basis. But if a new doctrine of form which could replace the Renaissance's descriptions of form is to have general and scientific validity, I am in agreement with Goethe that it must begin with a description of *the form of light*. In the following text I hope to be able to indicate this possibility without driving up all too many of the blind alleys of the speculative method.

The Copenhagen Interpretation. The Silkeborg Interpretation

Is it by chance that Bohr's theory is called the Copenhagen Interpretation? Is it by chance that it was postulated in Copenhagen or does it have natural roots in the Scandinavian mentality or pattern of thought? I am posing this quite absurd question because such a causal context will in the future automatically form part of the reflections on the problem of complementarity the world over simply because of the name on the label. The question is then whether one can imagine and construct such a Scandinavian principle of unity. If one can, this means that a specific Scandinavian philosophy exists, something no one had imagined before, and that one can talk of Scandinavian philosophy in the same way that one talks about Greek, German, French, English etc. philosophy. Is there a common denominator to, or a more profound connection between, for example, Søren Kierkegaard's situation philosophy and Swedenborg's fundamental principles, to take two of the North's thinkers whose teaching has had a fundamental significance for modern culture? Is this common denominator also valid for Tycho Brahe and can it also include Niels Bohr's philosophical viewpoint?

It has been shown to the point of triviality how analytical mathematics and geometry has its starting point in Euclid's geometry and in Greek logic, and that all this development is a result of the mentality and life pattern which developed in and with the Greek *polis*. No one disputes the logic and the experience of this development from this particular and clearly defined environment.

Can the same method be used for a Nordic development where the environment is ill-defined and imprecise and the aversion to unity appears to be inborn? To make the question concrete – is there a connection between Existentialism and Bohr's theory of complementarity? The answer must immediately be a clear no, as every attempt to combine Bohr's thesis with any

12   The Natural Order and Other Texts

already existent philosophical principle at all has led to a hopeless self-contradiction.

The only logical consequence must be that an inductive method cannot be created on the basis of the Copenhagen Interpretation, and, if this is accepted, then the inductive method is completely bankrupt. Several scientists have already taken the consequences of this attitude and agreed that it is no longer possible to form a model or a picture of the modern *Weltanschauung*. We do not at this moment wish to discuss the rights or wrongs of this postulate. We only want to draw attention to a simple fact and an unavoidable consequence in connection with this principle. From this perception, one can no longer allow oneself to talk about a 'an image of the world' or about 'images' on the whole, as according to this postulate they have no scientific relevance. If one then represents this bankruptcy as the 'new scientific image of the world', this can only be stamped as a swindle and a deceit. One could just as well call the lack of an image an image as call a world which no longer exists, which no longer possesses the context that could justify the label 'world', a world.

Every *image* is an *illusion* and thus exists in a complementary relationship to reality. The picture and the world have always been two complementary areas. Even a geometrical figure is an image, a picture, a work of art, a pure illusion, and scientists can no more suspect what humanity will be able to imagine in the future than can tram conductors or customs officers. The only thing scientists can establish today is that it is not possible to undertake a description of the most recent scientific experiences upon the basis of the classical form of description or even upon the basis of forms of description which have developed on a completely new foundation, apparently independently of the classical form of description. That is all.

It is here that the Copenhagen Interpretation begins by setting up an absolutely unforgivable taboo, a completely irrational prohibition, which Werner Heisenberg expresses in this way:

'The concepts of classical physics form the language by which we describe the arrangements of our experiments and state the results. We cannot and *should not* replace these concepts by any others... We must keep in mind this limited range of applicability of the classical concepts while using them, but *we cannot and should not try to improve them.*'[*]

Only on the basis of this stupid sanctification of the classical interpretation of the concepts of elementary physics and geometry does the conclusion automatically follow that the new physics is indescribable because *the descriptive form* is laid down. The prohibition against meddling with the elementary descriptive forms thus really becomes a prohibition against making

The Natural Order 13

a completely new elementary basis of description, a new pictorial form. By the maintenance of this prohibition, the Copenhagen Interpretation blocks the way it has itself scientifically opened up.

Here we turn back to the question I asked myself at the beginning of this section. Can an elementary philosophical basis as clear and simple as the classical one and with its roots in Scandinavian thought processes be found? Is it possible, for example, to describe the relationship between the dimensions in a quite different but just as simple way as Euclid's discursive account? Perhaps this is an idea that only my own personal imagination could reconcile, a vision I myself have discovered and of which only I can enjoy the fruits. But I have much pleasure in imagining a connection between Ole Rømer's statement of the constant called the speed of light, the characteristically right-angled clash which H.C. Ørsted demonstrated existed between electrical and magnetic poles and then Niels Bohr's demonstration of the constant he called the *quantum*.* What do we know about *forms* today, other than that they are constants? What difference is there between spatial *statics* and other forms of constants? It amuses me to imagine a world where topology or the so-called *analysis situ* is united with Kierkegaard's situation philosophy and this again with a plastic world picture which includes and explains all the elements of nature in a unity of time and space in unceasing transformation, where the constants are only metamorphoses.

As I, in order to satisfy such an irrational desire for logic on the basis of such extravagant wishes, am forced into criticizing the Copenhagen Interpretation, I have decided that I will modestly make do with calling my perception, which is above all a kind of corroboration of the Copenhagen Interpretation, the Silkeborg Interpretation.

The rules of the game

Against the postulation of Bohr and Heisenberg, I set the following statement of the scientist C.D. Darlington, quoted by John Dewey in his book *Reconstruction in Philosophy*, 'Scientific discovery is often carelessly looked upon as the creation of some new knowledge which can be added to the great body of old knowledge. This is true of the strictly trivial discoveries. It is not true of the fundamental discoveries, such as those of the laws of mechanics, of chemical combinations, of evolution on which scientific advance ultimately depends. *These always entail the destruction or disintegration of old knowledge before the new can be created.*'*

14 *The Natural Order and Other Texts*

Niels Bohr has done neither one thing nor the other. He has done a third thing, created a both-and. This solution may perhaps be of interim value because the problem is thereby pushed to one side and given time to mature, but it can never be a definitive solution. It is nothing other than an agreement to ignore a set of crucial problems which are gradually forcing themselves more and more upon the attention.

Einstein based his statements upon the classical definition of the concept of *the experiment* as an experience that could be expressed, communicated and understood. Bohr's scientific experiences went against Einstein's rational perception to the degree that Einstein felt himself forced to come out with the purely sentimental-religious argument that God did not play dice. However, with these new experiences the *concept of play* is irrevocably introduced into natural science. Interestingly enough, at precisely the same time Johan Huizinga was demonstrating on a purely humanistic basis the fundamental significance of play to human cultural life with the book *Homo Ludens*. At the turn of the century, the Norwegian-American author Thorstein Veblen had demonstrated with great irony that play is the foundation of every system of social hierarchy in his book *The Theory of the Leisure Class.*★

The consequences of the opposition between the ideas of Einstein and Bohr will not, to my mind, be fathomed before the basic concepts of classical physics and mathematics have been interpreted in a new way which makes it possible either to discard them completely or to integrate them into a new context with the world that opens up with the new physical experiences. Incidentally, the Copenhagen Interpretation, with its taboo, has been completely unable to stem the semantic disintegration taking place everywhere, something which is so obvious that even an old politician like Stalin was clear that something was wrong. The classical world picture belongs with the classical form of language and will vanish with it.

Thoughts, words and actions

Why do the Latin peoples think and express themselves far more rapidly and more precisely than others, and why do Englishmen only listen to a man who finds it difficult to express himself and whose thoughts move forwards with a boring long-windedness?★ Because the Latin peoples think exactly as they speak and because the starting point of their thoughts is *the word*. From a Latin or classical perception there exist no thoughts for which there are no words, as each thought has in a subtle way arisen *as words*. The characteristic of a

The Natural Order   15

thought is that it can be expressed. That it can be expressed is to say that it can be understood by others, that it is a *social reality*, and, as language is an accepted fellowship, that only communicated thoughts exist. Only *the socialized* thought exists in the Latin perception as thought, because only that thought which is expressed so that it is understood by others exists. However, this is not a definition of the activity of thought itself at all, but only of socialized thinking. From this it must be logically concluded that in the classical meaning no individual thinking exists. Therefore in the classical cultures each new word, each new concept, is a direct attack on the social unity of society itself, based as this is precisely upon the absolute meaning and context of concepts. This explains why Socrates and all creative Greek philosophers were 'enemies of society' because of their new ideas.

Any identification between thought and expression, their union in what we call a *concept*, is the standardization or rationalization of thought, the abolition of its variability as far as meaning is concerned. A concept can only have *one* meaning if it is to be understood, so that it can thus enter into intellectual communication, intellectual fellowship in dialogue. Therefore the identification of thought with word is nothing other than the standardization of thought, the maintenance of one uniquely permitted way of thought, of a particular set of meanings. He who does not follow these rules of the game, or at least allows it to appear that he does not, is simply not taken into account. He does not exist. The advantage of this systemization is that it gives a swift and very clear process of thought and expression and that the rules of this game can be learned by anyone who has sufficient aptitude. This is called *classical education*. However, it also prevents anyone who knows the combinatory possibilities of all the expressions (which is invariably the case as, after centuries of philosophizing, all the possibilities of the game have been revealed) having the possibility of setting out one single original thought, one single new idea, on the basis of the conceptual system. If one demands such a creative originality, then one has to begin to play with the concepts themselves.

If one says to a man, you are a hero, whilst at the same time thinking that he is a prat, then one is apparently thinking the opposite of what one is saying. In reality, one *means* the opposite of what one is saying, for it is not easy to explain what one has said as anything other than the expression of a thought, which thus must have had a reason, an *ulterior thought*, which is not the thought that the man is a prat, but that *it is advantageous to say something else*. One can thus think one's own thoughts without saying anything, or even whilst simultaneously saying a third thing. It is maintained that one can only think in words, but it is difficult to say how words and thoughts are connected. One can easily read a text aloud without hitting upon a single thought that is expressed in the text, just as one can act without thinking about what one is doing, or think without putting one's thoughts into action. It is this powerful play of possibilities which represents the individual creator and separates his being from all others. In order to orchestrate people in a social harmony, it is necessary to agree mutually, at least, to give up one or more of these characteristics. The more characteristics that are given up, the more the human being's individuality is abolished. Such a socialization of humanity produces different cultural types according to which individual characteristics have to be renounced in order to have the right to be a member of the society. Seen in this perspective, Scandinavian socialization appears to be based upon the socialization of *the thought*, Latin socialization upon the socialization of *the word* and that of the Slavs upon the socialization of *the action*. By socialization should be understood that which all the members of the society are theoretically agreed upon and perceive as common property.

The possible and the actual

One cannot answer anything that cannot be posed as a question, but it is surprising how much one cannot express in a concrete question. All posed questions are simply conditioned by the words we have available to form questions: *what, where, whom, how, why, when*. All of these questions can be starting points for a philosophical principle and can be interpreted in various ways, but the question still remains the same. The starting point is still the same. If, as far as elementary physics is concerned, one thus retains these classical interpretations, then these concepts *are not an isolated area peripheral to the conceptual area of modern physics but its foundation.*

The most hotly discussed concept today, which sooner or later will demand an unequivocal solution, is the interpretation of the concept of *actuality*. What is the Copenhagen Interpretation of *the actual*? There the actual is placed in opposition to the *possible* and it is stressed that the transformation from the possible to the actual takes place with a leap. What then is the possible according to the theory of relativity? The possible can be arranged in two opposing groups of possibilities. One is called *the past*, which contains all the events we know (at least in principle) and about which we have been able to hear (in principle). In the same way, we postulate by the concept of 'future' all events we could influence (in principle) and which we could attempt to change or prevent (in principle). In classical theory one postulates the future and the past as separated by an infinitesimally short interval of time we call now, *the present*, or the instant. In the theory of relativity we have come to understood that this is not so. Future and past are separated by an interval of time which exists, the length of which is dependent upon *the distance between the observed phenomenon and the observer.*

At any given point in time, the observer can find himself unable to recognize and influence a phenomenon taking place at a distant point in the period separating two clearly specified moments. One of these is the moment when a light signal has to be triggered at the point of the event in order to reach the observer at the instant of observation. The other is the instant when a light signal sent by the observer at the instant of observation reaches the place of the event.*

All events which take place between these two specific times can be called 'simultaneous' or *contemporaneous*, actual or timeless. *As past and future according to the Copenhagen Interpretation are the possible, thus the present must be the actual.* Here, without knowing it, the Copenhagen Interpretation is completely in agreement with dialectical materialism. There is just the difference that *dialectical materialism asserts that everything is simultaneous or actual and that the actual is the same as the objective*, whilst the objective in reality, like all experience, belongs to the past. That *the positivists identify actuality with future*, and therefore have to give the observer (the influencer) an unequivocal role in the process, is another error, which Niels Bohr attempts to avoid by simply cutting out the observer as an influencing element, to make him one with the conditions of the observations, with the instrument, without however managing to free himself from positivism.

The Marxist perception that everything is actuality was already formulated by Engels in the perception that *everything is process*. This perception was made even more precise by Lenin in his definition of *matter as that which is given to us by our senses*. As we cannot sense latent energy, only kinetic energy, this is really to say that this is *a statement that all energy is kinetic*, that mass and energy are the same. In Marxist terminology, drawing attention to the contrast between latent and kinetic energy is called formalism, which one could well say is correct. But as an object is just a formal thing or a form, this dialectical materialism works completely without objects.

The misunderstanding of the Copenhagen Interpretation is to drag around with it the classical identification of object and actuality instead of using the two concepts as opposites and acknowledging that three and not two complementary elements exist, namely the objective, the actual and the subjective or, to put it another way, *object, instrument and observer*. What in reality both dialectical materialism and the Copenhagen Interpretation are agreed upon is that *instrument and actuality are the same*. To instrumentate or to set up an experimental condition is really nothing other than to combine a simultaneity or contemporaneity.

Not long ago, Niels Bohr warned against wanting to define more precisely the dividing line between object and subject, as the mobility of this dividing line appears to advance development. The instrumental and the technical are the same and it is in reality 'actuality' that thrusts itself between object and subject, between past and future, between knowledge and influence. Hegel had already observed this strange development, which he called '*Entfremdung*', and which Marxists maintain is 'a capitalist fault that will vanish with the transition to socialism'.

I myself am of the opinion that it is immensely important to demarcate the scientific from the technical and the technical from the subjective or human, if we are not to run into the crazy catastrophe, of which this conscious blindness had led us to the edge. To clarify and define their relationship to technique is the one and only responsibility scientists have today, and this they fulfil in order not to be the ones with the prime responsibility.

Work demands an instrument, a tool. To look demands, if not a microscope, a telescope or a set of spectacles, then at any rate a pair of eyes to look with. But that which one has to look *with*, one cannot at the same time look *at*. I have the impression that it is this context that Bohr calls complementarity. Movement is the instrument with which one ascertains positions and positions are the instrument with which one ascertains movement. At any rate, to move or change something one must have the Archimedean point outside of that which is to be moved.

Interest, instrument and object

The critique of the complementarity principle propounded here is a purely artistic critique, a critique of the Copenhagen Interpretation as a work of art. In common with dialectical materialism, this way of looking at it situates *the subjective or interest* as the foundation for any observation.. Without interest, no attention. This attention can be compelled by other interests or be a pure and voluntary personal curiosity. From this attitude one can differentiate purely artistically between three forms of interest:

1. artistic or purely human interest,

The Natural Order 19

2. technical, pragmatic, methodical or purely instrumental interest,

3. scientific or purely empirical interest in experiences.

From these three complementary forms of interest, actuality or the instrument takes on three basically different meanings and purposes.

The instrument is neither object nor subject. As modern science has had to demonstrate that the instrument influences the object under observation, that the arrangement itself of the experiment changes the conditions of the object, then this relationship has nothing at all to do with *subjectivity*, for subjectivity is above all *will and wish*, and in this case one cannot say that it is *the observer's wishes* which influence the object, unless by *his interest in observing*. As far as the technician is concerned, the relationship is completely the opposite. He wishes to influence the object with his instrument, to operate, to generate a process. If the instrument cannot influence the object, it is of no use in the technical sense, it has no technical interest. This adversarial condition between the relationship of the scientist and the technician to the instrument is clear and unambiguous. This adversarial condition can only be clearly seen from the artist's angle, because he is not interested in the object at all, only in the subjective and in *instruments which can serve these subjective interests*, which are purely purposeless curiosity, the liberation from tedium. He wishes to play on or with the instruments, and anything at all that he sees or senses is therefore a possible instrument. In principle he cannot accept that the object, '*das Ding an sich*', exists at all. Instruments serve only one thing for him, pure subjectivity or '*das Ich an sich*'. *In the artistic sense the instrument is thus a means of expanding human activity and interest.*

From a technical viewpoint, the goal of instrumentalization is the instrument itself and a development identical with a growing instrumentation, the cementing of a practical causal relationship. *The instrument here is a replacement for human activity and interest, 'das Ding für mich'.*

In scientific observation, on the other hand, *the instrument* serves *to eliminate the influence of human interests and activities on the objective process.*

In relation to the causal world of technique or the logical object world of science, the contrasts are so sharp that unalloyed artistic activity has to be perceived as a purely destructive world, whilst the destructive in art has the opposite sign. It is this that I called the aesthetic world in my book *Luck and Chance*. This is the only one that gives the concept of *value* any meaning, a world that is deliberately ignored or resisted by all modern philosophers, politicians, economists, sociologists, psychologists, teachers and scientists, and which made C.D. Darlington add to the already quoted text, 'We need a

20   *The Natural Order and Other Texts*

Ministry of Disturbance, a regulated source of annoyance, a destroyer of routine, an underminer of complacency,' or, in other words, a ministry of aesthetic activity. The necessity of this centre for organized 'ill-doing' is perhaps above all conditioned by the destructive power of the military having become so widespread that it must be abolished or abolish itself.

The cultivation or dissolution of personality

How is the *present*, the actual, to be expanded to comprise ever greater ahistorical or eventless periods of time in a simultaneity, so that to an ever greater extent it *abolishes the meaning of time*? This can happen by coupling the events together into ever greater events where the whole of time becomes literally a waiting-period, '*en attendant Godot*'. At the same time the event one is building up becomes more and more monstrous.

'To be educated is to be observant', a Danish author has stressed recently. He could have added that to educate is to shape, and society's intellectual culture thus consists of shaping people to *concentrate their attention upon the same things*.

To be an artist is to create attention. Therefore a creative artist can only distract people from their forced attention. Only the inattentive person can observe and draw attention to something new. Artistic upbringing consists in uneducating the people and making them inattentive and instead opening their eyes, ears and other senses.

An artist cannot live where he is forced to concentrate his attention upon what any stupid idiot could hit upon, regardless of how educated such behaviour is. He has to leave.

I hereby declare that I only acknowledge a land as my fatherland if it consistently refuses to have anything at all to do with powers which own atom bombs. One could call this treason. As it is so, I owe it to my fatherland that I accept being called a traitor.

For me the event itself, the situation, the living instant in immediate contact with past and future, with what I *know*, is the only acceptable reality, the artistic and the intelligent reality and the realistic and intelligent art.

In the last century, Kierkegaard complained that Christianity was being abolished by its own spread. However, that this was at all possible demonstrates that in Kierkegaard's perception Christianity was not an eternal but a temporal phenomenon. If Kierkegaard identified the instant with the eternal, the present with the divine, then Marxists can safely maintain *that socialism is the secular realization of Christianity*, of the all embracing and eternal instant, as one of my old Communist comrades recently asserted to me, for what science is helping the technicians to develop today, what they in fellowship call progress, is the gradual evolution of the present in time and space.

Therefore I can today indicate that it is actuality itself, human reality, that is being abolished by the spread of industrialization. This human reality is no longer valid as quality but only as quantity, as amount. The mistake in Bohr's terminology lies to an even higher degree than the Marxists in identifying amount with mass, quantity with quality, and calling an amount that represents a determined unit or mass a quantum.

The profound and explosive conflict today growing within Communist and Socialist development is based upon the realizations that to an increasing degree are bringing to light a problem to which it has hitherto been more or less unnecessary to take a position. However, this development is splitting into two opposite tendencies of a completely new character, towards either a human or an inhuman evolution. Marxism's superiority over all earlier philosophies lies in it being the first attempt to unite the scientific *perception of truth* with human *ethics* and norms of action which, to use Høffding's definition,* are a *perception of health*. If, as Friedell and Nietzsche,* one perceives what I would call the aesthetic purely negatively, as the negation of both truth and health, then we will see that the modern philosophical and political struggle is to a greater and greater degree about how far aesthetics or the perception of beauty have any right to exist, about whether there should still be freedom for Loke as well as for Thor.*

Form and container

With the Copenhagen Interpretation's reservation of a place of honour for classical metaphysics and logic and the apparent commencement of a completely new construction by its side, the conflict between the new and the old physics is avoided. It is otherwise with its relationship to materialistic dialectics. Here it is war to the knife, even though Bohr carefully avoids saying anything concrete, making do with a head-shaking 'not understood'.

Dialectical materialism has been able to avoid discovering that it has abolished the object because there *matter* is only perceived and acknowledged as *substance for processes* and not as forms in itself, and thus only in its character of *raw material*. Hereby arises the peculiar and absurd theory about

22 The Natural Order and Other Texts

quality's sudden change into quantity, which, despite everything, is immensely effective in a *purely technical* sense as an explanation.

By dividing this dialectical opposition into three complementary forms of observation, the observation of *constants* or masses which we call *qualities* (and not like Bohr *quanta*) and the observation of *amounts* which we call *quantities* and finally the observation of *changes* or processes which we call *values* or variations, it is possible to acknowledge dialectics and the theory of complementarity as two of three complementary systems of experience, an artistic, a technical and a scientific system. However, this initially presupposes that one recognizes the limited field of dialectics and at the same time goes in for my postulate that in every complementary relationship there must be at least three complementary factors. Even if I have not been able to demonstrate that this is the case in the relationship object-instrument-subject in a sufficiently convincing way, it seems to me that we can, at any rate, request an explanation as to why.

When, after this first superficial tour around a number of problems, we turn back to our first problem, we can do so with a more comprehensive acquaintanceship with the framework in which I have arranged the knowledge and the elementary experiences I as an artist have had to gather in order to come in contact with the intellectual surroundings in which I live and which to an ever increasing degree are marked by the expressions, language and conceptual world of scientific thought.

In his collection of articles *Atom physics and human knowledge*, Niels Bohr emphasizes that in the *never ending striving* for harmony between content and form there is reason to remember that 'no content can be represented without a logical framework and that any form, however useful it has hitherto been, can become too narrow to include new experiences'.*

The word *form* can have several different meanings. In this case there can be no doubt that, in its adversarial relationship to the concept of content, the word form means *container*. Here Bohr does not make the Marxist mistake expressed in the dogma, 'the only true form is the form of the content', a mistake which, however, becomes *true* according to the definition of truth and reality given here, and as such makes necessary a supplementary statement that *the only actual form is the opposite of the content*. When Bohr talks about framework he is talking about actual form not true form.

The logical framework for scientific description is the forms of language. 'This attitude is also expressed in historical development, as one no longer discerns sharply between formal logic and studies of semantics or even philosophical syntax...,' says Bohr. 'In our discussion we will not regard

The Natural Order 23

mathematics as a separate branch of knowledge but rather as a refinement of the common language.'

The harmony between container and content, between the milk bottle and the milk, does not mean that the bottle is made of milk, but that its form holds the milk in place, gathers the milk into a three-dimensional form. Thus milk is given an actual form. If we had wished to give it a true form, an objective form identical with the content, we could have just quick-frozen it. But in our case the milk is framed by a container. This could be of metal, pot, cardboard, glass etc. and thus have its own *true* content of various characters. Such a container could be used not only for milk but for an endless number of fluids and powders *unless a prohibition is made from pure convention against using the container for anything other than one particular form of liquid by the application of a label.*

The container is an instrument. So are language and the philosophical concepts described. Werner Heisenberg says, 'the only thing one can say about philosophical concepts like causality, space, time etc. is that they are indispensable *instruments* for present scientific research', but to define the limits of their spheres of usefulness is impossible.*

Here Niels Bohr agrees with Heisenberg, as he says, 'The distinction between object and subject necessary for unambiguous description is upheld by the fact that with every communication that contains a reference to ourselves, we, so to speak, insert a new subject which does not appear as an element of the communication's content. It hardly needs stressing that it is precisely this freedom in the choice of the line of demarcation between subject and object which gives room for the phenomena of the manifoldness of consciousness and the possibilities of human life.'

In this form, the postulation does not separate the 'will' of the instrument from human will and must invariably lead to the blind alley in which Bohr finds himself when he says, 'The problem is how far we can talk about freedom to act in agreement with our possibilities.' No, we have no possibilities of action at all if they have to be identified with our instruments, and at a certain point this is the demand of science and in this case of Bohr, as he wishes all actions which cannot be described in words to be reckoned as non-existent. In agreement with Einstein, he calls this 'a clear logical demand, as the word *experiment* (which means attempt: A.J.) itself refers to a situation where we can tell others what we have done and what we have learnt'. This presupposes in the first place that one cannot or may not do something that one cannot express, that one cannot or may not attempt something that one cannot at the same time express, but it also means that one does not have leave to express oneself

24 The Natural Order and Other Texts

artistically, for *the artistic is precisely the telling to others what one has done without thereby having learnt anything at all or imparting any experience whatever to others.*

New consequences mean new logic

In his definition of the experiment, Bohr emphasizes that it is not a question of specialized experiments, scientific experiments, but that the definition should have a universal validity. As justification or reason for this demand he produces a new demand, *the demand for logic*, which Heisenberg has already described as an instrument. In reality, this demand is to the effect that human thinking should be identical with the framework in which it is traditionally organized, and that it is forbidden to take this apparatus to pieces to see how it works in order to make another. However, at the same time, this is what Bohr wants and regards as absolutely necessary when he says, 'It is precisely this impossibility of setting, by observation, a sharp distinction between subject and object that creates the necessary latitude for the expression of will,' and continues elsewhere, 'As far as the relationship between reason [logic? A.J.] and instinct [the reflex or unconditioned action without cause? A.J.] is concerned, it is above all decisive to understand that no human thought in the true sense is possible without the use of a conceptual construct based upon a language which each generation has to learn from the beginning again. This utilization of concepts represses to a large extent not just purely instinctive life, but even stands in a distinct complementary adversarial relationship to the display of inherited instincts. If we look with wonder at the superiority in relation to man with which the lowest animal can use the possibilities of nature for the necessities and propagation of life, the most correct explanation is often that *for these animals there is no question at all of conscious thought in our sense...* The execution of such actions is only possible, when refuge is not taken in *conceptual thought.'*

I am of another persuasion and associate myself with those biologists who maintain that the whole of biological development has happened through sparks of conscious thought, and, if this is so, is identified with *intelligence* and not with *conceptual* thinking. I assert that a concept is not a thought but a device, an instrument for thinking, and that a complementary form of thought thus exists to the *thought that constructs concepts* (philosophical thinking) as well as *pure quantitative thought* (scientific thinking) or calculation, and this is subjective thought, *willed thought* or wishful thinking.

There are thus two possibilities. Either such a purely wishful thinking does not exist, or it exists, but is *forbidden* on scientific grounds, stamped as anormal, unhealthy thought.

If science has use for a philosophical apparatus in order to undertake its experiments, then it is of course obvious that this apparatus must in perfect condition at the moment it is to be used as an instrument. However, if the apparatus is not good enough, and fortunately Bohr says that it may never be good enough, then it must be improved. But this in itself says that the scientist at the observatory cannot *at the same time* undertake his observations and enlarge the telescope with which he is to see. If science has thus use for *philosophy* as an instrument, it must find that what best suits it and protest if it is not good enough. However, if the philosophers on their part are to elaborate a set of meanings with universal validity, they must also have standardized their building materials, *words*. They cannot agree to them being pulled apart and used in a thousand ways meaningless to philosophy. But if the language is not rich enough, then there is only one way in which it can be enriched, through literary and poetic development, the only thing that can enrich and refine the language in itself as language, as expression. However, philosophy is not developed as an instrument for science nor poetry as an instrument for philosophy.

Bohr maintains that the logical framework for scientific description is in the forms of language and continues, 'This attitude is also expressed in historical development, as one no longer discerns sharply between formal logic and studies of semantics or even philosophical syntax... In our discussion we will not regard mathematics as a separate branch of knowledge but rather as a refinement of the common language.'

With this perception, Bohr has consigned the whole of language to one large container in which can be found an orientation from the sediment of daily speech towards refined language, mathematics. This simply means that Bohr accepts that one has use for instinct with which to make philosophy and one also has use for philosophy with which to make science. However, instinct must be confined and only those drops which philosophy distils in its alembic have the right to exist, and this same situation is 'necessary' as far as philosophy is concerned. Yet he does not think that the consciousness of society functions in such a way that the drops from the pure test-tube of science are directed straight back into the alembics of the primitive instincts where they act as huge, heaven-sent instruments. The facts show us that *it is the instincts which have use for scientific research and keep it going* and here only he who works directly with instincts, the artist, has positive *power*. No compromise is valid here.

26   The Natural Order and Other Texts

Dialectical materialism starts from the realistic perception that it is life that determines consciousness and not consciousness that determines life, but forgets that life shapes consciousness by developing it in a dialectical opposition to life, in a continuous protest against the conditions of life, and that an identification of life with consciousness is simply the death of intelligence, is an unconscious reflex. Classical scholars perpetrated another misunderstanding in perceiving life as something quite independent of practical existence. It appears to me that the theory of complementarity could give both a more correct and more effective and, at any rate, a more realistic picture of these conditions. However, if this is the case then we have to avoid, for example, J.P. Jacobsen's *Arabesques* being perceived either as 'daily speech' or as another mysterious form of mathematics.* Artistic refinement must be accepted as a spiritual development complementary to both the rationalistic development of instruments in daily life and to scientific and logical development. Everyday art does not exist, for art is celebration, and is so even if there is celebration every day and every instant of that day. *Art is the phenomenal itself and the phenomenal is the unique.* If the word 'phenomenon' can no longer be used in this meaning, then art no longer exists, and neither do the sensory phenomena.

Either phenomenal or functional

Niels Bohr maintains that 'it is impossible to distinguish between the behaviour of material bodies and our observations of it. In order to find a true parallel to this knowledge of the limited validity of the accustomed idealizations that the atomic theory has given us, we must turn to an area of science so far removed from physics as psychology or even to the kind of epistemological problems already posed by thinkers like Buddha and Lao Tze in their efforts to find an expression for the harmony in the great drama of existence in which we are simultaneously actors and spectators.' This old situation has, however, completely changed, for a role which is neither that of the actor nor the observer but that of the instrument is growing like lightning. More and more, we are all becoming instruments or functionaries, and those groups which can really call themselves active players as well as free spectators, whose freedom in one of these areas dominates all their other functions, are becoming less and less in relation to the total population. What is worse, even the concept that should cover these two groups, that of the elite, is in reality just an expression for the most rigid and responsible and immovable of functionaries who have not the least power, for *power is beauty, grace.* In modern society this is replaced by what is called impartiality, which is really no more than scientific control.

Bohr's anti-artistic position can be established from the following statement, 'As a more appropriate method of expression, I suggested that the word *phenomenon* be exclusively used to refer to observations gained under stated circumstances comprising an account of the whole experimental arrangement.' If this concept is to replace the simple description of sensory impressions in general and if Bohr's description is not merely to characterize *specialized* scientific phenomena or more correctly *scientifically treated* phenomena, then phenomena, the world of the senses in itself, will no longer exist.

I would therefore suggest that this definition is changed to *a phenomenon is a sensed or observed change.* This definition allows us to establish a new perception of the intermediate relationship, to establish the transition between causality and non-causality, a problem that first took on universal significance after the observations of Bohr forced science to give up the belief in absolute relativism, absolute process or absolute actuality. This paradox that the law of causation cannot be given general validity but at the same time cannot be deprived of any validity is really the reason for this new philosophical conflict, and this has also given me the opportunity to introduce the aesthetic, defined in agreement with Baumgarten as sensed or observed changes, as an integral part of human thought or intelligence without doing violence to that artistic autonomy which has hitherto been necessary to all philosophical systems.

Pawns, the other players and spectators

What Bohr has discovered, or rather the conclusion that Bohr should have reached from his observations, is that *conditions* and *laws* are not the same and never can be, that they are complementary opposites. Conditions are set in advance and rules are deduced. If the rules deduced from an experiment or a game are identical to those conditions set for the game, then nothing new at all has been experienced, and if they are in harmony with those conditions then anything novel is unimportant.

The conditions *for* an experiment can never be identical to the conditions *during* the experiment and must stand in a complementary adversarial relationship to them. *The condition of the experiment itself is that it can either succeed or fail. If this possibility is not present, the experiment cannot be recognized as a true experiment,* but must only be perceived as the purely experiment-free repetition of an already undertaken experiment. The experimental content of *the repetition* of an already undertaken experiment has only a purely subjective significance as an experiment for those who were not present at the time, but who have followed the instructions as to how it is to be undertaken, and are not therefore themselves experimenting. *The definition of experiment laid down by Bohr and Einstein really excludes any truly new scientific research from the area they call experiments and thus does not even cover the purely scientific experiment at all.* The fact alone of having proved that an experiment can be repeated is in itself a proof that it is no longer an experiment, and this proof is present when all Bohr's conditions are fulfilled.

Thus, if the validity of a scientific experiment is to be recognized, the general condition is that all the conditions which presuppose the possibility of the carrying out of the experiment are known, that the result of the experiment itself has hitherto been unknown, and that, when they are present, it can be repeated under the same conditions. The result of a scientific experiment is the description of the experiment.

The separation of laws and conditions, which is the separation between idea and experience, can only happen outside the field of the experiment, in the actuality where the game is under way.

Dialectics – triolectics. Dynamics and statics

What now remains is to give a presentation of the relationship between dialectics and the complementary system. My abilities and my knowledge only permit me to sketch the possibility of such a connection. As I have said before, I cannot nor will not attempt to prove it.

In its perception of history, dialectical materialism has, by involving the historical past in the present, celebrated great triumphs. No one can deny that I am the synthesis of my mother and my father. These *two* persons are not possibilities but necessary actualities in my existence in the same way as my *four* grandparents, my *eight* great-grandparents, *sixteen* great-great-grandparents, etc. back until in the fourteenth century, when I have over a million necessary kin. The whole dialectical apparatus functions irreproachably. However, if instead of moving into the past, I follow the family trees of these innumerable forefathers in the direction of the future, then the whole of the dialectical system dissolves in an impenetrable jungle of accidents. Certainty is lost. What in one direction is determinism is chance seen in the other.

The Natural Order 29

But what if one now wishes to force this same dialectical economy to be also valid into the future, then there is no longer anything that can be done, neither as *past* nor as *future*, for then the future has become identical with the past and the past identical with the present. This is what happens purely logically if the theory of dialectical materialism is followed up in its present form. That the Soviet Socialist Republics do not do this at all demonstrates their whole evolution and their philosophical silence. How far this break with the principles of dialectical materialism is unconscious or a hidden manoeuvre justified on its subjective basis, I will not say. However, the result is the same. We will have to find out for ourselves.

Dialectics is based upon a conviction about the endless union of polarizations or *two-sided* oppositions into syntheses, which then again produce dualities. That there is something correct about the unity of duality cannot be explained away as long as the polarity of electricity and magnetism has not been explained away. But if this principle is transferred to politics, and internal national polarization, right and left, is abolished, then a country has to seek its polarization outside itself. That such a polarization between East and West can be of high dynamic quality for the development of trade on both sides in a sort of naive competition or cold war, there can be no doubt. It is like a football match where both sides are trying to win. However, let us now imagine a whole new type of football field, where, instead of two teams and two goals, there are three teams in play and three goals. Now what would happen when the three teams began to play against each other? It would swiftly be discovered that it is impossible to control which of the two attacking enemies had scored. It would become necessary to invert the rules so that the victory was a negative one, so that it was the team that has defended itself best and had let in the least goals that was the victor. The victory becomes defensive and not offensive. The game would of course adjust itself accordingly. It would not be an exciting game at all. This is how a third power can neutralize a tension between two powers. Therefore two-sided opponents are always aggressive whilst three-sided ones are defensive. Whether this in itself describes the transition from dialectics to complementarity, I will leave unsaid. [...]* Whether a three-sided relationship is static or constant is dependant, however, upon whether a rising tension occurs. Then this could perhaps lead to an actual explosion, the possibilities of which are abreacted in a two-sided relationship by the *duel's* incessant consumption of energy. No political advice whatsoever lies in these observations. I am only trying to discover out what happens.

Two dialectical oppositions neutralize each other, like positive and negative. Where there are three mutual oppositions, such a synthesis cannot occur. Here we seem to be discovering the philosophical rule of Bohr's complementarity theory.

But let us move to the area which has my special interest as an artist, the character of light and colour. One can make a spherical model of every, absolutely every, colour possibility available in Runge's colour ball, with the spectral circle at an oblique angle on the black-white axis, and get all the colours lying in a rectilinear relationship to the centre of this sphere, at the same distance from the centre, to neutralize each other so that they, by mixing together, under all circumstances return to the grey colour in the centre. Here I ask science, how is this possible? Is this not the most perfect mechanical model one could imagine? What is the explanation of this polarity? Can it be a subjective accident with no foundation whatsoever in the order of nature and the physical characteristics of light?

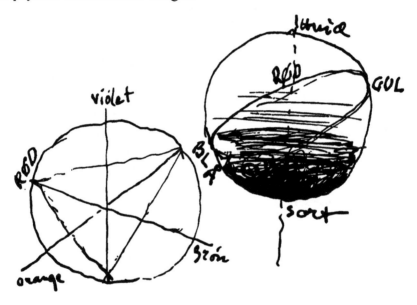

RØD = RED, BLÅ = BLUE, Grøn = Green, GUL = YELLOW, Hvid – White, Sort = Black.

FIG. 1. THE SPECTRAL DIALECTIC

If we now regard the three primary colours blue, yellow and red which slide harmoniously over each other in the spectral circle, and place them in a triangular relationship to each other, then we will see that even though all three

The Natural Order 31

are constant, irreducible colours, then *the complementary colour to one is the median proportional colour between the other two*, the evenly mixed colour of the other two. It is thus the three primary colours, which in accord with Bohr's definition of complementarity, relate complementarily to each other, whilst what have hitherto been called the complementary colours relate dialectically and not complementarily to each other, as their synthesis abolishes the colour effect. This observation lies at the root of my whole taxonomy and under any circumstance abolishes the possibility of using both the traditional interpretation and Bohr's interpretation of 'complementarity' within the world of colours.

According to recent information, the Swedes have established that gila tissue has significance as a constant in the nervous system, something that Fridtjof Nansen is said to have indicated as a possibility as early as 1886.* By this, they can be said to have in practice abolished the basis for the centuries-old conflict between the advocates of the three colour theory and the complementary colour theory and given a synthesized explanation for them both, in that the visual cells *are* trichromatic whilst the whole mechanism of sight *works* in accordance with the system of complementary colours. This shows that in this area there appears to be a connection between complementary statics and dynamic dialectics. But how does this model relate to the optical phenomena themselves?

When we observe nature, everything becomes greyer and greyer the more it spreads out and becomes distanced, whilst the grey in our model is in the centre. Could one imagine an inverted perspective where the things became smaller and smaller the closer they came, and thus an inverted space that would be the spatiality of light? Is our perception of space one-sided, like our perception of past and future and thus *oriented*? Should the idea of the expansion of the universe be supplemented with another about that same universe in the process of shrinking? I don't know. I only know that just as the Renaissance's perspective picture of the universe does not satisfy us any more and therefore art since Impressionism has sought to base itself upon completely new principles, so it now becomes a question about *pictorial art*, about how far new perspectives can be outlined for anything at all.

32   *The Natural Order and Other Texts*

Three world pictures

1. The variable entity
2. The process of creation
3. The process of liberation

At each corner of the borders of the old Chinese empire stood a stone on which was written 'World's End'. Society and universe were one, were the world. As it was discovered that there was a world outside Verona, so arose the problem of the extension of the world that classical culture had chosen for its own, *the accepted world*, society. However *the fission between the two worlds, society and universe,* had already been observed, and the recognition that the laws of the universe were different from those of society had been established, even though the tendency to harmonize will always be at work in human consciousness. The belief that the formula for this harmonization has been found is called religion. I do not believe in the possibility of an unambiguous world picture, but the lines of direction given here do permit the conjecture that it is possible to develop three mutually complementary world pictures, providing one keeps them strictly separate.

A picture can only be a picture of the process under which the picture came into existence, nothing more. This is true also of a world picture. At any rate, this is the reason why I, as an artist, dare postulate that there exist three complementary world pictures which cannot under any circumstances be identified with each other because they occur under three opponent processes, which I will briefly sketch here.

You take a lump of clay and shape it plastically into an image without losing any of the clay and without adding new clay. This method is the exact expression of the homeomorphic world picture, the *a priori* of which is that nothing gets lost and nothing is created, but where everything can be changed. I have the impression that this world picture is the foundation of what is called the wave interpretation.

When Heerup entered the Academy's Sculpture Department,* he used this method and was immediately thrown out, because he could not reconcile himself to the particle method, which consists of first securing an arbitrary number of small particles and then beginning to place these particles in position, one against the other, a development which is conditioned by the *number* of particles and stops when there are no more. This progressive process of development, the *a priori* of which is that new quantities can be constantly added, expresses the classical world picture that has to be established before the process begins, as if it were an imaginary container or mould into which the molten metal is poured.

Finally you can go in the exact opposite direction to the latter as you begin by removing those parts of a given material, for example a rock or a piece of wood, which do not belong in the picture. This comes into existence directly by the breaking down of the material, by the removal of the picture-less material from the pictorial material. Here the image-making is directly identical with destructive action, with pure action, with what we will call radiant action, effect or activity, phenomenal action. These are three different actions of creation.

If I have not talked of any specific world picture in the last two cases, it is because the expansive explanation of the universe is in reality a hybrid product where you paste on something here and remove something there. What in my opinion characterizes modern atomic physics is that it has certainly isolated the world picture constructed upon the wave interpretation, but only at the expense of an imprecision which arises through a fusion of the particle and the ray concepts. Only when one decides to set up a complementary description of all three observations, will the three world pictures clearly emerge. That they could emerge simultaneously seems to be excluded, however, as it would hardly be possible to describe a pure particle observation unless on the basis of a mixture of ray and wave description. Just as a pure description of the radiation phenomenon presupposes a mixture of wave and particle description, so a fission is conditioned by a fusion, not because of the lacking objectivity of the theory, but because we would otherwise be unable to observe, because there is no *place* for the observer. I would like to know if I am right about this interpretation.

What do we observe?

The empirical doctrine of classical physics constructs its proofs on the basis of direct observation. This is no longer possible today. What one uses as a basis for one's conclusions is no longer the sensation of the object itself but signs of the object's behaviour deciphered by measuring instruments, on photographic plates and so on. These signs and not the object itself have become the only criteria for the demonstrability of scientific statements. The postulate that matter is what is given to us by our senses is hereby given the *coup de grâce*, whilst the same thing has happened to the classical perception of reality.

If I stand by an aeroplane and it flies away, then I see that it getting smaller and smaller. The classical perception would say that this is imaginary. 'In

34 The Natural Order and Other Texts

reality', the aeroplane remains the same size. However, if I now set up ten cameras at my side and as the aeroplane distances itself and at regular intervals take photographs with the cameras, then I get ten uniform photographic proofs that the aeroplane really got smaller and smaller. This is the reason that the classical perception of actuality is no longer valid, also in daily life. By the perception of actuality here I mean *what one can use the word actuality for. The object has not become smaller, but actuality shows something different.* I will here ignore the lacking proof that it is the same flier the camera has taken, of the possibility that there could have been aeroplanes of differing sizes and that the various cameras could have photographed different machines. What interests us in this experiment are the possibilities for the most comprehensive explanation, the most logical explanation. Anyone can see that this is a problem that plays the greatest role in art, in the sense that it is the perspective problem itself that is at issue. The important thing is to demonstrate that *we do not see or sense what is at all, but what happens,* that the camera is completely unable to maintain a picture of the object, of what *is,* only of what *happens,* of the instant however long or short that is. Our senses do not perceive things, only changes of a quite specific limited kind or form.

Complementary semantics
Symptom versus signal

If we go back to the modern scientific explanation of the use of observation instruments, we see that, according to Susanne K. Langer (*Philosophy in a New Key*), they are classified in an explanatory series of three elements, *object, sign, subject.* In this connection, the object is what the subject is interested in observing. However, when he cannot observe it, he seeks a sensory phenomenon connected with the object which it is possible to observe. If he is sure that these two phenomena always appear together, then he is sure to have found a sure sign that can show him *where* the object is to be found at any rate. Such a relationship of actuality or simultaneity between a thing and its associated sensory phenomenon is called a *sign relationship.* Now it appears that both humans and animals use such sign relationships everywhere. Indeed, we can just as well establish right away that any sensation at all is a sensation not of objects but of signs of these objects' presence. *No one has ever seen an object. No one will ever see an object.* One only sees light rays in motion and the refraction of these movements and nothing else. This is what we take for objects, because we have always experienced the direct correlation of these two things with each other. As our sensations are paramount in relation to our experiences, this is the world of objects we encounter, the construction of sign combinations we will call *symptoms* in forms or gestalts. This perception forms the logical conclusion of the materialistic postulate that objects exist independently of our sensation of them.

This definition of the symptom is different from that of Langer, but has the advantage that it can be expressed logically in detail and form the basis for an unambiguous definition of the purpose of scientific research, as the revelation of symptoms, as *the demonstration of symptomatic relationships.*

In order for a symptom to be recognized as such, it must be absolutely 'true'. If the object is not always and under all circumstances present where the sign appears, then the sign is simply not a symptom. A mistake has been made and the whole thing must be scrapped. This mistake can only be due to the established sign relationship being false or one sign having been exchanged for another.

Just as a doctor defines a picture of illness by the combination of several different symptoms, we define our sensory pictures by combining sensory impulses in forms of objects or in images of forces and movements.

In contrast to the absolute unambiguity of the symptom, another form of sign combination, *the signal*, has a dual character which the former has not. If we set up an adversarial relationship between *the natural* and *the artificial*, then we are right to call symptoms natural signs and signals artificial signs.* This division which, against the background of our definition of the symptom, is, as far as I know, quite new in semantics, and which clashes with other definitions of what is called 'the natural sign', is based upon the clear separation that *symptoms in my definition are what one would call objective signs whilst signals in contrast are subjective signs,* willed or intentional signs. If this simple arrangement is wrong then a specialist should easily be able to pull it to pieces.

If a symptom is a sign relationship that is established by the hand of nature, as one might say, then in order to establish a signal it is necessary to produce a special device, a special instrument for the transmission of the signal. Regarded as a sign instrument, the relationship between the requirements of symptom and signal device is similar to that between the requirement to use only previously found stones to hammer with and the permission to make a specially constructed hammer. As an effect, the difference is like that between the tracks one leaves when walking and those one makes on purpose to mark the way with a stick. If there can be opposition to this definition of the signal as identical with the artificial sign, then it is because it indeed *covers all natural phenomena which have arisen as and exclusively have the function of sensory effects.* This is to say that the song and dance of the birds as well as the colour, scent and form of the flowers must be perceived as artificial signs or signals. This dissolves the old established adversarial relationship set up between the actual and the concept, or, if you will, the sensual and the 'actual', where everything apart from human ideas is perceived as 'nature'. From an actualistic perception, the artificial must naturally have its nature, together with the ideas, under all circumstances.

If we set up the symptomatic relationship object-sign-subject, then we can set up the signalistic relationship *subject-sign-subject*. Whilst symptoms exclusively serve as *the orientation* of a subject in motion in the objective world, signals serve as a subjective orientation in relation to the movements of another subject, either by indicating as symptoms the presence of the sign-transmitting subject, or by also influencing the sign-receiving subject's movements and changing them. The signal is artistic because it is artificial and free in relation to what is being described. The growling or barking of a dog is a sign that it is aggressive, but *is in no way identical with the aggressive action*. On the contrary, it is a sign it uses to avoid biting. The sign has become more important than the object. This contrast between action and the *sensual sign of the action's potency* cannot be established at all on the basis of a traditional philosophical use of language (see Benedetto Croce's aesthetics).

With symptoms one can only orient, but with signals one can orient and *direct* and thus force something to follow one's will. The orientation which the subject can establish through the signal is *data* about its own state and movements. However, by yet another element the signal can become *indicative*, as the signal-transmitting subject describes not itself but *an object*, for example an approaching danger, from which we get the series *subject (I) – sign – object – subject (II)*. Such a form of warning does not need to be directed towards one single subject, but could be a general broadcast. It must be noted that such an indicative signalling appears most often to have an accusatory, provocative or teasing function.

Signal versus symbol

Apart from this *insultative* characteristic of the signal transmission, another characteristic exists, albeit upon a parasitic basis, which is not in the most proper sense signalistic, but nevertheless is so, as it is what we call a *false signal, a fraud*. For example, the equipment of flesh-eating plants has to be perceived in this way. *At a more developed stage this trickery represents the ability to lie* and to pretend, to play-act. This is possible because, as already mentioned, the observer believes in the correctness of the signal and thus in the presence of an object which is not there. If he doesn't then the effort will be in vain. The observer reacts in this way, allowing himself to be fooled, because from experience he had *the concept* that where there was an object there was a sign. He has mistaken the signal for a real symptom. His critical sense is not functioning. His reaction to the signal has become a *conditioned reflex*. This is what happens when a fox allows himself to be enticed away from the ducklings by the apparently wounded mother duck.

Allowing oneself to be systematically fooled by such false signals is called conscious logic or symbolization. To symbolize is to say that one permits the presence of the object to be replaced with an idea or just a concept *x*. The difference between *idea* and *concept* is that the idea demands an imaginary signal, whilst this only hampers the concept. Only when any idea about a concrete object in connection with concept *x* is eliminated has one reached pure symbolism, pure concept. With this is determined not only the difference between symptom and signal but also that between signal and symbol. *A word can thus be used as a symptom as well as a signal or a symbol*. None of these uses can be dispensed with or identified with each other.

The difference between symptom and signal can thus reveal the difference between the natural and the artificial, and it is only by the representation of false signs or symbols that an adversarial relationship can be established between what we call lies and what we call truth. If, as is asserted, it is this ability of man to symbolize that lifts him above the animal world, then this is to say that the one who lies the best lifts himself the most. This may sound cynical, but it is at any rate what mathematics and classical philosophy teach us. Placed in correlation to the social requirement for truth it could well give a deal of trouble. When therefore we asserted in the beginning that a symptom should be absolutely true, this only has meaning if at the same time an absolute lie is cultivated, for without this the concept of truth would have no actuality any more. It would have vanished by dissemination.

New signals

What has happened in the relativistic experimental arrangement for the determination of the period of the present is that our sign system has been duplicated and that the two sets of signal systems have been placed in an adversarial relationship to each other so that signals can be exchanged. A

38 The Natural Order and Other Texts

dialogue has been established.

If we keep to the world of the senses in the artistic signal relationship we have an actor, an instrument (the sign) and an observer or spectator who, just like the scientist, has to collect his observations. In the exchange of the two light signals, the first signal becoming the most primitive form of question and the second the most primitive form of answer.

There is no meaning at all in sending a new sign before the answer has arrived. If questions are continually sent out without answers coming in, then in reality it is the same question being repeated constantly, regardless of whether its form changes. Time stands still until contact is made and communication or dialogue is set up.

The longer there is between question and answer, the longer time is wasted by having to wait. The interesting part of the relativistic explanation is namely what can be scientifically proved – that time can be wasted. This is an enormously important observation for the understanding of the principles of the Marxist economic doctrine, which is based upon the English principle of 'time is money'.

Symbol versus symptom

If there is a particular reason to perceive the world of the signal as identical with that of art or, to be quite precise, the world of the fine and beautiful arts, it is simply because for humanity the beautiful is when the signalistic becomes art. Let us put it this way, what we will call *magic* is an intermediate thing between what we call symptoms and what we call signals.

Let us first establish that a causal relationship between the symptom and its object has in no way been established. It is not thunder *because* there is lightning. It has not rained *because* it is wet everywhere. It is not *because* one has a fever that one is sick and so on. However, *it is quite different if one is able to change a movement with the help of signals.* This can only be explained as a causal connection. In order to operate, and thus for technical reasons, the revelation of such possibilities for the establishment of a causal connection is a consequence or a number of consequences or a chain of consequences with the help of another consequence which is the only one that has significance. It is therefore the technician's requirement from science that it will not only find symptoms, but above all establish causal connections, this in itself being the opposite of a scientific analysis. *The establishment of objectively operative causal relationships is technique. The establishment of subjectively operative causal relationships is magic* or art, is captivation. Simple-minded thought does not separate these two forms. The belief in an almighty god is the belief in a universally subjective causal relationship. The belief in justice is the belief in a socially subjective causal relationship and so on.

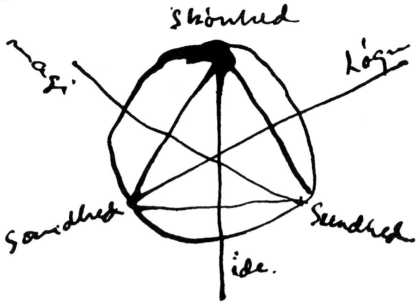

Skønhed = beauty, Løgn = Lie, Sundhed = Health,
ide = Idea, Sandhed = Truth, magi = magic

FIG. 2. THE FIRST TRIOLECTIC

That such causal systems are not true does not hamper the fact both that they are actual (if they are not mistaken) and that they function, help or hinder people in doing certain things. That the concept of magic has also been given a non-metaphysical interpretation in this account is a consequence of the remaining interpretations. Our definition simply says that *magic is doing what one wants and yet coming well out of it*, which one could also call the Faustian perception of art. In the classical view, magic is a pseudo-science constructed from particular concepts and ideas. It is only when one accepts this definition of magic that one can assert that runes, for example, do not have a magical origin. Metaphysical definition is necessary in classical philosophy because it has no place at all for non-conceptual thought, thought without tools, thought

40   *The Natural Order and Other Texts*

that is based only upon the talent of thinking.

Instead of magic, one could call this form of thought *introductory thought*, for it is not completely without context. One could just as well also call it seductive thought or aesthetic thought: one could call it thought for particular occasions or whatever. But it seems to me to be quite unnecessary here to describe this phenomenon, as I could never measure myself with the authorship of Søren Kierkegaard in this region.

The dialectical opposite to truth is lie. When Bohr sets up a complementary opposition between truth and clarity, then he has in reality given me the key to the acknowledgment of the triple character of complementarity, as imagination or illusion also exists in a complementary relationship to truth as well as to clarity, unless he does not reckon with fantasy as an important psychic activity at all.

If the dividing line between the symptomatic and the signalistic represents the opposition between the natural and the artificial, then the dividing line between the symptomatic and the symbolic represents the opposition between the real and the imaginary, and thus that which we call the truth and the mendacious, and is the mechanism itself which allows the setting-up of an adversarial relationship of truth-lie itself.*

It is here that the inner structure of modern science is about to fall apart. It is from this point that the sickness today is spreading into all science, for science has no conditions at all at its disposal for concepts such as actuality, reality, experiment or phenomenon. However, just one concept is to this degree identical with science, in that it fuses with the unambiguity of the concept, and that is *truth*. If science is not true then it is simply no more, it has vanished. Any attempt at a scientific approach to philosophy must pass through the control of truth. If science today wishes to appeal to philosophy, it must identify itself or we must identify it if it will not do so itself, and the question, 'What is truth?' is the same as the question, 'What is science?' In its modern evolution, science has appropriated truth, has identified itself with truth, but it cannot introduce scientific truth as an unidentified truism into philosophy, and cannot introduce itself into philosophy without examination.

What has happened today is that the natural sciences, the classical sciences, are no longer coherent, but have broken down the middle into two opposites. Classical natural science was symptomatic in its criterion of truth. We have clearly shown that the symbol in relation to the symptom is the definition of what we call lie, imagination or illusion. Universal approval of imagination is called convention or agreement, and an intellectual convention is called a concept. When therefore modern science clings to the demand for the constancy

The Natural Order 41

of the concepts, this means that it is demanding belief in the constancy of the imagination, in fixed lies. That this is simply a prohibition against a creative pictorial art we have already demonstrated. But even such a prohibition cannot save the situation, for the constancy of the concepts does not secure unambiguity in the concept of scientific truth, it does not abolish the self-contradiction.

Niels Bohr has laid down that 'it is the purpose of science to increase and order our experiences'. This statement, which is very unclear, is surely the reason for the general mobilization in the philosophy camp. That science gathers and increases our experiences is the very essence of science, but then comes the question of the ordering of these experiences. Here the question then is, do scientists believe that it is a scientific activity to order experiences, do scientists believe that a scientific method is to be found to order anything at all, and do scientists imagine that anything at all can be found which in a direct sense could be called a 'scientific order'? If this is the case then we are in a serious conflict.

Keeping order is a police affair, and the only thing that science can pronounce upon is the ascertainment of truths and nothing else. When science puts itself at the service of order, this means that it has to function as an authorized lie detector. It is said that the lie detectors which are used in the American forces do not react to Italians. They are too clever at lying. If science really demands participation in controlling the ordering of our experiences, then it is time that we set up Darlington's Ministry for the Destruction of International Understanding and Conformation and, as a focus, set up an institute for advanced lying with training in make-believe for ourselves and others, a central institute for artistic activity. This institute could also be called an institute for new ordering or for creative philosophy or simply the Folk High School, for imagination is just *discovering something for oneself*. Discovery and invention are two opposing activities. Any ordering is an invention. Every systemization is an art. If the meaning of Bohr's statement is that science does not have a purely intrinsic purpose because it cannot continue its research without the results achieved connecting with the public consciousness or, at any rate, with the consciousness of other research results, and that systematized development is therefore a necessary precondition for the development of scientific research, then a very painful controversy will have been removed. Humanity has always had to systematize its experiences quite independently of scientific research in order to be able to act with wisdom, in order to be able to transform its knowledge into something it perceives as wisdom, and this doctrine of wisdom is in reality philosophical activity. This activity has developed quite independently of modern science and has not been equal to constructing a systems theory that harmonizes with the experiences of modern science. However, today a philosophical science is necessary, as any philosophy which is contradicted by scientific experiences is without any actuality, except as an instrument for upholding *social* peace, order and stagnation, for supporting social *actuality* and avoiding events. Preserving the conceptual definitions of classical physics also involves preserving classical philosophy and classical forms of society. Or is the order of the factors reversed? Building a new world of concepts parallel to and independent of the old is only possible if one finds a new planet and begins *existence* in a completely new way. This is perhaps possible today, but we others who still wish to remain on the earth are not interested in having it reduced to a museum. We would rather discover something new for ourselves.

The rules of nature and the laws of society

A law must be kept, but a rule has to be followed. A rule is thus a regulation of order, but is not itself the order. A rule can be followed in different ways just as one can order in different ways, but within an order all details are fixed. One can ascertain if certain rules are being kept, and rules are thus also a kind of law, although they are not absolutely constant. A law is to be considered absolute in a given situation, but a rule is a law which one decides to follow or not follow, and in a given situation or a particular form of situations is thus still open to choice and decision.

Can there be an objective or scientific separation between laws and rules? Such a thing could only be arranged if one called all artificial rules discovered by man laws and only recognized the rules of nature, the rules that nature follows in and outside humanity's existence, independently of human will and impervious to human will, ability and knowledge. Attempts have been made to identify the laws of society with such natural laws, and attempts have been made to give them a divine, absolute character, all in vain. Today everyone has agreed to perceive all social laws, orders and rules as kinds of contracts which people agree to keep or follow or, at any rate, to behave as if they keep or follow them.

Herein lies the self-contradiction of modern science. We have already indicated that the '*laws*' of the natural sciences are, without exception, proof of symptomatic sign relationships. When science therefore talks of the laws of mathematics, it also destroys the unambiguity and truth of its statements about laws, for no concept, no mathematical formula is natural. They are all purely artificial rules which can be accepted or rejected at will and *their essential artificiality is that if they are rejected, they do not exist at all. The same is the case with words and writing.* An unknown writing, an unknown language, has no existence at all, even if its signs exist, unless its rules and meaning are known. This is the contrast between concepts and symptoms. The development of the natural sciences takes place according to certain rules, but nothing makes these rules absolute, nothing makes them natural laws, although this is what science tries to demonstrate. No one can prove that science could not develop according to absolutely different rules. Today science can no longer find out what the rules of its game are or even what the game is. Science has therefore lost its raison d'être as the unambiguous criterion of truth and thus exists no more as science. The re-erected unambiguity of this concept of truth will be necessary in order to accept science into philosophy.

What has brought confusion into the natural sciences is the discovery that one cannot perceive natural symptoms as absolute, that nature does not follow its own *'laws'* with absolute consistency, and that nature is a gambler marked to the highest degree both by chance and by rules of the game of its own, called *'natural laws'*. However, their absolute infallibility, in which no one believes anymore, takes from them nothing of their absolute character of being rules of the game for particular natural phenomena.

An answer that is already formulated and given before the question arises and is posed could, if it was a scientific answer, be called a precondition, or, where the question is of an ethical nature, is called a defence, and in both cases they take on the character of legality from repeated use. An essential feature of the original Nordic perception of law was that it was not perceived as a mutual agreement, a message, or a forced demand, but as a *vow* that was absolutely one-sided. Agreement only occurs when *belief* in the vow is declared. The relationship of trust is thus a relationship between both *belief and laws*.

A law is thus a decision or a prejudice. A defence is the same as a resistance or a defended point of view, a prohibition.

One can change a law by force whilst being elevated above the law oneself, and one can in fellowship work out a law that all vow to maintain. But what in reality are perceived as its basic laws are its theoretical *a prioris*, and one can demand of them that they are logical, that they are not self-contradictory, but even where this is achieved one cannot call them scientific, as they are just preconditions for talking about the results of scientific investigations, not for the results in themselves. In nature are found no laws, only rules.

In the most advanced circles of modern culture, games theory has already

44   *The Natural Order and Other Texts*

become an instrument with which one prepares oneself to play upon people's credulity. *A game is a process the end result of which is unknown, an experiment.* A superior power is one who can make an opponent play a game, the result of which he knows, and which is thus not a real game to him. An authority is one whose opposite number knows that he knows the result in advance, but nevertheless agrees to play. A winner is the one who plays the best, and a cheat is one who pretends to be following the rules of the game, but however does not. The only player who in the aesthetic sense could be an artist is the cheat, because his game is, without exception, *apparent,* and thus is pure sensory effect, pure intuition, a performance. The actor does not play. He plays the role of the player. In the same way, the virtuoso does not play music. He plays Mozart without being Mozart. The artist is the only one that is always conscious of this double game, wherever it is played. An artist never lets himself be fooled by a politician, unless he perceives him as an artist. Inorganic nature does not seem able to play the double game or fool anyone. This is the basis of the relative truth value of the symptom. If truth is symbolic then it cannot at the same time be symptomatic and vice versa. Truth must indivisible if it is to be a truth. An illusion is also a truth if it is defined as a true illusion. A lie is a form of truth: if its antagonistic relationship to the facts is defined then it is *a true picture.* To an artist this is obvious, indeed, it is even the monitor of his originality. In order to really imagine something, to be able to imagine, one must know precisely what is *not* imagination. It is in the symbolic area that the artist finds the concepts of truth of the modern scientist so deplorably unscientific and illusory – indeed, improbably poor and dilettantish in their illusionism or imagery. Only by handing over the control of universal imagery to creative artists can scientists today have order in the tabernacle. In this way, the artist's stance becomes that of an anti-symbolistic symbolist.

If we thus set up a theory about a complementary tripartition of *symptom – signal – symbol* and identify these with the criteria for *truth – beauty – health,*★ meaning by health only balance or legality, then we can construct a triangle similar to the colour triangle, and with this we can work out the dialectically antagonistic relationships.

If we perceive the symptomatic relationship as the criterion of truth and set up the lie as the dialectical opponent to truth, then we must maintain that a lie is half symbolic and half signalistic, that a lie is a hybrid product and thus as such more complicated and more interesting than truth. The great mistake of modern culture has been that, in its idealism, it has undervalued the cultural significance of the lie and worn itself out in an eternal hunt for truth, instead of investigating what a lie is. In a peculiar way, this investigation has been a taboo. The reason is the fear of losing those illusions that can make people conform to rules and customs. Nevertheless, at a time when scientific symbolism is stagnating into an irreplaceable implement, it is enormously important to define the mean between signal and symbol called pictorial art. In reality it is this, which, being the opposite of the symptom, places pictorial art in an antagonistic relationship to science. The recognition of this is of fundamental dynamic and dialectical significance for both art and science. In its antagonistic relationship to the symbol, pictorial art is a false symptom produced by signalistic and symbolic effects, and is in this sense pure illusion. The false symptom is a representation of the sensual signs that always describe the presence of an object without that object being there. It is the life-like picture of an apple on a dish, where in reality there is neither an apple nor a dish, but just a canvas and some paints. *Such a picture is not signalistic. Neither is it symbolic but more or less both.*

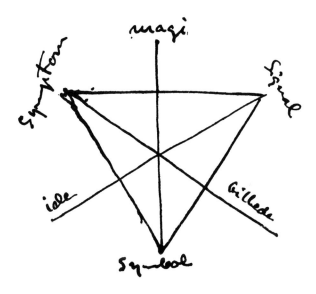

magi = magic, billede = image, ide = idea

FIG. 3. THE SECOND TRIOLECTIC

In the same way, if we seek the dialectically antagonistic relationship to the signal, then it must be a false signal that is a mixture of symbol and symptom. Such a hybrid product is called an ideal.* *Ideals are imaginary signals*, but are imageless, having nothing to do with the world of sensation, and cannot be produced pictorially. In the sensual sense, they are *anti-pictures*.

Similarly, the dialectical opposition to the symbol is a hybrid product of symptom and signal called magic. We can thus now polarize these phenomena in relationships where they mutually abolish each other, and establish that symptom and picture are deadly enemies just like signal and ideal and like symbol and magic.

In European culture, it looks as if three basic cultural types are being separated out, each of which in itself has a tendency to fall back to one of these antagonistic relationships which, as it were, form the basic tension in the intellectual structure. It is as if the Byzantine-Muscovite culture above all emanates from the opposition symptom-picture, as if the Romano-Latin culture first and foremost stretches between the opposition symbol-magic, and the Nordic culture above all orients itself along the opposition signal-ideal, and that the basic European conflicts are identical with the mutual competition and complementarity of these three orientations. At any rate, it is possible to explain certain conflicts in religious history from this viewpoint.

Part 2:
Expeditions to new worlds

A traditionally coherent description and critique can be elaborated only for the known. This we have attempted to do in the previous section. In the great unknown region now lying before us, we must use another method, if we are not to tie ourselves to forms which will hinder us from revising the perception of what we see through new observations. We must experiment forwards in leaps in order to collect material for study. The definitive conclusion can only be reached when far more comprehensive data becomes available.

The naive pictorial world of modern science

What have we now achieved by this initial analysis of Bohr's conceptual world? First and foremost, we have discovered that we can draw a picture of the perception of time lying at the heart of the scientific description of actuality. We can simply draw a line which symbolizes the time dimension and is thus theoretically infinite. On this line we draw a point and call it the present moment. On the side of the point all in the direction of the past is the past and on the opposite side of the point everything that has an opposing direction towards the future is the future. What science calls actuality occurs by an extension of the point which thus becomes a part of a line having its centre on the present moment, and is thus a symmetrical abolition of the orientation towards the past and towards the future within the part of the line delimited by the two end points and called actuality.

How are the opposingly oriented movements within the field of actuality abolished in a contemporaneity? *By the end point of the past from the present moment being shifted towards the future.* This is called 'the utilization of scientific experience', and by *moving the future orientation back in the past* to something called 'historical origin'. The length of actuality is the distance between question and answer, which is called *the communication interval*. The development of this interval thus occurs by a double projection, in part of the past's experiences out into the future and in part of exciting events back into the past, and by the establishment of an absolute communicative correlation between them.

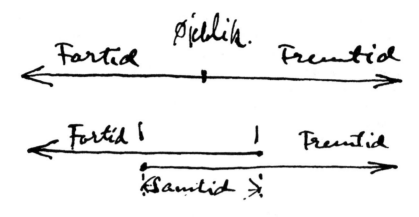

Fortid = Past, Øjeblik = Instant, Fremtid = Future, Samtid = Contemporaneous time

FIG. 4. THE NAIVE PICTORIAL WORLD OF MODERN SCIENCE

When such an instrumentation is undertaken by the scientist, it is to achieve a *result*, and this result is neither present nor past-future, it is something completely different. This is what one calls the objective result, actuality taken out of its context with past and future, so that it can be measured, checked and repeated, thus giving the possibility of *reproducing* an area of actuality exactly the same as before, indeed, preferably thousands of such identical areas of actuality completely independent of the time dimension. If it can be repeated and measured, this result is a *quantity*.

We have hereby seen that actuality is an abolition of the past-future orientation in a static opposition. If this static opposition can be repeated with precision, that means that it can be taken out of its position in the time dimension, liberated from its position in time, and that it has become what one calls an object.

If the length of actuality is the distance between question and answer, what then is the length of the future? The geometrical sign for the future is the half-line: that is to say, a line which is closed by a point at one end, whilst in the other direction there is just direction or orientation without end and thus theoretically infinity. What makes such a line a symbol of the future is simply that the end point is perceived as *the zero point of the beginning* and not of the end. Here it is astonishing that what gives the scientist faith in scientific results is their measurability, and this measurability consists in these statements being capable of reduction to purely numerical reckonings of repetitions of units disposed along a half-line, perhaps in a 'line of the future' (?), for no measuring apparatus in the world exists which is not ultimately and simply a half-line divided into regular divisions from the starting point out into the theoretically infinite. This is true for measurements in both space and time. Indeed, apart from it being impossible to separate what one calls measurements from what science calls 'the concept of the future', even though the latter cannot be measured, but is itself the yardstick and thus the *a priori* of all measurement, the concepts of both space and time become in reality quite absurd in this connection.

What, purely psychologically, is 'the future' or the *a priori* of measurement? This is the question that is awaiting an answer, and thus, in the most profound sense, our curiosity, our wonder, our *interest* or our attention. Time which stands still is either enormously long or so short that it slips between the fingers as an instant, depending upon whether the waiting time is used just waiting for something immensely significant or whether something enormously significant has to be finished in a limited time frame, upon whether one is thus waiting for an answer or has posed oneself a question to be solved and where thus the answer is only whether one can or cannot. That a phenomenon is measurable would thus in reality only mean that it can be inserted into the simple questionnaire that is the regularly divided line of the future, and one has the impression that the same primitive apparatus is a symbol of what is in modern society called progress. One surely hits the bull's eye if one maintains that *the only kind of question to which the answer is given in advance is quantitative measurement.* Posing a question to which there is already an answer is today called posing an 'intelligent' question. He who can pose questions that even the wisest cannot answer is a fool.

Science can only give answers to questions to which there is already an answer in the given conditions. The technical handicap of science is that its possibility of being answered is conditioned by the question being posed 'correctly'. It has been said that science is the answer to the question *what.* But one forgets that it can only answer if one has learned *how* the question is to be posed. All questions which do not answer to this instrumentation are simply scientifically irrelevant and are the reason for the sustained stagnation of science which makes the best scientists record that the scientific apparatus itself is the greatest opponent to scientific innovation. With the help of the Copenhagen thesis, this dilemma has been by-passed for a while.

50   *The Natural Order and Other Texts*

Science has no future before it

It is immensely easy to demonstrate that what Bohr and Heisenberg call 'the future' is completely fused with what they call the present or the actual, for *only the present can be influenced, changed or prevented* (in principle). Indeed this particular activity, the operation, the process, is the only thing we call presence or actuality. The true essence of the future as something complementary to the past, to what we know and can have heard about, and to the present which we can influence, change and prevent, has completely escaped their attention. We have already seen what a catastrophic effect this blindness has on their definition of what we call the experiment. What really represents the future, what makes it at all possible to talk about something which can be called the future, must be the presence of something we have never known before or have had the possibility of hearing about (in principle), which we cannot immediately change or prevent for that same reason, and which we thus would not be able to influence (in principle), except by running into it and thereby getting to know it.

Bohr's dilemma occurs here, for he has discovered that it is impossible to learn anything new except by running into it. Unfortunately, this collision appears to be an influence which changes the behaviour of that which one wishes to learn, so that it becomes impossible to advance towards this unknown. The effect is really that the future has to be defined as the impossible, the unknown and the ineffable and the uninfluenceable, the unchangeable, the intractable. However, at the same time, this only becomes the future if one is prepared for the impossible to be possible, the unknown to become knowable, the ineffable to become articulated, the uninfluenceable to become influenced, the unchangeable to become changed and the intractable to be managed. The future becomes actual by coming up against the past and becoming the present.

Here we have come back to the conclusion that the unthinkable must be capable of being thought and that the origin of the thought is not the convention but the creative thought, that the origin of the word is not the accepted definition but the creative word, and that the origin of the thought and the word is a process which takes place in a unique creation in the psyche of the individual.

The definition of actuality or contemporaneity by the theory of relativity and by dialectical materialism identifies it with communication, which is defined as the establishment of a *dialogue*, a mutual contact. Actuality is not, therefore, just the time the realization of such a mutual contact takes, but also the space that exists between the two points of contact, which thus becomes actual space.

The Natural Order 51

One could even go so far as to maintain that what is here called actuality is the transformation of time to space, as we know little more about space other than that it is contemporaneity.

A very big problem with this perception of actuality is defining what is really to be understood by the expressions past and future, especially when one begins to dig down under the expressions one is normally satisfied to use as an explanation, and tries to have these explanations explained instead of accepting them for what they apparently cover.

Thus if we are to discover what the consequences of modern development are, we must tackle basic principles that have hitherto been beyond dispute, have been sacred axioms. We must submit all the *a priori* or taboo conceptions of classical culture to analysis. We must reach a new perception of the relationship between thought, word and action, and come to a deeper understanding of what it is to think, what it is to talk and what it is to act. But as soon as we begin upon this, we discover that there is no unanimity at all about anything to do with these points. Discussion has been furious for centuries. If we are to find out, however, we have to avoid throwing ourselves into these discussions of opinion. Instead we must accept whatsoever opinions that can be put forward and then see if it is possible to explain each and every one in relation to the other, without excluding anything at all, and then see if we can progress to new ways of thinking. We must discover how one thinks, speaks and acts in different cultural circles, how they believe that they think, talk and act, and how they say that they think, talk and act, and then compare the results. That this is a task far beyond my abilities means that I am condemned in advance to be all at sea, but if only the beginning is correct, then it does not matter. It is a matter of beginning well.

A dialectical antagonistic relationship could be set up between the actual and the irrealizable. But then the question becomes what inner polarization the concept of the irrealizable contains. The relativists call the irrealizable the possible and divide possibility into two opposite groups that they call the past and the future, between that we could know and that we could affect. Here already, however, a contradiction lies hidden. We have no possibility of affecting the past, unless one deprives the concept of scientific experience of any meaning. An experience can be true or false, or replaced by another, but the experience in itself is not a possibility. It is determined in its being, is a necessity. No one can run from his past, not even a scientist.

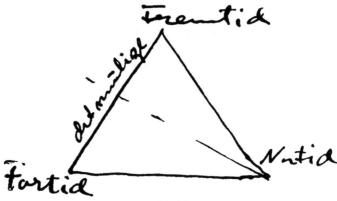

Fremtid = Future, Nutid = Present,
Fortid = Past, det mulige = the possible

FIG. 5. THE TEMPORAL TRIOLECTIC

If at the same time we take the expression *experiment* seriously, then we must demand that we learn something through scientific research which we have not had the possibility of knowing before, that the result is a new knowledge, and thus another impossibility. Thus the possibilities lie neither in the past nor in the future, but in the scale that connects them and which goes from the probable, which is not pure past, which is the necessary, to the improbable which is not pure future, which is the miraculous, the pure accident.

Through Bohr's investigations we are today allowed to include this side of the essence of phenomena in our observations, and this opens up a new philosophical horizon, widening the register from the secure to the problematic. Linguistically, what one could know means what one has already answered, and what we do not know but want to know is what is called a question. The future is the questions without answers, and the past is the answers which no longer have question marks. Actuality is dialogue.

Irresponsible causes and effects without causes

Science maintains that it is not possible to answer anything that is not posed as a question. This is just as great a misunderstanding as not wanting to reckon with questions that cannot be answered. An answer which is not provoked by or does not have any relationship at all to a question is what one calls *a precondition*, an *a priori* or an axiom. This is what is also called, with a pitying expression, a *necessity*, and for the whole of science all the past, everything we have been able to hear about and all the events we could know, and thus the whole of the area of scientific experience, is an *a priori*, a necessary answer, the precondition for being able to pose a new scientific question. That this area has been developed experimentally does not wipe out the fact that all this *a priori* has come to an end by being so. It is time that scientists liberated their statements about experimental science from a certain sentimentality, especially where it concerns their perception of the experimental.

Bohr's observations knocked the bottom out of the all-encompassing container of the principle of causality without, however, being able to assert that causes do not exist. No one could be made to take responsibility for anything at all except on the basis of the principle of the cause, and the weakness of Bohr's morality or philosophy is precisely his talk of the 'responsibility' of the scientist. If a responsibility is the actual or causal unit of question and answer, of effect and cause, then it is necessary, it is the condition, it is the same as what is called *the irresponsible cause,* and the proof that effectless causes are to be found. These are also called truisms. There are also *causeless effects*, that is, meaningless questions or problems. A measuring instrument is such a causeless effect, an *instrument for the answering of meaningless questions*. This is the only possible definition one can give for a measuring instrument.

Determinism versus Communism

The Marxists postulated the thesis that humanity never poses questions to which there are not answers in advance, that the posing of problems is just the human brain's reaction to answers already existent in matter and society. That a number of intelligent heads have rolled in the course of time before the rest of them discovered that questions which do not correspond to the given answers are 'counter-revolutionary' because they are stupid, does not seems to have advanced Soviet philosophy. But why waste time with intellectual problems, when the positive results of these can be imported free, whilst at the same time one can be indignant that so much energy is wasted abroad on *metaphysics*, art and aesthetics and other depravities?

If *Communism, or absolute actuality*, universal communication, is set up as a predetermined *necessity*, then this is cut off from ever being a *possibility*. The precondition for ever being able to realize this *possibility* must be by first *recognizing, purely theoretically, the absolute equivalence of all possible and impossible questions as questions and the equivalence of all possible and impossible answers as answers.* Within actuality no question and no answer can be more meaningful than any other question or answer, if actuality is not just a delusion. On the basis of Lord Kelvin's theory of equivalence, Alfred Jarry transformed this experience into the higher principle he called *pataphysics*, which, in its relationship to physics and metaphysics, must be described as the new universal religion, able to abolish the conflict with the scientific concept of truth, the victorious evolution of which the metaphysical religions have been unable to survive, and science has thus been released from a task it would not have been able to master without the help of artists.

The symbolism of temporal perspectives

We now go back to an earlier problem. How does one decide what the orientation is towards the past and towards the future by the introduction of a point on a theoretically infinite line, a dimension? In which direction does the future lie and in which the past? In which direction lies progress and in which retrogression?

If we take my own orientation, it all seems easy enough. If I follow my nose, that is progress, and if I have to go backwards, then that is retrogression. But then I begin to get a murky inkling that progress is surely an aspiration to something higher whilst retrogression has often been explained to me as a fall. But what is ascension and fall, cadence and decadence? It gets even worse if I begin to discuss these problems with others. Then I am suddenly told that progress is to the left and reaction to the right, whilst the man of the right explains that progress is to the right and to the left is decline.

Both swear to me that I should not listen to their opponents, but at the same time I cannot avoid drawing their attention to the fact that, from their front, they, each facing the other, must automatically be pointing in the same direction, though one is lifting the right and the other the left arm. For them both progress lies in the same direction. They have just chosen an opposite position in relation to the progress they both want, and I am not able to see that either one of the two positions is more correct than the other. But then I am told that the one who can crush his opponent can turn a quarter-circle, follow his nose and go straight ahead, that the liquidation of this system of opposition turns humanity directly in the direction of progress, and it is then that the majority can create its dictatorship and wipe out the opposition of the minority

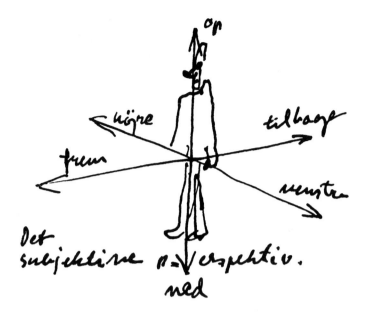

op = up, tilbage = back, venstre = left, frem = forward, højre = right, Det subjektive perspektiv = The subjective perspective

FIG. 6. THE SUBJECTIVE PERSPECTIVE

based upon privilege and the ownership of the means of production. When I then ask *the line of direction of this progress*, I am told that it is the way towards *the right for all to achieve the greatest yield for the least effort*, and then I can only answer that this is not a line of progress at all, as it has no starting point and is not infinite, but has a termination point which is the state where I can achieve everything without any effort whatsoever, and that, purely graphically, this must be a retrogression.

Then I am told by the other side that I have completely misunderstood the situation. The priest can tell me that the broad way, *the straight way*, the way of least effort, is nothing other than a fall straight to Hell. The right way, the way of the right, the shortest way between two points, is the exact opposite of the correct way, which is the thorny path against the stream upwards, *the way of the highest effort*. Everything else is perdition. Here I have to answer the same as I answered the socialist. I can see no true starting point for this journey. But I can see a termination point where I reach the absolute altruistic state where I offer the very best I can without enjoying anything at all and therefore kick the bucket. It is possible that this is the gateway to the highest salvation, but it says nothing to me about what progress is. Both perspectives seem only to be dialectical opposites in a double game where, in contrast to the capitalist system, the chosen elite sacrifices itself to the majority's wish for the least effort, where people instead of having masters now have servants, which most justly perceive as a revenge, an exploitation of the benefits, but which does not in the least explain to me what progress is, except that I do not want to be either master or servant.

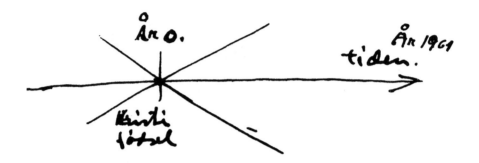

År 0 = Year 0, Kristi fødsel = Birth of Christ,
tiden = time, År 1961 = Year 1961

FIG. 7. THE BEGINNING OF THE CHRISTIAN PERSPECTIVE

I will simply turn back to my drawings and ask them for advice. I draw a point on a line. Something strange happens. I have made a station on the road, a stop. I could also have done the opposite: begun with the point and moved it like Euclid. But if I do that, then I get not a line but a half-line which stops at a certain point. Is this point now the start or the end point? That the beginning is in the drawing process itself is self-evident, but can this be thought of as an end-point at all? An end-point to what? No, it is impossible. I note that *the end-point of a half-line must always be perceived as the beginning, regardless in which direction I draw or think the line.* If I cannot thus find out what orientation I have to give the orientation past and the orientation future from a given point, then I have at any rate now established that I can make a future orientation without at the same time having a past orientation, whilst the opposite seems impossible, and that *the past orientation can simply only occur as a negation of the future orientation,* represented linearly as two opposite orientations from a central point.

If the shortest way from one point to another is a straight line and the same line, if it is followed in one direction, is the easiest way, whilst that followed in the opposite direction is the most difficult way, then the straight line in one direction must be the *line of fall* and in the opposite direction *the line of ascension*. If this line is a half-line with one end-point, then this end-point must be a centre and a half-line must be the same as a radius without a defined size of circle, a radiation. *Progress, orientation or radiation should thus be the same*. But this should mean that any point must be a centre without a circle and that a double-orientation past-future is a diameter without a circle. Why not?

Art and political geometry

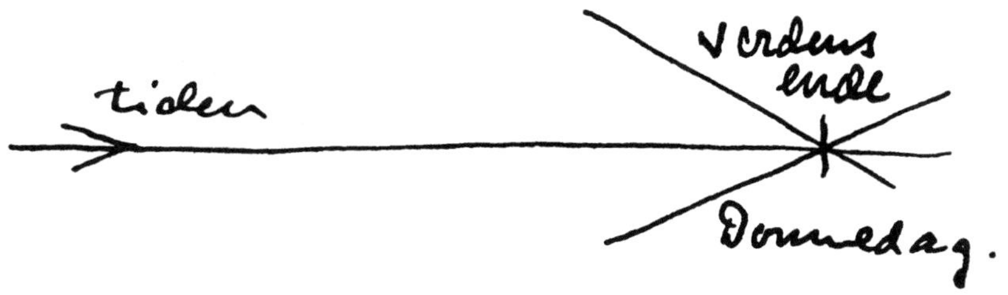

tiden = time, Verdens ende = The end of
the world, Dommedag = Judgement Day

FIG. 8. THE END OF THE CHRISTIAN PERSPECTIVE

If we now go back to our drawing of the line segment we called actuality, which has occurred by allowing the half-line from the past to overrun the future's half-line, then the two end-points in the resultant line thus have a meaning as two radiating centres. It is easy to demonstrate that this is the case and that we are here confronted with an ethical-scientific polarization, and that this polarization has played a quite extraordinarily large role in the political, technical development of recent centuries. Indeed, we will see that this is the key to the understanding of how this machinery in all its simplicity functions.

The purely geometrical turning-point or centre, the zero point of the modern reckoning of time is the birth of Christ, and his birthday has simply been moved a couple of days from the New Year in order not to make him a purely almanac

58 *The Natural Order and Other Texts*

principle. Others have vainly sought to move this zero point which secures Christianity a far more essential place in culture than any church could establish. With it Christianity has become a fixed point with the effect that everything that happened before the birth of Christ is the past, whilst everything that has happened since the birth of Christ is the future. Such a dividing line is, however, without social actuality. This actuality or waiting period is established by placing a point in the future where the judgement on the past will take place at the resurrection of Christ and *the end of the world*. With this, every worldly event within this space of time from the birth of Christ *to Judgement Day* is made absolutely meaningless. *Only then will the future begin.*

What was represented here was a doubly opposed central perspective in the dimension of time, and thus on the same axis. One central perspective was towards the future, where all the lines converged in the fall of the world, and from where the radiating lines beamed out towards an unknown paradisaical anti-world. At the same time, the birth of Christ became the illuminating focus in the perspective of the past, from whence new hope was beamed over the earth. But what makes the whole system so interesting is that the beginning, the birth of Christ, and thus the future perspective, is placed in the past, whilst the end, Judgement Day, the definitive past, is projected out into the future. With this the system for the area of modern actuality, the waiting time, was worked out in an absolute or ideal form. Only when, with the Renaissance, they began to investigate the apparatus itself and refused to believe blindly in it as something absolute, did they become at all convinced that it was just an instrument, and only at the turn of the century did Sorel discover how this instrument could be utilized for other purposes, that ideals could be transformed to instruments. He thus gave Mussolini, Lenin and Hitler the blueprint from which they could shape their concentrations of power and open the way to the establishment of a purely technical condition of tension, where the system works by force, without anything being built upon belief. This system has today become so purified that the atom bomb expert only needs to press a button if humanity does not wait in peace and good order. The opposite pole to this point about which the expectations of the world have literally gathered lies in the scientific perspectives of nature. The birth of Christ no longer plays a greater role than the zero point on a thermometer. Points of origin are established in the past, right back to the reckoning of the moment of the origin of the universe itself. The past becomes more and more illuminated as the future gradually looks blacker and blacker. As a threat, the tension between the displacement of the past into the perspective of the future is an enormous scourge, a process which paradoxically enough is nourished by

The Natural Order 59

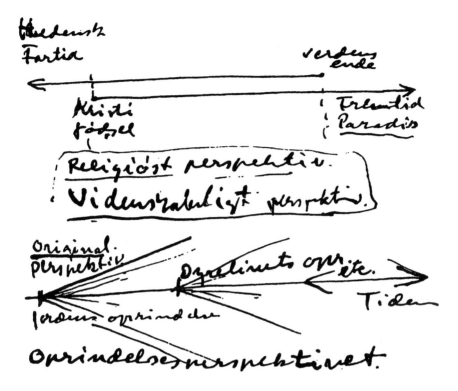

Hedensk Fortid = Pagan past, Verdens ende = End of the world,
Kristi fødsel = Birth of Christ, Fremtid Paradis = Future Paradise
Religiøst perspektiv = Religious perspective
Videnskabeligt perspektiv = Scientific perspective
Original perspectiv = Original perspective
Dyrelivets opr. etc. = The origin of animal life, etc.
Jordens oprindelse = The origin of the world, Tiden = Time

FIG. 9. THE PERSPECTIVE OF ORIGIN

humanity's exaggerated exertion to achieve the least effort, which will exhaust the generation of human energy, but has an unknown breaking point. The only consistent enemy of this perspective, its only implacable opponent, appears to have been modern art, which has persistently been working to break it into pieces and demonstrate its absurdity since Impressionism. It is, at any rate, difficult to free oneself from the suspicion that even eminent scientists are duped by this primitive and banal blueprint.

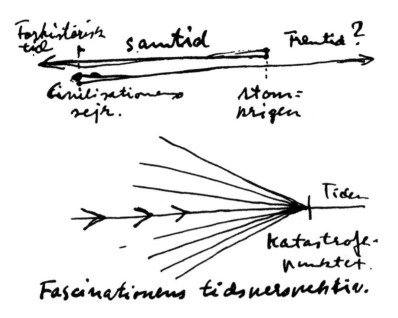

Forhistorisk tid = Prehistoric time, samtid = contemporaneous time, Fremtid = Future, Civilisationens sejr = The victory of civilization, Atomkrigen = Nuclear war, Tiden = Time, Katastrofepunktet = catastrophe point

FIG. 10. THE TEMPORAL PERSPECTIVE OF FASCINATION

What Sorel discovered was the geometrical formula for idealism. With this, idealism became reduced to an absolute idea-less instrument based upon scientific experience and utilizable regardless of which particular goal a large number of people are required to gather their interest around. This is the absolute unartistic and idea-forsaken basis for modern propaganda and advertisement, an apparatus to make people want something without coming to that decision via personal thinking, criticism or the taking of positions to the problem, without even suspecting at all that these represent an endeavour or that it is a question of problems or that they have any responsibility. The colossal effectiveness of this apparatus in Germany under the Nazi regime, the system that has today left us a people who stand open-mouthed at what they themselves agreed to and can hardly be made responsible for, is in reality a far more dangerous phenomenon in itself than any of the horrors the collision of these concentrations of energy has invoked up to now. It could be called *scientific idealism* or objective idealism. It is poor art. Cheap wallpaper.

Modern art's struggle against this idea-forsaken acceptance of the most banal form of images will become more and more unequal, because artistic pictorial creation has been officially reduced to an unnecessary entertainment if it does not serve these primitive perspectives and the artist is to create spontaneously like a child and not worry about *the ideas*. There is no longer any use for them except as clichés. The moment has now come when art, in order to avoid being reduced to a simple advertisement technique, must break through in the same way as in the Renaissance with people like da Vinci and Dürer and draw up the perspectives and symbols which today rule the large majority, in order by this to see and demonstrate what they really look like and what they will result in, to complete that break with the Renaissance's compositional formulas of central perspective which began purely destructively with the breakthrough of modern art, and to create a new foundation for the perception or observation of images which *is not only naive and spontaneous, but also able to capture all the modern intelligence and express the modern consciousness in all its nuances*. This can only happen in a remorseless battle against objective idealism.

How can the dimension of time be depicted?

Orientation towards the future is the primary direction and the orientation towards the past is the secondary counter-movement in the other direction derived from it. But how can I immediately ascertain what is motion and what is counter-motion? For the central zero-point is also apparently the beginning of a series of numbers towards the past. Only this series is negative. But if my attention is not drawn to this negativity, then I could imagine that the backward step is an advance. If I mark a point on an endless line symbolizing the dimension of time, then I can myself decide in which direction the future lies. The opposite direction then becomes the past. *But I cannot treat my lifetime from the cradle to the grave in this way.* Here I can reverse nothing. The orientation is, as they say, irreversible. *If time is to be perceived as a dimension like the other three, it must neither have a beginning nor an end determined in a particular orientation.* Time must be reversible, unless *time, orientation or irreversibility should be the same*, which is to say, that *time is always future* and can never be anything else. But then it does not delineate a dimension. Should time then have something called the beginning of time and thus be an oriented half-line out towards infinity? Should eternity thus not have existed always, but will exist only in the future which is the only true infinity? But then what about the decay of the universe? Does real infinity begin then? How can there be a real infinity when it also has a beginning at a particular moment? Or does time no longer exist when the world no longer exists? In that case, time is not a half-line but a line segment just like actuality. A line segment is a line limited by two end points. But what does such a line segment consist of? Logically it is impossible for it to consist of a series of points as the point cannot have special extension like the line segment. *Regardless of how many points one puts together, they will remain points* and it is unthinkable that they can be laid side by side to form a line, for then a line necessarily has to be defined as *the spaces between a series of points*. The line loses any significance if it is not a symbol for a context and this context can be only described as a *possibility of motion*. A line must be something absolutely essentially different from a point. The point only exists at the end of the line when one cuts it short, and appears as the termination of the line, its negation. If a line has in principle neither beginning nor end and thus no orientation, then a half-line has a decided orientation and *a line segment, which must have two end points, must thus also have two opposite orientations* and thus be two lines of the same size located in the same place, which is not impossible because they have no mass, and with two opposite directions of motion. But if this is correct and time has two end points, then time must be able to go forwards and backwards, but not simultaneously, simply because the only thing we know about time is that it is apparently something that cannot go in several different directions at once, or that it is what makes us able to separate directions from positions, sequence from simultaneity. Finally, time seems to be a special form of experience of what we call motion, just as space appears to be a special vision of what we call statics.

The original point – fascination

If attention is concentrated upon a point, then attention is, in the classical sense, fascination, something that Erik Lundberg has set out with such great genius in his description of the method for deciphering a Greek or Persian building in *The Formal Language of Architecture*.* Art is playing with fascination, and this play must contain a quantity of unwritten and original information for it to be practised at all. That Bohr is so fascinated by the superior character of mathematics, that this for him is the focal point, is understandable and natural. But if it is made the focus of *everyone's* attention, which is perhaps

The Natural Order 63

unconsciously what the Copenhagen Interpretation sets out to demand, then the arrangement that leads in that direction appears, at any rate from an artistic point of view, just as naive as my own incursion into scientific problems. For it is precisely fascinations, their elaboration and interplay that are the artist's special area.

Let us now go back to the experimental arrangement that relativism postulated in order to describe simultaneity. Let us do it by imagining a man sitting on a sphere in space. He lights a flare. The light beams from this strike an apparatus on another sphere lying several million light-years away and release a mechanism which lights a corresponding light, which after the same number of light-years is captured by the apparatus on the first sphere. The man who sent the light is long since dead but the two signals are simultaneous. But how can we now get out of this simultaneity, and how can we achieve the sharpest contrast to this simultaneity? We can do this either by being outside the field of action or by placing ourselves midway between the two phenomena and measuring the time difference between the interception of the two signals. This shows that *a field of actuality is something one chooses. What is to be simultaneous is something one decides oneself* or, more correctly, everything exists under particular conditions seen from a particular point of view in an absolute simultaneity. Establishing oneself in this absolute view of simultaneity is called mysticism in a Swedenborgian sense. But the strange thing is that absolute simultaneity cannot be explained as anything but absolute space.

Instant in time – point of intersection

We started by cheerfully accepting time as a dimension like that of space and drawing it as a line, and we have seen that further explanations involve us in more and more complications. It becomes even more difficult if we want also to enrol the dimension of time into our system of spatial coordinates of height, breadth and depth. By projection we can extend space to as many dimensions as we wish, but the dimension of time must have another character which has not hitherto been discovered or noticed. My solution of the problem is this, that *the dimension of time has always been included in any system of coordinates, just as the dimension of time or motion has always been smuggled into any geometrical description, even of purely spatial phenomena.* One only needs ask oneself the question, where is the point of intersection of the three dimensions of space? *Is it at all possible to fix a point of intersection for the three dimensions of spaces at one particular point,* as is done in any system of coordinates, without doing violence to these dimensions or introducing a phenomenon which has nothing at all to do with these dimensions in themselves. No points at all are to be found in the three infinite dimensions of space. If they were, they would not be dimensions but finite magnitudes.

The interesting thing in the establishment of time as a dimension is that, purely graphically, it can be treated and described by a line in the same way as the three dimensions of space. If a line is defined as a dimension and this as infinite, it is impossible to decide what is forwards and what is backwards on the line. *Our dimensional line cannot have an orientation. The same must be true of the dimension of time.* What is the future and what is the past cannot be determined. Just as progress and retrogression, forward and backward only have relevance to the nose and to the tail if one stays in one position. (Central perspective is just a right-angled projection of one's own system of coordinates of right, left, up, down, forward and backward.) Thus the future too only has relevance to the subject's progress or advance, and the past to what the subject leaves by this displacement. *If time belongs to the past and the future, then it is identical with subjective motion in space. If the observer does not move in relation to his environment, then time does not exist.* However, time does not disappear because of this. It is just reduced to a point, to *the instant in time*.

The result of Einstein's introduction of the time dimension as a fourth dimension thus means that *everything that can be reduced to a point in geometry is transformed from being a spatial phenomenon to a time dimension,* as *the Euclidean definition of the point as a purely abstract phenomenon in space, without dimension, must be replaced by the definition that a point in space is the introduction of the time dimension into space,* because *a fixed point at any rate has the dimension of duration or time.*

Beginning from this definition, I am of the opinion that we can construct a new anti-Euclidean geometry if, instead of starting with the point, we go in the opposite direction and begin with that purely abstract principle of three-dimensionality, the sphere or the globe. Imagine a sphere, the only abstract property of which is homeomorphology. This sphere has a precise diameter, shall we say 10 centimetres. We press this sphere one centimetre flatter and measure the ensuing enlargement in the breadth of the incipient ellipse form. We continue the process with yet another centimetre, continuing with our calculations until we have pressed the sphere to the thickness of one centimetre. Through these nine stages we have achieved *a curve which shows us precisely how big the sphere is when it no longer has thickness, when it has become a surface.* From being infinite it has become finite. But if we have thereby been able to calculate the homeomorphic equivalence between a three-dimensional

The Natural Order 65

and a two-dimensional figure, then this homeomorphology is not absolute, as the meeting of the two pressed together poles has reduced two points to one and *has liberated one point from the whole.* We have defined this point as an instant in time, as *a time dimension.*

If, instead of pressing the sphere flat, we had begun with liberating it from this point in the middle, we would have been able to establish the homeomorphic equivalence between a sphere and a corresponding spherical surface plus the centre.

However, if we now go back to the circular surface and under measurement begin to stretch it out in length, we will in the same way be able to establish the homeomorphic equivalence between a surface of a particular size and a line of a particular size, and we liberate yet another point by this process. With this we now have two points and we must thereby conclude that there exist three dimensions of time just as there exist three dimensions of space and that the difference between a three-dimensional figure and a two-dimensional one is that the first has no temporal dimension, whilst the spatial two-dimensional figure has had a spatial dimension replaced by a dimension of motion or time. In the same way, the spatial line must have two dimensions of motion. The problem then is how I am to transform the line into a point. I can do this by changing it to pure motion. If I thus let this determined line segment be projected in the direction of the line with sufficient speed through space, it should thus be reduced to a point, and a point will be geometrically liberated. This is also what Einstein maintains, if it is projected with the speed of light. If the particular speed could be achieved by rotation, this would mean that *a space can be reduced to a point by rotation at the speed of light* if it does not move in space, or that light is matter transformed to rotation. This, according to my impressions, is the elementary geometrical consequence of Einstein's and Bohr's definitions.

According to this definition, time and motion should thus be the same and a point in space pure motion without spatial extent, and thus a nothing rotating about itself, pure rotation.

When one has established this definition of pure rotation, one begins to speculate about how pure rotation can really be, and attempts to imagine a purely non-spatial rotation. Such a rotation must normally or probably only be able to spin one way, otherwise one has to have a double rotation. But that cannot simultaneously have an axis firmly oriented in space, for then it would be part of a straight line, a definition of the straight line given by Gauss. This, incidentally, is the only positive definition of a true line that exists: a series of points that can rotate about themselves without moving from their place. That

66   *The Natural Order and Other Texts*

the point's rotation is far freer than the rotation of the points on an axis where all have to rotate in the same way is self-evident. *The points have thus become a line segment or have been integrated in a spatial dimension by having lost one of their freedoms of movement.*

By the axis it is even clearer than by the point that it is impossible to get it to rotate, unless this rotation goes only one way without the rotation being oriented. If it is to rotate the other way, for there is only one other way the line can rotate, it has to stop, and the new rotation will then act in relation to the other as a turning back, as the passage from one side of a surface to the other.

What we have done here is to leave the motion of the subject completely out of consideration, ignoring completely any absolute conception of forward or backward, and have laid the foundation for an elementary non-oriented geometry, or more correctly a dynamic *situmetry.*

From this angle, development or expansion is complementary to progress. I would not call this relationship an antagonistic relationship. *As far as I can see, this is what Bohr calls the 'complementary antagonistic relationship', identical to the special form of 'opposition' that exists between two dimensions in a right-angled context,* a context for which, as far as I know, there is no precise expression, a context where two factors go *across each other.*

If we conceive the universe as an infinite sphere, it must be immobile. If we conceive it as expansion, we must conceive it as the surface of a globe, which must have a centre. If we investigate how linear motion, progress, is related purely subjectively to evolution, our own linear motion, our own progress, then two possibilities exist, either that *the focus lies in the past,* so evolution is conceived as a dissemination from a point of origin, or that it lies *in the future as a central perspectival point* we are approaching, a goal. The whole of the scientific description of nature is based upon such a series of dramatic points of fascination in the past: original zero points in the past from whence the whole development spreads. The metaphysical zero point, the aim, the goal, beyond which we can know nothing about events, lies on the other hand in the future, whether it be the destruction of the world, death, the social revolution or any other purely traditional goal.

I have drawn my pictorial or situmetric consequences of the principles of Einstein and Bohr and thus come to the conclusion that I can establish a quantitative equivalence between a particular three-dimensional sphere x, a surface which thus purely mathematically must be called x, a line segment which also purely mathematically must be called x and a point x.

If I now go back with this variable x to the world of Euclidean geometry, then I discover that this formula simply works as a magic wand that makes all of this world gradually vanish as I go forward. This is thus not a non-Euclidean geometry but a directly anti-Euclidean geometry and an anti-mathematical geometry, if one perceives symmetry or the equal sign as the backbone of mathematics. For what I have demonstrated is a system according to which I can change x in agreement with all the fundamental variations of geometry, and show to how great a degree x can be different from x without ceasing to be x.

Turning point – the centre

I have often asked myself if it is possible to perceive a point as a definitive end point except as the centre of a circle. *By a definitive end point I mean a necessary turning point.*

For me, this question arose by speculating on what really happens geometrically when one describes a surface as two-sided, when, for example, the Möbius strip in any particular direction is called one-sided just because the motion is unbroken. One could easily fold the Möbius strip into angles and get the same result. Thus this is not a question of a break but of the size of the angles. I have noticed that the right angle and the straight line are the two critical phases, and all that I know about a right angle is that it is the form that a circle's diameter takes when it is seen from an arbitrary point *on the circle's circumference,* whilst seen from the centre, or anywhere else on the line itself, it is a straight line with two orientations. Except where the line strikes the surface. There the diameter begins, there it has only one orientation and there the right angle disappears. This context explains to me all I know about the properties that are ascribed to these geometrical symbols.

If I perceive the centre as such a definitive turning point, for a straight-lined movement as well, and if I accept the formula of the constancy of the speed of light, and I imagine a hollow glass sphere, the walls of which have an absolute reflexive action, and throw a flash of light into the centre of this sphere, then it should never be possible to extinguish this as long as this arrangement is sustained, for it should be a perpetuum mobile, as the light-beams sent out from this centre will always be reflected back to the centre. This light will thus always stay lit. This is a description based upon the antagonistic relationship between content and container or 'form'.

If I now wish to describe the same phenomenon without taking refuge in the idea of such a counter-positioning of two different materials, what would the explanation be then? Then it must be that the light-beams are sent out from the

68   The Natural Order and Other Texts

centre but simultaneously held back by a force that has the same character as if the light particles were attached fast to the centre by a rubber band that could be stretched to one particular point where the elastic force turns and pulls the particle back again to the centre. Or, more correctly, when the particle is sent out again, it acts as if the centre for this motion does not lie in the centre of the circle, but represents an area round about it, formed by the mid-point of the backward and forward movements, and all these points of intersection together form a sphere-surface, and if one could see what was happening on the other side of it, then it would look as if the particles were thrown back from this sphere-surface. Thus it must appear to an observation made inside 'the light-sphere'. Seen from without, they circle about.

The precondition for the correctness of the first explanation is the adoption of *the constancy of energy*, but, as a consequence of such an undemonstrable *a priori* having been created, one is forced to espouse the *constancy of the speed of light*. The one automatically gives the other or, more correctly, it is the latter which gives the former, for in reality the speed of light is perhaps the only real measure by which other speeds can be measured.

Only by maintaining that light cannot become three-dimensional material is there any basis whatever for proving the objective constancy of light. What is called the expansion of the universe has been explained either by the objects, in fact everything, shrinking and making space appear larger, or also by the objects moving away from each other and putting more and more space between themselves. But as we cannot actually say anything at all about either space or the objects, only about the sensory impressions, and in science these are reduced to *visible* signs, *then we cannot really say anything at all about anything but light*. If, bit by bit, the speed of light were therefore to become quite slow, then no one would be able to discover it, for we would accustom ourselves to it and have nothing to measure it against. This third explanation is at any rate just as good as the two other. Which is chosen is only conditioned by what the hypothesis is to be used for.

It is my impression that throughout the whole of scientific evolution there has been a large number of observations that have been discarded and ignored because they do not suit the logical framework which conditioned the development of an unambiguous explanation of the phenomena.

Only when confronted by two unambiguous explanations which were both satisfactory and yet mutually excluded each other, was it understood that one absolute unambiguity for the whole of scientific description was an impossibility. However, the way was thereby opened to gather up those previously ignored observations and investigate whether they too could form an independent unambiguous description.

This area is precisely the never elaborated artistic science, the science of magic or the doctrine of artificial causes. It is necessary to make a systematic treatment of this area.

The materiality of light

There can be no doubt that this latter perception is the basis of Goethe's theory of colour, or, more correctly, the conclusion of the observations for which he wished an explanation. This is the outline of a conception of *the colours* of light as a gradual *fatigue* becoming at the same time a gradual *materialization*. In order to understand the meaning of this, it is first necessary to understand what it is that becomes fatigued in light. It must be the rotation. The light particle has perhaps changed size, has become larger. Finally, we must try to find a description of what a gradual materialization means.

The precondition for a theory that justifies such hypotheses must be that light and three-dimensional matter are exactly the same, only in different states of existence, and that all types of matter have their own quite special character in the state of light as well. *Spectral analysis uses the fact that one can determine the spectrum of any three-dimensional matter, of all minerals.* Each different form of matter has a different spectrum, and to that degree this is identical with being able to infer an unknown form of matter from an unknown spectrum. All this has been developed since Goethe's time. But an explanation, what about that?

What is light in relation to dark and what is transparency in relation to impermeability? The only thing we know about an object is the circumstances under which it is impermeable, and it would therefore be more correct merely to call the constancy of the speed of light *the light barrier*, just as the constancy of the speed of sound is called *the sound barrier*.

In order to complete the image, the pictorial form of matter, of which we have here generated the basic elements, all that is left to conclude is that what we call the material world does not just appear as a purely spatial three-dimensionality, but that it also possesses three dimensions of motion and that these are incessantly being exchanged with each other, thereby creating forms of matter with three, two, or one spatial dimensions or none at all, where these are replaced by dimensions of motion. This gives us a logical and simple explanation for the separation between the four so-called elements, the character of which modern physics has not clearly accounted for, but which is,

70 *The Natural Order and Other Texts*

however, one of the most essential actualities in our existence. A liquid ought then to be a three-dimensional form of matter which has lost a spatial dimension, which has been replaced by a dimension of motion. Instead of a three-dimensional spatial constancy possessed by crystals, any liquid should only possess a *surface constancy* which should thus be the thickness of a meniscus. Furthermore, all types of gas should be spatially one-dimensional or linear and have two dimensions of motion. Science must ascertain whether this is correct. I would only point out that *the surface constancy of a liquid in this context must be just as important as the motional constancy of light* and, in this way of looking at it, the same, because the ascertainment of the actual *one-sided surface* on the water or in a one-sided mirror is the light phenomenon identical with reflection.

Radius and radiation

According to our definition, a half-line and a radius are the same, if we understand a radius as an independent geometrical object and not as a special function of the circle. A radius is thus that half of a line we define as infinite. Inscribed in a circle, a radius is half of the diameter, but in our definition *a circle's radius is only a determined piece of a radius* which in reality projects beyond the circumference of the circle and continues into infinity. Indeed, what makes this definition even more remarkable is that the correct radius can only really begin outside the circumference of the circle, as that part of radius between the centre and the circumference is a line segment and not a half-line. Our radius is thus a half-line the end point of which is the centre of a circle, but which first begins where it cuts the circumference of the circle. But how should we define it if we allow the part of the radius inscribed within the circle to disappear? *Then a radius or a half-line become that line which from a given point on the circumference of the circle stands at right angles to the tangent on this point and is pulled out from the exterior of the circle.*

If we keep to this definition, something very strange has happened. We have made a planiform geometry where *a point and a sphere are the same* and a three-dimensional geometry where we *cannot distinguish between a point and a sphere*. We have commenced upon a geometry outside actuality or what modern physics calls the field of actuality. We can now see that three geometries can be made; one for what happens within the circumference, or a geometry for everything that can be inscribed in a circle, or, for three-dimensional geometry, everything that can be contained in a sphere or on the circumference of the circle; another for everything that happens upon the surface of the sphere; and finally a geometry for everything that projects beyond it. But if one is outside the circle, this becomes a point. How will it now be possible to distinguish between a point and a circle or a sphere, seen from without? One can only imagine that if one asks *how many radii can emanate from a point*. In the abstract, this must be infinitely many, but this theory is not tenable in reality. If there is no distance between the radii at a point, then it is impossible that an increasing distance does not occur between them the more they are elongated into space. However, *if there are infinitely many, a distance can never occur between them*. But if it doesn't, it is the point itself that extends into the infinite, *and the point has no existence*. There must thus be a limit to how many lines can intersect in a point, for if it is infinitely many, *all the lines can intersect each other in one point and everything is a point and nothing else exists but the point*. But if we assume that the radiations from a point are limited in number, then theoretically this point's extension to a circle or a sphere will give a rising number of possibilities for radiation the more the circle's surface grows, and one could thus calculate the size of the circle or sphere according to the total of radiating radii. But as these radii necessarily become a greater and greater mutual distance apart the further they get from the radiation point, one would thus *perceive fewer and fewer radii the further one moves away from the point*, which is to say, that the globe or sphere more and more approaches the magnitude of a point the further away one gets from it. Of course, this explanation is like a purely optical theory of perspective, but the question is if it could not be elaborated into a purely geometrical formulation without being connected with a concept of light effects, and thus where the explanation is advanced exclusively on the basis of the observance of a severe inner logic in the geometrical conclusions. This is, of course, a task to which only mathematicians can give a definitive form. That I have come to these conclusions is only because I have started from the basic definition of activity that activity and radiation are the same, that all activity must, so to speak, be radio-active, that the radiant is the same as pure action, which again is what we have defined as the aesthetic.

Everything that can be inscribed in a circle or contained in a sphere can be *terminated*, everything that can be inscribed upon the surface of a sphere or in the ring of a circle can be continued into *infinity* and everything that can be described as radiation can be described as *commencement*. This is our purely geometrical formulation of the philosophical tripartition.

72   *The Natural Order and Other Texts*

The absurdity of the classical world picture

An equals sign is two parallel lines and equality is parallelism, which is the same as symmetry.

Two uniformities are characterized by the fact that they can be laid together and the result thereby becomes *the sum of two entities*, that the parallelism can be abolished and that it has become a new entity. The description of this process is that a + sign, which is called plus, can be placed between two uniform phenomena that can be laid together.

Now one would think that it would have been much more simple to abolish one of the lines and use just a single line as an addition sign, as the two have become one. Curiously enough, however, this individual line is used for the opposite, for the subtraction sign. What is the reason that these signs have necessarily to have this form in classical mathematics and geometry and what is the reason that these signs have to be replaced in accord with modern mathematical usage? I pose this question without ever having been able to undertake even the most stupid form of mathematical calculation.

The reason simply lies in the purely imperative preconditions that are the condition for Euclidean geometry, and also for the analytical method in mathematics, that only one theory exists, the equivalence theory, that on the basis of this an unmentionable lie is established, and that the parallelism is only apparently abolished, but not in reality.

By lie we mean, in a purely logical sense, an insuperable self-contradiction about which there is agreement not to do anything, as it is the condition by which the whole concept is able to develop. With a beautiful expression, it is called an *a priori*, and is a taboo. The fundamental self-contradiction in Euclidean geometry consists of the postulate that *one and several are the same and yet are not so.* When we talk about one plus one plus one, and so on, still remaining *one* thing and thus *an entity*, yet at the same time about them becoming more and more, and thus a *plurality*, a *quantity*, and about what Bohr called a *quantum* having no other definition than that of being *a subdivided entity*, these are thus treated as if they were identical with the number one, but at the same time are not so.

The paradoxical thing about the classical world description, the limitations of which were already suggested in Newton's primitive relativism, is that *it is not possible at all to establish an equivalence if this is absolute, for absolute equivalence or equality would mean that the equivalent magnitudes are the same size, are identical. One can only work with equivalence at all if there is a lack of equivalence, either in the spatially or the temporally determined position, or, if this not so, if there is then no equivalence between the positions of the observer during the observation.* The latter variability is the artistic one. The variability of a spatially constant form observed in time is called topology, and the measurement of a fixed body undertaken through spatial motion is called geometry.

Where Euclidean geometry vanishes into a hole is where the experiments that are to *prove* its basic axioms have to be taken too *literally* in the logical sense. If I have five line segments and am to demonstrate that they are equivalent or uniform, *then this can only be done by placing them all in the same place*. If they then cover each other, they are uniform. But as four of them have vanished, as they have no extension except in length. The one-sided or oriented Euclidean explanation does not allow me to get my line segments back after this operation by an opposite operation. If I lift the line segment at the same time as it remains where it is, then I am depicting a surface instead of two line segments, and if I pull it out at one end it just becomes longer without any logical reason, as a line segment cannot become any longer than it is. In the same way, I can reduce thousands of points to one, but there is no Euclidean method to recover the thousand points from the one point again.

If we can only sense changes, where do our ideas about static phenomena, about immutable elements, about the presence of things, come from? We get them from the variability or difference of the changes. If everything changed in the same way, then we would not distinguish any change. This diversity in ways of changing creates the opportunity within a limited area of observation in time and space to perceive those changes that are so small or so large that they cannot be directly observed as purely 'static' states. It is these apparently static states we call objects and which we perceive as forms. We perceive them as forms because they offer resistance to an arbitrary change. Forms, resistances or objects are thus three forms of expression for the static phenomenon.

If, in the same way, we could gather this side of the essence of matter under the concept of statics, then we could polarize mutability in relation to this and call it dynamics. Just as statics in its purity can be described abstractly by the concept of unity, so dynamics in its pure, abstract form has to be designated as variability. But just as it is possible to perceive *unity* and *variability* only as the opposite of each other, a third factor comes into our observations that can only be perceived, that is to say be given a logical meaning, if it is placed in an antagonistic relationship to the two mentioned concepts. This concept, which is science's basic concept in its classical elaboration, is the concept of *equality*. Equality can only be imagined where one can compare, and one can only compare if one has at least two things to compare. This equality between two

74 The Natural Order and Other Texts

things is called symmetry or equivalence.

Causal relationship cannot be traced from either equality or from difference. That a causal relationship between two situations exists is really a presupposition that it is a question of the same entity in which changes have occurred. *The concept of causality is the belief in a changeable entity.* Purely quantitative variability is and must remain without cause, and can only achieve a purely statistical order.

Computation is a means with which equalities and differences can be described. In their simplest form, these equalities and differences can be one-dimensional, corresponding to the numeric series and calculated by simple addition and subtraction, but they always stand in an irreversible relationship to the number *zero*, on the other side of which they unfold into the negative numeric series. Moreover, they can be two-dimensional from the point of zero and then calculated by simple multiplication and division. Moreover, they can have three, four, indeed, infinitely many dimensions and be calculated through the square root etc. But no number says anything whatsoever about the entity the written total represents. This entity is described as a rule by a letter, x, y, z, etc. In mathematics the letter describes nothing more than a fixed sum or quantity, the identity of which one wishes to establish without wanting or being able to reveal its character, and is thus only an abstract way of writing numbers. Nevertheless these letters do not describe the numbers but *entities*, but as these entities are abstract they cannot change. This is their whole meaning. x is and must remain identical during the whole operation. x *says nothing other than what the entity* x *is except that it is constant.*

If two line segments are to be able to cover each other and afterwards to be separated, if two magnitudes x are to added together and then taken from each other again, then there must be a boundary which *stops them from completely coinciding and becoming one. There must be an absolute opposition between all parts of a quantum in order for it to be called a quantum,* for what comes out is identical with what is put in. But the question immediately arises: what is it then that keeps them together? Can the neutral entity be divided into two halves, of which one that separates is held in equilibrium by the other which adheres, and can one liberate the half that separates and thereby achieve an absolute unity?

It is not difficult to see that this relates exactly to mathematics. Only if x is identical to x can $\frac{1}{2}x$ be identical to $\frac{1}{2}x$ and $2x$ be *identical* to $2x$, but in order for x *plus* x to give $2x$ and in order to be able to divide x into 2 *times* $\frac{1}{2}x$, x must be *different* from x. x must form an entity, the division of which can only be explained by this entity, and *the next* x *must form another entity which cannot however be identified with the first without vanishing.* Logically, therefore, the whole of the mathematical as well as the geometrical system is nothing more than an imaginary construct according to certain rules of the game, without logical basis but with logico-absurd method.

Law is equality which is not based on equality but upon absolute identity, upon the entity. If I am to give a picture of what is meant by this, let us then suppose that I witness a motorist suddenly turn in over the pavement and flatten a man standing up against a wall and afterwards hurriedly vanish.

I investigate whether there is any hope for the flattened man and as this is not the case, I get hold of the police in order to get the two men, the victim and the criminal, identified. This means that I have to compare the dead man with the information about another man, and, even though the various parts have been, purely spatially, somewhat displaced in relation to the man's natural appearance, nevertheless have to place him in an equivalent relationship to the form of the man who exists under a particular name and in particular surroundings by discovering particular characteristics which are unique and which we recognize despite their sadly flattened circumstances. Such identification is called topological.

As I am the only witness to the accident, I am the only one who can identify the criminal. I am therefore sent around to find him. I had taken a quite precise and unforgettable impression of the man because I was lucky enough to have had a camera with me and to have taken a precise picture of the man, whose appearance was quite distinctive. Of course, the man I then indicate to be guilty, who corresponds exactly to the photograph, is arrested on the basis of my identification, and, in spite of his violent protests, is indicted and a trial prepares his sentence, until it can be proved that he could not have been at that place at the given moment, but that it could have been possible for his twin brother, who is as alike to him as a pin, and who travelled to America the following day. With this the case is concluded. But if it had been based upon the truth formula of *classical* science, then this absolute identification would not have been necessary. The resemblance would have been enough for him to be convicted.

This is not to execute smith for baker, which is a purely utilitarian method. This is to sentence a smith because another smith has committed a crime, a principle not unknown in law. Science can do no other.

Modern science has dissolved the significance of the basic concepts in the classical perception of our surroundings and their laws. The Copenhagen Interpretation wishes to hinder this dissolution spreading in its natural consequences over the old classical world-picture. As a stop on the way, as the

76 *The Natural Order and Other Texts*

establishment of a period for contemplation and reflection, this taboo has been of extraordinary value. But only if the period liberated in this way is used precisely for experiments in new forms of treatment, for the setting up of new methods for dealing with the classical and elemental world, without these treatments having to be used immediately, and thus for experiments without context. And who is closer to being able to use this period than those that have liberated it. I am sending out these ideas to a Scandinavian public in order to incite and to warn against the belief that the Copenhagen Interpretation can be used as a pillow.

I have sought to discover a natural connection between geometry and mechanics. I believe that the goal of a revision should be the setting-up of a logical conceptual unity which no longer accepts an unbridgeable chasm between a dynamic and a static description of phenomena. One could still have great interest in a classical geometry, but only if one is made aware that this is an abstraction and *it is established where one is abstracting from.* However, this is not done.

I believe that the whole principle of motion in geometry, and thus what I believe I have defined as dimensions of time, is ignored, without consciously defining that this side of the affair is being disregarded. This is clear in Euclidean geometry. One moves the point and creates the line, one moves the line and creates the surface. One moves the surface and creates volume, but what these movements are *in themselves* is a problem that can no longer be ignored.

The same is the case with projection. Two surfaces are identified by moving them so that they cover each other, but what is such a movement in itself? A form is turned around a point or about an axis, even about several axes, but even this movement demands its explanation in itself and in relation to the form independently of the result. Today, mechanics is an abstraction just as irreal as geometry, but no one can separate these two worlds purely abstractly any more.

What one calls mechanical physics is in reality today just as abstract as geometry. The only difference between geometry and mechanics is that classical geometry excludes any preoccupation with the temporal dimension and works only with spatial dimensions. That such a science is possible and will always remain so, is just as obvious as that a purely abstract science which is isolated around the concept of time will, in the future, have the possibility of developing new systems of coordinates of temporal dimensions. But now that Einstein's theory of relativity has abolished the concept of independence between time and space, a purely *spatial* geometry is reduced to an inferior phenomenon which can no longer form the point of departure for a general world-picture. If, however, the time dimension is drawn into geometry, then it is no longer separate from mechanics. This fusion will become more and more distinct in the coming evolution.

This is, of course, a critique from without, where no regard whatever has been taken of the inner demands placed on geometry and mathematics by experts, but scientists today have suddenly begun to take an interest in philosophy and logic, and I await a logical critique of my postulate about the lacking logic in what is being presented to us as a logic satisfactory to science. Not because either science or logic interests me. But in for a penny, in for a pound, and let us see how much we can believe, how many new ideas we can form, how many pictures we can create on this theme.

The scientific *a priori* is beautifully expressed by Werner Heisenberg in his book *Physics and Philosophy* 'The *symmetrical* characteristics always constitute the most essential characteristic of a theory.'* This means that *theorizing* is first and foremost *symmetrization*. This is valid for scientific theorizing and is even *the basic scientific definition of truth*. That something is true in the scientific sense is really only to say that the phenomenon's symmetrical relationship to another phenomenon can be established. This symmetrical relationship is called equivalence or *equality*, which is to say *equally valid*, equal validity, equivalence.

The equal validity of phenomena is thus the starting point for and the goal of any scientific theory and the demonstration of such an equal validity is called truth. This principle of truth is today accepted as a proof of truth in all social legislation the world over. The acceptance of the principle of equivalence, that two *identical actions* are identical and must be treated *identically*, is the basis of the whole legal system. One can discuss whether two actions have identical value and thus are really identical, but once this is established in relation to the rule then the hammer falls automatically. Therefore *one cannot under any circumstances today refer to a higher truth than the scientific principle of truth*, one can only postulate that equivalence of value is not always established correctly and never can be except according to the law, that on the one side there are *in reality higher values* than on the other and thus a higher *justice*. But this changes nothing in the principle of the scientific knowledge of truth.

What Bohr discovered and what toppled classical physics was a situation where two worlds both explained the same thing – physics, but which could not in any detailed way be mutually established in equivalence or symmetry. This was the catastrophe. In what relationship do these worlds stand to each other? Are they two physical worlds? Are they in a dialectical sense *dissymetrical*? Are they identical with the dissymetrical phenomena observed by Pasteur and

78   The Natural Order and Other Texts

Curie in the structure of biological salts? Or a third thing? All this is a completely new question which both can and will be answered. But one thing is certain. The formula of equality, the formula of symmetry or the formula of equivalence is no longer theoretically absolute. It must be united with other completely complementary theoretical principles like the *unity or integral theory* and the *differential or convertible theory*, and it must be established that the bases for these theories are mutually complementary and must be completely independent, which they are not today.

Equivalence is the equal value or significance of phenomena. The establishment of an actuality or event abolishes the possibility of placing any divide at all between essentials and inessentials within the event or the actuality. Everything is equally essential because everything belongs to the event which as a whole has been chosen to be the essential one.

But outside the event absolutely *everything* is essential in a polarized relationship to the event or actuality for its establishment, and the closer the external lies to the event's focal point – *for the event is a focal point* (the bigger it is the colder it is)* – the more essential becomes the event's environment both in time and space. *It is this regularly increasing essentiality or significance we call perspective.*

If we throw a stone into the water, it is the striking of the stone against the water which is the event itself. We can say the same about a blow on a cymbal. If we change the sound recording of what happens during and after this blow, if we change this sound image to a visual image, then we see the same phenomenon spreading over the water's surface, repeating itself in the sound image, only here linearly. The blow itself, just like the stone touching the water, creates a complete chaos. *This chaos is actuality, the incident.* This then provokes an echo, a sound perspective, which completely resembles the waves' gradual and regular spread on the water's surface, where they become lower and lower and at the same time broader and broader, until they spread out and are completely united with the water's surface. We then say that they vanish into the distance. Waves thus lie outside the region of actuality's sphere of simultaneity.

If, from the centre of the event, we then observe the movements of a particle as we assume it following the wave's height movement as the wave gradually distances itself from the place of the event, then, if the particle moves in a straight line away from the location of the event, I can only see its vertical movement up and *down. The farther the particle distances itself from the centre of the event, the smaller becomes the vertical line.* If I am now sure that the particle follows and indicates the top and bottom of the wave, then I

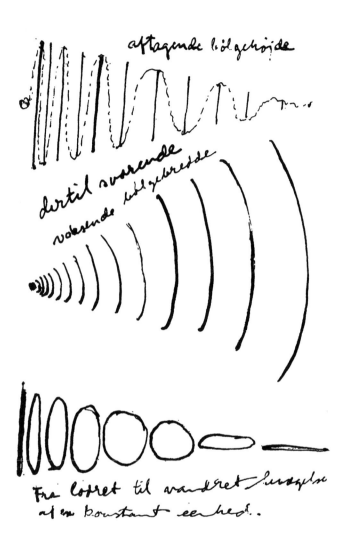

aftagende bølgehøjde = decreasing wavelength
dertil svarende voksende bølgebredde = corresponding wavebreadth
Fra lodret til vandret bevægelse af en konstant eenhed =
movement of a constant unit from vertical to horizontal

FIG. 11. WAVELENGTHS AND WAVEBREADTHS

80　*The Natural Order and Other Texts*

conclude that the wave is therefore gradually becoming smaller and smaller the farther it gets. But if I observe the same wave from above and measure its length the other way, thus its breadth, then I can show that *the same wave has become broader and broader and thus bigger and bigger*, if I at the same time ignore that it has become lower and lower. This shows that an observation of length of a wave *from the centre of the event and thus across the wave's motion* gives an opposite result to an observation of the same wave in a perspective that follows the high points of a wave. A third result must come to light if I regard the waves from a point where the wavelength is abolished by the light's perspective. These three observations must then, if one ignores the different instrumentation, lead to the result that there are three kinds of waves, cross-waves, length-waves and high waves, just as *by not perceiving the head as an entity* one has to come to the conclusion that there are three kinds of head – faces, profiles and crowns. From an artist's point of view, this is the basis for Einstein's characteristic distinction between longitudinal waves and cross-waves, but perhaps this is just a fancy. I have never pretended that it is anything else. However, it shows that the reason why an aeroplane becomes smaller and smaller the farther away it gets *can* be explained by the light waves by which it can be seen becoming lower and lower.

One can perceive Newton's primitive principle of relativity as the beginning of an *experience*, but one can also perceive it as the beginning of a *prohibition* or the statement of an impossibility.

The great service of dialectical materialism is the indication that no *absolute* values exist. The betrayal of socialism on the other hand has been to want to establish only one value. The great service of science is to have established *the principle of equivalence*. Its betrayal on the other hand is in wanting to infuse this principle with value.

As science and dialectical materialism have said this positively, then they may develop these principles as far as they wish, but on the question of the establishment of *values* they will have just to hold their tongue, because they have cut themselves off in advance from any possibility of undertaking such an operation. This has become *a purely artistic matter*. That these newly established values can be criticized, and that materialism is right that such a critique can only be established in relation to actuality is just as correct as it is correct that any artistic effort, any demand for new values, is a direct result of a critique, and is conditioned by an enmity towards phenomena within the same actuality. The only thing science can do in this connection is to investigate where there really is a correspondence between the stated value and the actual value, and this can only be demonstrated when the wish is realized, unless there

The Natural Order 81

is some instrumentation in the project, the results of which must *necessarily* lead to other results than those for which one has a use in order to realize one's wish.

The principles of perspectival science. Calculation of attraction versus calculation of distraction

With Einstein's theory of relativity *time* became a concept perceived as a *dimension* just like the three spatial dimensions. To understand what this means it is necessary to find out what time was before this perception prevailed. This can hardly be done until we have established what is meant by a dimension. Let us say that *a dimension is the objective basis for the establishment of a scale of uniform amounts*. In this way a dimension can be defined as an infinite and an indivisible amount. The dimension of time is eternity.

The question now is: for what can such an infinite and indivisible dimension be used? It can be used to measure with, as it can be divided without dissolving into its parts. The scale can thus also be used for the calculation of *uniform quantities or what Bohr calls quanta*. Now what is a measurement? It is a line identical with the series of Greek numbers 1-2-3-4-5-6-7-8 and so on. *A satisfactory measurement is an unambiguous statement about a phenomena's relationship to this series of numbers*. This can be depicted as a line terminated at one end and infinite at the other. But it was not long before it was discovered that this series of numbers did not need to be straight at all. *The linear movement can be transformed to a rotary motion* where each number corresponds to a rotation. One only needs to count the rotations to measure the total of the uniform lengths. This is true of measurements in time as well as in space. One cannot imagine an end to the number series by which one measures, as it will always be possible to add another number. In this way the dimension must, on the one hand, be perceived as finite as it has the form of a circle, whilst, at the same time, however, this wheel has to be infinitely large. *The only thing we can say about the measurable world is that it is oriented from a particular point in a particular direction*. But at the same time this point does not exist as it is zero point and one cannot measure with less than a unit of one. Indeed, *as to measure is to compare, any measurement is impossible unless at least two equal amounts are set up*. Thus in the world of measurements, neither zero nor one can exist except in relation to others. A measurement can only make a statement about the *equality* of amounts. This is the reason why the Arabs first found the number zero. With the introduction of this number or

82 *The Natural Order and Other Texts*

anti-number a new world-picture was opened up. One was no longer oriented in one direction, but could just as well orient oneself in the other direction. Instead of the wheel always going in the same direction during the measurement, another principle was discovered, which was that of the pendulum, where a movement is neutralized by a counter-movement, and it became apparent that this pendulum movement, just as occurs in a clock, could be transformed into a one-sided movement, an oriented movement, and could be oriented and measured.

With this we have reached the revelation of the scientific swindle we have hitherto pretended to accept, *measurable progress*. We have seen that a measurable progress is nothing more than a constant repetition of a cycle. *Only absolutely uniform cycles can be measured*. To make a half-line into a kind of tape measure, which has a beginning but is theoretically infinite, seems to be the same as to combine the half-line's oriented motion with a movement in the circumference of a circle.

If we assume that we place the end point of a half-line on a point on a circumference then by making the circle rotate we will be able to get the half-line simply to vanish in the circle. This seems to be what happens during measurement. The same thing happens when a thread is spooled on to a spindle, only with the difference that during this spooling nothing is taken up on the spindle. The half-line simply vanishes and is transformed into numbers which describe rotations, and is decided by the encounter between two points, one on the circumference and one that does not rotate. Measurement is thus description that can only be concerned with surfaces and not an orientation in itself, only *an imaginary future*. Measurement is simply the systematic and automatic abolition of the future, its integration into actuality as an absolutely neutralized element, a quantity. One can only measure what can in some way or other be encompassed or what has been already encompassed in some way or other and the only thing one measures is the phenomenon's relationship to this encompassment. This is the reason why science has to identify present and future, for the measurable future is only *a particular orientation within the experimental field*, and thus in that particular time. This is the illusion of the measurable future.

If we draw the purely quantitative form of the numeric sequence, we see that this is identical with the angle of perspective. If we perceive this unit as an ordinary image, then one splits into two and two becomes three and three four and so on. This process cannot be called division. It must be called distraction. If one goes in the opposite direction, nine become eight, eight seven, seven six, six five, five four, four three, three two, two one, and then what happens? We have reached the point of highest tension, of greatest attraction, after which something has to happen. This is *the perspective of significance*, the calculation of events. If one wishes to concentrate upon an event, one has to count in the opposite direction to normal: 9-8-7-6-5-4-3-2-1-bump.

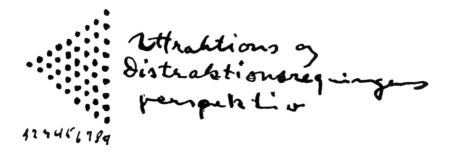

FIG.12. THE PERSPECTIVE OF ATTRACTION AND DISTRACTION

The contrast between counting forwards and backwards in series of numbers is thus a process which is completely different from the manipulation of positive and negative numeric amounts. Instead of something being taken away or added, either a concentration or a dissolution occurs. It is this process which is the model for dialectical materialism's theory of the transformation of quantity to quality. Dialectical opposition has not been discovered in the process because the quantitative reduction is parallel to the reduction of the form, although in reverse proportion to the explosive effect.

Freedom, equality and fraternity

Any establishment of a difference in significance is the establishment of a difference in size in a context, and thus of a perspective, of a break in actuality's extent and unity.

Now one should beware of labels. They are set up from other experiences to interpret them, but the polarized description is the one that *opposites attract each other and likenesses (equalities) reject each other*. From this it follows that *equality and unity are opposites* whilst clear, pure opposition is unity.

The formula that plus and minus neutralize each other is of fundamental significance in classical mathematics. This is to say in a dialectical sense that a confirmation is neutralized by a negation so that nothing is left. That this rule is not universal in actuality, that it is not true for calculations of variability, the zero points of which lie more or less centrally, can be understood if one represents a difference in temperature from -5° to +7° = 12°. If minus had neutralized plus here the temperature difference would have been just 2°.

Dialectical materialism has never manifested itself as a scientific principle because it has never been expressed in a consistent mathematical formula, for the statement that thesis creates antithesis purely mathematically means that plus invokes minus and together they form a new entity (+-) and that this entity is different in property from the two factors which have shaped it. The unscientific character of this statement has been preserved on purely political grounds because the French socialist Lasalle came out with the magic formula, so valuable to modern revolutionary socialism, that a synthesis is always greater than the sum of the parts. Herein lies the propaganda value of this socialist superstition, which is called quantity's change into quality, because with a good conscience one can maintain that any synthesis that is quantitatively greater than another also automatically becomes qualitatively superior. That even the most gifted thinkers allow themselves to be fooled by this formula is because it is correct if one identifies quantity with *number* and quality with *mass*, and thus perceives *quality as a unit's resistance to disintegration or dissolution*. But if quality is identified with value, then both these concepts become completely meaningless. This is what is normally done. On the other hand, if one defines *value as the latent possibilities for the liberation of energy* in contrast to quality, which in any circumstance has to be defined as constancy or inertia, then the whole arrangement has a meaning, as *value becomes the negation of quality*. This contrary entity is what we call the object. Therefore when Marx differentiates between latent and constant capital, we will then simply deny that there is anything called constant capital. The transition to constant capital is the transition to socialism, the devaluation of capital.

The abolition of variability in one area is thus the establishment of *an absolute condition of equilibrium between plus and minus*, and thus polarized equivalence. This polarized equivalence is what the dialecticians call synthesis. Everyone knows that such a synthesis is not valid in classical mathematics. The synthesis x-x is not a mathematical synthesis today, and yet no one can get around the fact that + attracts - and repels + in physics, and that the whole physical context is explained on the basis of this simple arrangement. That the number zero only has a meaning if one maintains this entity (+-) does not seem to have troubled anyone. My lack of knowledge of mathematics hinders me from knowing if, for example, we should say that the calculation of integers is concerned with numbers on such a basis, but this is also quite immaterial, as the philosophical and logical consequences of such developments have not been clearly and simply formulated.

My assertion then is this. Absolute equilibrium or polarization creates a positive-negative object that can only be observed and only has actual existence if the object is destroyed. We have hereby reached beyond a dualistic perception, whilst preserving its integrity as one of three explanations: the mutual relationships of the conditions of equilibrium, the mutual relationships of the conditions of evolution or extension and constriction or concentration, and the relationship of the movement of progress or one-sided 'positivist' movement to the immobile.

If we now test the meaning of the statements 'you should love your neighbour like yourself' and 'you should love your enemy' against these demonstrations, and we perceive *to love as sympathy, emotion or need for unity*, then it should not be possible to love anyone but one's opponent or enemy. Thus the latter injunction 'to love your enemy' must be a banality, because love becomes enmity and hatred should either be the opposite of enmity or the highest form of love, or *equality should be the same as hatred* as well, because likenesses repel. Thus if I love my neighbour as myself and so establish an equivalence between my sympathy for myself and my neighbour, this is to say that I have established a situation where we mutually repel each other or where we in fellowship are attracted to a third person. It is not necessary to explain that this is the case in democratic societies. This message therefore has no meaning at all except as *a prohibition upon either loving oneself or one's neighbour*, whilst loving god with a full heart. But if you do that, then you have established god as your permanent enemy or opponent, and if you love him then you must hate yourself as well as your neighbour. The result must be that you no longer wish to live or that you will consequently fight against everything that is sympathetic in life, or that you understand that art is god and god is art.

These reflections are in no way new and have never been explained away. The only thing one can do to neutralize them is to set up an earthly *authority* which by prohibition neutralizes their meaning in this meaning's own name and to this meaning's earthly 'best', or, to take the same explanations up in a new way, if we do not wish to take the risk of open sandwiches being called food instead of mere sandwiches. For the only thing we know about love is that it is not hatred, but we know that *love and hatred can be abolished in a state called indifference or equivalence.* We get nowhere if we do not reckon with

86 *The Natural Order and Other Texts*

all three of these positions. If we transfer these to a pictorial idiom this becomes the asubjective, perspectiveless image, where *the indifference means that everything is parallel, everything is just as great*, having the same significance regardless of how far it is from our centre in time and space, and even that the centre called ego does not exist at all. *Put artistically, one does not care either way.*

In an aesthetic respect, the perspectival laws of pictorial art are universally valid in the description of our direct sensations. The further a phenomenon is from the absolute ego, the more meaningless, the *less* it becomes as a sensory phenomenon. This is true in time about our oblivion, and in space with our sensory impressions.

The question then becomes whether in the area which is neither that of direct sensation nor that of scientific observation, there can be found *an area where the phenomena appear to grow in significance the farther they get from one's own egoistic centre*, whether this is the natural perspective for the *critical*, whether our critical sense functions in a reverse perspective where one is oneself a point and what is sensed as the furthest part here takes on the most enormous fullness of significance, and whether what one hates is identical with the strange, the unknown.

That the splinter in your neighbour's eye is meaningful, whilst you does not see the beam in your own, appears to indicate such a critical perspective is the reverse of that of direct sensation. The pain of the beam in your neighbour's head is, of course, nothing in relation to the sensory significance of the splinter in your own arse.*

If you now obstinately endure your own pain and help your neighbour, then you are a Martha. But if the two accidents are occasioned by the same effect, then the wail about your neighbour's crushed head is used as a sign for and an expression of hidden sufferings, which thereby can appear in a significant and valuable indirect form to others. If you content yourself with giving out signals about your own state, then these signals will be compared with what has happened to your neighbour and of course have a great significance, but the reaction could be divided, causing either laughter or irritation. But if your neighbour is now your opponent and you have yourself swung the beam and he has directed the splinter, what then?

Then any cry of pain about the state of your neighbour would be an accusation against oneself, whereas just one word about your own state would be absurd. Therefore all heroes have to keep quiet, and therefore an artist cannot be a hero, even though he is eminently qualified to go foremost. He must be something even more central – the impulse that starts it all, an enemy.

What is a situation?

Triolectics or the doctrine about *the necessity and the sufficiency of three complementary pieces of information to describe what we shall call a situation* is nothing new. It goes back to pre-Christian gnostic ideas that possibly had their origin in Pythagorean principles and which also form the basis of the Christian doctrine of the Trinity maintained as a principle by the Cathars, who were decimated in the 12th century by the Catholics and burnt in a series of persecutions that made the old Roman persecutions of Christians look like children's games. The crusading armies of the Nordic nobility were used for this dirty work. In the name of moral rearmament, a dialectical opposition between 'holy' and 'worldly' powers was set up and when the knights had done their duty, they too were cut down.* This did not, however, stop the inquisition continuing nor a revolution allowing a third class to appear.

In modern democratic society, the Christian doctrine of the Trinity has been replaced by the doctrine of liberty, equality and fraternity, by the doctrine of hope, faith and love, which has now become an expression for the way, the truth and the life or for the spiritual, the worldly and the psychological. It was the Cathars' doctrine about the complementary relationship of the spiritual or psychical to the psychological or the organic that the Catholics refused to accept. Modern scientists are also attempting their own betrayal on this point when they talk of science's 'responsibility', which becomes 'scientific responsibility', which then becomes *faith* in science, where there is nothing whatsoever to believe in and even less to hope for. What is left is the absurd, love. *You shall love science with a full heart.* However ridiculous this formula sounds, it is a quite logical consequence of the Christian doctrine of love, a doctrine that merely outbids Christianity in consistency, as it maintains that you shall love truth above all things.

Beautiful are the things we can see, even more beautiful are the things we understand, but by far the most beautiful are assuredly those we do not comprehend, said Niels Steno. This is the reason that *we see the things we do not comprehend with the greatest intensity*, that things become more and more indistinct, the better we know them. This is the perspective of meaning that has to be abolished in the dialogue of the field of actuality. The more often an action is repeated, the more our attention is blunted. *An action is therefore never repeated under the same subjective conditions.* The doctrine of scientific forgiveness consists of ignoring this condition and formulating the high Christian principle of *disinterested love* in its extreme absurdity. This can only

88 *The Natural Order and Other Texts*

be done definitively by forbidding all artistic interest. We stress this only to show the hopeless confusion of our basic concepts.

This absurdity can only be hidden if one throws suspicion on the ability to think independently. However, it does occur to me that the superiority of Scandinavian philosophy consists in its ability to integrate absurdity into the complete picture without losing contact either with nature or ideas.*

Actuality and reality

The word actuality is often identified with the word reality and it is with that meaning we have frequently used the word here.* But it is a big question whether these two concepts really cover each other or whether they are not in reality opposites [...] That this lack of clarity must profoundly affect the whole of our presentation is obvious. But I have never thought to represent something perfectly. The only thing I can indicate is the fact that the word *actuality* can mean *action*, that the word *reality* can mean what happens, and thus the *effect*, but that the word actuality can also mean *cause* and thus in reality reaction to an effect, if this is identified with the concept of object. Further, it can be perceived, as we have done to a large extent here, as *the relationship between action and reaction, the present*. This whole problem demonstrates to how high a degree these reflections here must be perceived as experiments.

If the world of the actualities is placed against that *of names*, concepts or symbols, then we draw attention here to the fact that this 'actuality' is a composite product, that the world of *things* is not the same world as the one we sense, that the world of *sensation* is the world of constant genesis and dissolution, whilst the world of things is a world of objects, of constancies, and that these two worlds are complementary. This is the reason that we separate the world of things from that of actualities.

The world of names is the world of language and the world of language is the world of conversation. To be able to converse you must speak the same language. That is simple. The profound misunderstandings only come when one believes that one is talking about the same thing when in reality it is something different, even the opposite. This is to a high degree the case in relation to the basic concepts of philosophy in Germanic and Latin usage [...] Until the philosophers stop fighting about what the various concepts *should* mean and concentrate instead on *presenting all the meanings each concept in the philosophical systems could ever have or have the possibility of having*, then any talk of the unambiguity of concepts is just hot air.*

You asked, my boy

What can we then say about this arrangement which is called the field of actuality regardless of its placing in time? We have shown that the first signal must be identical with a *question* and the second with an *answer*, but is this not the same as the establishment of a causal context? *The establishment of an actuality is the establishment of a causal context.* We have now in reality reached a completely new way of treating causal contexts, because we can distribute them in different groups, one for each kind of question that could be posed. It then appears that all questions must be gathered into three main questions:

The artistically subjective *who*?

The instrumentally oriented *where*?*

And the scientifically identified *what*?

As all questions must be a kind of causal expression and instrumentation is the establishment of causal context, it is no wonder that, with the oriented expression *where*, we cannot only answer with a *here*, and thereby pinpoint a place on a line, a plane or in space, but also, with the question *when*, pinpoint moments. We can even pinpoint the order in the event's relationship to experience and the past through the question *why*, which is really only the question about what has gone before or should have gone before or what is the precondition for something. In the same way one can order the possibilities of also repeating something in the future by answering the question *how*. It has been shown that a whole philosophy can be constructed around just one such question. Pragmatism or functionalism is in reality nothing other than such a *how*-philosophy, just as determinism is merely a *why*-philosophy and what there is of philosophy in Christianity is just a *when*-philosophy, and they are thus all purely technical philosophies, which, mark you, is and must be the main pillar of philosophy, as it is above all a technique of thinking.

The question *what* is correctly perceived as the scientific question because it can only be answered satisfactorily when we have already answered the technical questions satisfactorily. If we have the answer to the question *what* is happening, then in reality nothing more happens, for then we know also *where, how and why*.

What? is also the concluding question if one asks, 'What should we do?' Only there is no scientific answer at all as to what we should do. Science knows nothing of the future. It only knows about the past. Therefore it can only speak of what we should not do. The question 'what should we do?' can only be answered with a suggestion, or with an order, and thus either aesthetically or ethically. An order always stands in a causal relationship to a *why*, whilst a suggestion abolishes the principle of causality by the free will utterance, *why not*.

The most characteristic and significant aestheticizing of the causal principle is not however its rejection but the question and answer: '*Why?*' – '*Because I want to.*' This is the shortest possible casual connection, but not the only one. In innumerable cases, we make do with such elementary answers to our questions: 'Why do you believe what he says?' 'Because he is a scientist.' Such a relationship of trust is purely magical. *Any establishing of an authority is pure magic*, nothing more. The reason the social authorities in their time burned all the magicians they could get hold of was just because they did not want disloyal competition. *Any demand for the observance of a rule or the acceptance of an* a priori *is pure magic*. The comical thing is that those who use the magic system today no longer know this, for what is called magic today consists only of experiments to establish causal connections that no longer function, but which it was believed worked at one time, or which some believe still work. All magical causal connections really lead back to a simple 'because I want to'. Only it can be difficult at times to find out who wants to and thus who is directing the performance. The agency wishing to is a *who*, is an artist, but does not need to be an individual, and could be a group.

The human utterance of will can be imprecise and could then gather itself in the decision, 'I will or I won't', but this direct utterance of human will can never be directly identified with an order, for the transformation of the utterance of will to an order is its transformation from free and unconditional will to instrumented, reason-conditioned will, a socialized will even, as an order does not begin with *I* but with *you* and is not *will* but *shall* or *must not*. To assume a *responsibility* is to use the formula, *You shall, because I wish it so*. If one gives a reason for an order, then one's own responsibility weakens with the length of the series of reasons, if one is not lying. This is true of both individual and collective responsibility.

We have seen how those words recognized as interrogatives condition what can be answered, and in what form and in which direction the whole net of contacts develops, and we have seen that the whole thing is really built up in relation to the answer. A pure question that cannot be answered must then be posed outside this net. But is it possible to ask questions in another way? 'To be or not to be, that is the question.' Is this really a question? Yes, it is a question to the degree that the question must express an interested reaction to something one does not know. As science is knowledge, any question at all is unscientific, because it is an expression of ignorance. Science has difficulty in understanding the significance of this precise limit.

A question that cannot be framed in the normal interrogative form has the nature of a paradox, and the more essential the problem the more significant the question. Such a question is called a puzzle. Giving forms and presence to the puzzling in life is what one calls the fine arts. There is nothing so lacking in current interest as a poetry of ideas, the problems of which have been solved. Nothing is so puzzling as an art-work in front of which one cannot pose one single question. All art is built upon enigmatic propositions, which only contain problems at the moment they are created, but the puzzling thing about art is that through these problems it cultivates its own problematic essence, which becomes clearer and freer the more temporal problems it works with and works itself out of. The most important liberation appears to be the release from having to serve masters who give art orders to formulate their own orders, indeed to be liberated from the aesthetic rule that in *the principle of* order the principle of beauty itself appears to be crystallized. The only question to which art really seems to be able to give an answer is the question, *who* are we, whilst the answer only seems clear where art refuses to take any position at all in posing such a question, as if the human being could only demonstrate who he is by constantly escaping any identification, by hiding what happens and just showing what has already been done, what he has chosen. The day that all people are identified, are identical, *who* will no longer exist.

The artist sees and evaluates or appreciates. If the artist's appreciation is not accepted and criticized by placing it against another appreciation that is perceived to be higher, then the artist can only go on his way and exclude this area from his art, the area having become without artistic value or interest. Up to now no one has been able to hinder this development, which is automatic. What the artist has declared dead and without interest remains dead and without interest, even if it has been possible to force people to behave as if they had filled it with art.

In this way, art has been pushed out of more and more areas of human experience. But art has never surrendered a terrain without a struggle, and the tragic termination of these struggles can be read in the three forms of drama that mark the great battles of the retreats. First there is the refusal of art and humanity to allow their struggle to be made identical with the struggle of *the universe* and nature, as expressed in the Greek tragedies, next the giving up of the identification of humanity's struggle with *society's* struggle, as reflected in the Renaissance tragedies, which they later tried in vain to reduce to a human identification with the social *class struggle*. This defeat was called the liberation of *the individual* and this liberation became the beginning of the

92 *The Natural Order and Other Texts*

psychological drama, the stage for which is reduced to the inner life of the individual, which has today been sold to the psychiatrists. Today there is nothing left. Nothing to lose. Therefore the artistic struggle is about everything or nothing. The development is irreversible. There is only one way out, to regain everything on a higher plane or perish as artist and human being.

Are majority and right the same? Or complementary?

Science cannot question, for questions are ignorance. But can science then deal with questions at all, *can science answer*? Is there anything called scientific answers?

Here we are at one of those points where scientists today are again utilizing magic, for science can really only answer a quite specific kind of question, namely whether the answer already given to a question is right or wrong. In reality there is no method at all for finding scientific answers. *There is only a scientific method for the control of answers.* This control aims to *repeat the question, investigate the answer and see if it is the same as the first one,* nothing more. The more times the same answer emerges from the same question, the more satisfactory it is in the scientific respect, and the surer science is that the question and answer belong to each other. But what science answers is not whether the question or the answer is right. *The only concrete thing science really answers is whether a particular combination of question and answer can be repeated.* If it can be infinitely repeated, the combination is said to have objective validity, to be a scientific truth. *Scientific truth is thus nothing more that the truth of repetition* and the criterion for scientific statements about truth is absolute similarity between the so-called objects. If this similarity is absolute, then one can simple ignore the objects' character as sensory phenomena and just give them the same name or number. *Scientific research is therefore exclusively research for identical numerical dimensions or quantities, nothing more.*

But now we have pinpointed that it is not a scientific activity to answer or to demand answers to questions, that it is a *technique*, what then in an intellectual sense is a technique? It is *philosophy* and philosophy is above all *ethics*. But, you will protest, ethics stands then in a harmonious relationship to science. If we pose a question and find the answer, then we have postulated an equation that can even be controlled scientifically. This is a complete misunderstanding, however, for what we have found is perhaps an equivalence or equal value, an *equilibrium*, a *similarity*, but this similarity is at the same time a difference, because it is the similarity of two *opposites*, and the similarity only consists of the two opposites holding each other in equilibrium in a certain way, nothing more.

However, if scales are the symbol of justice, then this instrument plays a fundamental role in the truth criterion of science itself. This is, of course, correct. One must only understand that science is not at all interested in what happens between the two scale pans. *Science can only be summoned in the instant equilibrium is perfect, to check if it really is perfect.* To find this out, the scales are investigated thoroughly and reproduced in as many examples as possible. Exactly the same amount of all those weights will be placed in the scale pans and if the same equilibrium is repeated then science begins to be able to use this weighing.

If we wish to weigh something and to find out *how*, then we have to discover how *one* weighing can be established, and here science gives us only the purely magical answer – yes, that this is something that has been agreed – a convention that one should observe, an order, for *science can never do other than follow the orders it is given*. Knowledge has no morals.

The advantage of dialectical materialism over the Western European sciences is that it has discovered a moral science, a moral criterion of truth, just as objective and controllable as the scientific *criterion of equality*, which is the objective *criterion of the entity* or *the truth of the controllable opposite.* Here it has simply established that an entity is a constant opposite, and for an opposite to be constant the two opposites must be *polarized equivalences*. Western European science cannot find a scientific formulation for this polarization simply because moral judgement must not be objective in Western Europe. The reason is simply that in Western Europe *the artistic criterion of truth* has not yet been given up, and there is not yet a wish to renounce *the significance of allowing oneself to be weighed* in order to find the answer to the question *who*, because a fundamental role in democratic objectives is still assigned to the cultivation of personality, called in Eastern Europe 'the cult of personality'.

If one controls whether a million measurements are the same or whether there is equilibrium between two scale pans or sits in one of them oneself, then the problem of equivalence looks devilishly different from each of the three views. This does not, however, hinder the fact that a judgement of equivalence in all three cases must be submitted to scientific control, wherever this is possible. This shows that *the preconditions for* this control and *the consequences* of it are far more important than the control itself, and even that the control in itself is and must be *the abolition of everything important*, that the scientific

94 The Natural Order and Other Texts

principle and the meaningless principle are the same – disinterestedness.

But how can one now criticize dialectical materialism when it in reality is an advance in relation to logical materialism? One can do it by pinpointing how self-contradictory principles of opposition have been hitherto. If I say that the opposite of right is left, then I cannot at the same time say that the opposite of horizontal is vertical, even more so as depth too stands in a kind of opponent relationship to the two other coordinates, for the opposition right-left has 180° whilst the other oppositions have only 90°. A system of coordinates has thus three right-angled oppositions which from the point of intersection result in 6 opposed orientations of 180° but produce 12 right angles. The broaching of the problem *what is an opposition* is just the posing of a question, a new fundamental question, which is first and foremost open to a welter of new questions, as *an answer is just a means by which one can stop a question, an opposition to a question.* The only thing one seems to be able to establish is that dimensions must stand in a right-angled relationship to each other whilst orientations must stand in a straight-line condition of opposition to each other, and it occurs to me that the complementary theory of Bohr is dimensional but lacks a dimension, whilst dialectical materialism is oriented but believes it is dimensional.

When modern scientists agree to set up a prohibition, such a prohibition becomes an order. The unscientific element in the Copenhagen Interpretation is that it begins with an order, and when this order is pronounced by some of the world's most significant scientists, then these appear as authorities and not as scientists.

What does a scientific attitude become when it is framed as an order? A scientific order cannot just argue that *you must because you must.* It has to be based upon the requirement to follow the method of scientific evaluation that truth value is measured in probability, and the probability grows with the number of identical answers. Here this basic scientific principle fits like a glove the democratic principle that *the majority is right,* which, posed purely morally in a purely dialectical opponent relationship, must lead to the conclusion that *the minority is wrong.* Indeed, a transposition of the scientific principle of evaluation to the juridical-ethical area, and thus the area of orders, must simply end in pure justice being achieved by eradicating any minority. No scientist can sneak around this argument, which could be correctly called scientific socialism or simply the triumph of science in intellectual life.

There is absolute danger in this triumphal procession of science, not least in politics. At any rate, above all in the Germanic cultures, the scientific background for the *demand for normalization* dominates social ethics and law.

The demand: *You must, because it is normal! You must not because it is abnormal! You must be normal! You must not be abnormal!* and the innumerable other methods that can be found to make people behave normally, that is to say, *in the same way*, become intermingled with the scientific criterion of truth that the most normal people are the most 'truthful', and with the requirement that one must be truthful. This results in he who best fits in with the conventional hypocrisy being perceived as the most truthful, and truthful pronouncements, because they are rare or abnormal, being perceived as a kind of mental sickness, as delusions, psychoses. Science has no arguments at all to set against this. On the contrary, this boloney can work with scientific and statistical methods and arguments.

This necessary moral conclusion of the general recognition of the scientific criterion of truth is the reason for the immense popularity that modern science enjoys in the modern democracies, be they socialist or capitalist, and, although scientists are in the minority, this apparently does not matter, for science does not concern itself with law and right, with good and evil. It just so happens that a way to make atom bombs has now been found, and, as those who gave orders for their production will not take the blame, the politicians all push the blame on to the scientists who discovered how to split atoms, and suddenly the scientists see themselves as a minority placed in the dock for poking into things that do not interest the majority and invoking catastrophes for the whole of humanity. Thus the scientists' own method is beginning to turn against them and devour them.

Much has been said about scapegoats and they are used to draw the attention away from those who really should be attacked. I am not so sure that it is possible to use a completely innocent person as a scapegoat. It seems to me that in the choice of scapegoats people have an astonishing instinct for finding the right one and pouncing on the tenderest spot. However, this is always from the precondition that 'the majority is right', and from the unavoidable experience that value, when all is said and done, is decided by the majority, even though it is first discovered by rare individuals.

Science comes into conflict with the judgement of the majority not because it is the majority that judges, but because science stands in an insurmountable oppositional relationship to judgement on the whole, because judgement is a decision, and a decision is an instantaneity, and because majority in science is not just space, but above all time. *In reality science wishes for unlimited time, wishes to have the disposal of all time, in order to establish its calculation of majority*, whilst the majority is the most impatient thing in existence. Public opinion is the most capricious thing in existence. Public opinion is the public's judgement, and the public forgets its own judgement just as swiftly as it was made, changing its opinion faster than a woman. In this regard, we are all the public, for the public's judgement is our own judgement in cases where we have no personal interest, and this is only conditioned by our interest in being excused from unnecessary difficulties, whilst at the same time having as much free entertainment as possible.

Everyone is equal before the law, for a law is the establishment of an equilibrium, a condition of equal value, an equivalence, a uniformity in process. Order is something quite different. Order is a particular succession, a particular way, and one does not have to conform to but to move in accordance with it. It is my impression that it is the Scandinavians' absolute rejection of any order in their ideas, the absolute rejection of fixed ideas or of the fixing of ideas, that gives them their sharp eye for order outside themselves in nature or in other cultures. This sharp eye for natural order, which for example resulted in Niels Steno's geology,* in Carl von Linné's botany,* and in the archaeological tripartition,* is always confused with scientific methodology, but is really something quite different. It is an eye for the technique of nature, for the order of nature, an openness precisely conditioned by an absolute lack of personal interest in artificial order.

I have followed up this whole argument in order to indicate that Kierkegaard's great effort in modern philosophy lies to my mind in having demonstrated the natural order, the natural succession in the modern philosophical tripartition, to have shown that what one calls aesthetics is nothing other than what one also calls introduction or *cause*,* that *the constant of aesthetics is the constant of the commencement*, and that *ethics is the constant of continuation* or the *constant of constants*. This means that aesthetics is orientation and represents the constant of orientation, whilst ethics is motion and represents the constant of motion, and logic is immobility and represents the constant of immobility. When Kierkegaard, instead of perceiving the three basic philosophical forms beauty, health and truth as constants, as three complementary and incompatible entities, orients them as stages and thus gives them their orientation, this means that he in reality perceives *ethics and logic purely aesthetically*, and thus not as health and truth but as sickness unto death and religion.* This is clearly apparent in his unscientific and purely artistic perception of truth, in the perception of truth as something that must be personally attested. *With Kierkegaard is created for the first time in the history of philosophy a complete, purely aesthetic picture of the world which is at the same time a purely aesthetic attitude to life.* This is what the

The Natural Order 97

Existentialists have never found out. They have just discovered that Kierkegaard reduced Christianity *ad absurdum.*

Either or

An image is a fixation. The development of our world-picture can only happen by the revision of the old one. Any religion is the belief in a particular picture of the world. The atom-bomb perspective is the direct result of the attachment of the newest scientific and technical results to the classical world-picture dominating philosophy in both East and West. Modern humanity has only one alternative, either an atom bomb conflict or a universal agreement to unite all the progressive forces of the Earth in the conquest of space opening for us today, between a new international Middle Ages or a universal renaissance. Anyone refusing to choose the latter in an absolute condemnation of the former has already chosen the former. Any Scandinavian with respect for his culture must choose the latter.

When an artist wishes to locate science within his own area as a kind of art, he need not reduce it to something it is not in order to incorporate it.

Newton's mechanics and all the other parts of classical physics are constructed upon a model based on the hypothesis that the world can be described without talking about god or ourselves. This could be transferred to the religious perspective and form the same model by saying, in other words, that classical physics is constructed on the conviction that the truth can be known without knowing anything about either the way or the life. In philosophical expressions, classical physics is based upon truth's absolute independence from aesthetics and ethics.

If an artist cannot answer *what* the truth, the way and the life are nor explain *why* they are there, he can at any rate describe *how* they look and function purely pictorially in relation to each other and in relation to our traditional system of description, indicating their form of motion and thus the road they are taking.

What was new in the Renaissance, the new situation which arose with Newton's classic model of physics, was that, at the same time, this became both a classic and a static model of truth. If we accept this perception of truth, then we can add that not the truth but the evolution of truth, the dynamics of truth, is dependent upon *the way and the life* being perceived as one unit in an oppositional relationship to truth, so that this opposition becomes *half-way and*

98 *The Natural Order and Other Texts*

half-dead. The other half of the way and the life has to be used secretly by science to get things going again.

But scientific truth becomes thereby more than a truth. It becomes *the extension of a principle of truth,* an instrument for the accumulation of experiences. This *extension,* which in itself has nothing to do with scientific truth and is only a technique (if the truth criterion of Einstein and Bohr is to be taken seriously and thus as a *truth in itself* and not as a cunning instrument) which simply puts a stop not on scientific truth but on scientific *evolution.*

This stagnation has occurred because Einstein and Bohr, perhaps unknown to themselves, have established science as the religion of our time, for their definition contains science (the conditions) or the truth, as well as ethics (reality or state) or the life, and aesthetics (the event, the sequence) or the way. These are not my definitions, but those used to perfect science as a religion or picture of the world or outlook on life.

Artistically, this is to say that science reckons neither with the spiritual nor the psychological, with neither the imaginary, the imagined, nor the vital, the living, the organic (which natural science would like to call the biological, but does not know what this is). These two areas are also often called the individual and the social.

When scientists today step out of their isolation they suddenly discover the world has not stood still since they left it, and that the rest of the world has accepted their isolation and independently of the world of science has developed a discussion about how far the way and the life are really the same, or whether there is also the possibility here of two different, mutually independent ways of describing the world: *whether it is not possible to describe the world by merely describing ourselves,* without talking about either god or science, or whether, on the other hand, it is possible to *describe the world constructed from a model that is god,* defined in the metaphysical sense as pure imagination, the pure art-work, without talking of either physics or ourselves, in this case the purely biological, and thus whether one could describe the world as an art-work because god and artist are in this sense the same.

This has not only been attempted in the intervening time, but has been successful in creating a basis for the development of these two constructions, exactly, however, in the same way as the scientists threw *the way and the life* together, but here throwing *the life and the truth* together in order, with the help of *a half-dead truth, not to find the way, but to get ahead of it,* to create a pure art that is *god,* and, in the same way, by creating a dialectical opponent condition to the synthesis of *a half truth and a half way* to develop *the purely vitally biological.* The latter has been made by *dialectical materialism,* the

The Natural Order 99

former by *the modern Northern European evolution of art*. These two forces are therefore today the only ones that can set up an effective resistance to the transformation of science to religion. At the same time they are mortal mutual enemies and must remain so.

The area of experience of science is the past and the more it extends our area of experience, the further away it moves the zero point of this past, the point of origin. That this is the case in investigations into the past itself is easy to understand. One can also understand that the same is the case with the spread of our knowledge in space. The further from our globe the pieces of information come, the older they are, so the pieces of information we are able to obtain from the farthest globe come also from the farthest past.

It is more difficult to understand that progress towards microcosmic experience is also a removal towards the past. This can only be understood in the perspective of *significance*, in the perspective where the concern with smaller and smaller phenomena, with more and more insignificant trifles, precisely because of this character of increasing insignificance, is a movement towards the past, as significance can be actual or present, and be potential or future. Therefore the past, seen at its most profound, cannot be defined as anything other than being without significance. In the scientific perspective everything must be insignificant.

The scientific observer is the perfect spectator. He sees the whole thing from above, from the centre or from below. But his guideline for the observation is the angle that space's third dimension forms in relation to the surface he is observing, and the further one can distance oneself from the event, the more this is transformed to a point.

I have defined the artist as the most explosive human when confronted with sensory influences, and thus the most event-creating one. This explosive capacity can either have a quantitative character, which has the effect of the release happening at the least provocation, [or] can be constantly generated. That the amount of energy released each time has to become smaller and smaller, the greater the available force necessary for the reciprocation of influence, is obvious. Therefore the perfect spectator is the person who releases the least energy at each provocation, but responds to the most provocations. The greatest artist is just the opposite. The direction of the two developments is opposed. However, the development of the observer's special ability also conditions him to try more and more to avoid influences that take too much out of him, and to seek more and more events without significance. For the artist the condition is the opposite.

The logical consequence drawn here from Bohr's complementary theory,

100   The Natural Order and Other Texts

which at the moment only comprises the description of elemental or microcosmic phenomena within physics, is then this:

If classical logic cannot be used as a frame for the explanation or ordering of these experiences, then the experiences which fit this frame must be isolated from the others. If a satisfactory new frame cannot be found for the remaining phenomena, then it must first and foremost be investigated whether these new experiences can be set up again as two mutually complementary explanations which permit their division into two opposite groups, each fitting its own logical frame, and whether these three logical frames then stand in a mutually satisfactory complementary relationship to each other. It is this that I have attempted, and hope that I have demonstrated the possibility of. As it is only the artist's task to create possibilities and not to realize them, my task is thereby resolved, if the solution is satisfactory.

The consequence of this arrangement must then be that, for a satisfactory *explanation* of what confronts us today there must exist at least three explanations. Bohr himself has indicated that these explanations, regarded as explanation, must in themselves be the opposite of science, because he places *clarity* in a complementary relationship to *the truth*. Clarity is just a question of order and consequently, as scientists cannot put things in order and the *upholders* of order are also debarred by reason of their work, only the artists are left with the necessary superiority, freedom or cheek (use what word you like) to undertake the operation.

Uno intuito – conclusion

'The whole is greater than the parts.' This basic axiom of analytical mathematics has been perceived as a form of the principle of identity. We have demonstrated that the principle of identity is absolutely incompatible with this axiom. Because one realizes that Euclid's proof that an arbitrary number of line segments are uniform by identifying them with each other, that is to say, by letting them cover each other, by this process reduces them to just one line segment that is identical with and neither greater or smaller than one of the parts, regardless of how many line segments are concerned, *the whole is not greater than one of the arbitrary number of uniform line segments*. If the 1st is identical with the 1st, then 5793 must be identical with 1, whether one perceives this number as a unit or an entity, as there are no other forms of entity than the unit. An entity can thus never be a sum. Any theory of unity is complementary to any theory of equality. If a line is perceived as an entity, then it can never be identified with anything but itself. This is the reason why equality-geometry can never work with lines but only with rows of points on an imaginary line that has no existence. An entity cannot have a magnitude as it does not represent a sum. As the point is the only entity with which Euclidean geometry works, it cannot have a magnitude either. The point is indivisible. The self-contradiction lies in having to maintain that a point has to resemble all other points, that something which does not exist has to be something else that does not exist. If one point really has to resemble another point and together they form two points, then a point has to have a size. Then one also has to have points that do *not* resemble each other and thus points of different sizes. In their absolute forms, everything and nothing are the same.

The analytical method proceeds by division, dissolution and amplification, by developing the possibilities for variability. The synthetic method works in the opposite direction by the encapsulation or establishment of more and more widespread units. The illusion lies in the belief that a unit that is more widespread than another is also larger. In reality the synthesis acts reductively, as by the proof of identity. In order to understand the absolute independence required for the description of such processes, it will be necessary to elaborate a logistical method as a dynamic negation of logic, an inductive logic. We will investigate a typical example of the method by laying out the syllogism – all humans are mortal – Jorn is a human – Jorn is mortal. We can draw a cycle of everything mortal: plants, animals and humans are parts of this entity, are entities in the entity, and within the entity of humanity there is an entity, Jorn. The characterization of mortal beings, of plants, animals and humans is absolutely independent of how many examples of the species are to be found. Quantity has absolutely nothing to do with the entity, perceived as a unit. The entity is only quantity if one perceives it as sum and then it does not matter what one counts, but only that it has been counted correctly. The extent of this unit can thus be reduced to a point. At the same time, however, it cannot be denied that here we have dealt with two sides of exactly the same case, and we just have to accept that these areas of experience are complementary.

With the theory of complementarity we should be able to arrive at a scientific critique of formal induction or the jigsaw puzzle, at a natural philosophy controllable by scientific method or typology. With this we have reached the concretization of the philosophical problem I posed myself in the beginning. Is Scandinavian philosophy first and foremost typology, and is the Copenhagen Interpretation just a new result of a traditional activity that could be called Scandinavian philosophy? If this thesis is to be maintained, then the Germanic races, which a couple of thousand years ago swept down over Europe, must not

102   *The Natural Order and Other Texts*

just have been, as is preached in the rest of Europe, a flock of destructive barbarians, whose only cultural value consisted in giving fresh blood to decadent Rome by re-introducing primitive forms of life, but must have been specialists in a natural typologizing, which in turn would be to say that it was they who built up and shaped scholasticism in its vital form.

We have set up a tripartite complementary theory and will now see if its use against the European cultural picture supports such a theory. Our fundamental complementary tripartition consists in the doctrine of *symptoms* which we call science or the doctrine of descriptions, *significations* or artistic or intentional sensuous signs and finally the science about *symbols* or the legal concepts. These three complementary areas are liberated from their static isolation the instant one of them is placed in an opponent relationship to the mean between the two other complementary views and thereby enters the dynamic chain of processes called the dialectic. The mean between symptom and signification is called the magical or *model*. The mean between signification and symbol is called the figurative or *fanciful*, whilst the mean between symbol and symptom is called the *imageless idea*, abstraction, or the tenets of the typological. The model, the fantasy and the abstract idea are three widely different worlds which are unfortunately, however, often confused and mixed together.

Our schema gives us the possibility of establishing three dialectical combinations that are mutually complementary, one that arises with the opposition *symptom-fantasy*, one that works in the dynamics of *signification-abstract idea* and finally one that opposes *symbol-model*.

Europe is perceived by many as the work of Christianity. With just as great justice or injustice one could maintain that the three oppositions that divide Europe into a Slav, a Latin and a Germanic culture are the work of Christianity, as this separation has followed three fundamentally different perceptions of religion which are all maintained to be Christian, the Greco-Byzantine today called the Russian, the Roman Catholic that could be called Latin and the Nordic Protestantism which can be perceived as Germanic, a division that has nothing at all to do with the race problem, or, at its most profound, with Christianity either, but which is a result of language forms, which again are the expression of distinctly different life rhythms which, in their dramatic interplay, have developed the immensely vital field of tension called European culture, the starting point of the whole of modern culture.

The perception of Christ as *the redeemer* or saviour who has atoned for our sins and the perception of Christ as the great *model* to be copied and followed mutually exclude each other's meaning and represent the fundamental complementarity between the Byzantine and the Roman perception of

Christianity's earthly or worldly significance. This opposition is well-known and well-elucidated. Nordic Protestantism, which in vain attempts to approach one or other of the two oppositions mentioned without, however, the perspectives of either '*In tyrannos*' or 'Europe or not' being felt to be convincing,* behaves differently. This vacillating attitude must, of course, be regarded by the other two sides as a weakness, a lacking sense of the meaning of religion and a lack of ability to choose and maintain a standpoint. Nordic theologians, apart from Söderblom,* all too easily seem merely to go in for this criticism without investigating *what* hinders us from choosing, and without posing the question if this really is due to a third point of view, just as essential and indissolubly tied in with a special Nordic form of dynamics, yet complementary to the two others.

Now the concept of religious dynamics is just as absurd as the concept of Moral Rearmament. But behind such labels lurk deep-lying norms of behaviour. The opposition between imagination or pictorial cult and symptomatology, and between science or the desire for truth, is posed so clearly in the presentation '*In tyrannos*' that we hardly need hesitate in characterizing this opposition as something characteristic to Byzantine-Muscovite culture. Everyone who has studied classical culture a little knows that the opposition between symbol (law and ethics) on the one hand and the idealizing tendency towards models or exemplars on the other is typical of Latin culture, especially the Roman. What remains is thus the opposition between the signalistic and ideas about the order of nature. That this opposition is typically Nordic has perhaps never been directly established, but if one accepts it here, then the way is open for a new and more profound understanding of what we do, how and why, and thus who we are.

This opposition reveals us in all our ridiculous frailty, in our crazy effectiveness as well as in our irresolute doubt, in our intellectual and practical efforts, but above all in the opposition between our unconditional approach to immediate artistic expression and on the other hand our conditional approach to science and to ethics.

According to our explanation, Russo-Byzantine culture should be the only one in Europe that is able to maintain a naturally objective scientific character, whilst Latin culture is the only one permitting a constant unconditional conception of justice or ethics, which is the purely technical instrumental attitude. At the same time Northerners are the only ones who comprehend what pure subjectivity is and who maintain it in its absolutely unique intentionality, the only ones who are able to live aesthetically in the full and absurd meaning of this word. Thus our three complementary basic principles ought to be

104 *The Natural Order and Other Texts*

distributed in the European cultural group in this way.

As far as mixed products are concerned, then in Russo-Byzantine culture it ought to appear that one seldom comes across a purely ethical or a purely aesthetic attitude and instead encounters, as a rule, a mixed product of imagined morality and moralizing images. On the other hand, ought knowledge and aesthetics seriously and consistently be separated in Latin culture? I have never experienced such a thing, but have seen in this context that the requirement placed on the aesthetic that it also demonstrates knowledge, and on science that it is judged in accordance with principles of harmonious beauty.

The ambiguity in the Nordic way of thinking ought then to lie in an intermingling of science and ethics that makes the desire for truth something moral, an intermingling of experience and law, or science and philosophy. You could hardly find a more characteristic example of this way of thinking than Niels Bohr's theory. This intermingling is what is called an idealism or ideology, and it is characteristic of Bohr's theory that it is not a metaphysical but a scientific ideology, and thus a union of empiricism and articles of faith. If this activity is something typically Nordic, that is, the disposition of knowledge that one can believe in and thus that one has a special interest in *learning*, then the teaching principle also must be dominant in the Nordic attitude to Christianity, as on the whole to everything else. So Northerners must be not only the most teachable of all peoples but also set up teachability itself as the moral virtue.

The perception of Christianity as a teaching stands of course in a sharp opponent relationship to the theory of redemption, where any teaching is absolutely unnecessary. The absolute idealization of Christ's conduct in the exemplar theory must even be directly hostile to any attempt at acquisition and criticism.

We therefore think that we can allow ourselves to state that here we are confronted with a third complementary attitude, and that the significance the Protestants have always ascribed to bible translations and bible criticism indicates that here we have a special Nordic dynamic within Christianity. This must mean that it was Northerners who constructed the teaching system within the Christian evolution of the Middle Ages and that such a tendency had already existed in Scandinavia in pre-Christian times. In my book *Golden Horn and Wheel of Fortune* I have already shown what the rune-stick and probably even the *futhark* might have meant as a *popular* textbook.* The probability that the Nordic *thing* or moot had great instructive significance is also quite large. However, the attempt at coupling together *Weltanschauung and attitude to life* which Bohr has sketched, and which I have here sought to draw on further, can hardly be characterized in any other way than a draft for a new scholasticism, if the concept's purely historical meaning is peeled away and the reservations the Catholics have to the subjective side of scholasticism, a doctrine to which they, from a Latin perception, can only give a purely realistic significance as an instrument, are abolished.

Today there is every probability that the separation between the Nordic and the Latin cultural groups will again be abolished, and there is reason to ask what would have happened if Gustav Adolphus's victory over the Catholic armies had not resulted in the practical division of Europe.[*]

The Latin perception of ethics and laws as something *constant* is intensified to an *absolute degree* within Catholicism. This makes it impossible in advance to come out with changes to the perception of the laws of nature, which is why it is necessary to condemn this side of scholasticism where it abuts the scientific investigation of new and unknown natural laws. Catholicism's distortion of scholasticism consists in the setting-up of the category of *illegal knowledge*. Undoubtedly Bohr's complementary theory about constant oppositions or, put another way, about *the necessity of contradiction* belongs to this illegal knowledge. It is even possible that the preconditions for such a doctrine of investigation were already to be found in the father of scholasticism in the ninth century, the heretic Johannes Scotus Erigena,[*] with his remarkable Nordic name. In this connection, neither will I omit directing attention to Thomas Aquinas's doctrine of intuition, which seems to be a reflex from his Nordic origin,[*] and which Catholics would rather avoid discussing.

What this is about is evident from a French book about Thomas Aquinas by J. Jugnet which goes in for the viewpoint that 'through the experiences gathered, the difficulties, the exertions and the dangers endured, as well as the inspiring resolution and intellectual consciousness, certain imitations become *just as valuable as the creative itself.* Resolve is the true human privilege.'[*] This craftsman's or industrial mentality is not particularly unknown and would obviously be good enough for anyone who cannot see the difference, if only Jugnet did not demand the same obtuseness of others. It leads him of course to the conclusion that *production and reproduction are the same*, a thesis which is basic to Marxist socialism, where it has been developed in an absolute form. This belief that a saint's martyrdom can be just as valuable as Christ's martyrdom is one of the most distinct signs that Kierkegaard was right about Christianity dissolving itself by its spread. This lack of a sense of quality is *fundamentally* incompatible with the Nordic way of thinking, which has always been hostile to this phenomenon. Hegel called it '*Entfremdung*' in the demand for absolute origionality, something which Bohr did not notice in his definition

106   The Natural Order and Other Texts

of the experiment, because he must have perceived it as a truism.

This, to us, greater truism is, however, completely unknown if one looks outside our cultural group. Indeed, *it is simply denied as a possibility.* If, therefore, we cannot clearly and unambiguously formulate our own truisms about others, then they will just be perceived as a manifestation of a special form of Nordic madness and neurosis. This is especially true within the Latin system of thought, where the concept of misunderstanding is an impossibility because of the dominant position of the authoritarian method. Any departure from this critical systemization simply has to be perceived by its adherents as bad manners, contrariness, mischievous distortion and hair-splitting, and thus as irrational and arrogant aggressiveness that can only be answered with a pure aggressiveness. There is simply no possibility that this can happen any other way, and conflict is unavoidable.

As there are complaints that Denmark is prone to preaching, it is thus possible that this is nothing new, and that schoolmasters have annoyed the rest of the Danish population right from the Stone Age, even though schools in the modern sense are a new phenomenon. This is a passion that Danes will need to curb in the coming period, especially where the free high schools are concerned, if we are to get in step with the rest of Europe. A people that puts all its energy into calculating its knowledge and hindering a calculation of actions could, if they were coupled with a population group who calculated their actions and arranged their information in relation to them, easily be forced to do the other group's errands, especially if its own experiential system were suppressed in favour of a belief in that of its opposite number. This modern development is, however, so far advanced in Scandinavia that a new crusader mentality, regardless of how big an attempt to rearm morals is made, could hardly be developed. A rising enmity between northern and southern European states will, on the contrary, be a probability and with unavoidable consequences it will appear that the USA, which has hindered Western Europe's opposition in the two groups of six and seven states by affording Latin Western Europe all its support,* will, after a union and in the event of this tension being strengthened, immediately change course and according to good gangster principles offer Northern Europe all its support against the Latin countries, by reviving the political attitude of its northern Union states, which is really no more than a vapid watering-down of the Scandinavian dialectic. By the consequent homogenization of the Western block invoked by the total subjection of Western Europe to the USA, a big new step towards a new world war will have been reached.

England under Roman rule adapted itself to an anti-subjective instrumental perception of existence which was given the name of pragmatism and which in the USA became even more realistic so that the danger is that it seems as if the United States could take over a Latin way of thinking. The conflict will first show itself when Latin America has developed enough to present its own dynamic principles, today hidden behind the Cuba problem, which is far more complex that the simple opposition between capitalism and socialism.

That I today say no to the question of whether The Seven should seek admittance to the organization they call The Six, but which calls itself Little Europe or more succinctly the European part of Europe, is because such an affiliation in the form it is taking today would be an affiliation, absolutely crippling to Northern Europe, to the special dynamics of this group, which work upon the basis of oppositions not included therein. The choice presented in this way between 'Europe or not' is to my mind a fraud, as this form of dynamics is not that of Europe. On the other hand, the specific dynamics of the European northern states is just as unlike Europe as that of the southern states, and if I here purely personally set out an ineffectual little 'no', then it is so that I can later have the right to set out a far more momentous 'no' the day Northern Europe seeks help from without to 'defend' its dynamics against the Latin methods. That day I will no longer have a fatherland.

United Europe cannot be resurrected. It can only be *created* by a whole new future perspective being opened up. Our past and our classic concepts must be taken up and revised. They must neither be sanctified in a museum nor thrown away, for the fate we afford our past we afford Europe as a whole. We have all the necessary preconditions to give Europe a new future, if we remorselessly reduce realism or the waste of time to what, of course, it is and must remain to us, an instrument, whilst we as people refuse to be instruments. He who today asserts that he is a European must be able to raise himself above his acquired prejudices and master all the three typical basic forms of European dialectics mentioned here without renouncing the ownership rights to the one that is his own.

Art and science

Just as the old grey photographs will gradually be replaced by colour reproductions of the same subject in yellow, red and blue and reproduce reality in altogether richer nuances than before, so we too are learning that the universe today must be seen in an interplay of different viewpoints which mutually contradict and complement each other and can, each on its own, be 'correct'.

108 The Natural Order and Other Texts

If it could be said that in my aesthetic study *Luck and Chance* I have reproduced something of art's yellow, radiant and glaring spectrum, then it could perhaps be said that in my first book *Golden Horn and Wheel of Fortune* I concentrated on the quietly smouldering gleam of warm red also reflected by the world of art, which approaches what one could call an artistic ethics, art as the expression of law and legality. This third treatment of the same subject, in which, completely out of the blue, we have come to the postulate about artistic nature of the scientific spirit, has hereby come into existence. Whether, with this work, I have opened up the possibility of the establishment of a whole new kind of humanism, a Nordic humanism, will not depend on me, but on those who have the ability and education to put this ball, with which I have been playing, systematically into play. I hereby hand it over to the university people.

With this act, I hope to end a century old cultural struggle, which has been going on from Grundtvig's time under the name of the struggle between popular national culture and aristocratic intellectual culture but which in reality is the struggle between two perceptions of reason.* Of these, the classical-Latin perception, through its point of departure in the measurement system of analytical geometry, secured the *hierarchical systemization* that was the backbone of the Roman societal structure. By emphasizing topology's close connection with a spiritual tendency that had its richest flowering in the zoomorphic ornamentation of the Viking era and in Old Icelandic poetry, we are able to understand that this spirit within literature had its focus in *the living word*, the greatest masters of which in our time have been the poets N.F.S. Grundtvig and James Joyce. After these authors' works have taken effect, it is no longer possible to maintain the classical hierarchy of concepts that scientists have hitherto clung to. On the other hand, neither is it any longer possible to preserve the previous century's illusion about the broad popular character of the wider evolution necessary on the lines indicated by these artists. The Grundtvigian principle of Nordic humanism was not really humanistic but rather scholastic in the form it took in the Folk High School. Grundtvig himself was a Nordic humanist, but the Grundtvigians were not. We have both Aakjær's and Andersen Nexø's words for that.* But as they liberate the creative spirit in the High School movement and allow poets and artists to become the spiritual leaders of these centres, they could become so.

Enthusiasm excludes objectivity. Objectivity excludes enthusiasm. Reason excludes enthusiasm as well as objectivity. But the person who does not encompass enthusiasm, reason *and* objectivity could perhaps in the classical sense be called a humanist, but he is not a fully formed person.

This recognition is what I call Nordic humanism, and the big new thing in the

Folk High School is not its enthusiasm for either Edda nor Bible but its *enthusiasm for enthusiasm*, no less. The right of the people to enthusiasm, and everything that could deepen and enrich it, is the right of the people to the aesthetic for its own sake, and this popular demand is one of the greatest contributions to modern democracy. But no enthusiasm can appear without having an influence on something. Therefore any development of enthusiasm is united with a creative philosophy and the sharpest analytical scientific spirit. If enthusiasm, in accord with the Greek meaning, is defined as 'divine transport' then we can in our godless time translate this as *the transport of forces*,★ as what we called *value*, and thus in this case as the transport of intellectual forces. One thing becomes clearer and clearer as one studies the whole thing and this is to what a high degree *transport is the Scandinavians' dearest occupation*, our traditional way to praise and power, a power that cannot rule over anything, but which moves mountains, and one marvels how this special ability of the Scandinavians is overlooked to such a high degree in the political and economic calculations of our relationship to the surrounding world. However, this is a subject that does not concern us here, apart from the difficulty of understanding Nordic philosophy without keeping the transportable side of this philosophy in mind. I would even go as far as to assert that there is something seamanlike in every Nordic peasant, so that it is not to be wondered at that he one day runs off to the open sea.

In order to understand correctly what I mean by this, it is interesting to look at the role an ordinary French book on logic by Paul Mouy ascribes to this Nordic effort in scientific philosophy.★

The first discussion is on Tycho Brahe's observations, which made it possible for Kepler to establish the elliptical orbit which the planet Mars describes around the Sun and which is the track of the planets as a whole, with Kepler stressing that 'Tycho Brahe is such a precise observer that a mistake of 8 minutes is impossible'.★

Then we come to Ole Rømer, the Danish astronomer, member of the Academy of Sciences in Paris, who discovered in 1676 that Jupiter's first satellite revolves about the planet in a variable period of time (about fifteen minutes a week). By investigating the conditions of his observations on the Earth, he found out that the satellite was *before* its normal time when the Earth was close to Jupiter and *late* as the Earth distanced itself. He concluded from this that light must have a particular speed that could be calculated. If Rømer is discussed in this book, it is to demonstrate that it was *the idea of relativity* that gave the impulse to the discovery of the speed of light, as 'relativism is the solution which appears if during observation one reckons with the observer

110 *The Natural Order and Other Texts*

(man, Earth) and gives this a calculable place, as far as possible, in order to eliminate the observer's influence on the observation'.

It is curious to see how far Niels Bohr is able to plunge deeper into precisely the same viewpoint. The context is quite striking when it is stressed that 'With Niels Bohr a new scientific era of great philosophical extent opens, as the observations of matter, energy and light (or more generally the rays: infra-red, ultra-violet, X-rays) are coordinated into a new doctrine.

In the first form of Bohr's theory, the atom's electrons are ascribed movements around a nucleus. The electrons circulate in the same way as the planets circle the sun. From this stems name *the planetary model*, which is the name Bohr's theory has been given. However, this planetary motion has no effect outside the atom. The electron only produces a *phenomenon* when it abruptly changes cycles. This is what one calls the *quantum* leap. This quantum leap *liberates a quantum of energy which is exactly the quantum energy we find in the radiation*. By energy quantum is to be understood a certain amount of energy that one can not divide. The energy variation is thus neither even nor continual.

Philosophical thought must learn to comprehend the extent and precision of this powerful synthesis which unites light and matter under one and the same law.'

What has interested me in this work is not the energy's quantum but *the phenomenon's type of motion, which is what I have called value*.

When I learnt in the following pages that the English scientist Dirac has established, on the basis of very abstract mathematical calculations, a particular *energy of rotation called spin*, I could have concluded that my amateur observations in this book have been a waste of time, as this is already a solved problem. This is what I should have studied first. However, I can also perceive this as a proof that in an artistic way of thinking I have been able to understand what it was all about to the degree that I *intuitively* understood what the next step had to be. From this optimistic attitude, I will allow myself to point out the strange thing that H.C. Ørsted's laws of electro-magnetism have not had such a great philosophical significance that he has been mentioned in the French book, and maintain that the question of the relationship between gravitational laws, right angles and concepts of coordination on the whole could perhaps derive something new from the rule of thumb.

All this lies outside my area. What I have sought to clarify is the special character of the common Nordic presentation of problems, together with the continued existence of these problems in constantly renewed form. For my own use, at any rate, the model of Nordic thought patterns I have set up is useful as

The Natural Order 111

an instrument for a more searching investigation of the rules for the Nordic reaction to European development on the whole. An analysis of this relationship is reserved for a later treatment in the same book series.

I have especially drawn notice to something unsolved in connection with H.C. Ørsted's results, because this is connected with unsolved problems around the phenomenon we call the system of coordinates, which is the foundation for the doctrine of symmetry as well as the doctrine of perspective. In the beginning of the previous century, Scandinavia made a powerful drive to comprehend Hellenic culture in depth. Thorvaldsen's fame shows us that we were successful in identifying ourselves wholly and completely with the world which at that moment was regarded as the Greek.* That this understanding went even deeper is demonstrated by the international recognition that Julius Lange's frontal principle still enjoys.* The reaction to Classicism was necessary and created a renewed knowledge in the opposite direction. But today we must distance ourselves from the one-sidedness of the Romantic reaction, not to Classicism, but to the specific Nordic advance that was achieved with Classicism as an instrument. The law of frontality is a *rule for reading pictures*, an elementary perspective of reading, consisting only in establishing the simplest right-angled relationship between observer and object, and thus the rule that allowed the later establishment of central perspective.

Today we are faced with having to establish new rules. We could, in part, move from the principle of frontality to the even simpler principle of symmetry. If we investigate the principles for symmetrical structuring modern scientists developed after they had discovered the principle called *dissymmetry*, then we have to acknowledge that all the concepts that still go under the name of symmetry within art-life are hopelessly antiquated. The whole of this world of concepts must be re-defined in a way that allows a sharp separation between what could be called symmetrical *opposition* and what could be called symmetrical *similarity*. The greatest self-contradiction exists here.

Furthermore, we must replace the principle of central perspective with a new doctrine of perspective which explains the concept called '*Entfremdung*', or the apparent change of size to number, and which gives a clear picture of what happens in what is called the calculations of probabilities. This can be sketched briefly if we again take up the photographing of the aeroplanes. This time there are not one but innumerable planes in the sky, all at a regular distance from each other and all identical. We take a photograph and see in the photograph that one machine covers the whole foreground. Behind it the same width is filled by two, behind them by four, behind them eight machines, until *the one machine in the foreground has become a line of thousands of machines on the horizon*, all reduced to small dots. Even though we know that all the machines are equally large, we can thus demonstrate that under observation the *mass* of the phenomenon is in reverse proportion to the *quantity* of the phenomena. This form of observation is, however, not the Nordic speciality. It is *observation undertaken from a machine*. But more of that another time.

Appendix

Triolectic schemas

Jorn further elaborated his 'triolectic schemas' in his study of ancient graffiti upon Norman churches published in 1963 (*Signes gravés sur les églises de l'Eure et du Calvados*, Copenhagen, Borgen/Paris, Minotaure, pp. 202, 206).

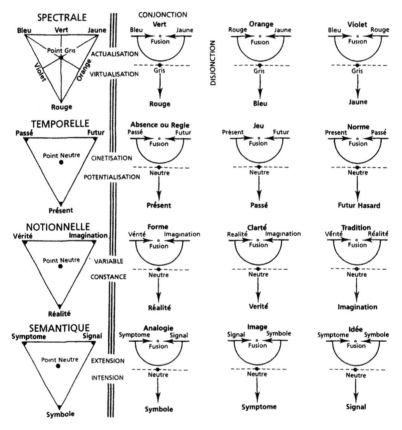

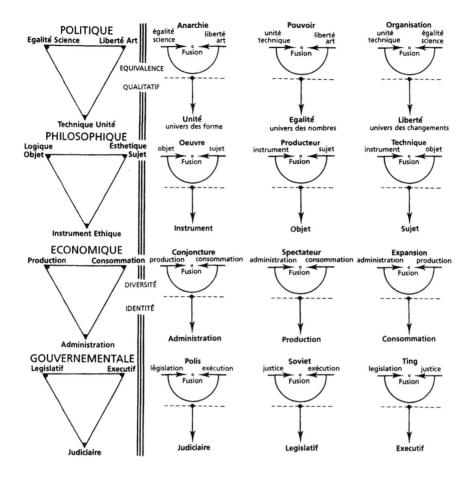

'SOME EXAMPLES OF TRIOLECTIC COMPLEMENTARITY
We here present some models of triolectic equilibriums applied to different conceptual domains. We emphasize these are simple working bases, totally undogmatic, which could be modified or extended. It is in their nature to be open, to start, for example, with more than three relations, this method not being based upon any numerological mystique. Its purpose is to liberate the dialectical movements constrained either in sub-Marxist determinism or in the arbitrary antagonisms where Lupasco founders.'

ASGER JORN

VALUE AND ECONOMY

CRITIQUE OF POLITICAL ECONOMY
and
THE EXPLOITATION OF THE UNIQUE

Report no. 2 of the Scandinavian Institute of Comparative Vandalism, 1962

Following-up the success

Left-wing artists and intellectuals have played a rather peculiar role in popular modern progress, full of significance but at the same time regarded with a strong distrust. One did not know what to make of them and at the same time there was a need for them. The materialistically oriented workers' movement especially had difficulty in understanding these vague idealists struggling for something that only seemed to impoverish their own position. That capitalist economists like Adam Smith regarded the whole of this group as a flock of worthless parasites in society is so well known that it is hardly worth mentioning. The point of view could also be advanced that one could at least demand of a group calling itself intellectual and fighting for a new economic system that they were intelligent enough to demonstrate the economic basis to which they themselves were entitled. This is what I have tried to do here.

I have not included the group of intellectuals who are occupied with teaching, upbringing and technical training in the group I call *the creative elite*, because I cannot see that they have anything to do with it at all, as school-work is not generally creative but a continued reproduction of certain skills and of a particular attitude. The training necessary for the maintenance of society is the task of the state's administrative body of functionaries, in the same way as traditional academics and the church's people act in the maintenance of order, and is as a rule in the sharpest contrast to the creative elite.

In spite of this I give prominence to the Folk High School as the natural anchorage of the creative elite, because it is not in this sense a school. This is therefore at once a demand to have normal school teaching as well as technical training removed from this organization to the ordinary vocational and further education colleges or to rename all the so-called 'Folk High Schools' concerned with practical purposes, and to establish a progressive, intellectual, poetic, artistic, philosophical and Scandinavian-philological leadership of the remaining centres by the side of, or rather above, the administration of purely practical and economic schooling and, instead of the ridiculous academy for the distribution of prizes at the intellectual cattle show that has now been set up on the French pattern, to get a really active academy for creative intellectual life as was projected in its time in Sorø.*

The economic rationalization of our cultural life, the basic principles of which are here presented in a clear and logical form, is based upon the tripartite principle of stabilization I advanced in my first report *The Natural Order* with such great success that there has been no criticism of it whatsoever. This tacit recognition shows that in principle I am in accord with the thinking and reading section of the Danish people. As the economic triolectic advanced here is only a precise use in a special area where I am demonstrating how the principle is to be utilized, there should be no hindrance to us getting to work at once and ordering this affair in the correct manner, whilst we are preparing more comprehensive and searching operations.

Despite the fact that art and humanity are as they have always been, the question 'What is wrong with art today?' is still being asked. Only something has come between art and humanity. The direct connection between the best and the popular or the vulgar no longer exists and the old connecting lines have become obsolescent. A breakthrough must be planned and an independent social structure constructed *which would take care of this alone,* in a direct contact between the highest and the broadest for the enrichment of peoples' lives. The natural conditions to undertake this step, which is of universal significance, are to be found in Denmark today. When 121 French artists and intellectuals signed the demand that everyone should decide with his own conscience whether he wanted to kill the North Africans, they were excluded from their positions, for example in the world of entertainment.* This lockout was so crippling that they had to be recalled. This shows what a little strike of the elite could accomplish. It is time that the creative elite was clear about its power, demanded its rights and did its duty by the people.

Part 1:
Critique of political economy

This section, apart from a few rearrangements, was published in French by the Situationist Internationale in 1959 and dedicated to the Danish syndicalist and workers' leader Christian Christensen, who in my youth, when he lived in Sejs near Silkeborg, was like a father to me and taught me what economics, economic critique and organization are.*

The Marxism which is criticized here is what made Marx maintain that he was not a Marxist. The old basis for international communism has today definitively broken down. Here I could say to all those who are seeking pure socialism, 'If you are going to the right, then I'll go to the left.' I have already indicated in my book The Natural Order *that this statement should not be perceived in the traditional sense. The illusion that progress and evolution are the same has come to an end. This has meant that the communist movement is dissolving. I go in for progress, but in order to progress one must be able to regress. In his cultural history, Hartvig Frisch has demonstrated that the forces of progress do not always evolve from the top, but can shoot out as side-shoots from the trunk.* My idea of progress is therefore based upon an out-and-out revolutionary conservatism, for I am going back to the composition of the First Internationale and maintaining that none of its three basic principles – anarchism or the principle of the evolution of personal freedom, syndicalism or the evolution of wise, social organizations and socialism or the knowledge of the context of all social phenomena – can be done without today.*

The main points in my critique*

Production and reproduction are, like progress and evolution, two complementary oppositions.

Neither commodity value nor work can comprise the elemental concept of social value, which must base itself upon the human being as the source of value.

Raw material cannot be constant or free capital, as capitalists and socialists maintain. Raw material is in a continual reductive process.

Use value is the opposite and negation of the article of utility, as quality is the opposite of value.

Value in itself and forms of value

The common criterion for truth for any socialist or anti-capitalist politics, the basis that is still recognized as valid by socialists as well as communists, is the Marxist analysis and critique of the capitalist form of value, *the commodity*, perceived as the elemental form of the wealth existent in a society where the capitalist form of production is dominant. This manifests itself as an immense accumulation of commodities.

This analysis was carried out by Karl Marx in his 'critique of political economy', a work that was given the name of *Das Kapital*. Marx does not just demonstrate that the capitalist form of wealth is the commodity, for that demonstration cannot take place at all without a precondition that wealth and value are the same.

As wealth exists as the opposite of poverty, it is precisely this opposition between rich and poor that socialist politics wants to remove. However, as, according to dialectics, an opposition cannot be removed without thereby achieving the removal of or the neutralization of both oppositions, socialism abolishes wealth along with poverty. If wealth continues to blossom one can simply demonstrate that socialism does not exist. The idea of a socialist wealth is not just utopia. It is simply rubbish.

The present crisis of socialism has its starting point in the fact that Marxism's identification of commodity, wealth and value make the abolition of value as such the ideological goal of socialism. Thus the concept of value itself becomes an absurdity in socialist terminology, whilst socialist politics is forced to become a permanent politics of devaluation, the end purpose of which can only be the absolute abolition of all values. Nothing in Marxist economic dogma contradicts this goal in a scientifically logical way. This absolute and all-embracing devaluation is, indeed, altogether unavoidable and will happen of its own accord whether people wish it or not. This natural evolution forms the scientific basis of socialist theory. This tendency is the basic definition of socialist development itself, the one by which the consequences of all socialist actions are justified, and is the justification in itself of socialist politics.

We will here attempt to indicate that it is possible to accept the Marxist analysis and critique of the *capitalist* form of value, the commodity, without thereby taking over the identification of this form with value itself as a concept and a reality. This is to say that it is possible to accept the purely scientific side of *Das Kapital* without thereby automatically taking over the political conclusions that Marx drew from it.* It consists of perceiving the Marxist critique not as a critique of value in itself but of a specially occurring form of

124 *The Natural Order and Other Texts*

value limited in time and space. To get to this new form of critique, it is first necessary to lay down a new and precise concept of value which does not contradict itself, and which is at the same time far more comprehensive than the Marxist one, a concept of value that harmonizes with the conceptual world of the natural sciences, something which the Marxist concept of value clearly does not do. In order to do this, we must find a corresponding definition of the concept of form so that we can clearly and unambiguously lay down what is meant by different forms of value. This leads directly to a necessary critique of the concept which in dialectical materialism goes under the name of 'objective quality'. This is the purpose of this study.

Concepts are concepts – actualities are actualities

In order to avoid a thorough discussion about this question of concepts, Marx was obliged to exclude the whole question by saying that it did not exist at all, that it was irreal. He stated that value is not a concept but an actuality, namely the commodity or the exchange value. Thereby he is really stating that all value is exchange value. Concepts are words which everyone has agreed to give one and only one meaning. This socialization of the concepts is altogether necessary to make it possible to explain something to each other that we can agree on in fellowship. Therefore the whole socialist theory stands or falls on this tool, with which this theory is transformed to an ideology, becoming clearly and unambiguously socialized. In this argument Marx forgets, however, that he himself in *Das Kapital* defines value as a purely *metaphysical* and thus immaterial phenomenon, as an *agreement by convention*, and thus as nothing other than a concept.

However, even this Marxist refusal to discuss concepts does not hinder the rising depreciation in all areas which becomes a result of socialist politics. On the contrary. As the actual goal of socialism is the practical abolition of exchange value, socialism is not just moving towards an eradication of possible new value theories but towards a state where even the actual objects vanish, towards a state without actual values.

Marx was himself the first to see this evolution and to go in for it at full throttle. He even perceived his own Marxist philosophy as the last philosophy for which there would be a use, and that only in the period of transition to the socialist society, where all philosophy, even the Marxist, would be abolished. Here one sees his own economic philosophy replaced by the greatest economy, as far as philosophy is concerned. His goal was to make all philosophy unnecessary, including Marxism. Thus this growing devaluation of everything, of even Marxism itself, is not anything unexpected. It is both the conscious and unconscious goal of socialism.

Marx's conceptual confusion is too great to be able to demonstrate the overall consequences of this consistently anti-progressive ideology. For example, he talks of the commodity's factors, the use value (defined as the substance of value) and the exchange value or 'value in itself' (which he identifies with the dimension of value). There can be no doubt that dimension and value are here perceived as the same. However, he thereafter divides exchange value into two completely different factors, as he says, 'Any article of utility can be perceived from a double viewpoint, from that of the quantity and from that of the quality.' As dimension and quantity are the same, value and quantity must also be so. In dialectical materialism, the concepts of *quantity* and *quality* are themselves the key concepts. It is therefore strange that Marx cannot keep to them when he has to talk of value and commodities. The reason hits one in the eye. It is altogether impossible to classify considerations of value, be it under the concept of quantity or the concept of quality. Even the most diligent materialistic dialectician falls down here. Is value then really, as Marx himself suggests, just a purely metaphysical concept? There are only two possibilities. Either this is the case and then Marxism is neither materialistic nor scientific in the strict meaning of that expression, or Marxism's concept of value is out-of-date and must be replaced by a new one. It is this latter perception that I want to attempt to develop here. In order to do this we must look a little closer at what could lie in the concepts that Marx is manipulating. What do, for example, *substance and dimension*, the two concepts which in Marxist doctrine are the two factors of form, mean?

Substance and process are in the Marxist sense the same

In order to able to understand Marx's concept of substance, it is necessary to place it in relation to what he calls form. As we are keeping to a purely materialistic evaluation and conceptual world, we can in the main confirm that what the Marxists call matter is perceived as substance, and is normally perceived as being the same as the material's characteristic of *raw material* for something, and not in a true sense as an *element*. In the Marxist sense, all material is actually or possibly raw material and nothing else. On the other hand, the form of the material designates its character as a material different from all other materials, which can be determined or united in a special object. In this ways one talks of different forms of energy, etc.

126   *The Natural Order and Other Texts*

These forms of energy stand in a dialectical opponent relationship to the substance of the same energies. But it is here that Marx is wrong. In Marx, the concept of form is, so to speak, never placed in relation to the concept of substance. He prefers to operate with a completely different opposition: form and content. Thus he talks of the value's form and the value's content. A content is what is enclosed in a form. Thus Marx declares that the content of value is work and adds to this description that *the true form is the form of the content*, which logically makes formal truth identical with work or with content in the value question.

However, he also says somewhere, 'We now know the substance of value. It is work!' We must thus state that in Marx, *substance and content are the same*. However, he also declares that use value is 'the value's' (the exchange value's) substance and at the same time explains that 'work is not the only source of value for the use values it creates, for material wealth. It is the father. The earth is the mother.' But in order for a use value to be able to be transformed into a true 'value', an exchange value, he himself emphasizes that it is necessary to eliminate or completely devalue one factor, the material character of the commodity, to deny the mother, the earth, which is the original source. *The transition from use value to exchange value happens by the devaluation of the article of utility's material actuality.*

The lacking understanding of the materialistic significance of this operation can be seen even more clearly in Marxist theory, if one goes a little closer into the Marxist perception of form. Here it is stated that *the use value is the natural form of the commodity*. What does that mean? Marx adds, however, that the commodity possesses a form of value of a quite special kind that contrasts sharply with the various natural forms of the commodity, namely the form of money. If we accept that the use value is the commodity's actual *substance*, then it is impossible to perceive an article of utility as being identical with a natural form. An article of utility is not a natural form but a cultural form, otherwise a wooden table would have the same form as a tree. The more one reads Marx, the more one becomes clear that he hasn't an inkling of what a use value and an article of utility are. He believes that they are the same. One can excuse him. In spite of his unique efforts in the cultural history of humanity, it was not given to him in practice to immerse himself in either the world of wealth or of use values.

Nevertheless it is precisely this lack of knowledge of the artistic and the artificial elements in the article of utility's character of wealth that reduces the extent of the Marxist theories to a limited period in history which is now past.

We can accept the fact that articles of utility represent the substance or raw material of commodities. There is, however, just the important thing that use value is something more and something more essential than just commodity substance. It is in itself a value that is certainly devalued in the instant of barter, but immediately takes up its intrinsic value again in the consumer's hand, when the exchange has taken place. *Once bought by the consumer the article of utility is no longer a commodity. It has again become an article of utility.* This determination is necessary for all articles of utility except money.

He who manufactures articles of utility does it primarily because he has use for them. If he makes more than he can use himself, then he has created a utilitarian surplus value. This surplus production is directly valueless to himself. If others are interested in it, then he can give it away. This is called potlatch.* However, it is this productive *surplus value*, and only this, which is made into commodities, first by the exchange of surplus products in barter and then by the surplus production being exchanged for money, this again being exchanged for other articles of utility. Exploitation arises when a person is not allowed to give his surplus production away to whom he will. Slavery consists in the person no longer being allowed to decide what he has a use for himself. One can thus be exploited before one becomes a slave. The Marxists have not discovered this. However, if one has no right whatever to decide what, how much and why one produces, then one is simply an instrument.

What Marx discovered was that all the process mentioned here is *artificial*, that is, discovered by people, and that *the article of utility also has its substance which is the forms of nature.* However, nature exists, as Lenin maintains, independent of our sensing it and our use of it. This means that nature is not in itself a substance. It is so only in its relation to the human wishes and abilities that create the articles of utility. Nature itself is not a means, and has not in itself an end that serves humanity. Nature is simply the first unavoidable condition for all production. Nature exists in natural forms. The destruction of these natural forms is the process we call the manufacture of articles of utility. One can destroy natural forms without manufacturing anything. But the manufacture of articles of utility is impossible except by a destructive incursion into the natural order. This incursion is called culture. So the foundation of socialism in the order of *nature* makes its theory a denial of art and culture. This is apparent above all in socialism's complete lack of understanding of the agriculture problem.

Use value is the negation of the article of utility

Marx is forced to eliminate the whole problem of consumption to avoid seeing the holes in his theory. He does this by simply and primitively maintaining obstinately that there is nothing at all that one could call use value and what one does call use value is in reality what should be called the article of utility. If Marx in the beginning maintains that value and dimension are the same, then he also ends by identifying value with quality or article, which in reality abolishes the difference between quality and quantity upon which dialectical materialism is built. In no other place has Marx used such an agitated tone and such cheap arguments as in this question and, oddly enough, no postulates have been lapped up with greater joy than precisely this rubbish, be it by communists, socialists or capitalists, priests and popes and artists, the whole caboodle.

Marx asserts that the use of the word *value* in connection with articles of utility is just as crazy and pre-scientific as the pre-chemical use of the word salt not just for true salt but also for substances like sugar because there is a purely external similarity between sugar and salt. This parallelization is not, however, a scientific argument but a piece of chicanery that the socialists have also used recently in Denmark to assert that one cannot compare the amounts from the national wealth used for military purposes with those used for cultural institutions like the National Museum, because the military, as everyone can clearly see, has nothing to do with culture. No arguments seem to have so great a carrying capacity as such mental short-circuits.

Of course, Marx himself believed in his own argument. However, he did not follow it. He could not solve the problem. But if he had really followed his own theory in *Das Kapital* and written *article of utility* every time he wrote *use value*, then he would have swiftly discovered the absurdity. But he was careful not to do that, and Marxists since have not dared to do the experiment, but have all faithfully continued to swallow his assertion. One has to hinder discussions about this problem. When Marx says, '*Use value is realized in use or consumption*', then it would be quite meaningless to imagine that he is talking of the article of utility, for the realization of the article of utility is after all because of its production and not its consumption. One does not realize a roll by eating it.

The use value of bread is realized in the digestion, in the dissolution and thus in the process of digestion. This is all that can be said directly about use value. Use value must therefore be exactly the opposite of article of utility, *the negation of the article of utility* as article or object, or as actual form.

Marx elaborates, 'As use value, the commodity is above all of differing quality. As exchange value, it can only be of differing quantity.' Here we have arrived back at the concepts of quality and quantity. Does anyone, after this presentation, doubt that use value cannot be the same as the article of utility? If one uses an article of utility one cannot at the same time preserve it as a commodity. In order for an article of utility to be recognized as a commodity in the modern sense, it must be *unused*, remain intact, and it is thus this intact object that Marx calls quality. We will keep to this unambiguous definition of the concept of quality.

However, it is thereby impossible for use value to be the quality of an article as one likes to maintain. Quality, if this word is to have one unambiguous meaning, must simply mean the article in itself, the extent and duration of its body, which in reality are the same, its *condition.*

If I buy myself a pair of shoes, then their consumption and destruction by wear cannot really be their quality. On the contrary, one perceives their *quality as their resistance to destruction*, their permanence or constancy as an article. It is obvious that the shoes will hold their quality best if one never uses them, if one puts them in a cupboard. This is the way the shopkeeper has to treat them. The least use diminishes their price to a degree that no Marxist law can explain. However, if I don't use my shoes, then they are at the same time without value to me. *The value is created in the use* but not by the wear or consumption in itself. I buy good quality shoes precisely to avoid them being swiftly worn out, even though this is, despite everything, unavoidable, if I am to use them. One cannot thus directly identify use or consumption. For bread the problem is even more complex. I do not bite the bread into pieces to destroy it but to produce thereby strength with which to build myself up. Only that part of the bread that gives me strength is a value to me. The rest is pure garbage.

Value is process

Marx says that 'as an article of utility the commodity is quality and as exchange value it is quantity'. This formula, perceived by dialectical materialism as a renewal of the scientific concepts, would, however, remain completely static and unusable, if Marxism did not reckon with what it calls the transition from quality to quantity and vice versa. This process has not been given a clear scientific formulation in the ideology of dialectical materialism.

What evades the attention of Marxists in this formulation is that Marx's so-called exchange value has no more to do with value than the article of utility has to do with use value. The Marxist pseudo-value, *exchange value, is nothing other than the neutralization of two values in a condition of equilibrium* which is called equivalence or equal value – equal validity. Two values which are equally valid abolish each other's value and make each other valueless until they are again torn from their established opposite number. This opposition is fixed in the object we call *currency*. Money in itself as an object is valueless. But it is an article of utility, a form. The special thing about it, however, is that as it is gradually liberated in its pure form, where there is no material covering for it, it has only a purely metaphysical value based exclusively upon belief, upon everyone believing in it. *In the socialist society the banknotes themselves become the measure of what people believe and value*, nothing more. One could abruptly agree that one no longer wanted to believe in the particular banknotes. One could make others and the first ones could be ripped up. They would be valueless, on the metaphysical ground alone that as a matter of pure convention one has agreed not to believe in them anymore.

The market value of things is not conditioned by their quality, far less by their amount. It is conditioned by their *differences*, their variability. To reduce this variability, to standardize a commodity is therefore to say that one is devaluing it. This process of standardization is called economics. The exchange value of two commodities is thus not their equivalence but the dissimilarity in the conditions they offer and this is expressed in the price difference. By reducing this difference to a price difference of a purely quantitative nature, one can fix the price. In reality this means that everything has the same price and thereby there is nothing that has a price anymore. The price no longer exists. The real exchange value exists exclusively in the change or variability in price. When all prices are fixed, trade has become meaningless. The commodity no longer exists. This is the purpose of socialism.

It should thus be correct to put forward the perception that *value and process are the same* and that which Marx calls the value's substance is the true value and not the dimension of the value as he claims. Dimension is nothing more than the quantity of a particular quality. However, *value is a particular quantity of qualities undergoing process or change.*

Matter or natural forms first become substance in the process that changes them not to quantity but to other forms or qualities. Outside the process each substance is, in its own nature, just a special quality or form. The concept of substance is thus characteristic of nothing other than the process itself or the transition between two states. Substance is the material actuality of the change or the transformation. Let us test the possibilities for a deeper knowledge of the production problem that this opens up.

The cycle of production and consumption

Marx declares that barter implies the following change of form:
Commodity – Money – Commodity (C–M–C)
But this process necessarily presupposes a deeper lying change of form:
Article of Utility – Commodity – Article of Utility (A–C–A)
Behind this lies a third change of form:
Natural Form – Article of Utility – Natural Product (N–A–N)
The most primitive human life form was based on this simple cycle: N–A–N. The city society's trade added a new element to the chain in a cycle N–A–C–A–N. The Greco–Roman money system made the cycle one notch longer: N–A–C–M–C–A–N.* What new element have the socialists added to this cycle? It is not our task here to indicate this. We would just like to stress that only the study of this cycle is able to give us a real scientific picture of the relationship between production and consumption in modern society. At the same time, it has, however, to be pointed out that, in contrast to agriculture, industry gives nothing back to nature in a rebirth of the values it consumes. Industry's consumption of nature is *irreversible*, as the natural products it leaves behind have always been definitively devalued in human and cultural terms. Industry therefore has a direct contact with that rising depreciation of matter which is called the expansion of the universe. This is the reason why its advocates do not see their own place in a cyclic development, and this is the reason that those who are not in the running must be wary of whichever cycle industry may now find to launch itself into, for behind that grows no grass.

A commodity is a socialized article of utility

The bourgeois revolution against the nobility, the court and the Catholic Church had its point of departure in indignation at the wealth, plenty and luxurious living of these privileged groups, and it set up against them the bourgeois virtues of modest simplicity of conduct, of thrift and frugality. Marx did not even discover that it was this sudden and compulsory thrift in consumption which was the source of capital-creating savings. This tendency did not come on the agenda at all in the revolutionary ideas of socialism. On the

132 The Natural Order and Other Texts

contrary, there was a tendency to promise all the people what the privileged classes had before the bourgeois revolution. According to Marx, the luxury consumption of the individual capitalist plays no role at all in economic considerations.

It is only against the background of this fact that one can understand why socialists feel themselves so dependent upon capitalists that they assume a bourgeois-capitalist revolution to be a necessary prelude to a socialist one. The two revolutions are just two sides of the same affair. Of course, there are purely tactical reasons for not getting too close to the problem. No one makes a revolution to be frugal, especially not poor people. But the reason that it is at all possible for socialists to suppress this problem is that they already assume certain bourgeois-capitalist traits of character as an obvious necessity amongst the people who are to shape socialism. This means that what is called capitalism is nothing other than a particular form of socialism or socialization: a form of socialization really just as deep-seated as the working class's socialization of industry's means of production and what complements it, namely, the socialization of the means of consumption, for *a commodity is nothing other than a socialized means of consumption*, a socialized article of utility. In this way the socialist revolution is nothing other than the completion of the capitalist revolution. The only element removed from capitalism by this completion is private savings, nothing else, for the true wealth in the course of life, its variability in consumption, has already been reduced through the capitalistic mass production of the same article. It is rare today to find a capitalist whose consumption exceeds a petty and bigoted life-form. The difference in the standard of living of a grand duke in the 17th century and a great capitalist in Rockefeller's period is grotesque and is becoming steadily greater.

If socialists do not therefore need to deal with the socialization of the article of utility, it is simply because the capitalists have already saved them the labour. This socialization allowing the characterization of an article of utility as a commodity has the three following characteristics:

a) Only articles of utility of a common interest to the members of society can find a sufficiently large market to be able to be used as commodities. The ideal commodity is the article that everyone wants.

b) Only an article of utility which is found in sufficiently large numbers of uniform examples can be recognized as a true commodity in the Marxist sense. Industry is only interested in serial production and the interest rises with the number. To open the way for industrial production to such a socialization, *capitalism has had to fight the idea of rarity value* and make people believe that the special value of handcrafted and individual production was a formalist superstition. This is the reason for Marx's remark about the enmity of capitalism to art, an enmity that has become absolute only in the socialist society, where one maintains that the reproduction is just as valuable as the original.

c) Finally, capitalist production is characterized by the use of art to an immense extent for propaganda on behalf of popular mass production. The advertisement for socialized production is therefore only the natural consequence of the capitalists' advertisement for a socialized consumption. Socialists also avoid taking this economic significance of art into consideration. Therefore they cannot explain why there are types of wine in France that are half as dear as others even though they are just as good. The explanation is that because of the lack of advertisement they are not known and cannot therefore be sold for a high price. The lack of advertisement is due to the limited number of commodities.

The container principle and the concept of form

When we maintain that socialism excludes savings from the capitalist consumption system, then this is really just a propaganda cliché without meaning, for *socialism is in reality constructed on the principle of absolute savings.*

This can only be understood if one includes the article of utility in the economic considerations, and this is probably the most important reason why socialists avoid it. We have been able to establish that the article of utility becomes a commodity in the instant the producer cannot use it himself and it thus becomes directly or immediately of no use to him, and therefore where the direct causal relationship between production and consumption is broken. Only the article of utility saved up in this way (placed in reserve) becomes a commodity, and this happens only in the event of a sufficiently large number of uniform articles of utility existing in the depot. This system of accumulation is the process of commodity genesis and is not eliminated by socialism. On the contrary, it has become an absolutely common principle for all production. The socialist system is based upon a common accumulation of the whole production, without exception, before it is distributed. This occurs with the intention of achieving complete control by such a distribution.

No one up to now has analysed accumulation, which is the same as saving, in its own form, which is the form of the container. Accumulation is dialectical interplay between container and content. We have noticed that substance is often identified with the concept of content, but it is really nothing more than process. *Substance, in the form of a real content, means the latent power,* restrained energy or matter available to be used in a process. But we have always perceived form as constancy or stability. A container's form is a form that exists only as a direct opposite to the content, its function being to prevent the content entering into a process except under controlled and severely limited conditions. In this way, the container form is thus something completely different from the form of the material in itself, where only the content's own form exists. It is only in the biological world that the container becomes an elemental function. The whole of biological life has, so to speak, occurred on the basis of a development of this opponent relationship between container form and the material's own form. It is this path that technology is continuing in an artificial way and is definitively systematizing through what we call the measurement processes, for any goal whatsoever is nothing other than a form of container, and what is called by that strange expression scientific control is only the establishment of a constant relationship between objective forms and artificial container forms manufactured by man.

These measurements or container forms are established as purely conventional oppositions to the forms being measured. Generally the container hides the content's own form and thus possesses a third form, the sensual form or the apparent form. In the discussion about forms, these three forms are never clearly separated. But all three forms are actual and make up sides of our experience of matter. They make up a scale of oppositions that allow us to distinguish between the matter of the unorganized world, the forms of biological nature and our own purely sensory world. But another world unites with these three actual forms, the world of imagined forms, formed by thought and fantasy, the symbolic forms.

Scientific and philosophical systems differ from each other in the way they confuse and mix up these forms, which, as forms, have nothing to do with each other, if the descriptions are shaped into clear and unambiguous concepts. If one can establish that there is an opposition between *quality* and *quantity* as two opposite characteristics of matter which is also the opposition that exists between *units* and *similarities*, then it is precisely the principle of container form which permits people to be fooled that this opposition can be abolished as *the similarity and uniformity of the content is neutralized by the container's function as a unit.* By this one comes to the formula; the greater the unit or quality, the greater the similarity or quantity, as the law of probability abolishes the *meaning* of the differences to the same degree as the units are increased in number. In the unit *container-content* the opposition between mass and amount is abolished.

This storage of accumulation or box principle, this insurance or savings principle, is the basis for the whole of the modern tin-can philosophy which sees progress as the tendency towards greater and greater similarities. One has just to extend the container, to make it bigger and bigger, which isn't so difficult as it can be changed independently of the content because its form has nothing at all to do with the form of the content. This is the capitalist as well as the socialist principle of development and all their reflections about the relationship between form and content only serve the purpose of developing this tinned goods industry.

Surplus and economics

The word *state* means condition, the static, the quality or the form. The great discrepancy of Marxism is that it has not understood what the state in its innermost being is, that it is that purely biological form, the container. The biological cycle in nature is called *ecology* and it is the mistake of the Marxists not to have seen that unpolitical economics, ecology and the pure doctrine of the state are the same. Despite the opposite being maintained, socialism therefore becomes the society of the pure state. This cannot be otherwise. The day that the lie is rooted out, everything is true and then truth is abolished. Really this is the way that the socialists wish to abolish the state.

Marxism is the first philosophy that has stressed the economic problem as the most important, as the basic condition for human conduct. In order to avoid the direct consequences of this theory's fusion with socialism, a distinction was discovered between higher Marxism and what was called vulgar Marxism. *Vulgus* means people, just like *populus*, and this more lowly regarded popular Marxism, which in reality is not taken into account, probably corresponds to what were called the vulgar or folk democracies in eastern Europe after the war. I here have to make this absolutely vulgar perception of Marxism my own, for I am an adherent of democracy.

Since industrialization, economics and economic problems have played a steadily rising role in human activity. It is therefore appropriate for once to examine thoroughly what this new dominant concept truly covers. If one goes back to the original speculations about economics, one discovers that they limited themselves to only one of the three sides that today comprise economics, namely the ordering of *expenditures* in a housekeeping. Neither incomes nor

136   The Natural Order and Other Texts

savings were dealt with at that time. Only later was the concept of economics moved over to the savings achieved by limiting expenditures.

These savings are called economizing. The question of from where the savings that are to be made or distributed are to come has not yet been posed. This undefined dimension is called *wealth*. However once the economic question is posed in its entirety as the relationship between income, saving and expenditure, the basis has been created for the development of what is called *political economics*, which deals with the question of the production, distribution and consumption of *wealth*.

Expenditure – saving – income

We have already indicated at the beginning that wealth has nothing to do with what is necessary for the maintenance of life, and thus to the economic in its true sense. Wealth is surplus, abundance, multiplicity or what modern economics calls surplus value. If this wealth had always been used from the dawn of time in accordance with its own essence, as waste, unprofitable consumption and superfluous luxury, then an economic problem would never have existed, but neither would technical development. Economic problems first arise the moment wealth is saved, collected and stored, thus taking on the character of a reserve. It is through the accumulation of wealth that one economizes. Thus this is immediately just a question of a choice between consumption and non-consumption and it is this problem that occupies the thoughts of most people.

Karl Marx was the first person to move the main interest in economic considerations consistently over to the relationship between production and saving. He maintained that the saving of products from time immemorial has been the source of all humanity's misfortunes and that the equivalence between human production and consumption is the formula for happiness, as it hinders the accumulation of wealth. Strangely enough this leads to the demand for absolute saving.

A completely equable economics would thereby arise, a true economy, and a new economic science, no longer interested in wealth, but, on a purely economic basis, able to control the harmony between the various parts of the economic whole. This would make economics an absolute unit, a quality, by excluding the problem of variability or what we call the concept of value. *Human economics* has hereby become identified with *biological ecology* and can be perceived as natural, and an integrated part of the natural sciences. This socialist economics is far more superior in its theory than political economics, because the latter systematically avoids analyzing the source of wealth. Its success has led to a pure doctrine of political economics hardly being found anywhere in the world anymore. Everything is consciously or unconsciously stamped with the principles of socialist economics.

Economic politics versus political economics

In order to understand this development, it is necessary to understand what the concept of *politics* really means in its basic essence. What in Hellenic city society was called politics, and is still the fundamental meaning today, are those actions carried out within a social community *without any regard whatever to economic considerations*. Politics is surplus fellowship or a social unit's anti-economic actions, the variability in the actions of a social group. Gathering the description of all these unique and incessantly changing events together is called the writing of history. Politics is thus the medium for introducing something new and unexpected into the pattern of actions of a whole group. This is called historical development and is a purely artificial or artistic phenomenon.

The 'Critique of political economics' of *Das Kapital* is in no way a critique of economics as such. On the contrary, it is a critique of the control of economics through the purely uneconomical activity called politics that is still frustrating all objective economic calculations. As an antidote to the political consequences, which are always uncertainty, instability, crises, social and productive disorder, Marx suggests a socialist politics or more precisely an anti-political economic system, which must necessarily remove any possibility or necessity of making politics.

As communists see that the state is used as a political instrument, the socialist movement reckons that one can dissolve the state by rooting out the class which dominates politics. The political goal of Marxism is therefore to replace the state with an inoffensive and automatic administration or a system of distribution of those things which could be of common interest. As in socialist terms that is everything, this is to say that this administrative apparatus would control everything. Statistics robots will compute, guided by effective soundings of public opinion, in accord with the wishes or otherwise of the majority, and in the society of the future secure us a perfect and effective dictatorship of the majority, without the least possibility of fooling the people, that is to say, of making politics with them and thereby allowing people to dominate other people. The problem will be solved.

138 *The Natural Order and Other Texts*

There is just the snag that this technical administration which today has developed with growing speed all over the world to the east and the west, although it abolishes the politics of cultivating politics, does not at the same time, as was believed, abolish the state. On the contrary. *Everything becomes the state.* What was overlooked was the fact that *the state is not and never has been a directly political instrument.* The state's function has always been to avoid or at any rate diminish and even out the misfortunes that politics brought with it. The state was created to create stability and this stability is precisely the same as what is called economics. The statesman in his pure form appears neither as emperor, nobleman nor capitalist. He comes into history under the name of '*major domus*', the householder or the economist. In this category we will find all the really great statesmen of Europe. He is the economist, the bureaucrat, the first model for the statistics robot, even though he is encumbered with faults because he is only a human being and not a machine. If the socialist goal is itself in this way in absolute conflict with the progressive ideas of the working classes, this is because of this misunderstanding of the concept of the state, and their great illusion about being able to liberate themselves from this apparatus by perfecting it.

In order to come to power, the socialists have worked out a political programme. They are therefore forced to accept the political perception of the state, a perception which contrasts completely with those perspectives in which Marx believed and which came from the theory of the swift dissolution of the state. They wish to utilize the apparatus of the state and thereby become themselves utilized for just the opposite of what they aspired to. In the Soviet Union, they believed that they were on the way to abolishing surplus value, but without knowing it they have created the greatest and most sensational completely unusable surplus value in the history of humanity, a star that could lift humanity above its attachment to the earth. The danger of this situation is that they themselves believe that they have done this of necessity, to defend themselves, and thus for military reasons. For this reason, they are blind to the fact that this new human possibility for expansion could not under any circumstances be coupled with the production of H-bombs, but on the contrary must definitively close this chapter of the history of humanity as the final mistake for this new perspective to have any possibility at all of development.

Instead, however, bureaucracy swarms everywhere. As the true so-called 'power factors' within the areas of capitalism, socialism and communism, these snotty little functionaries are increasing more and more. Like the counter-revolutionary armies of socialism, they are spreading out over all branches of human existence, for *bureaucracy is the container system of society.* In the name of economic control, and to preserve their own meaningless little existence, they sit by the innumerable screws and taps of the whole system of pipes. They have all 'the power' except one, the one able to change anything at all, and this is really the only power that counts. That the social justification for the sputnik and the atom bomb is the same everywhere, even though they open two quite opposite perspectives, is the fault of that ridiculous flock of politicians, economists and generals which in the USA carries the delicious name of *the power elite.*

Value is inconstancy – quality is immutability

What must now be the consequence of our new definition of value? Firstly it must be that we can maintain that value never under any circumstances can be a *state* of things, a constant. Thus value does not exist in the same way as things. Values arise and pass away. One cannot therefore own values, as it is so nicely put. One can only own objects containing a latent value, a possible value. A substance is a possibility of value. Thus in theory all objects in the world possess values, if people are able to extract them. This is thus dependent exclusively upon people themselves. On the other hand, one could say that everything is value in itself, because everything is in process. This is just not in peoples' direct interest. All matter is in constant emergence and disappearance. Value can therefore be characterized as an objective property of matter. Or, more correctly, if quality is the property of matter then value is the material characteristics or abilities, the dynamics of matter. The value of a form or a quality thus depends upon *the ease with which one can dissolve the form and liberate its latent energies,* whilst its character of quality consists in its resistance to this. The ease with which a quality is transformed to another quality is thus its value. The socialist attack upon the right of private ownership thus comes from the will to destroy a system that blocks the free play of values by making them private, which is to say socially inaccessible. However, the law of mechanics says that a form of energy cannot be counteracted without the energy gathering itself after its liberation into an even more inaccessible form or quality, which thus becomes *more valueless and precisely therefore of higher quality.* It is this opposition to which the socialists close their eyes.

Fixed values do not exist. If they are fixed, that is to say that they are qualities and not values. In his analysis of industrial society, Marx demonstrates how *variable capital* is transformed to *constant capital,* that capital from being a value is transformed into a quality, and that it is precisely

140 *The Natural Order and Other Texts*

this transformation that shows that the transformation of the capitalist society into a socialist society is unavoidable and necessary. The socialists have shown their theoretical superiority for it is extremely easy to demonstrate this process purely scientifically

Value perceived as process can only be progressive or regressive. It is here that the socialists have allowed themselves to be fooled, for this means that value can only exist in the form of rising surplus value or depreciation, as inflation and deflation. The fixation of a form through a rising reproduction of the same form is the neutralization of its value, its transformation to quantity or '*Entfremdung*'.

Uniform work is valueless – only new ideas create surplus value

Marx maintains that what is called *constant capital is the apparatus of production*, and thus the industrial machinery. This apparatus is in itself unable to enter into a process, to create wealth or surplus value. It can only repeat the same production in the same tempo. The more industrial production develops its technical apparatus the more production becomes valueless as a commodity, until complete automation makes the product completely free of charge. In this way Marx has shown that it is not the machines that produce value, in this case surplus value. *Surplus value arises exclusively in variable capital* and this variable capital is manpower, *the human being.*

This statement makes Marx draw the conclusion that it is the worker that creates surplus value. But it is of significance to investigate more closely where this surplus value really comes from. Where is the variable, the element of variation that makes the rising profit possible?

It cannot exist in the abilities and diligence of the individual worker, his personal and professional characteristics. Neither capitalists nor socialists reckon with this in the industrial production. The workers are not exploited in their abilities or in the quality and value of the work, but exclusively on the basis of the *amount of work*, the quantity. Work is measured in man-hours. As it is thus in the exploitation of man and not of machine that profit and wealth occurs, Marx perceives the content of value as the work put into it and the standard of measurement for the object is one hour's human work in capitalist as well as socialist industry.

But even Marx was clear that it was not because the workers could be made to labour for longer and longer periods that profit rose. This has become even more distinct after the organization of the working class and the reduction in working time, for profit is still rising. How do the Marxists explain this condition? The explanation is enormously simple.

The precondition for this explanation is *that every producing human in the world has the right to what he himself produces.* If this basis, which is Marxism's great, humanistic achievement in world history, is removed, then the whole meaning of Marxism vanishes. Now it is demonstrable that the industrial worker can produce far more than he himself consumes to maintain life, and with technical development he takes less and less time to achieve the production necessary for himself. As he nevertheless continues to work at the same tempo, there is, however, a steadily increasing surplus of production, and as this is taken from him he is exploited to an ever increasing degree.

If we now stick to the capitalist and socialist evaluation of industrial labour as a purely quantitative dimension, where human characteristics play no role, then it is also quite obvious that the purely mechanical work could be carried out to a greater and greater degree by machines and thus carried out free of charge. Then the conclusion becomes in reality that *in principle mechanical work is valueless.*

Within mechanics the concept of work is *the product of quantity or tension.* If it is possible to disregard tension as a factor in industrial labour and to perceive labour purely quantitatively, then this is because *the whole of the factory installation keeps production in a constant tension* common to all. This is the reason that there is an equivalence between one man-hour and another. No variability of any significance is possible in the tempo of work. Thus the machine represents the inertia or the resistance to changes in the working process. The valuelessness of labour is conditioned by this constancy in tension. If one man-hour is equivalent to another man-hour, then all human labour is free of charge or valueless. This is the weakness in the Marxist theory of exploitation, for if industrial labour is without value in itself, then the worker represents a higher human value than other human classes, not as maintained because of his work achievement, but on the contrary because he has preserved his human values intact despite the work, because these values are not utilized or introduced in the process.

If there is something correct in Marxism's theory of value, it is in no way connected with work. If the measurement of value is perceived as man-hours and this has nothing to do with work, then it simply has to be *the human being's time* and nothing else that is the variable capital to which he himself owns the property rights.

Surplus value is not created in the work but in the variability of the work. In reality this is well known. Movement, change, and not the price dimension,

142 *The Natural Order and Other Texts*

creates the profit. But where does this variability come from? It cannot come from the machines working with clockwork precision. It cannot come from the workers either, who labour with their accustomed constancy. It is just as unlikely to come from the capitalist or the manufacturer who makes the factory yield its utmost, which is also constant. It is thus the transformation of industry itself as such that creates surplus value. Therefore surplus value is, as we have seen, the result of a rising acceleration of production. But who creates this acceleration? It is those who have a new idea, those who discover new machines and processes, *the inventors.* Here we are at *the true source of rising surplus value, human ingenuity* and imagination. A new invention has already lost its ability to create surplus value the day all the competitors own the machine, when it is common to all. The socialist countries have been able to overlook this question because they have been able to exploit the exploiters in the capitalist countries for their inventions. But this problem has become topical today.

Time – space – and event

Trade is exchange. Transport is displacement. These two processes are basically different. *Unilateral or what is called irreversible transport, and thus a transport where neither interchange nor return transport takes place, is called progress.* Progress is thus pure transport. This progressive movement is necessary in order for a movement to be *oriented.* Without it, a rudder has no function at all, even though a boat without a rudder is also oriented by the advance of the water, as it drifts with the current. In order to give possibilities of orientation, progressive movement must be movement collected from within in relation to the surrounding element.

Progress is neither necessary, absolute nor ideal. Einstein explains that a uniform movement in space is without orientation, and that in a space speeding off into outer space we can only locate up and down, as we do on the earth's surface, if the speed is still rising. This explains why what is called general progress also appears as a general increase in speed, a constant acceleration. The whole of our conscious orientation is conditioned by this rising acceleration, which unites our universal experiences with our most primary conditions and thereby creates our ability to experience the connection called causality. If the idealistic belief in progress is bankrupt stock today, this, however, in no way abolishes the significance progress still has for us. We have just lost certain illusions and must in the future base our perception of the whole question upon quite new principles, which have to be combined with the three basic factors, time, space and event.

We have to demonstrate that time becomes space and space time. We now know that a star observed at a distance of 40 light years is just as old in time as the distance is long. To observe through the instrument of time or of space is thus a simple interchange.

Time is change which can be regarded as a progressive movement in space whilst space appears as a constant which can only be observed if one is participating in that movement called time. Thus neither time nor space possess an actuality, existence or value outside this change or process, that is to say, outside the active combination called the time-space continuum. The action of time-space is the process and this process is in itself the transformation of time to space and space to time. These transformations are called events.

The rigidity, inertia, constancy or quality in matter rises with the speed of movement to the degree that one could put forward the claim that quality and speed are the same. Value is thus found not in the speed but in the transformation of the speed, and the less this speed is the easier the speed and the direction can be changed. The general acceleration thus creates a rising progress but is in itself the tendency to greater and greater inertia. This is the double-edged effect of the general tendency of progress. A real development of value thus cannot be identical with rising devaluation or acceleration even if it is dependent upon the same.

A person's lifetime or span of years is his personal property. But this property only becomes value if this lifetime is realized, and the realization of a lifetime happens through its variation, its changeability. Therefore the perfect industrial worker realizes nothing of his life during the working process, as this is completely eventless. Seen in purely human terms, working time in its industrial form is active waiting time. Therefore the abolition of the right to private activity only makes the person more and more valueless. This is the reason why socialization can only have a standard of value in the activization of humanity's leisure time, if socialization is to have any human purpose, something which is not necessary. *Leisure time* is therefore the only thing that has value in modern society and the modern form of exploitation is concentrated upon precisely this one point: how can we steal the individual's free time from him? This is the greatest problem of modern state politics.

144 *The Natural Order and Other Texts*

Progress and change. Value is transport

That I bother at all to concern myself with something as deadly boring as economics and into the bargain do myself the even more killing inconvenience of translating what I have written and then publishing it in Danish, then, of course, this is from the conviction that this ought to be enormously significant to the Scandinavian people. Whether this is right or wrong is not my business. With me any responsibility stops at the purely personal question of conscience, to get it said and especially to get it said at a moment where it could, if wished, be included in the economic deliberations which it seems are to bring in their wake deep-seated political changes in Scandinavia's relationship to the surrounding world, and because these political deliberations are said to have been concluded upon a purely economic basis.

As I set out my theory of value in connection with my theory about the natural order, it is very evident that this is created from an analysis of the Scandinavian cultural tradition as compared with other cultural traditions, and that it is an attempt to take the fundamental Scandinavian attitude to these problems. If I therefore make the assertion that *value is the transport of forces* and not the size of these forces, nor their quantity, then this is a direct critique of economic policy in postwar Scandinavia, for, by tying itself to the belief in the superiority of dimension and quantity over variability, this policy has denied the economic principle which I am setting out here as a Scandinavian contribution to the problem. If this theory does not have general validity, then there is always a chance that it has Scandinavian validity. The unique context of Scandinavian cultural development from the Stone Age to the present day makes it enormously simple to demonstrate that our periods of full bloom have always coincided with those periods when we have concentrated all our wealth, our surplus of human enthusiasm around the problem of transport. This is especially apparent in the Nordic Bronze Age, the art of which is one long tribute to the holy transport, and it is apparent in the Viking period, where the positive element was not the plundering, rapine or trade but transport and especially the transport of precious goods. We have already indicated previously that the great humanistic discovery that Marx made was that *only in humanity, never in machines or instruments, arises wealth or surplus value*. This is the reason that human transport, especially if it is superfluous or unnecessary, is the best source of human wealth. This can be studied in the immense pilgrim transactions of the Catholic Church in the Middle Ages, which created all our wonderful church art. The same is also true today where, with its rising surplus, the car industry is on the way to making car traffic impossible.

I have found, however, the most shattering commentary to what is being prepared today in Scandinavian politics in Palle Lauring's fantastically clear analysis of Scandinavia's economic decline at the end of the Middle Ages in his book about *The Sons of Valdemar and the Union*.* Every Scandinavian politician ought to read the section on our childishly rash indifference to the transport problem: our self-important Viking conservatism and chivalrous enthusiasm for the *fata morgana* of the German regional farmer. History repeats itself. Nothing is learnt. Nothing is forgotten. I will not go into historical considerations here. The only thing I would indicate is that a people that voluntarily renounces valuing what is the most precious element in its own being, in which it has shown itself to be superior to all other peoples over millennia, has thereby sinned not only against itself but against all humanity, which develops precisely through the wealth of differing abilities and contributions to the development of humanity by the various peoples and cultures. Only by the development of this our special ability are Danes and Scandinavians as a whole in the same boat. This is the only boat we have. Without it we are wreckage and bodies washed ashore. And with uncomfortable clarity this too can be read in our history. To an overwhelming degree our fame abroad is unfortunately a stressing of this side of our existence and hardly without reason. However, this is outweighed by Scandinavians having, on the strength of our special culture, all the natural preconditions for being the best and most secure transporters in the world.

Who owns whom?

Let us now sort right from wrong. In *Das Kapital*, Karl Marx has shaped a scientific analysis of the economic character of the commodity. The treatment of this concrete subject is a scientific achievement which can never be shaken. In this limited area, Karl Marx has realized a scientific knowledge that corresponds to Heisenberg's demand 'that it has universal validity and can be neither changed nor improved'.

At the same time, with the economic perspective gradually being realized more and more, as Marx foresaw, the *political* programme of Marxism has lost its interest. In the focus of events, it has already become past and history. A third value in this work, which can never be diminished, is hereby liberated, the artistic value, the literary human value.

146 *The Natural Order and Other Texts*

In human sympathy, even, I dare to say, in poetic and dramatic force, this work surpasses most of what the poets of the same period have depicted. If, through the rich knowledge and the careful documentation, one is able to decipher the terrible tension of this striking document of its time, then one cannot avoid seeing life in a different way. I mention this not to appear as a literary critic, but as just the truism it is for me as it must be for all humanity. In this area too the value of *Das Kapital* is universal. It forms a stage in the history of humanity.

In its demand for the protection of the weak against the thoughtless and violent exploitation of the strong, it is an accusation and at the same time a rule of conduct in direct continuation of the doctrine of the New Testament, which it outdoes at exactly the same point that Christ outdid the Pharisees of the Old Testament. This is why Christianity is just as little able to condemn Marxist socialism with any right as the Pharisees were able to shape a legal judgement over Christ. In the struggle against socialism, the Christian church has had to use the same means as the Pharisees used against Christ. The Pharisees' demand for forgiveness was outdone by Christ. Marx simply maintains that no individual has the right to draw up accounts over his efforts in the community. Everything must be forgiven when everything is owed by all to all. Against this demand, the champions of Christianity stand just as disarmed as the Pharisees did before Christ. This why the principle of socialism is spreading all over the world.

'Communism is a classless societal system with uniform ownership by the people of the means of production and complete equality of the members of society,' it says in the Soviet Union's Communist Party programme. This resembles what is also in the American constitution and no one can ignore the fact that the means of production in the West are being more and socialized.

But what about the exploitation of the strong by the weak?

Part 2:
The exploitation of the unique

Noteworthy insights and outcomes with inserted remarks

P.H.

This section has never been published before. It is dedicated to the critic and architect Poul Henningsen, a cultural personality whose range and breath of vision will possibly one day outshine those of Gropius, le Corbusier and Frank Lloyd Wright. Danes frequently remark that it is easy to criticize, which proves that the Danish people lack a critical sense. Poul Henningsen's repeated criticism of the exploitation of art and culture by the state and the holders of power (including the broad public) is elucidated here in dry, scientific calculations, that show the method by which this exploitation takes place.*

The transformation of the proletariat from value to quality

The struggle to elevate the proletariat without property to conditions of human worth, and to give the working class weapons and arguments in its fight for human rights that has been carried on since the rise of industrialization, has been waged with the help of artists and authors. One could even say that what recognition, what dignity there has been about this struggle is to the highest degree due to the efforts on the part of artists and intellectuals.

It is obvious that such a creative solidarity with the working class from a social group not working in industry could never be explained as idealism, as the theory that explains and justifies the working class's takeover of power in society is in itself anti-idealistic, materialistic and based on demonstrating the significance of economic interests as the basis of society. If what is called the left-wing intelligentsia has supported this struggle, then the working class must reckon that this has happened because one possesses a certain degree of intelligence.

Consequently this group must itself feel utilized by this prevailing class, at any rate, if it forms solidarity with those who wish, according to the programme, to hinder people using other people. As all the artificial privileges derived from inheritance of property, titles of social rank, capital and other means of exploitation are now or in the process of being abolished and as the powers of the nobility, the church and capitalism are gradually diminished by revolution or by a quiet development connected with it, it has become apparent that the formula for justice and economic balance that satisfies the worker in industry cannot be used at all for the creative activity. A place for this within the capitalist and socialist system has simply been forgotten, and it is regarded as a waste of time. However, this activity has a certain parasitic right to live on in the shadows within the bounds of capitalism, on the basis of a certain liberalism. But in the socialist system this right is definitively eliminated.

This condition results in two opposite tendencies within modern art today. One is about finding a purely ideological justification even for this removal of creative activity, and the other is about justifying our rights to economic existence by the rules of economic computation that are today adopted in modern society. We have no right at all to complain about being excluded from the economic whole if we are unable to demonstrate the rules by which an indisputable fairness could be shown and how exploitation goes on. The broader population have the greatest grounds for suspicion about an intelligentsia unable to provide an elementary form of intelligence sufficient to demonstrate its own economic basis for existence.

If the proletariat without property has been the dominant factor in creative life for a century, then this is not, as the politicians believe, because of this class's unity or quality. On the contrary, it is because of its value, its unique availability and openness, conditioned by owning nothing and therefore having nothing to look after, nothing to lose, and thus having everything to win. This unique availability gave the working class a human surplus value that contrasted rawly and harshly with the bourgeoisie's self-centred petty little home-life.

So what did this class win? Here arose the socialist theory of the takeover by the proletariat of the means of production. This was realized in a limited geographical area and there was thereby a change from availability to its opposite, absolute engagement. *Value was transformed to quality.* The working class's interest and mentality was also transformed in a thought process that is the exact opposite of that which had ruled the proletariat without property, and the understanding between the worker in a capitalist and a socialist society only became possible to the degree that capitalist society became socialized and the working class in the capitalist countries changed mentality. From being absolutely without property, in their own perception they became the absolute propertied class. The only ones who continued to have everything to win and nothing to lose were the artists, who are today the only population group that has preserved its complete availability. Every trick has been tried to abolish this too. But as this is itself the precondition for creative work, the result has just been that though art continues to be made, it is without value. For the artists who have preserved their free availability and creative ability, life has become more and more dramatic and lawless. One could say homeless.

At the same time rising automation in industry has meant that the work lacking quality that was the basis of calculation for social production is carried out more and more by machines. Hereby the very basis for continued development is slipping towards a calculation of equivalence based upon one hour's industrial work lacking in quality. The undifferentiated working class is coming unstuck and losing its unity, whilst specialization is spreading.

So one comes to the interesting alternative! *Is one to be paid for consuming as well as producing, and is one thus to be paid for living in society?* This must be the logical consequence of society owning individuals. One no longer has the right to decide what one wants to consume or produce. This seems to be the current tendency in modern politics the world over. We will not bother to indicate the completely absurd consequences of this tendency here. It is only necessary to point out that the starting point for Marxism's criticism of capitalist exploitation of the individual is the postulate about the individual's property being his own productivity. If one abolishes this property right, then the individual will, of course, never under any circumstances be exploited again, for then there will be nothing that belongs to him. As an argument against exploitation, this solution is, however, more than absurd, for it abolishes any possibility of establishing a relationship between production and consumption. Only the abolition of any variability in consumption, an absolute uniformity of consumption, permits the reduction of the consumption question to a pure question of numbers where the individual freely uses *as much* as he needs because he cannot decide *what* he needs. But even in this case one does not avoid a problem, as, for example, it appears to be of great significance in the USA.

The lacking respect for the valueless product invokes a quite idiotic and meaningless waste that is simply due to this indifference.

Romain Rolland tells somewhere of a wood-carver who decorated a castle with figures which the prince amused himself by using for target practice. That the great majority reacts in any other way is a big illusion. Thus even in the case of everyone having to consume exactly the same, a control of consumption is still indispensable. The idea of free and uncontrolled consumption is stuff and nonsense. Standardization only makes the possibility of perfect control easier, nothing more.

The secret knowledge

The triolectic theory of complementarity is based on the recognition of the observer's relationship to the observed. Carried over to the economic problem this gives a clear perception of what it means when something is perceived as 'free of charge'.

If we perceive the air as free of charge, it is because we are living in the atmosphere. If we were imprisoned and locked into a larder, then we would also perceive food as free of charge, if we did not begin to speculate how long the stores would last and if there was plenty of everything in relation to the time of one's confinement. All the different things would then be of equal value, equivalent, just like the various things on a *smorgåsbord*. Unless everyone sequestered their own favourite dish, then it would not be possible to start bartering at all.

If the larder, on the other hand, is locked so securely that one cannot get in and so stands hungry outside, then there is no possibility of barter either. But then the larder is valued at a higher and higher price the hungrier one becomes.

It becomes an unattainable 'ideal', which in a desperate situation one would risk one's life to reach. 'Idealism' is nothing more than such an actual or imagined larder.

If therefore socialists assert that they are against idealism, then this is only 'true' in the sense that they are just acknowledging realism and value in their own 'ideal'.

If one is sitting in the container and it is big enough, then everything there is in the container, and all that is not locked into other containers, appears to be free of charge. But if this is an *artificial* container, then it has to be constantly maintained. Then the container *in itself* is not free of charge. Only an agreement to build and maintain the container leads to the artificial container being built. If such a container is a building not needing much attention then that building costs nothing, when the building costs have been paid. But this is an excellent object for exploitation, by rent, interest or tax. Today it is all the same whether one pays the first, the second or the third. It costs just as much and it all goes by and large into the same treasury. Thus exploitation can take place outside barter.

If one maintains that quality and value are the same, then what has to be paid for art and culture must be an exploitation of exactly the same kind. This exploitation, which is common in both East and West, is the reason why it has not hitherto been possible to demonstrate how art is milked by the holders of social power, whether they represent the people or an upper class. If this triolectic method is acknowledged, then its economic consequences must also be acknowledged. If the economic consequences are not acknowledged, then it will be necessary to forbid all philosophical use of the method or to prove that it is false.

No human knowledge can be locked into a container, unless it is called a *secret*. If the proletariat had kept secret the knowledge that Karl Marx had discovered, then the working class's takeover of power would have become an *absolute* takeover of power. But Marx was working above all for humanity, and Marxism has therefore changed the whole world. An idea became a social force, *whilst* it streamed out to the masses. No one, either in the East or the West, wishes to acknowledge the change that Marxism has wrought in the thought processes of all, and thereby in their mode of action. It is the strength of this idea's radiant power that neither Marx nor the Marxists have taken into consideration. Not even those who call themselves Marxists have the patent for Marxism any longer, and not even the anti-Marxists can stop thinking in a Marxist way. This is especially true of the most eminent capitalists. The day an idea is known and used by all, it no longer has value.

Communism is the negation of socialism

By adopting the principle of keeping knowledge secret, the Soviet Union has taken over the Roman or Latin power dialectic, which is based upon an opposition between ethical rights and, on the other hand, the united principle of aesthetics and knowledge. A stagnation of the development of human social rights hereby occurs, whilst the whole of science is placed at the service of chance expansion. Progress thereby becomes more and more asocial as society's productive powers have to be utilized more and more effectively to maintain this expansion's front rank above the research of other countries.

The competitive relationship between the USSR and the USA that is established directly by the division of Europe into an American and a Russian colony, separated by an imaginary Iron Curtain and the atom-bomb competition, has now led to the USA, with ruthless consistency, being sucked up in space. It will not be long before the colony-areas of these two countries are tied to that wagon each in its own area. In relation to the immense victory that this new development means for humanity, I can easily take the consequences of this sucking-in lightly. It is too magnificent for an artist, at any rate, to have any desire to look pettily at this problem.

But there is a but! From the knowledge about social and economic structuration we have today, we can indicate in advance that the initial basis of this development, a mutually aggressive, militarily competitive relationship, is in the long run unsustainable. At a certain moment, this endless perspective will only be able to be carried further if the whole of humanity voluntarily or without any form of force, betrayal or threat of war goes in for the task. This will happen only if the task is directly allotted to humanity in concert and not to an increasing degree arrogated by an aristocratic power elite, which will not even be able to avoid starting racial manipulations in a far more rational and consistent way than the Nazis, because the selection will have quite precise and controllable goals.*

If those nations that have not up to now been directly involved in the system of military opposition in control today do not begin to prepare from now on for such a future re-adjustment of this whole future perspective on a universally human, humanistic basis through a systematic critique of the imperialistic colonization programme as it developed in the last century, then the whole of this fantastic perspective will one day subside. Unless opposition to and absolute independence from the whole of the old military programme and above all from that of the atom bomb is asserted, and the whole of this threatening apparatus is abolished, all progress will fall back into an indissoluble conflict situation.

In its relationship to capitalism, socialism is an opposition, a negation. But the Russians have not yet discovered that the transition from socialism to communism must also manifest itself as a negation, that communism is the complete negation of socialism. As this communistic stage is reached, socialism and capitalism become exactly the same. This is what has happened today. In more and more areas, separation between socialism and capitalism is becoming, as we have seen in the previous text, more and more impossible. They have formed a synthesis, a synthesis that today is neither one thing nor the other, neither capitalism nor socialism. This is the reason that all the talk about their opposition fills humanity more and more with loathing, because of the obvious emptiness of the platitudes.

So there was Stalin. But there is no Stalingrad

Czesław Milosz, a Polish author, has sent an open letter to Picasso through the Grove Press of New York. Part of this reads:

'Like each one of us, you are responsible for what happens on our planet and *your special responsibility is measured in the distance between your fame and the anonymity of the ordinary citizen.*

I accuse you, Picasso, and not just you, but all the artists and intellectuals in the West who have allowed themselves to be snared by words. In this period of atrocities and suffering you all chose, free as you were to choose, the most careful conformity. This gave you – perhaps also your conscience – an appearance of men who belonged on the side of progress. But in reality your weight counted in the scales and stole hope from those in the East who did not wish to subordinate themselves to absurdity. No one can say what would have been the consequence of a categorical protest made by you all against the official doctrine forced upon art in the East. If the support you gave to the terror counts, then your indignation would also have counted. It is therefore just that your irresponsibility is revealed, *so* that your future biographers do not forget it.

I hardly need tell you what your name, which the Stalinists appropriated as their property, has been used to conceal.

Imagine, Picasso, that your biography contained the following passage: At the height of Hitler's power Picasso painted his portrait. You painted Stalin's portrait and it called forth the party's rejection because it did not conform, etc.

154   *The Natural Order and Other Texts*

– If you answer that, in spite of everything, Stalin was not so bad as is said, then you reject the witness made public in the press in the East by people who know what they are writing.

Why should you and so many others be exempted from duties that weigh upon us all? *

This writer reveals that he was cultural attaché for the Polish Peoples' Democracy in 1948 and thus had had a lightning official bureaucratic career, like those we saw springing up in that period in communist and socialist organisations all over the world. A representative of the new Eastern power elite is thus here attacking the creative elite in Western Europe because it is irresponsible and does not fight the absurd and ridiculous, yet wishes to give the appearance of being progressive.

Should the creative elite of Western Europe fight this ridiculous absurdity, then it will have enough to do, and then it will go hard on Czesław Milosz and similar red tape merchants.*

How can the responsibility of famous people be in a proportional relationship to their fame whilst at the same time it being a requirement that they should have the same responsibility as an anonymous person? Here we find the bureaucratic and popular absurd concept of the creative elite expressed in all its royal absurdity. Like all bureaucrats, Milosz has obviously lost all sense of humour. He hardly knows about Ubu or that Picasso has a high rank within the *College de 'Pataphysique*, the praises of which have been sung by the afore-mentioned Grove Press.* Just as the Munich verdict on Gruppe Spur for blasphemy and pornography has been issued by this excellent organization as a highly-comical document,* so the Milosz letter is in the same context.

Milosz maintains that the poor geniuses in Eastern Europe have only the choice between 'subordinating themselves to conformism or to emigrate'. He forgets that Picasso has been an emigrant since the Spanish Civil War. Picasso has never been Spanish cultural attaché and Stalin has never invited him to exhibit in Moscow.

What Picasso and we others are accused of today is our solidarity with the Soviet Union during the period that Stalin was leader and that we swallowed the thesis about 'historical necessity' which, according to Milosz, only served as a debasement that *almost* delivered Russia into the hands of Hitler. Yes, we know well that the Russian generals today, who are to save the cause of peace with their atom bombs, have become pure-washed angels so that the good, little citizen can sleep peacefully in his little bed with his sweet wife without risking being sent to Siberia, without his responsibility being measuring according to his fame.

Value and Economy 155

There is no difference in thought process at all between Milosz and the Russian writer P.S. Mstislavski, whose article 'Communism for Equality' has now been issued as 'Facts on the Soviet Union'.* In this, it says:

'Today in the West there are also scientists who assure their fellow men that capitalism can be democratized and the class difference between people made to disappear. These myths have already been torn apart by Marx and Engels, not to speak of Lenin. History has long since dispersed these illusions. It has shown that private ownership of the means of production invariably and constantly develops and concentrates the inequality of people.'

To the intelligent person this is pure twaddle. Marx has demonstrated that variable capital always tends to become constant capital and is thus socialized. Only if Mstislavski could prove that this tendency towards socialization of the industrial means of production could have in any way been *avoided* in Western Europe, does his inference have any meaning. But he is just as unable as the capitalists to do so.

The difference between the bureaucrats in Stalin's period and today is that the former were forced to know Marxism inside out. Today they only need to pretend that they know what Marxism is. But they just don't.

A near miss is still a miss. It is perhaps worth remarking that Stalingrad was the turning point of the last World War, perhaps a turning point with the effect that a new World War will be an impossibility in the future. War is dirty work and it is perhaps best to forget it. Perhaps it is best that everyone forgets that such a place called Stalingrad ever existed on earth.* We who took part in the struggle of the time are no longer suitable for a Sunday School and we were too ·tired to see what was happening in the offices behind the scenes. There was fatigue was the world over and everywhere the seats were filled with the holy ones of the final days. Let them sit. But they bore us. We know what it costs. We know too much.

Mstislavski writes further:

'The American sociologist Charles Boyer maintains that unequal demands and differences in human talent are the natural foundation for the existence of classes. For its part, the *New York Post* frightens its readers that all motives for human activity will vanish under economic equality. Greater incomes, greater duties – monopolists recognize no other stimuli, and therefore everything done in the socialistic countries with regard to creating social and economic equality is called a painful experiment. What has been achieved in the Soviet Union and the other socialist countries is, however, *no experiment* but a result of the best experiences of humanity.'

'*Keine experimente*,' says Adenauer.* Statesmen say the same the world over. We are undertaking painless tooth extraction everywhere. Now the revolutionary construction of the industrialized socialist countries is no longer a painful experiment, indeed, it has never been so. If there has been pain, then it is because of the cruelty of a blind tyrant, nothing else. See, this is the new tone.

But all those whose whole life was one great painful experiment, *the creative elite* – yes, we had sympathy for the Soviet Union, because we perceived this whole development precisely as a painful experiment. Now we suddenly discover that we have been fooled. *Keine experimente*, only the peaceful results of 'the best experiences of humanity.' But all who seek to renew the sum of these best experiences know how much it has cost: how many unsuccessful experiments, how many crushed fates they cost and will continue to cost. The Soviet Union suddenly shows us that it would like to harvest the experiences without cost, so that it can be offended by the criminals who talk about them.

In 'Facts on the Soviet Union', the president of the Soviet Academy of Sciences, M. Keldyjs, writes, 'The resolve and goal of science consists in placing new natural phenomena at the service of humanity.' *To place a natural phenomenon at the service of humanity is an invention, not a discovery, and thus is a technique.* What the Russians call science is only technique. When the Russians say 'science', they mean technique. Why? Are they bad scientists? No, they are excellent. The Russians know very well what is technique and what is science. Why do they come out with this rubbish? There can only be one reason. *The Soviet Union refuses to socialize its own science, to place its scientific results at the disposition of humanity.* They want only to force their technique upon the world. Their science is secret. On this important point, they are in league with the American statesmen. If one perceives *scientific socialism* as realistic and materialistic, then this means that *everyone in the world has right of access to the experiences of science.* That the opposite could become the case amongst so-called socialists is a possibility that Marx never dreamt of in his wildest imagination.

That one hangs honours on idiots, and that the social class division and ranking list is not identical with the differences between the talents and unequal needs of people, this we know in Scandinavia.* One reads Hans Christian Andersen in the Soviet Union too. We also knew and found it in order that the building up of the Soviet Union was able to move so rapidly because the best and the most costly experiences could be taken over free of charge.

But when the Russian revolution happened, we were promised that a completely new development would happen from then on, and everything that happened thereafter in the capitalist countries would just be decadence and degeneration. The communist countries had taken over the best that capitalism had made and now nothing further could grow from that direction. This fantastic new experiment attracted the creative elite on the whole world. With this precondition, I can say that my admiration for the Russian people has been without limits for decades, knowing well the cost in sweat, blood, tears and injustice.

Today clean people wash their clean hands and say, 'Experiment – did someone say experiment? We have never experimented and do not intend to do so in the future. It must be a misunderstanding.'

Then we know how bad things are, and it is a great relief to me to be shown that it was a fantasy that I ever should have fought for the Soviet Union. It is just as good to read in modern archaeological books from Russia that all that about the plundering and rule by force of the Vikings, that about the empire of the Goths and so on, now in the true light of history reveals itself as a good old lie. They never were in Russia – apart from a few insignificant mercenaries. So that is one less unpleasant reckoning for the Northerners.

I am convinced that Picasso, just as little as I, would not relinquish a jot of the responsibility attached to our past. Not even if it cost us our heads. For the whole thing was too exciting and significant. But the exciting thing was the enormous work of art we dreamt of, and not the Soviet Union as such, and this dream will live on without the Soviet Union so long as it refuses to socialize its science.

If the new leadership of the Soviet Union comes to us as says: 'You have been fooled. But we are not fooling you', then of course we must pay for naivety. But the same trick cannot, of course, be performed twice. Then we must have the cards on the table. To the progressive population today current Russian propaganda material seems just as sterile as *The Readers' Digest* because in its naive mendacity it is an insult to our intelligence. We found it very heroic that Russians have up to now had a pre-1914 life-style. But when they now begin to introduce 'the best' of what has been popularized in America during the so-called 'decadent and depraved period of bourgeois decline', on the basis of what has been created in Western Europe – and this is what is happening – then we here in Western Europe cannot describe either them or the Americans as anything other than a bunch of untruthful parasites and hypocritical boasters. If the so-called welfare tendency in Northern Europe in the areas of articles of utility and art has created a popular renewal that these states could take over and learn from, then we cannot also put up with being disdained and spat upon precisely because we have arranged our existence to advance humanity. In this shabby process, we have no longer any

158   The Natural Order and Other Texts

responsibility, for we know that it only extends to making people believe that being the poorest of the poor is 'the best' and therefore free of charge.

No one can be blind to the rising Americanization of the Soviet Union's way of life or to the relaxation of tension between America and Russia. The reason is that both countries know that the threat of the atom bomb today is just as empty a political means of terror as the gas war in 'no more war' times. At the same time they are both agreed on hindering the world from becoming aware of the central significance of inter-planetary space travel to the economic structure of the future until they have established their monopolies in that area. *A relaxation actualizes another tension,* and this new tension, which is today automatically growing in strength, is the opposition between the Latin cultural circle and the rest. It is there to be swallowed up, but by whom?

It cannot be done without war, and the USA is trying to establish an advantageous position in this war by promoting a United Europe. Without understanding this, Scandinavia will become a blind plaything in the game. There is dynamite in the problem about the European Common Market.

I am not writing this to meddle in politics in any way. On the contrary, it is to demonstrate clearly that the experiences we have harvested in recent decades have definitively proved that the creative elite can have nothing to do with the power elite. It must establish itself as an independent organism antagonistic to the state but on an equal footing with the state apparatus, although strictly separated from it, if the dynamic of human culture is to preserve its strength. This development is already under way and cannot be stopped. It can gush forth in the anarchic panic of a raging youth or be formed organically in a vital evolution. It is Scandinavia that has the next move in this affair.*

UNESCO in Prague
Both national and international politics belong to the past.
The politics of the future will be cosmopolitan and independent of the state apparatuses.

We can separate social activity into three fundamentally different functions, *maintenance, distribution* and *renewal.* The reproductive, working group in society maintains the vital cycle of society, the state institutions in connection with special organizations, which are private in the capitalist countries, look after distribution or administration, whilst the artists, inventors and researchers create the possibilities for renewal. These three tendencies are complementary, which is to say, that one cannot derive one from the other. This does not mean, however, that it is impossible to combine two of these three complementary activities, but then one is confronted by a hybrid product.

Dynamism in the modern social structuring, as it has developed with the colonizations since the Renaissance, has given social administration the opportunity of also tying itself to a high degree in with the renewing activities. This possibility for inner renewal vanished with the worldwide grip of imperialism and we now see the various state leaderships more and more tied to stabilizing administrative tasks. This was what the socialist theories had foreseen and were able to calculate.

Today, all this calculation has broken down because of the Russians' invention of the *sputnik*. An expansion has hereby been opened up which makes the whole development of colonialism a small provincial intermezzo. Whether modern politicians, industrialists and military leaderships today already know this, and the social power elite, without telling to the people and the leadership of the lesser states, are already about to alter their economies on this basis is not known. Much indicates that this is so. At any rate, this and nothing else is the economic perspective of the future, and the small states who relinquish their economic integrity will be anonymously sucked of all strength when this new dynamism gradually gets going. Only by recognizing with foresight the inevitability of this new perspective and by avoiding being threatened into turbid combinations, can this expansion also become an inspiration and advantage to cultural development on earth. Otherwise it will just become a state driven impoverishment. It must be separated from the administration of the national states.

As the international power elite is already today a comprehensive net independent of any iron curtains that could be set up, only the development of a corresponding organization with an independent economic basis can secure a movement also being created for the elevation and enrichment of human existence on earth. This combination must consist of a direct collaboration between the renewing and the reproductive groups in society, of artists, scientists and the various organizations for production, and thus between the people and the so-called 'professional celebrities'. In the superstitious and handcrafted period of the Middle Ages, the monks and the adherent part of the Catholic Church were the guarantee and mainspring of this development. Today, where such a work has to be international and in accordance with the most modern thinking and science, this medieval organization is completely powerless. We have no use for more churches. That solves no problems.

It is here I believe that Scandinavia, in contrast to the forces of social violence, has fostered the basic structure for the development of humanity with

160   *The Natural Order and Other Texts*

its system of Folk High Schools and public buildings for community or cultural centres.

I mention *the buildings* deliberately, for it has struck me that Professor Hal Koch in his astonishing admiration for Constantine the Great makes an even more astonishing reservation about 'his disastrous need to build', the only worthwhile side of him.*

No economy without containers. Houses, countries, organizations and nations are containers. If the Scandinavian labour movement comes to have a surplus working force at its disposal, then it is to be hoped that it will not allow this to remain unused, but that it will be precisely informed of the current requirements, even where there is funny business about this or that being 'necessary', so that it can discern what is in the interests of the people and what is not. Advancing this development does not mean doing anything other than is being done in other countries. It just means beginning *before* the others, and this can be done precisely because as a tendency it was already sketched out in Scandinavia with the development of democracy in the previous century.

That this development is also the only thing that can bring life to the mortally sick UNESCO justifies us in demanding that the principles of the Folk High School and the communal buildings be adopted as the basic tenet of this organization. At the same time we could demand that the inter-planetary experiments are taken from the social power combinations which have threatened the public with atom bombs since the end of the war and administrated by the same organization in accordance with the dynamic requirements of human life

In order to avoid the UNESCO centre being unilaterally influenced by one great power, we could demand that it be moved to a neutral country, and as *Prague* throughout the whole of European history has always shown itself to be the neutral point, then we could demand of the Soviet Union that Czechoslovakia be made into a practically autonomous economic area, where all the peoples of the world could freely meet, regardless of their ideas and opinions. If these demands are not in accordance with the opinion of the Scandinavian people, then I can safely say that the Scandinavian people have no meaning any more.

The whole of Scandinavia's position as a pioneering territory in certain areas is based upon the idea that a so-called 'under-developed' land has use not for investment but for *knowledge, ability* and *self-respect*. Scandinavians today are confronted with the choice of betraying this idea in favour of establishing a European monopoly in this area, the so-called Eurocracy, or bravely allowing the world take part in its experiences and relying upon its own abilities in such an open competition without artificial privileges. We have already shown that our centuries-old tradition is unsuitable for administering colonies.★ Is it really necessary for us to discover by experience that we are not suitable to be colonized either?

Scandinavians today are choosing between a peaceful, progressive situcracy,★ the lines of direction of which are given here, and a military Eurocracy without any perspectives of progress

What is the difference between Eurocracy and situcracy?

Eurocracy is the establishment of a common military, political and economic structure for Western Europe, planned according to classical Latin patterns, where it is impossible to take any regard of the modernization of the structure of society that has taken place in the Scandinavian countries in the last century, and even less of the ancient norms of action and customs of thought in the North.

Situcracy is a new social structuring based upon the possibility of uniting the oppositions in the structure of European society in a vital dynamic which uses them for a mutual elevation and enrichment, instead of for the mutual destruction which must automatically occur from a refusal to recognize their character and significance. Such a refusal would allow these forces to act blindly and without restraint.

England and Denmark are preparing a Western European conflict

The dangerous secret huckstering in Denmark around the Common Market has meant that most people, even intelligent people, just cannot find out what is going on. However, if one is not entangled in the threads oneself, the whole thing looks quite simple.★

The whole lack of clarity arose when England left the Nordic group without warning.★ It was the same story when they at one time took our fleet without a declaration of war.★ Danish politicians have such an admiration for English cunning that they have not enough honour to protest strongly. As they are not smart enough to do the same themselves, they run after the English like a dog after its master. They do not realize that he who is a dog for a master who acts without merit gets all the kicks intended for the master when no one dares attack him directly. To The Six who call themselves 'Europe', this is the

162 *The Natural Order and Other Texts*

position of Danish politicians, and it is to a great degree a deserved position.

The English forsook the Scandinavian group to go on their knees humbly to The Six. This has been an enormous moral victory for that group which did not have not many feathers left in its tail after the war. Our Lord has arranged that they got their privilege without either fighting or weeping. This can be said in truth, for the tie that binds The Six is the Catholic Church. But one is only given so much in heaven, and Europe is not heaven. This humble flock of Englishmen, with an even more crawling flock of Scandinavians in its train, is an all too appetizing sight for The Six, especially the Germans.

The French are objective and cynical in politics, but their allies are not. The conditions for admission are cunning, humbling and clearly disadvantageous, but the English and the Danes are swallowing the lot, if only they can be allowed into the henhouse, sorry, I meant paradise.

Of course both the English and the Danes protest, to save face, that they will also get the necessary insignificant modifications to provide the requisite raw material for the Nordic propaganda apparatus's empty victory bulletins. But in reality they are swallowing it whole.

It seems even more astonishing that England and Denmark should be so broke that they have to throw away all concepts of honour, all self-respect, overboard to get some money in. Any talk of national traditions and Nordic attitudes to life has suddenly become so reactionary that it defies description. It also sounds too good to be true. No, we know what is going on. Those who believe in this comedy have forgotten their history, especially about England. When the game is first set up, then you will see the whole of the nationalist life-guard mobilize. Nationalism is not antiquated today. It is *ill-timed*. It does not suit the politicians' book at the moment. We must lie low a little until the whole thing is in order. Then we can take a grip, and thus one of the greatest dirty tricks in the history of Western Europe is prepared.

The French understand politics. One cannot therefore treat France with impunity as England has treated Scandinavia. Thus it is in earnest that The Six demand that no one can leave the Common Market once they have entered it. Because of this, I have long made it public in Denmark that Denmark should refuse to sign this passage from the point of view that what comes easily, should also go easily. But the politicians in Denmark say one cannot take that kind of thing so solemnly. If we wish to leave, then there is nothing to hold us back. That is correct. We have nothing to ignore other than our given word and the honesty of the Danish people. If one has understood this idea thoroughly, then one has also understood that the whole of England's and Denmark's interest in a united Europe is a swindle and betrayal from the start. For those interested in the fate of Europe, this situation is threatening. Denmark is going completely in for England's antiquated political method, which only works under colonization. Behind them stands the United States, and it is easy to see what this is all about. There just remains to be said, that the development that England and Denmark are preparing today cannot be carried out without a bloody war between the southern and the northern European states.

My knowledge of the whole of Latin civilization makes me say: *it is not on!*

Why did The Seven fall apart and why is the unity with The Six being developed? Because Latin culture is specialized in building up such a unity, Scandinavia is not. Today the English newspapers write that England does not possess a technical and administrative elite able to undertake the administrative tasks that the Common Market demands, Denmark even less so, but that both the Italians and the French possess the best trained and chosen elite ready to take all the demanding key posts. *England and Denmark have to accept them, for there is a use for them,* but when the whole thing has been put on its feet, will they allow them to remain? Will they go, if required? Why should they? Here we have the coming conflict. It can be calculated in advance. It is the shabbiness of the whole perspective.

It is doubly shabby because the precondition for picking up the art from the French is that Scandinavia begins by imitating the Latin system. This can only be done by denying our own best features in order to take them up later with fanaticism, a fanaticism that will only benefit the Americans. Both are pretence and bluff. From their military alliances, the English are known for the self-sacrifice by which they fight to the last Frenchman. Today USA has taken over England's role and will let us fight till the last European. The ridiculous thing about the whole situation is that we will just be fighting with ourselves. It is even more idiotic that it is those who are the sharpest opponents of Latin culture in Scandinavia who today have to mobilize to protect it, because it is simply a condition for also protecting our own ground.

When Gustav Adolphus won, he stopped at the border between the mental oppositions in Western Europe. This mental opposition is based upon an economic, political and practical opposition that more or less follows the borders of the old Roman Empire. It is here that England, after the invasions of the Anglo-Saxons, Vikings and Normans, comes to play its peculiar cultural double game, which the Danes can neither copy nor take advantage of. This double game is made impossible in a united Europe. The two oppositions will enter into a direct conflict, the result of which can only be negative for both sides.

As Germany is today a militarily occupied area, it has no independent attitude. The whole of European opposition is centred around the position of the Scandinavians. Latin egocentricism is bounded by *geographical space*, and is concentrated around Paris and Rome. Scandinavian egocentricism is decided *historically* by time and is concentrated around our historical traditions. Conflict between these two points of departure is unavoidable, if Scandinavians do not maintain their geographical integrity and build it up according to Latin patterns and let those in the South take care of their own. This would advance cooperation.

The programme for a harmonious, united Europe was torpedoed when France prevented Brussels becoming the centre of Europe. European politics today is just a struggle between great powers, nothing more, and what has been lost cannot be recovered. The only thing Scandinavians can do now, if they do not want to keep to themselves, is to get the English to respect them and stop playing blind man's bluff with themselves, but perhaps this is also too late. It does not concern me. The creative elite in Northern Europe no longer wish to be placed under an official policy according to Latin patterns. To an all too high degree, we have learned to value the freedom that was forced upon us, and, as we know its conditions, we will fight to the last to preserve it.

The Danish Ministry of Culture and international scientific socialism

The *Kulturkammer* of the German Nazis, who understood so thoroughly how to distinguish between well-behaved and decadent art, is still so much with us that the judicial authorities in Germany are maintaining its principles about modern German art.[*]

Today a Danish Ministry of Culture has been set up. What this instrument is to be used for depends not upon the men who have set it up or their intentions. It depends solely on the lines of direction that are laid down for the activities of this ministry, on its right to dispose freely of the economic means that exist in and arise from culture, and on its direct contact with the broader population, independent of the power elite's political, industrial and military demands. If this independence is not secured by law, then the setting up of this ministry will probably be the hardest blow directed against Danish art and culture for many centuries.

Georg Brandes perceived the greatest advantage of the French Revolution to be freedom of research.[*] We must today demand of the Danish Ministry of Culture that it be confirmed by law that the Danish nation requires that all scientific results are and should be universal common property, that it will not relinquish the principle of the international socialization of science, that this is our perception of what is called international scientific socialism, and that Denmark will maintain this rule independently of whatever position other countries take to the problem. If the Ministry of Culture cannot prevent Denmark entering into an economic community with other nations who refuse to follow this rule, then this ministry is not an institution for the protection of Danish culture, but an instrument for the foreign exploitation of it, and has nothing to do with either socialism or democracy.

By separating the Ministry of Culture from the Ministry of Education, an organ has been created which, if this independence of ordinary and technical education as well as of religious belief is maintained, has the possibility of making the development of popular culture independent and of counteracting the gulf between the masses and the personalities. With the setting up of the academy suggested by Grundtvig in Sorø, and with the support of those Folk High Schools which still maintain Grundtvig's High School programme and all the philosophical and humanistic faculties, there would be the possibility of developing a completely new and necessary structure in Danish society which could be a model for the whole world. If only a half-step is taken on this point, then the whole is lost. Here for once no compromise is possible. It is either – or, kill or cure.

Who owns culture?

Exploitation consists of extracting the value of a so-called raw material or a substance and leaving it an empty and worthless shell. The best object for exploitation in human society is human desire and enthusiasm and the creative results of this, our cultural past.

What is special about the methods of modern industrial society is their unique effectiveness, and in the development period of this society creative enthusiasm was exploited to the utmost. The last mortal blood-letting was realized, not by gangsters and unscrupulous capitalists, but by state apparatuses, to the degree that no one with a drop of intelligence could mobilize even the least grain of sympathy for them. Even their most stupid threats are taken with a shrug.

In the Latin countries, where artistic prestige has never been completely disparaged, attempts are being made to retie the connection between the power elite and the creative elite with the help of the aesthetic traditions of the Catholic Church. This has succeeded to an astonishing degree and has created

166   The Natural Order and Other Texts

a dynamic flowering, noticeable by everyone who has anything to do with French or Italian culture. However, it has been precisely the strength of North American science and industry that the power elite has perceived the creative elite as free of charge for a century. This has at once made the creative elite independent in relation to the power elite, and given this independent elite a strong centre in Bohemian Paris, that remarkable no-man's-land where so much incredible new stuff has flourished.

For these many years, the creative elite has fought for its freedom by combining frugality with richness. It is the strength of this struggle that the modern state apparatus, even with the help of the Church, is more and more unable to control, in the East as well as in the West and North. If this problem is far more controlled in Southern Europe, then this is because of a cultural structuring that can no longer be introduced into Scandinavia, and which will also in the South turn out to be insufficient in the long run.

If N.F.S. Grundtvig, who thundered against things Latin, was nevertheless wrongly perceived by Georg Brandes as a clandestine Catholic, then this was because he clearly saw both the advantages and the lacks in the structure of Latin culture and struck at precisely the weak point both of us and in the Latin area, projecting a new development that could take advantage, on the basis of modern democracy, of what was valuable for the people in both systems. However, this new cultural creation is incompatible with the old both in the South and in the North. But what is far more significant to us, it is incompatible with all perceptions of economics hitherto. It presupposes that the people are both able to save and themselves use what they have saved.

Since the end of the war, there has only been disdain and scorn for the Scandinavian welfare state from American and Southern European sides, and our politicians and economic leaders are gradually acknowledging our inferiority, and asking whether we could get *the foreigners* to direct us in the right ways, just as in the Middle Ages, when German nobility was called in to rule the people. I have not heard much else than this abroad and have had to admit that I myself only found elbow room outside Scandinavia. Yet I have never for a minute doubted that this could be changed and will be changed the day the Scandinavians themselves become clear that they are a source of amusement the world over and about what it is that is being mocked. I think that Scandinavians are traditionally no slaves to the hierarchy of riches, and are perhaps the only people in Western Europe who lose none of their dignity because of poverty. In Denmark and Norway this characteristic is about to be lost, and precisely where it is most important, in the peasantry. If Sweden is able to stand today out in its relationship to the rest of the world, then it is above all because of the free and worthy mind of the Swedish peasantry.

What the Swedish poet C.J.L. Almqvist wrote a hundred and twenty years ago, and what today turns outs itself to be the wealth of the Swedish people, is that they possess the free person's superiority over poverty. This is an old commentary on Swedish foreign policy that is valid up to the present day:

'THE SIGNIFICANCE OF SWEDISH POVERTY

The Swede is unpatriotic to the degree that he seeks *help* outside himself. He has done so now and then, and what has he got? By himself, he has always been helped. This does not mean that the Swede wilfully should relinquish "literary, political or commercial" context with the rest of Europe (that would be to seek poverty), but he should not look to any other country for his assistance in his hour of need. He should firmly maintain that state of mind – to be able to do without Europe without loss and pain.

This state of mind "of finding oneself strong in poverty", makes up one of the secrets, although often deeply hidden, in the Swedish being. The Swedish peasant, on the other hand, has learnt to be poor. He can work and he can even accumulate, but for the most part he squanders all the accumulation away. "The Swede lives above his capacity" has become a proverb. He is almost never cautious in the French or German sense, even less is he frugal like the Russian or the Jew. If foreigners accumulate money to own it, then the Swede collects it to distribute it. Poverty is his basic state, affluence just his interim, and wealth a little game he has now and then.'

*C.J.L. Almqvist 1838**

Welfare is a *journey*. Well-being is a *state*. Welfare is a *luxury*, but well-being is a *comfort*. To be equipped for welfare one must be master of the conditions that are offered during the journey, and only allow oneself the luxury of living in the utmost poverty, as well as in the greatest lavishness, without ever becoming a slave of either one state or the other, but by taking them both with the same superiority. The day a person loses his freedom in relation to life's external conditions and ties his fate to a particular pleasant form, he has become a slave of the external world. No one needs this superiority more than the Scandinavians, for it is the only thing we have. When the Americans emphasize that it is the Norwegian Thorstein Veblen who founded American sociology with his book *The Theory of the Leisure Class*, but that his biting criticism of the snob-hierarchy built upon types of enjoyment is *un-American* and without reality, then we Scandinavians in retaliation must emphasize that we sympathize with precisely the part that the Americans will not acknowledge

168 *The Natural Order and Other Texts*

today. What Veblen criticized in Americans was that they did not seek the various pleasures that life offers for their own sake but because they belonged to a particular social rung on the ladder. That he himself had *joie de vivre* meant that he never got a position that recognized his work. Modern American sociology no longer wishes to attach the social hierarchy to pleasures. Instead they now wish to construct a hierarchy on the Latin pattern without any form of pleasure, and to combat 'the professional celebrities' who, like Veblen, prefer their pleasures without hierarchy or fame, and who want to develop the pleasant on the basis of the ability to amuse oneself and others and nothing more. We will probably be treated in the same way.

This Scandinavian ability to prefer luxury above comfort has today gradually acquired chains, and these chains are called *the trade unions and employers' organizations.* In their fight to give the working population an existence of human value, these organizations have today been blocked in their struggle against each other to the degree that they dare not say a word about whether or not it is advantageous to renounce anything voluntarily. The result is that the Danish people as a whole today are unable to take an independent decision on anything. It is on this that these organizations today should be tested *in Scandinavia.* If they fail, then they will be smashed and crushed, regardless of whether they seek help abroad to stabilize their immobility.

The working population of town and country created the Danish Folk High School in order to take part in intellectual and artistic culture, to take possession of humanity's noblest forms of enjoyment. One would have thought that this century-long development would have preserved the working classes's superiority to the most superficial perception of the economic routine. But no. The trade unions and employers' organizations in Denmark have become completely will-less robots, subordinated to timeless and perspective-less 'public opinion'. How could the Folk High School become bankrupt in such a crushing way? That is easy to explain. The Folk High School is dead from metaphysical idealism and the lack of an independent economic basis. This basis exists neither in industry nor the state treasury, but in what is earned in popular culture, art and entertainment. We have discovered this now, so let's get down to it before it is too late. Either that or subordination to the American entertainment industry. *There is no alternative.* The Church cannot make a difference either way.

In a war, in a cultural struggle even, it is always the last minute that counts, and in that minute it looks as if all is lost. 'But all good ideas, they cannot die before even better ideas have grown from their seed'.* Let this be a matter of faith. Seed can fall on stony ground. I believe *the ground is in the people.*

Value and Economy *169*

Weeds can drift over the hedge, but I am not afraid that they will not be pulled out. The only thing I am afraid of is that *the even better* ideas will be confused with the weeds, because they are unknown. But if this happens, then they will throw roots out in alien soil, where they will be looked after and valued, like the work of Tycho Brahe. So I ask the Danish people, if history is to repeat itself today on this point. Has the hundred-year-old existence of the Folk High School in Denmark been in vain?

Money is the unit of measurement for the general tempo of society

How should socialists justify their demand that inventors work for them without pay? This can only be done by continuing to allow the old metaphysical and idealistic superstition to serve as a means of compulsion against anyone possessing extraordinary abilities. Such a compulsion can only be carried out by religious means. This is the reason that modern socialist governments are so busy polishing up the church facades again. But here the basic Marxist thesis that everyone has the right to what he created himself is also given up. Only by inventing a god to whom everything is owed can society find an argument to abolish this right. Only the painful thing is that if this right is abolished, it will not be long before invention also has to be abolished, because it is precisely this right that is the condition for the development of invention. This characterizes the opposition between the Middle Ages and the Renaissance.

This inventiveness or condition for variability is strongly threatened by the constancies developed by the capitalist and socialist systems. This will become noticeable above all through the increasing socialization of finance, for money is nothing other than the completely socialized commodity compelling the same standard of values upon all. This is a consequence of money only being able to measure social or common values. Values in their individual character of variability cannot be measured in money at all. Now the gold standard has been forsaken, monetary value just rests upon a concept. But what is the actuality behind this measurement, which cannot be a value in itself? It is not work. Neither is it use value nor the usefulness of things. Everything points to *money being the measure of social or common time.* But if this measure is to be just, which every measure seeks to be, then money will work towards a levelling of variations in the social tempo. Money thus neutralizes the tensions. The Anglo-Saxons say, 'time is money'. This is not correct. 'Money is time', but time of a quite particular kind. Not all time can be measured in money. Only the common tempo of social space corresponds to money. Outside this, money is

170 *The Natural Order and Other Texts*

absolutely nothing. The discovery of money is the foundation of 'scientific' socialism. To break the power of money as the framework for humanity and society is to surpass socialism. Money is nothing other than art transformed to numbers. Artistic communism will transform life to a natural, all-embracing work of art.

One of the reasons that the economic question today is logically inaccessible is the lack of understanding that there are three complementary ways in which one can *study* it. However, it is not possible to *work with* this question unless it is posed in a two-part opposition, in a dialectic. Hereby arises the war between the dialectical systems, each of which maintains it is correct, whilst the others are wrong.

Wealth is and remains surplus, and, being extraordinary, can never be a part of an order, not even at the top. Then it would no longer be a surplus, but a part of an economic hierarchy. Wealth has to be chance and directly futile, something I have defined as the aesthetic, variability or change, the unstable and fleeting in existence, represented socially by an irresponsible upper class.[*]

Economics must, on the other hand, be the neutralization of a variability or of wealth in a constancy, an equilibrium, between production and consumption – socially represented by a responsible state.

The gratis or free of charge can definitively arise if an equilibrium can be repeated, taken out of its context and reproduced. We in Scandinavia especially misunderstand the situation here, as we do not have a clear perception of the opposition between the economic and the free of charge. However, this relationship is quite simple. We have seen that surplus value is created by the newly discovered object which represents a new quality. This quality becomes value through its use, and the industrial use of this article is as a model for reproduction. Through this reproduction the quality becomes more and more devalued, until by achieving a sufficiently great number of reproductions it must be considered free of charge. It is this process which is perceived by Marxists as the transformation of quality to quantity.

If the *Scandinavian* dialectic is based upon a fusion of the economic and the gratis, then, in contrast, the *Latin* dialectic is based upon a clear perception of the purely economic or order, where no distinction is made between wealth and the gratis. As it is precisely the Latin doctrine of economics which is the starting point for all this science, then we find in the expression of the gratis itself the Latin perception of wealth or the beautiful, as the word gratis comes from the concept of *gratie*. This beauty is perceived simply as the *gift* of God or the gods. That such a perception has come to prevail is because the primitive form of surplus is used to be given away, as gifts, and this is called *the Potlatch system.*

Gift – debt and sacrifice

Professor K.E. Løgstrup has committed the feat of writing a book about the philosophy of art without ever touching on the concept of aesthetics.* As a work of art it is reminiscent of Heiberg's *No*,* but, although its objective method is commendable, as philosophy this doctrine of unaesthetic art is so shallow that only one point of the concept of beauty remains, that life is a *gift*. However, this is completely sufficient to open up an artistic perspective going in exactly the opposite direction to the one Løgstrup is pursuing.

There is not room here to develop an acquaintance with the pre-economic system of barter called Potlatch, so strictly pursued today by the modern tax authorities. Neither can we go into the materialistic origin of the principle of sacrifice and its later social utilization, and even less into its definitive establishment as a debt system. The opening of the dimension of the gift, its grace or beauty, between the precious and the gratis, between the unique and the ordinary, would perhaps have given Løgstrup an interest in reworking this material, to which he is closer than I am.

Today the question of art's relationship to ethics has come to a head in a series of problems, from which we can choose a concrete example. The Mexican state is currently sending an exhibition of the most ancient Mexican art through to the artists of our time around the world to show off the best in their possession. One room is dedicated to pictures by a painter who is at this very moment sitting behind the bars of a Mexican prison, condemned to be punished by the same state. His name is Siqueiros.*

If a politician, organization's man or military person is accused of a crime, he is instantly suspended from his position, and if he is condemned his work is denied any value. So we can see that the artist lives in a quite different world from that of the power elite, the power of whose members depends upon their moral renown. One could throw the artist or the research scholar into the most humiliating situation and yet at the same time value his work as outstanding. Thus what the artist is condemned for is completely irrelevant. One is obliged to acknowledge his 'criminal' disposition whilst giving him high honour.

The question then is this. Has an artist's artistic value anything at all to do with his moral and legal make-up? Then there should be no more people amongst the artists who have been condemned by the courts or psychiatrists

172 The Natural Order and Other Texts

than amongst those from other activities. This is, however, not the case and creative ability therefore has something to do with the individual's uncommon behaviour, and cannot be classified according to the general moral and legal yardstick. If one investigates this thoroughly, one will see that it has always been so. *The moral, legal and psychiatric yardstick has thus only a limited validity.* The church addressed this problem in its time, and anyone pursued by the authorities could seek protection from the law in the interior of the church itself. But with the increasing demand for justice, the church has in practise lost this concrete right to establish a higher court on aesthetic principles. They then went over to killing the criminal and afterwards raising a monument to him, thereby ascribing to themselves the right to value his efforts. But, with the modern demand for tempo, there is no time for that kind of thing. One has to *at the same time judge and imprison, value and press the best out of the man.* This is also the consequence of the concealment of scientific results.

I hardly need recount that the political, military and economic elites have in certain periods also been evaluated as artists or beneficial criminals and bandits who were first decapitated and then honoured, nor that the process by which the myth of Christ was glorified as a general social pattern. It just so happens that the criminal potency of the power elite has become so great that it could wipe out the whole of humanity and is difficult to reduce, even if what can be done to vary its effect is done, and just as Christianity became indissolubly united with the power elite against the artists through the efforts of Constantine the Great, so today the Christian elite finds itself in the same position as the power elite.

The result is that the Church has to be sympathetic to an extension of the power elite's 'artistic' freedom, whilst having to move into a sharper and sharper oppositional relationship to the world of free art. The result is that he who today chooses or follows the call for a free creation, must prepare himself in advance to be persecuted to the very end with threats and persuasions and, if they do not work, with condemnation. There is no longer any way around this. One often wonders why the small criminals are condemned, but the great ones go free. The explanation is that great crimes happen in the name of 'justice', and either the majority or progress profit, whilst at the same time washing their hands. In relation to the political game, artists can never be other than small criminals – and therefore absolutely punishable.

This split evaluation of the artist is a purely schizoid method of presentation, which is systematically used against art life. The cultivation of an unconscious schizophrenia is clearly apparent in the postulation by Løgstrup and other philosophers that an *identification* operates between the spectator and the hero in a drama. If this were really true and actual, and not just apparent, the performance of Shakespeare's *Hamlet* would not just require the death of the players, as in the Roman arenas, but also those of the public. But it is only the play of the politicians which automatically transfers the dramatic consequences to the public. This is the direct difference between the definition of politics and what in the classical sense is called art.

The precious, the economic and the free of charge are complementary concepts

The strange thing about Scandinavian economic doctrine is that the fusion of the beautiful and the free of charge or gratis cannot take place at all without the whole dialectic dissolving into a crippling confusion. Christians believe that God's grace and forgiveness are the same as what the French call '*grâce de Dieu*'. This is a fundamental misunderstanding that led to the Thirty Years War, and in the USA to the war between the northern and southern states, and what, with unavoidable consistency, will lead to a new civil war because of Western Europe's economic union. This is the reason why Russia is taking the steps towards Western Europe's economic union with astonishing peace and goodwill. They know that we can only harm ourselves.

The Eastern European dialectic works upon a third opposition between the completely free of charge on the one hand and on the other the fusion of the surplus and the economic, which has given birth to the *sputnik*. However, if the Soviet Union is not itself able to consume the extraordinary advantage that this system has created, then this is because the Russian system has cheated its own dialectical principle, as there is no longer anything in the Soviet Union that is free of charge.

The only thing at all that can take the shape of something free of charge is the past or experience, that is to say repetition, pure science. Had the Soviet Union been able to maintain the source of its own dynamic, then it would have been on the basis of the international socialization of the results of science and of universal information. The Soviet Union should have been the purest information centre in the world. By barring information to the outside, the demand automatically arose to limit more and more the circulation of information until today scientific information is a state secret the people are not allowed to know, and the scientists are state prisoners with the duty of silence just as in the USA. The whole development from the Komintern over the Kominform to nothing is sufficiently well-known.[*]

174 *The Natural Order and Other Texts*

One cannot distinguish between the precious and the valueless within Latin culture because it is impossible to measure the value of the extraordinary. The only peoples in Europe who have a clear and unequivocal perception of the precious as the opposite of the normal, and the whole of whose life dynamics are constructed upon this opposition, are the Scandinavians and the Jews. This is the reason why the whole development of free artists in Europe after the Renaissance is above all the work of Jews. On the other hand, the Nordic dialectic led to the first purely aesthetic philosophy, founded by Kierkegaard. However, this did not lead to artistic realizations because any realization is a normalization, and here the leap can only occur in conflict with the Nordic dialectic. This is the reason for the desperate asocial position of art-life in Northern Europe and North America, a position that the Jews have even made their religious ideal. Despite this, art-life has nevertheless been able to develop in an independent Scandinavian form because the artist has been accepted as *a necessary enemy of the people.** Here the contrast to the modern USA is clear.

Where Marx cheats his materialism is in his endorsement of the classical perception of art, in the Greco-Roman principle of beauty, which made him believe that he was talking about economics whilst in reality he was talking of wealth or surplus. This perception starts from the principle that what we cannot all see and thereby in community know has no existence. To see and know results in a conscious statement. However, Marxists fall in the trap that they over-value our ability to see, for people see only what attracts our attention or interest, and only changes do this. It is not the strange but the all too accustomed that loses the ability to catch our attention. This superficiality of our interests means that *from this perception what is most obvious has no existence because we are no longer aware of it.*

This process can be called devaluation. *The free of charge is in itself is absolutely uninteresting because it is obvious.* This obviousness is what is called the purely quantitative. But as everything has a purely quantitative character and everything thus also has the form of an object or a purely qualitative character, and as everything is in one way or another in an uninterrupted process at the same time, then the transition from quality to value and to quantity is a relationship only systematized in humanity's relationship to matter, not in matter itself, nor in humanity itself. Quantities can be observed. This observation becomes more and more precise the more objects that are observed at any one time. The quality can be observed. This happens with greater and greater precision the more the individual objects can be isolated. The process can be observed. This happens with greater and greater precision the more the objects can be influenced. These different observations can be compared and combined. But this is *art*, not science. *A thing's lack of meaning is the futility of being conscious or being aware of the thing*, and thus something completely subjective, nothing else, and the lack of necessity of being aware of a necessary and obvious thing means that it has become gratuitous, that it has become a natural part of one's existence, and that it has lost its sensory or artistic value. Politics consists of catching people's attention and is thus an art.

The game without risk

Only changes can catch people's attention. To create changes is what is called to play or vary. Establishing an area on the basis of the necessity principle is to say that in this area the possibility of play or variation is abolished. The game can be perceived as the very foundation of what are called the fine arts, because the attraction lies in the dangers we run in this game, which thus demand that one gathers all one's abilities and achieves the ultimate piece of work. Only when something is at stake can top performances occur. *In the principle of equivalence one gets like for like. In the game the opposite principle is valid, here one wins or loses all. Either – or, black or white.*

The institution of the state in society has to secure tranquillity, order, security and peace. On the other hand, the ruling class, if there is such a thing, secures tension, change or the game. This game can be artistic or unartistic, creative or unproductive. The peculiar thing about Byzantine culture was that its politics were ruled by a completely unartistic game, by the sport that occurred on the hippodrome. The political dislocations of power were decided by horse races, so to speak, and the political parties were just adherents of one or other of the competing groups. The emperor also had to belong to one or other of these groups. The whole affair could just as well have been decided by the casting of dice. This created the strange ahistorical equilibrium in Byzantine culture.

In Roman culture the game became absolutely safe for society as the game had justification only as a performance or the entertainment of the people. The consul was raised above the people, who were again raised above the players, who were all prisoners of war and gladiators. The consul was the referee, but only in an aesthetic sense. *He could not condemn a player to death, only pardon a player who was beaten.* This hierarchy is the model for the Roman Catholic perception of Christianity, just as the Byzantine attitude to the game

176 *The Natural Order and Other Texts*

is the foundation for the Greek Orthodox perception of Christianity, where it is the spectator, not the referee, who sits in the high seat.

Nordic or Germanic culture has always placed the game highest. Only what went on in the arena in Byzantium and Rome found a place in Nordic art. When the Christians refused to play and fight in the Roman arena, their entertainment lost any artistic character and became meaningless slaughter, which only awakened the public's disgust and sense of shame. The Roman hierarchy thereby collapsed like a house of cards. Only with Catholicism was a new interpretation of the same picture found. The condemning God was enthroned uppermost instead of the consul. Under him spread the heavenly hosts of saved souls instead of the public in the amphitheatre. At the bottom, the lost souls writhed in the tortures of hell instead of the heroic struggles of the gladiators in the arena.

However, this arrangement came in conflict with the image of the principle of justice, according to which heaven and hell were placed side by side, separated by the scales controlled by the archangel and the devil, so that the sheep and the goats could be distinguished. This principle of equivalence took on greater and greater power up to the Renaissance.

Arians – Donatists
Grundtvig – Kierkegaard

That the Germanic tribes refused to subordinate themselves to these two systems and chose Arianism instead has hitherto been explained as an accident, based upon the Arians being the only group who had any missionary activity. How great a role was played by accidents in history is in this case quite immaterial, but a rule cannot be explained by accidents. Then it was explained that the Germans found in Arianism a principle that protected them from being swallowed up by the Roman and Byzantine civilization. This explanation is also a good one, but it does not explain why the Germans kept strictly to this third European combination and have maintained it to this day. The astonishing superficiality with which Nordic religious historians treat this Scandinavian perception of religion is seen in its right light when it is discovered that Arius was poisoned the day before he was to take up his place as the supreme head of the Christian Church, and that all the Arian texts without exception have long since been burnt. Today not a single book on Arianism is to be found, even in Scandinavia, despite the Germans, and thereby the largest part of Europe, having been Arians for several centuries. This is probably the greatest and the most inexplicable hole in the history of Europe, but if it is filled, it will perhaps be seen that Grundtvig's teaching has to be described as a renewal of Arianism. In the current political situation, it is, however, important to point out the interesting fact that the English historian Moss stresses in his book of the origin of the Middle Ages,* that the special position of the French in medieval Europe was because they had produced the strange combination of Arianism and Catholicism that is reflected in the Avignon disturbances and which brought out that extraordinary Catholic chauvinism which we here in Denmark experienced with Absalon, whose fate is tied in with the Hvide family in such a singular way that Palle Lauring imagines that the whole thing is a matter of a banal family feud.* We find this same contempt for the specifically Scandinavian in Hal Koch's admiration of Constantine the Great's opposition to those who were to rescue Greek culture throughout the darkness of the Middle Ages, the Muslims and the Germans.* In North Africa, the Vandals were greeted as liberators by the Donatists. The disturbances that could spring up between the Arians and the Donatists seem to a high degree to be reflected in the opposition between Søren Kierkegaard and Grundtvig. *Søren Kierkegaard's demand for witnesses to truth was exactly the same as the Donatists demanded from the Catholic Church.* [...]

It is typical of Germanic culture that only the player who dares run the risk, and preferably risks all, is recognized as belonging to the elite, and this is what makes it so dangerous. This has the effect that we can never allow ourselves to get involved in a game where we are not consulted about the stakes. When the game has started, the Northerner commits himself with such violent energy that he can no longer control anything at all. To those who organize a game without taking part themselves, in order to profit from the game's results, the Northerners are the most welcome players, but the Northerners' fate always becomes the fate of the game itself. As a rule, they forget to be interested in what happens afterwards. If one has this gambling nature and is confronted with the unknown, then one is drawn to it precisely because it is unknown and therefore offers an opportunity for play and risk. So as not to be drawn into fixed games, it is therefore an unavoidable necessity for Northerners to be able to withdraw from such a situation.

Today the political game is made up by the social authorities, who secure the peace and order of society, at the same time giving the public to understand that they do this work with valour, that they have risked the most incredible dangers in the struggle for this order that they have become national heroes. As the capitalist and the socialist administrations are becoming more and more monotonous and tiresome, both systems have a mutual advantage in giving each

178 The Natural Order and Other Texts

other a role as the great danger. The power elite of the Eastern block is daily seen depicted in the newspapers of the West as an ugly face, whilst the West's power elite appears as the devil on the front-pages in the East. Then they meet in bloody feuds, where each number calls down destruction and annihilation upon the heads of the people. Then they can return home from the peace conferences as victors. Everyone breathes a sigh of relief. It had not gone as badly as one had feared. This fascinating game is called 'The Cold War'. However, it gets a little boring in the long run. Adenauer had to put off his election because there was an international football match. When people would rather see striptease on the TV than politicians, what can one do?

The heads of state know that the Nazi leaders were condemned for crimes against humanity. They must also be able to understand that whichever power uses apparatuses like the atom bomb for the destruction of the people, whether provoked by other powers or not, will be judged by the people as war criminals, and that any member of a government possessing bombs meant for human mass destruction must be seen as latent criminals, and that all governments connected to military groups which develop atomic weapons are accessories to the use of these weapons and will be judged in accordance with that responsibility. That will weigh on the conscience.

One hesitates, and the time comes where artistic entertainment takes up its place in this heroic drama – a few monuments here, some portraits in Greek draperies there, some well-turned novels and poems. The artist is useful, but he no longer believes in this comedy. This where we stand today.

Eisenhower has dismissed Scandinavians as a flock of drunken psychopaths with a tendency to suicide,* and now we are given to understand that Kennedy wants to send American artists to Europe to create prestige for the USA. So we can be delighted that the Americans wish to pay their best artists to entertain us and be pleased to see Ezra Pound and Henry Miller appearing in the name of the American people. Kennedy obviously seems to be blissfully unaware that the creative American elite has long since fled to Europe, where they are perhaps better known than in their homeland.

Before there can be talk of these politico-cultural arrangements, a little account has to be settled. We are owed a lot. This is not what depresses us. We can easily cross that out. But when they come and turn the affair on its head and maintain that it is us that owe the power elite and the people something, and base this on some poetic drivel about the gift of ability and the duty of talent, then we can only answer that this is a talentless composition, and within our own area everything can be forgiven except lack of talent combined with cheek.

If we are to talk about cultural politics, let us do it objectively. We will take care of the poetry.

It is especially comic when Eisenhower today declares that what he says as a statesman is not his *private* opinion. As if we did not know. But perhaps this new 'private' confession is also a political move to wipe out the fact that the Scandinavian stamp on the United Nations is fortunately being liquidated.*

Servants of the people – the majority's exploitation of the elite

Art consists of demonstrating and invoking differences of value and therefore stands in the sharpest oppositional relationship to the principle of equality. Capitalists believed that they could tie art to occupying itself exclusively with the inequality of objects, with the emphasis on the value of one commodity in relation to another. They got only a pseudo-art out of this, for they did not themselves believe for a minute in this pseudo-difference between one commodity and another. In the meanwhile, art vegetated and flowered on small canvasses in artists' attics.

At the same time, the politicians with their *theory of social equality*, which was adopted in the American constitution, had dug their own graves. Even when reduced to one person's *working hour* being equivalent to another person's working hour, the principle that an hour of one person's life is equivalent to one hour of another person's life makes the whole parliamentary voting system a meaningless farce, as the only reasonable thing would be to draw lots about who should do what.

The only thing one does at a political election is to agree in community about *the difference in the social value of two different people*. Political choice is therefore a break with the principle of human equivalence and un-Marxist. It was possible to avoid taking a position to this idiotic condition so long as there were still remnants left of the old aristocratic traditions which allowed the chosen to defend themselves against the ruthless exploitation of their abilities. But as this armour has gradually crumbled away, modern politicians are more and more subject to what one can call the exploitation of the diligent by the majority. So we have now reached that point where one can reckon that a good and conscientious prime minister (and the people have an increasing ability to discover them) can be carried to the graveyard after three to five years' service. This is true the world over, from Mao Tse Tung to Maurice Thorez, from Denmark to America.

Here it is then that the politicians, the industrialists and the military are gradually about to discover that they have committed a tremendous howler, for the same condition rules within industry. They will discover that the powerful can relax a little by allowing artists to perform before the people in their name. This is the reason for the great interest politicians and industrialists have in art today. This is the reason why they have again begun to dig up the old Roman principle, 'bread and circuses'. However, it just so happens that in Northern Europe there has sprung up an art of a completely new kind, which does not allow itself to be brought to heel and which is superior to subservient art, being more than simple popular entertainment or authoritarian propaganda. In contrast to most modern French artists, they have set up a directly inspirational relationship with the people, and they will not give up this again.*

A true art is the transmission of a true enthusiasm that develops in an artist, and before an artist can be enthused by the politicians, he has to be enthused by the methods, the art these politicians use to advance political events. These methods all result in the threat of war, and today this war is an atomic war. When war was an expression of *human* strength, then the artists could be enthused about such an elementary form of vitality. But not an artist is to be found in the world who today would lift a brush in enthusiasm for the little Jack-in-office who is to press the button in the East and the West every time the atom bomb is to go boom. Nothing at all can be done about this, even if a prime minister has to be carried to his grave every fortnight. Tøk weeps with dry eyes.* To make art *well-behaved* again is impossible. There is nothing more to be done than to copy the Germans and declare all modern art *decadent* and forbid it. But even such a precaution would not help, for there is also a demand on the side of the people upon the arts for liberation from the valueless existence being offered, and it is from here that the surprises will come in the future.

The gold standard and the artistic yardstick

In a previous passage we have set up the economic problem in three mutual complementary areas, the precious, the economic and the free of charge. Everything that can be controlled is economic. If something is placed under control then it is no longer free of charge. As the precious also lies outside control, generally one has a tendency to perceive the precious as free of charge. But if one does this, then it is no longer possible to set up a scale of values that has to go from the precious to the free of charge. It is this scale of values that the socialist doctrine of economics throws away, as it makes the economic value of an article identical with the working time necessary to produce it, and abolishes the value of the working hour by ignoring the variability of work effort, so one hour can only be calculated according to time, and the clock thus becomes the standard for the article produced. The basic structure is hereby set up for the clock-watcher mentality, to which the modern citizen must learn to dedicate himself, if he is to be reconciled to his fellow man.

There is so much of the free of charge that one does not need to save it at all. The precious is what is desired, but is rare. The most precious is the unique, which is passionately desired by all: in its indivisible form some have called this principle god. If such a unique thing has quality or constancy in time and yet can be divided, then it can be used as a unit of measurement for the scale between the precious and the free of charge. Diamonds, pearls and above all gold have been used as such a standard, but industry today can produce these things on as large a scale as one wishes, and this objectivized standard has thereby become so unstable that it is being given up in the capitalist countries too. That the gold coin standard is being forsaken is above all connected with the rising socialization. The result of having nothing by which the value of money can be measured has been that the various conflicting economic advantages of the different societal groups cancel each other out so that only the number on the note increases to such an extent that a couple of noughts have to be knocked off now and then.*

Before currency was invented, all precious things were artistic and aesthetic, and now after the war, strangely enough, economists have discovered that art works of an acknowledged value are the most stable of all precious objects. The Suez crisis revealed that a couple of big art collectors survived a collapse that made other firms break up, because they possessed two of the world's largest art collections. This has awakened the interest of economists in art to a high degree. Every art work is an absolute original and at the same time part of an artist's output, so the advantages of having gone over from the gold standard to an art standard are quite big. But the artists hereby take on a quite grotesque role as producers of the most precious things in society. The question is if it is an illusion that art is the most precious thing, or whether it really is traditionally identified as the precious itself by the people. Here I can refer to Karl Marx, who has proved that what can be perceived as social values never can be created by machines, only by people, and that humanity is thus the only real value-creating factor in society. A work's value is the direct expression of the interest the members of society show it. As the fine arts have no other meaning at all than to make people immediately and directly interested and interesting,

182 *The Natural Order and Other Texts*

art thus represents the highest value in society, as it is the result of unique achievement. What, in the narrowest sense, are called the fine arts are those arts the special essence of which consists in being and remaining unique. This is not the case with technical inventions characterized by being able to be reproduced without changing character, or even being directly meant for this.

As art can also be used to throw an interesting light upon phenomena that are not interesting in themselves, it has always been in the interests of the powers-that-be to set up the social task of art precisely as that of being their servant in this way. But as the bond with the transition to the monetary system's final victory has been broken and an independent artistic development thereby created, it will not again be possible to reduce art to this subservient role. So there are only two other ways to go, either the social powers-that-be have to forbid and destroy art, or the economic means that stand special groups in art-life in good stead must be dispersed into the general art life where the economic income is poor. The first possibility has already been attempted without success by the social powers-that-be.

Distribution without conversion

The opposition between the inventor – the artist in this connection is a kind of inventor – and the worker is that the worker's reproduced product can be *compared* with another product and evaluated on the basis of their *common* characteristics. The new cannot be compared with anything at all in this way. If it can, it is not new. It can only be compared in its *dissimilarity*. The doctrine of value that Karl Marx, and before him the capitalists, set up is based upon equalities in comparison. Its principle is the dialogue, exchange. *For the new there is no given equivalence.* The new is, as one says, irreversible, just like progress. What is called reversible is the basis for what is called communication or community. This reversibility is called dialogue in the intellectual sphere. Only where there is dialogue is it correct to talk of communication. Only on a telephone, where one can talk and hear from both sides, only on a train, which goes in both directions, can one talk of a communication. If the movement is only one way, then it is called transmission or distribution. Therefore when the press, the radio, the television, the film, even the whole of art life are called communication, this is a giant swindle. Here there is only radiation. Once one has understood this, then one understands why the whole of this colossal activity cannot be calculated on the basis of an exchange of goods, for there is simply no place for exchange.

Capitalism and socialism maintain that value occurs the instant an object is recognized as a commodity and is exchanged with another commodity. In the amount of commodity that can be obtained for this commodity occurs its social value. The Danish painter Carl-Henning Pedersen has gone against this postulate in an enormously effective and illuminating way by allowing his pictures to be exhibited but refusing to sell them.* The rising interest in his pictures demonstrates the whole absurdity of this capitalist/socialist principle of economics. Carl-Henning Pedersen's pictures have never been commodities. Their price cannot be reckoned in working time and yet there is a question how he can inhibit them ever being used as commodities and so reaching a high price. The only thing Carl-Henning Pedersen could get for his pictures is commodities and he does not like commodities. The only thing he really does like are his own pictures and he therefore retains them. But as his pictures are highly valued as commodities, then one could say that he possesses a great capital. It is not constant, for its value rises constantly. It cannot be evaluated as a fortune and cannot therefore be taxed. He likes exhibiting the pictures if he gets the chance and if one day he wanted to burn them all, then he is also allowed to do that. But that Carl-Henning Pedersen's pictures are *wealth and at the same time not a commodity* is proof that artistic value, even if at a given time it can be reckoned in money, and thus as a commodity, can nevertheless not be a commodity value. So the problem is: where is the natural home of art in the perception of social value?

The art work as counter-value

It is in the fight for humanity's leisure and interest that Northern European art and cultural development is today showing those strengths that it developed after the Reformation, which was first and foremost the detachment of art and leisure from the hands of the Church. The stakes today are about the wider existence of this development or its annihilation. To date the only instrument that has been found for the protection of this liberated leisure was found by N.F.S. Grundtvig and called 'the free Folk High School'. That, just like that of socialism, this organization has up to now only been used for just the opposite of this purpose changes nothing about the interest both of these ideas in their original forms must have for all thinking people.

In order to understand how this game works, it is first necessary to get a purely materialistic explanation of what art and what is called artistic value is

184   *The Natural Order and Other Texts*

and has to be in relation to what is called practical value, with which it is often confused.

The art work in its highest form is *valuable quality*: the form that always distributes its content without even being exhausted. It fills itself up in the most wonderful way. Art is the spiritual creation which preserves its quality simultaneously with spreading its value. This singularity has provided material for innumerable explanations about the metaphysical and religious essence of art, whilst at the same time the rationalists have simply denied that there is anything called art. The reason for this special character of art, which Marx was the first to acknowledge but the last to understand, is, however, quite a simple condition. Art never supplies values. Art gives nothing. It takes all. Art is the strength needed to influence a body and liberate the values confined in that body. Art is thus a destroyer of human quality and integrity, and it is this destruction of one's own absolute integrity that one experiences as beauty. The secret of art consists of the simple fact that it is more blessed to give than to take, but also that this blessedness is dependent upon a *voluntary* giving, so that what is given is felt as a *surplus*, a wealth, and not a duty. This is the simple materialistic explanation of the value of the art work and for all the other things called spiritual values. Art is opium for the people. It undoes, subverts, liberates.

In relation to the practical values, art is thus a counter-value, the value of productive pleasure. *Art is the call for a discharge of energy* without a precise goal, except the one that the receiver can discover. In this way, art is the source of benevolence, is what is called *grace*. By making God the origin of all grace, God has become identical with the artist, and by perceiving the artist's demand for the ownership of what he creates as blasphemy, creative art has been killed. In a practical sense, art is a meaningless value. At the same time, to the individual it is the very proof of his own freedom of action. This does not mean, of course, that the viewer can do what he likes with the art work. What he is freely and independently determining is the energies he has liberated in himself through the artistic experience. No one is able to control these energies except himself. If the viewer has no energies to liberate in this area, then he will see or hear nothing at all. *The most primitive answer to artistic provocation is the will to crush the art work that has brought one out of balance.* This is the reason why so many artists are at first persecuted and then later mourned. Politicians have always been incredibly diligent at manipulating this natural reaction whenever an art has occurred that has worked against their interests, for art is the most disquieting element of all in society, and yet, at the same time, the element that has the greatest political interest because it is the method of enthusiasm, of revival, of inspiration, and *nothing is so valuable to exploit as the enthusiasm of a people.* This is the highest form of politics.

As the industrial process is built upon the principle of equivalence or indifference, artistic enthusiasm was the worst enemy of the industrialists. The only art they could accept was that which could provoke a popular enthusiasm for the commodity that was produced and was to be sold. These advertising methods are so well known that they do not need to be discussed here.

Seen objectively or scientifically, one interest cannot be of a higher kind than another. Any accentuation of an interest at the expense of another is thus absolutely unscientific. *Even the most ancient city society understood the utility of art as an advertisement for the authorities,* and the subservient function given to this art shadowed developments from this point on right up to modern industrial society. If at the same time this art happens to be some of the most wonderful in the history of the development of art, then this is not because the art served the authorities, but because those authorities were able to identify their position with something central to the development of the world-picture itself. It was this character of universal authority that was able to inspire all the artistic capabilities, and that was suddenly split asunder by Christianity's distinction between universal and secular power, which were set in an opponent relationship from then on. From that moment, art becomes an expression of the independence of the universal idea from the secular powers, and any attempt to set the old unity up again falls to earth as a baroque and forlorn absurdity. However, as Christianity in its opposition to the secular powers became an *absolute* or unchangeable symbol world, the artists in their ceaseless need to create had to forsake it too in order to carry on their work completely on their own basis. These are the stages of the development of the independence of art.

Enthusiasm is the spirit of self-sacrifice, is artistic experience. If it is to be true, this experience can only take place as a *voluntary* action. In order to advance the industrial system, that artistic capability of the people, popular enthusiasm, had to be made ridiculous and forbidden in the name of economics, and gradually as this development has advanced and demonstrated its very limited significance, politicians have become more and more afraid of the artistic strength of the people, of the people's spirit of self-sacrifice. *After the war*, in which this spirit of self-sacrifice was put to its hardest test, politics in the East and in the West were directed exclusively towards reducing the significance of the people's enthusiasm to nothing. When the war was over, the people stood prepared to make sacrifices for the advancement of life, which during the war had been sacrificed for the advancement of death. As our country was one of the few that retained its production apparatus intact after

186 The Natural Order and Other Texts

the war, the greatest insult to the Danish population was that it suddenly had to have Marshall Aid from outside. That this aid was only a trick is evident from the fact that we had then to help the so-called 'under-developed countries', then we had to be helped militarily, and now we cannot even take care of our own housekeeping, but have to have help with our own administration. *How could such a thing be at all possible?* Because only one thing was forbidden, to appeal to the Danish people's artistic sense or spirit of self-sacrifice about our own. If there were tendencies towards self-sacrifice, then they had to be exported immediately, whilst at the same time we too received our import of 'self-sacrificing souls'. The whole of this enormous anti-Scandinavian swindle could not have been carried out so deftly and without friction, if we had not had that pillow that is called the Folk High School, which has had *a monopoly on Scandinavian enthusiasm and popular revival*, but which has only administered sleeping pills, every time someone snored.*

We have now come to the end of the road, and if Scandinavian reflection and resolve is to be awakened in time, then it must be done with such hard means that the anger of the people will probably at first be directed at whoever is trying to shake it out of its sweet dreams. But this is the risk that has to be run, for the Nordic peoples have previously shown before that, if they just understood *what* was going on, then they were the quickest to take decisions in fellowship, and with artistic magnanimity to get a change of system going rapidly and with intelligence.

The symmetry between production and consumption

With the quite insignificant variations that exist between wages, the capitalist and socialist economies that rule modern society can on the whole maintain that one hour's work in the machinery of society is uniform in pay to all. If one ignores all insignificant special cases and reckons with large numbers, the effort is uniform, for all individuals have the same value, and one hour's work is, as they say, equivalent to one hour's work. In this way the productive ability of all individuals is of equal value.

In order to avoid a saving which remains in the pocket of the working class, it is necessary that what is spent on consumption corresponds exactly to what is paid for production, and that on the whole there is also an equilibrium or equivalence between the production and consumption of the individual. If we set this up schematically, then this would show that *one hour's production corresponds to one hour's consumption.* This is the foundation on which every modern capitalist or socialist society bases its economic equilibrium. What is given for work is taken back for consumption.

The proletariat without property had as a political goal to make this equivalence between production and consumption really actual, so *anyone who worked an hour, really got the equivalent for his work, as he had the right to an hour's production of another individual.* If this equivalence is achieved, then exploitation no longer exists within social production. Everyone is equal, and all share equally.

This system functions irreproachably when it is a matter of the practical, necessary production for the establishment of life. This is also the reason that the Marxist doctrine of economics, as well as the capitalist one, can only account for the necessary. Now it just so happens that a person can normally only eat for three hours and his need for clothes and shelter are covered by one hour's daily work. Let us say that he works eight hours, rests for the other eight hours, then he has eight hours' consumption, of which only four cover his necessary needs. He then demands the *right to a luxury need in the remaining four hours. He wants to be entertained.* He has the right to be distracted by another person for four hours. He has paid for this with four hours' work. That is just.

Let us say that he wishes to play chess. He then seeks out another and asks him to play chess. We have now suddenly entered a world where all the theories of capitalist and socialist economics break completely down. If the other man has worked eight hours and hates chess, then he can refuse to play, but if he says 'yes' but is a complete duffer at chess, then it is the other man who gets angry. Or let us assume that they can both play chess well and that they like to do so, then they have entertained each other and both have saved an hour's production. Then they should both pay this in tax.

But society, seeing that these people have plenty of energy left, now squeezes production up so that everyone is tired. Let us now suppose that they are interested in chess but too tired to play. Well then, they can amuse themselves by watching the game. Let us suppose that two players entertain a hundred spectators. Then they have, in accordance with the economic rules that are valid in modern society, the right to one hour's production from each of the spectators, if they play for an hour. This becomes exactly one hundred hours' productive work that they earn in an hour.

Of course, those who wish to be entertained gladly go along with this, and thus it goes. But suddenly someone cries cheat when the two collect the money. This cannot be right. These players are not even production workers, they live like good-for-nothings and in no time at all earn enormous sums. How can that

188 *The Natural Order and Other Texts*

be? They have the right to one hour's production and no more.

Yes, but the one who wishes to be entertained would be the first to protest in rage and indignation if one said that anyone could then be allowed to perform as entertainers. No, the criticizing, choosing, rejecting and praising, elevating one above another alone is one of the greatest enjoyments, especially in sport. *In the entertainment branch the theory of equivalence has not a shadow of existence.* There just the opposite rules are valid. Only the best is accepted, and the better they are, the more people come to their entertainment, and if it is especially fine, it can be sent out on radio, television, film, gramophone record etc. filling up thousands and thousands of hours of entertainment, and what is more, everyone will pay with pleasure if the entertainment is good, and do it absolutely voluntarily. Thus there can be no talk of exploitation or force. In this way, all the modern means of production have multiplied the efficiency of the entertainment activity, have industrialized it. But this thus means that everyone who is able to do something that other people gladly devote their leisure to cultivating must become enormously rich. This is, however, seldom the case. Almost all the money that is paid for unnecessary consumption or entertainment goes into the pockets of the various governments, whether in the East or the West.

The socially productive people can be indifferent to this as they get their entertainment any way and even, on the strength of somehow representing the government in a democratic society, can be quite satisfied. Just, however, it is not. How then should one explain to the entertainer that he is going to be cheated of the money that in justice's name he should have had? This can only be done by maintaining that his talent is a *gift* which others don't have, and which he is *obliged* to use for the betterment of others. But who then has given him this gift? This is where *having to invent a god, who will compel certain individuals to achieve, not the normal, but their utmost,* comes in, whilst everyone else just has to achieve the normal. Today such an argument is, of course, perceived as pure rubbish. But it is nevertheless the only explanation that, even in the countries which lead in Marxist theory, they have to take refuge in, if they will not look at the affair in a purely scientific way and admit that the majority exploit those with unique abilities.

The enjoyment of output and output versus enjoyment

If we are thus forced to recognize the foundation of social justice as the establishment of an equivalence between production and consumption according to the old method that one reaps as one sows, then this does not lead to a universal solution unless one forbids both art and entertainment. I wonder if there is anyone who would deny that the greatest happiness of humanity consists in having done one's best in the area one loves to develop, that the highest output here is identical with the highest enjoyment. It is here the people are cheated by trying to kid them that they love something that is unimportant to them, and that what they really want to do is or ought to be unimportant to them. In industry everyone has to work at the same tempo. Those who desire to work more than others destroy the rhythm and are called to order and have to seek an outlet for their strengths and abilities in their leisure time. But if industrial production is to be absolutely universal, then they are simply forbidden to produce anything. They have to make do with sport and non-productive work. Because it is a joy to them, their special effort is perceived as an enjoyment and is treated as consumption. The result of this unartistic perception of work is that only the most boring work is the foundation for the judgement of value, and the most boring is monotonous reproduction, which is not creative. One therefore sees that a researcher who has had the same education as a teacher gets less in salary because his work is in itself interesting. *What creates value is here prized less than the purely reproductive.* The more boring it is the dearer it is.

How money is earned from art and culture

If it is an abstract generalization that we accept the principle that one hour's reproductive work has the same value as one hour's reproductive work, regardless of what is made and who does it, and that one hour's reproductive work has the same value as an hour's consumption, then it is still a fact that an hour's reproduction will be paid for an hour's entertainment, regardless of who is paying. Nothing in this system can hinder huge sums being earned from entertainment, without entertainment simply being forbidden.

You have probably been asking for some time what the whole of this problem of recreation has to do with art and culture. This is because, as in the question of public opinion, one only thinks of the present moment and does not value the length of the recreation. It is here that the fraud goes on, taking from art and culture the money which rightly belongs to them. If I amuse myself with a book for an hour, then I owe the author one hour's productive work. The longer an author preserves his actuality, the more money he will realize for art

190 *The Natural Order and Other Texts*

and culture. Try to imagine how many hours have been utilized in the course of time in the reading of Hans Christian Andersen's fairy tales.

The artistic culture of a people is in this way a directly measurable source of economic income. When it is said that something is sacrificed for art and culture, this is a pure economic and political swindle. Art and culture retain only a minimal part of the sums they earn. If therefore it is at all possible to be discussing how far a country's prehistorical collections should be preserved under accountable conditions that give humanity the greatest returns, then it is time that the people in artistic, cultural and entertainment life went on strike and refused to give the Finance Ministry the money that rightfully belongs to us. All great popular entertainers draw nourishment from the creative activity that can only be experienced by making an effort. Popular entertainment is only a facade. Behind it extend enormous constructions. This is human culture. Tearing down and building up, researching and re-making go on, and money is paid in abundance by those who enjoy it all. If the Americans just paid according to the tariff for the time they occupy themselves with European culture, then the whole of Europe could live off it. But then our artistic culture would stagnate.

Creative culture is not gratis, but it can only live in beauty or grace. An unartistic world is a graceless world.

Grace belongs to artistic people and no one else. Culture belongs only to those who do something for culture, but art is full of grace and culture is grace. It is this fact that the power elite try to utilize and hide from people. No means are too dirty in this work. The greatest American poet in America in our time, the pacifist Ezra Pound, champion of American neutrality during the last World War, was after the war placed by the American military in an open cage in a square in Milan and then put in a mental hospital because he was too intelligent, and because the American military could not have him killed for high treason. Here at home, children sing, 'I know a lark's nest', but I will not say more about this affair, as Bergstedt's film *The Feast of St. George* is not played today either in Russia or anywhere else.* It is a little too revealing for the whole comedy. There is no book about one of Denmark's greatest writers, Martin Andersen Nexø. On the contrary, his clothes were covered with spit at the time of the Finland war because he did not follow public opinion.* Today the value of Hans Kirk's books is explained by him having two faces, one beautiful, one ugly.* We have gradually become so used to this that it seems to be part of the conditions of cultural life. Perhaps it has always been so. The only new thing that industry appears to have brought to culture is increased productivity and mass effect. The threatening thing about the German

Value and Economy *191*

concentration camps as well as about the American Hiroshima explosion lies in no way in the atrocities, which are no worse than those happening in many other places on earth. The shattering thing is their colossal and blind mass effect that makes humanity more and more valueless. The great crime against humanity today is therefore the belief in the right of the mass effect to dominate. The mass effect is the graceless effect.

One of the strangest phenomena in medieval art is what I will call the art of indignation. This anti-artistic art aims at frightening people away from everything that is beautiful here in life. The perfidiousness of this art consists in it uniting the enjoyment of beauty with a remorseless indignation about what is enjoyed. This art form, to which we here from the North must admit having been godfather, has in America today developed into forms, the cynicism of which paralyses the whole civilized world with admiration, as it has been combined with the old Roman insistence on the people's desire for amusement. The zenith must have been reached with the so-called Chessmann affair.* A young man is accused of having raped a woman. This is the prelude to an entertainment in the name of indignation that lasted twenty years. Probably no woman in California will ever again report a man for rape. If it was calculated what the entertainment industry earned during the trials of these twenty years, then it would be better understand why they were kept going in the name of so-called justice. When the woman had finally been so besmirched by the public that she went mad, they could find no other way to absolve themselves of the responsibility for their crime than to declare Chessmann guilty and kill him. This last show number was carried out with dazzling brio. But that was a postlude. As Chessmann was an excellent author, he left a series of books. Like all other so-called and supposed criminals, he had in life served as popular amusement in the stocks of the modern information media. But today the American state is earning money from his books. Purely economically, it is this amount that can be called grace. *Chessmann has graced the Americans.* A graceless people void of beauty is an uncultivated people without anything to fall back on. One has to beware of that – but also to beware above all of those who maintain that culture has nothing to do with economics, for they are swindlers and demagogues.

Valueless output

If it is possible to allow a person to give of his utmost in an area he loves without his output having any productive result at all, then it is possible to

192 *The Natural Order and Other Texts*

perceive this output as a purely personal output without social consequences. He must therefore pay an hour's production for this pleasure, if it lasts an hour. This is possible in gaming and sport. We will assume that the man wants to play chess and that he finds an opponent who beats him, then he has had the enjoyment of giving his utmost, whilst his opponent could have played a better player. He thus owes his opponent an hour's production. Neither more not less.

If they both perform for an audience, then in fellowship they have the right to an hour's production from each of the spectators, as well as each of them having won an hour from the other. But what would the result be if all entertainment were paid in this way? The result would be the same as we are experiencing today, for money is paid out in such a way. It is just not the players but also those who own the organizations that rule this economy and shovel in the money. In this game, one can even win fortunes. However, care is taken that this is not conditioned by ability but by chance. Pools and lotteries.

It was believed that the whole question could be solved by distinguishing between professional production and amateur activity. That has been the Nordic solution. Here much has already been gained, as this side of entertainment is freed from speculation. One just loses in another way, for, despite everything, some speculation does lie behind it, namely, that of stopping money being mixed up with recreational life. This is the Protestant solution. It is not brilliant.

It is said that the Italians, who are some of the world's worst football players, have not lost an international since 1910. They buy their players abroad. Thus here we have another method. However, regardless of how one twists and turns it, the modern life form has called forth a broad popular demand for entertainment that is of such strength that the politicians and the rest of the leadership of society are powerless before this so-called public opinion, which has more sympathy for racing cyclists, film stars, artists, musicians, etc., than for 'the power elite'. Amongst other things, this condition has created a rising opposition between recreational life and politicians in the USA. That this opposition is hardly so banal in Europe is because a greater culture has accumulated.

Only the day that it is acknowledged that recreational life can not be arranged on either a professional or an amateur basis in the economic sense, will it be possible to give an enriching leisure back to humanity. Art is not craft, but it cannot be separated from it either. Art is the anti-professional profession. The artist is a professional amateur, and his output has the greatest value in society, also economically, regardless of who gets the money. Money-free amateur activity is a sheer metaphysical fraud.

The opposition of mass and tension

This short survey of the problems shows that here we have suddenly come into an area that neither sociologists nor economists really understand. The problem around this question cannot be explained by old-fashioned individualism. The selection of the individual who performs the best entertainment cannot in general be identified with the selection of the best individual. One wants to see the best performer, but at the same time he has to give of his utmost, in contrast to the normally working person who works to a common cadence, that must not be faster than the slowest can keep up with. *Society is not interested in individuals who entertain, it is only interested in abilities that have an interest to others.* If one knows something about top performances in recreational life, then one will also discover that the public are the hardest and most pitiless employers in existence. That the entertainer is forced to stimulate himself by artificial means that systematically destroy his physique does not move them. Harshly and systematically they demand the best of him, and the day he falls apart only scorn and oblivion remain. The public would rather see blood.

Mechanical work is the product of amount and tension. In normal production the tension is so uniform that one can ignore this factor and calculate the work as a pure amount or quantity. This is surely the reason that entertainment takes on an exactly opposite character. As compensation for tension-less work, spiritual equilibrium requires being able to swing over into an activity that *gives the greatest tension, but demands the least amount of work effort.* This is the reason for the colossal significance of the entertainment industry in modern society: the mass production of impotent tension.

We can demonstrate that this same industrial development, which to a greater and greater degree is developing *the principle of equality*, is within reproductive work developing a world of entertainment where only anarchy's law about the *difference* of people is valid. If industrial work tends towards indifference, then here only the law of the difference of values is valid, and the tendency is going towards higher and higher tension with a lower and lower input of work amount. As the scientific definition of the concept of work in mechanics covers both amount and tension, we are correct in stressing that we are confronted with two opposing forms of work carried out by two opposing types of worker whose life conditions are fundamentally different. This difference can be taken to the point where an entertainment uses a man up in one go, so to speak. To reach this high point he could perhaps have been preparing himself for decades. The question is what becomes of the man when he is used up and is no longer of any use. One could imagine a man becoming

194   The Natural Order and Other Texts

world champion at boxing and at the same time being destroyed. Similar cases are more common than one believes.

Even if every citizen only pays a fair price to experience a top performance these days, incredible sums are being scooped up from those entertainments that achieve the interest of world opinion because of modern means of transmission. It is obvious that the money earned in this way justly belongs to the one who has given the performance, but he just does not get it. Rising socialization makes entertainment or recreation the best instrument for the exploitation of the masses by the state apparatuses. At the same time, it is obvious that he who hereby gives of his best is only able to do so if his way of life is strictly adapted in such a way that, in relation to a well-paid worker, he lives as a rule the life of an ascetic. Thus if the entertainer himself had the right to the money earned from his entertainment for his personal consumption, he would, however, be terrified if he had personally to consume to such a degree. As his entertainment is at the same time an expression of a passionate interest in the area in which he is giving his performance, the money naturally and justly has, of course, to be invested in the raising of the level of his performance. The working population today must take a clear and unambiguous position to this requirement, if they wish to create the best conditions for the best performance.

The known and the anonymous – the remarkable and the normal

Does society not have the right to demand that the best give of their best? No. Democratic society has the right to demand that all offer exactly the same. If this is valid only for the great majority, then society is automatically established in two classes. If it is the majority that decides in which region and how the best are to give of their best, then the best form an exploited class, a subservient class, an under-class, regardless how this is twisted and turned, regardless of whether the selected group of people is perceived as an elite, as the best. Perhaps they are perceived as a higher class by the rest, but it is far from certain that they perceive themselves in the same way. Their highest endeavours are perhaps perceived by themselves as a most degrading and dangerous activity. What is called higher in their endeavours is only what *the others* perceive as higher, and they themselves are perhaps so intelligent that they can see that the things one can get them to do are sheer madness.

Without any right at all, modern society thus selects a group of people especially useful to the majority because of their special characteristics. These perhaps stem from original or special talents, but in all circumstances they are developed through upbringing and cultivated with the intention of suiting them to as higher a degree as possible to practising what is called their best. As this system gradually reveals its character more and more in the modern democracies, both in the East and in the West, a crisis is about to occur, as it has become a disaster for a person if it is discovered that he is particularly intelligent and diligent. The result is that in Moscow academics would rather sweep the streets and meditate on existence than take the responsibility for the management of factories. On the other hand, there are protests that many years of education having been invested in them and the money is required back, but as these people have probably not asked for such an education, the argument has no moral force. The interesting thing about this crisis is that it is common to both the socialist and the capitalist countries and is already so far advanced that it is extremely rare today to find what one calls an eminent personality in any significant post. An American industrial leader can perhaps earn as much as he likes, but the whole of his time is tied up in his efforts in industry and in social representation to the degree that he can be fairly sure that it is only his wife who can enjoy the advantages of his fortune before and after his death around the age of 45. One can understand when it is said that pretty women in America are the real power factor. They own most of both the leisure and of the capital, and are called the gold-diggers of our time.

However, this condition does not hinder increasing investment everywhere in developing what is called an elite to be placed in the various key positions. In America this group is called, curiously enough, 'the power elite', the secular power, and is the only elite that has social justification in the United States and the Soviet Union. It is divided into three intertwining groups, the political, the military and the industrial or commercial elites. The comical thing about modern American sociology is that, having excluded the artist from this goodly company, it has been discovered that the so-called power elite is completely powerless if the people do not have an idealized picture and a personal conception of them. People have to know them. They have therefore become strong competitors to commodity advertising. It has been discovered that the most important thing is to be known. Now, however, the total of people who can be said to be known in a particular period and in a particular place is limited by people's ability to maintain the name and image of a personality. The limit seems to lie about 500. This gives the pleasing fact that all the people in a village are personalities. In a larger provincial town, there is only a limited number of people who can be seen as personalities, the rest being perceived as more or less anonymous. The colossal increase in population has thus not increased the number of personalities. On the contrary, the increased knowledge

196 *The Natural Order and Other Texts*

of the population of other parts of the world lessens the chance on the home market. We see, for example, that the great number of literary translations clearly give far less scope for the development of literary personalities than in the previous century, especially when it began. There can reign no doubt that the severe isolation during the war played a great role in the development of the strong character features of modern Danish art.

What one does – what one is and what one has

Of course, it is completely meaningless to believe that only known people have a personality. Every person who is born on the earth is, just like his fingerprints, different from all others, but only known people have the right to have a social personality. *In every historical period known people have represented human society's elite.* It is about this elite that historical writing weaves its images of vanished times and makes our past human.

If one looks at history from a socialist viewpoint, the 'same thing would have happened' if other personalities had been in place. This is probably correct on the macro-level. What interest then do the personalities have? We will simply reverse the question. What do the innumerable series of numbers in the different five-year plans mean to us, when we cannot discern one human life in them? In themselves they are just as boring and uninteresting as the dirty stories that are told about Stalin are interesting. This is entertainment of rank, this is history, inhumanly human. The world becomes unknown if one does not know the people in it. The same is the case with history. It is the relationship between people and events that interests us. Not the events in themselves nor the people in themselves. The idea that the human elite, the known personalities, represents individuals in contact with events who are higher, more effective and nobler than all others, that history collects human events and gathers together material of a higher significance independently of the individual's position on the social ladder, whether rich or poor, popularly known or unknown, admired or despised, represents the ideology of European humanism. Today this idea has been completely removed from sociological observations in the United States as well as the socialist societies, and this is not absolutely without reason.

It is completely abstract to talk of an unknown elite, an elite that cannot be situated anywhere. In order to be able to talk of an elite, there must exist certain facts attached to it and obvious to the consciousness of others. The concept of an elite can thus never be attached to certain beings of remarkable character, only to certain *actions*. With individuals, others can only evaluate their actions.

The American sociologist C. Wright Mills is therefore completely correct in his book *The Power Elite* when he perceives the old humanistic attitude as pure sophism.* Only he makes the attitude to the problem even more absurd by replacing the perception of the individual's human power, the question of what one *is* into the question of what one *has*, instead of moving it over to the question of what one *does*, and thus to the personal dynamic, which is precisely the historical value of power, a strength in activity and never a latent power.

Human abilities that remain unutilized in their latent state, people who remain unknown because they have never had occasion to realize their abilities, have no reality. In spite of this, humanity's quality of latent genius is the very essence and substance of our strength of development. No instrument, no property, no social possession, no money, no social position, is in itself of human or social value. They are just as lacking in intelligence and sensitivity as what is called 'the power elite'. Power is the manifestation of strength and consists only in the will, ability and right to transform and change something, the right to vary or gamble with something.

Thus against secular power we place the power of art.

This arrangement of the problem seems simple, but it is not. What is perceived as most precious is *the art work*, and thus the article, the quality. It is something one *has*. One could easily develop this interest without being interested in *the artist*, for an artist is something one *is*, and one cannot evaluate the full value of an artist before he is dead and has completed his work. Consequently, there lies a great risk in buying the work of a living artist. But even recognition of the artist is just a recognition of a quality, of what he is, and thus of a momentary evaluation that could change. It is not a direct evaluation of the original, of what he *does*, of *the creative development of art*, which disturbs fixed evaluations all the time. If one wishes to value an artist for what he is, then one is at the same time forbidding him to change. Only a direct interest in the creative artistic process itself (and only creative artists themselves can have this completely) gives an unhampered artistic renewal. This engages, if one may say so, *everyone* to take part in the creative process of art. This is what this new development implicates humanity in, and it demands a common social framework similar to that which has been developed for sport and other light entertainment.

The only alternative to this development is the tendency that is today taken care of by the state apparatus and the power elite, and which depends on the standard for humanity being the human himself, as he *is*. Where it is perceived materialistically, this perception must either be an aristocratic tendency towards the raising of humanity's *quality*, a tendency which, if it is to be taken

198 *The Natural Order and Other Texts*

seriously, must end in racism, or be a real democratic tendency and thus has to set its target in the purely *quantitative* development of humanity. This last tendency is dominant the world over. One needs only to investigate the birth statistics. This is in context with the family being the basic community, where any productive surplus the individual possesses has to be distributed. In human terms, states and the power elite can only offer us these two perspectives – work to give birth to children or to kill each other.

On to be able and to know

The American sociologist we have already mentioned stresses that it can be statistically proved that 'the societal power that possesses the greatest destructive force, has also the greatest power',* and thus is the greatest power factor. This is the reason why the Americans maintain the production of atom bombs, not because they feel threatened, but because they are thereby able to threaten. Public opinion permits itself to be frightened, it seems. This cynical statement places the Europeans' subordination to the American military, politics and economics in a glaring light, as it shows that the Americans are clear that we have done it out of dread and respect for them. At any rate, this is how Americans themselves ought to see the affair according to their own statements.

It was believed that the German Nazis had reached the highest effectiveness in popular destruction with their crematorium ovens. But this shows how craft oriented the thinking of Europe still is. When the atom bomb was exploded over Hiroshima, the modern destruction of people was invented, where mass destruction takes place without the law of 'the survival of the fittest' having any validity any more. Hereby the personal characteristics of the individual in the struggle for life have finally become meaningless.

What, however, fooled the Americans and which today creates their greatest problem is the discovery that the power elite's power has, at the same time, become unusable because it is too great. The effect is too great and what does one do then? Remarkably enough, one works energetically to make it even bigger. It was discovered that the power elite has to be known by public opinion to have any significance at all. People have always lived on the edge of Vesuvius. The whole of Holland lies below sea level. Million of people live in constant mortal danger to this day, but feel themselves in no way subordinate to the forces apparently threatening them. Obviously one takes care, but one does not interest oneself in it at all. *For a group of people really to have power over others, it seems that these others have to be interested in them.* It is this interest that gives social value. Today it is difficult for the American and Russian power elites to attract the people's interest and, as they have colonized Europe, the same thing is happening here. Interest is beginning to be shown in the problem, and on the American side to collect around the method that has shown itself so effective in the fight about consumption. Like any other commodity, the elite has to be sold by the most hard-handed advertising. In order to avoid seeing what is really hidden in this problem, academics have made a false separation between what they call art and what they call advertisement. They simply refuse to admit the obvious that all art, even that of Beethoven and Rembrandt, is art because, amongst other things, it is an advertisement for something, and that to advertise is to give a sensory experience an extraordinary significance. That a sensory experience is given an extraordinary significance is first and foremost to say that one is conscious of it as something important and something present. This conscious reaction is what in the most elementary sense could be called intelligence. In order to avoid acknowledging the intellectual element in this process, academics have simply denied that intelligence occurs in this psychic sphere and that intelligence does not occupy itself with experiences of reality but only with concepts, even the concept of reality being defined as something that cannot be experienced but only comprehended.

Art is to be able, but to be able is also to know. To maintain the above-mentioned crippled concept of art, academics have had to remove knowledge from art. The achievement here is the isolation of direct knowledge from the problem of intelligence. That this formulation is commonly carried out in America demonstrates the above mentioned sociology, where everyone who is publicly known without belonging to the power elite is simply defined as a 'professional celebrity', which means that they are known only because their work 'depends upon being known'. Into this bag one can throw film stars together with scientists, pin-ups and fighters for enlightenment, artists, racing cyclists, religious preachers, boxers etc. and complain that these so-called clowns are taking the limelight more and more from the power elite, so that they too are required to clown for the public in order to attract attention. Eisenhower's speeches on television are repeated exactly like a play, without a spark of interest in what he is saying. Texan politicians have to perform in cowboy clothes and have no chance if they do not know how to handle a lasso. No wonder that the power elite has become more and more angry about these so-called 'professional celebrities'.

Where modern capitalists and socialists lack understanding only becomes

200 *The Natural Order and Other Texts*

clear from our definition of value. The citizenry took over from Greek materialism the conviction that only the known has existence. Strangely enough, Marxism is probably constructed on the same principle. We have to maintain that it is only the consciousness of a phenomenon that confirms its existence. However, it has been overlooked that it is only those phenomena that interest people as sensory phenomena, only those that, as we say, attract their attention, that have meaning to them. This invokes the illusion that phenomena that can be ignored also vanish. *Everything that has become necessary becomes at the same time without direct significance, without interest as it no longer invokes problems. From being significant it has become obvious.* One need think of it no longer. Ruling ideas, ideologies, societal groups and individuals are what have significance, the unusual. Those who are governed are those that have become obvious. As the lacking interest in the significance of a necessary thing is the same as the lack of the necessity of being aware of it and of being oneself conscious of it, this means that Marxism's disdain for free intellectual life and its development of the principle of necessity makes humanity's existence more and more unconscious and meaningless. What really happens when a phenomenon is made necessary is what is called its '*Entfremdung*', its removal from human attention, the diminution of its interest in relation to humanity. The process in itself has, however, neither changed character nor essence.

Public opinion or the slavery of the moment

Modern democratic society has become a complete slave of a strange, awe-inspiring being called public opinion. Even the power elite is more and more subordinated to its judgement. To perceive this as the opinion of the masses in opposition to the understanding of the intellectual aristocracy is completely mistaken, for we correspond to everyone and daily realize all public opinion, for public opinion is nothing other than our momentarily requested meaning, without precondition and without consequence about affairs about which we have neither time, desire nor ability to inform ourselves, but where we are nevertheless required to pass judgement.

Public opinion is thus nothing other than everyone's opinion at a certain point in time, and thus a cross-section of a popular instant. It is for this public opinion that there has to be new information at every moment of the day and this pours in such amounts that the new impression erases the previous one, and this makes people dafter and dafter from too much and too indifferent information. The amount and the rapidity hamper anything weighty getting a place in the current. This is even true of thought. A new form of newspaper philosophy of a quite special, non-contextual sort has arisen, so self-contradictory and windbagological that it excludes any form of overview.

The greater significance public opinion gets, the more timeless becomes modern civilization, and the more it is stripped of culture, which is the patience to cultivate characteristics.

The same is the case with the adaptation of practical production to instant consumption. This too is actualized to the degree that production and consumption have to follow each other in a faster and faster cadence. The Scandinavian resistance to this tendency is identical to the quality of Nordic production. This resistance can only be made economically understandable and calculable if the dimension of duration is also reckoned into the evaluation of value. *To reckon with the dimension of duration is what one calls culture.* When Danish politicians today say that culture has nothing to do with economics, then this is a denial of the economic structure of Scandinavia. I am not the only one to feel a premonition that this structure is richer than the one we will be forced to accept. The discussion around the activity of radio, television and other information and transmission organizations shows that the instinct is there, but the arguments are too weak. The latter is what I want to attempt to alter. But I cannot do it alone. I can only open the discussion on a new basis.

Ought a cinema ticket not to be cheaper than a theatre ticket, and a television presentation cheaper than a cinema ticket? Ought a gramophone record not to be cheaper than a concert, the reproduction of a painting cheaper than the original? Ought classic books not to be free? Apart from the purely technical question that creates a variation in price, the answer in principle has to be a no. The only way by which a diminution of the indifferent mass of information and the just as sickening amount of farcical entertainment is possible, is to make people pay directly for it and thereby force them to criticize, as the money they have to give out should then go directly towards raising the level of entertainment. Amateur sportsmen are actors without cost to the spectators. The sports presentations of television are experiences of the moment which take all significance from sport. Culture is context in time and it both costs and brings in money. By utilizing this without breaking new ground one eats up human history without renewing it. This is what is happening today.

202 *The Natural Order and Other Texts*

Technical cadence is artistic decadence

The position of the artist, the inventor and the discoverer is superior to that of the power elite, because the latter only exists the instant that it has forced itself upon the attention of the whole of society. Only when this universal attention has been established, does the power elite begin to be able to do something. Whether this attention is compelled by violence and threats or by charm and the invocation of sympathy is in itself irrelevant. It is established on two opposite emotions, anxiety and confidence. Only an infantile person can unite anxiety with confidence about the same power.

On the other hand, the artist has use for neither anxiety, confidence nor attention established in advance. On the contrary, in itself his work consists precisely of *creating anxiety and confidence*, of creating attention. If this exists in advance, then he will either believe that his art is stronger than it really is or be acknowledging that he has lost contact with his creative activity. This is why the modern form of success, which is not based upon the direct effect of art itself but on a purely mythological recognition through indirect (in artistic terms) sources of information, can be inhibiting to artistic development, if one is not able to look behind the scenes and locate direct experience again.

However, as it is precisely the instant artist reaches this personal or indirect success that he gets in the way of the power elite's demand for attention, it is here that the power elite must either get him in its service as its charming representative or have him stamped as a criminal. The latter solution seems to be the least damaging to artistic development today.

On the other hand, the power elite cannot itself create attention around it. It has to have the apparatus that *advertises* under its control, and as this apparatus has been today industrially perfected to the degree that it can distribute its opinions to the great mass of people at a moment's notice, the power elite has become a slave of its own perfect apparatus incessantly demanding novelty from hour to hour. Because of its quantity, the new thus becomes more and more meaningless to the degree that there is no longer any place for the meaningful. The power elite has hereby become just as cheap and uninteresting as the data it needs to deliver. For this reason the artistic and creative elite is distancing itself more and more from this apparatus and simply refusing to read the newspapers regularly, listen to the radio or to see television and film, except on chance occasions. *To improve the level of these institutions would just be to trivialize the real creative areas, which demand a far narrower and more intense form of attention.* Therefore the development of art after the war can be seen not to have had its real creative development in the changing tendencies one called '-isms' before the war. Instead it is decentralizing itself, not into movements but into more or less closed *circles*. It is this necessary hermeticism that has protected the development of art in these years from the attention of the public, which has rather been gathered around a number of superficial pseudo-isms. Today the results of this long confined activity are beginning to spring up and overturn all the concepts. I believe that in this new development Nordic culture, in the shape of the Folk High School, possesses a perspective that can offer the soundest fertile ground, being a bulwark against the otherwise unavoidable aristocratizing of this movement, a movement which cannot be stopped anywhere in the world, even with imprisonments or bloody violence, because it has the strength and right to life.

The poor – the good – the best. The disorderly – the orderly – the extraordinary

Capitalist society's transition to socialism is above all characterized by the power elite's transformation from a force working against the masses, an upper class, to a group of officials administering for and ministering to the majority.

For an elite to have real power it must have rights and regulations other than those of the rest of the population, it must form an extraordinary order. As this monopoly is abolished in modern democratic society, the administrative posts can only be occupied by the best amongst the mediocre, chosen from the good citizens. The disorderly and the extraordinary, the poor and the best are excluded automatically by the administrative hierarchy, except in crisis situations where normal people give up because they are confronted with the abnormal they have learnt only to hate and fear. There is indeed no test that can indicate the extraordinary, because, in relation to the good, the best as a rule resembles the poorest. No doctor would be able to foresee who would become the best sports people. Not even something that simple can be ascertained and it is far less likely in more complicated areas. A chance X-ray investigation once revealed that all the Dutch football team had bone deformations, a weakness that perhaps in fact drove them to achieve the extraordinary. Thus the best are met by the poorest. It is almost a rule. Therefore good and proper people literally never offer anything extraordinary.

This fact has produced the strangest results in the United States, where there is a demand that known people, who thus represent the extraordinary societal group, are immediately displaced if it comes to the people's notice that they are

204 The Natural Order and Other Texts

not at the same time more proper and normal than the great majority. This results in the public having the right to nose into the most intimate private affairs of known personalities, and the most unattractive form of hypocrisy we have yet experienced. This tendency to socialize the so-called private lives of known people has spread to Europe too, and in its false 'humanity' plays an enormous role as a means of keeping in the broader population's eye. The 'power elite' has gradually had to give in to the fact that so-called 'public opinion' plays a more and more dominating role in modern society and do what it can to appeal to it. It is here that it then suddenly collides with another group that it has hitherto been able to avoid noticing, a group it calls 'the professional celebrities', and which is simply those people that one likes and is interested in, not for what they are or have, but for what they do directly.

The human being owns himself*

A human being's variable capital is his life. If this life were not his own personal property, then the concept of exploitation could not be formulated at all, and a socialist idea would never have come to light. This does not, however, mean that socialism would thereby have been excluded. There are primitive socialistic societies where no one has any inkling what socialism is. Indeed, even highly cultured societies like the Egyptians and the Peruvians seem, in certain periods at any rate, to have had a socialistic structure.

The human being's only value is the development of his own life possibilities and of whatsoever else interests him. Every hour that he is forced to do something that does not amuse him is stolen from him, if he has to act in others' interests and not work voluntarily as a gift to others. The rules for this course of action have already been laid down: it is a matter of the production of things that are seen to be necessary for the maintenance of life. If, on the other hand, it is a matter of entertaining others, of amusing and carrying out something that is not useful, then the whole affair is arranged differently. No one has the right to force people to do that kind of thing. This is the reason for the rising opposition towards phenomena like prostitution. On the other hand, one cannot force people to be entertained by something they do not wish. Here freedom rules. Therefore no one can be exploited by entertainment, regardless of how dearly he has paid for it. He can be cheated, fooled and swindled by the entertainment not being as promised. But that is something quite different. This is part of his right to and possibility of criticism.

Artistic critique and scientific control are two dialectical activities that work directly against each other. What characterizes the newest industrial development is that through automation it has become more and more subordinated to scientific control. The results of this control can be compared with actuality to give a basis for a scientific critique, and it is this scientific critique which is more and more identified with the concept of the critique itself, so there is agreement that a critique can be rejected because it is not scientific. That a critique is scientific is to say that it is unartistic, and therefore the rising monopoly of science as a critical activity is a growing indifference and downright disdain for artistic critique. We can therefore see that it is artistic critique which is in rapid dissolution to a far higher degree than art itself.

Control is *constant* attention, an attention without variation, which is thus changed from a value to a quality. Now it so happens that a machine can achieve a constant of attention that no human being can approach. The old opposition between the worker and the inspector hereby begins to crumble away. If society has been divided between the known and the unknown who have to know the known, then we become aware that *the relationship between master and slave is based upon the master having to know his slave and to direct his attention incessantly at him,* whilst the slave must do his job without having his attention directed at anything other than the things he is working on. Thus the master has to have his attention constantly directed at the slave, but also finds himself in the humiliating situation that every time he needs to attract the slave's attention he has to shout loudly. At the same time this attraction of attention acts as a cessation of production and is thus always something negative and irritating to both parties. This is both disturbing and unjust.

On the other hand, scientific control has no direct critical effect. It just states. Instead of being unjust it is absolutely ruthless. It has become unartistic. In the belief that the master is a slave-driver by desire and need and lust for power, the working class, which has never been interested in psychology, has made its catastrophically wrong calculation. On the strength of its own programme, it has brought about the development towards scientific control which is taking place today, and therefore has to see itself being reduced to a more and more insignificant social phenomenon to which no one need direct his attention. It will either find itself implicated in this new development or there are only two other possible reactions: that it will want to hinder a natural advance that cannot be avoided in the long run and so become a reactionary and braking factor, just as when the craftsmen in their time attempted to storm the factories and destroy the machines, or it will demand the opportunity to lead *a new productive double existence* in automated industry as well as in an artistically creative production. This tendency is not unknown either. It was in this

206 The Natural Order and Other Texts

direction that the Englishmen Ruskin and Morris pushed the opposition to the industrial degradation of people as well as of objects of utility. *It is today generally recognized that the beginnings of all modern design came via Jugendstil and Functionalism.*

Artists have never given up their critiques and for once the modern working class is now standing on the dividing line. Is it to take up again the connection with artistic critique and participate in giving it a creative development, or what?

I would like at the same time to stress that such a development appears impossible except on the basis of the Folk High School movement and by a radical development of its structure, and thus, together with the English, *uniting* the two critical tendencies, the artistic and the intellectual, which each on its own has meant so much in the development of modern Western European democracy, but is today played out as an individual role.

When after the last war there was a desire to rebuild the old Bauhaus under auspices of the Scholl Foundation, this was done in connection with a Folk High School on the Nordic pattern. The leader of this so-called new 'Bauhaus' was the Swiss architect Max Bill. As this combination is precisely the only possible solution with perspectives for the future, I went in for a collaboration when it was about to open in 1953. This was refused with the reason that the new 'Bauhaus' should be a 'technical craft school' without any connection at all with the Folk High School. Modern design could not have anything to do with free and spontaneous creative artists.*

The lack of foresight that characterizes all the so-called left-wing intelligentsia in its patterns of action after the war has thrown Germany into the arms of the most conservative intellectual movements. My critique of Max Bill was only utilized – by an efficient intrigue – to get him chucked out of the school he had built himself and have it given over to an absolutely undangerous reactionary nullity, and the same thing has happened with the Folk High School. Today in Germany, Nordic thought is oppressed with all available means. Even the books of Vilhelm Grønbech,* which are officially in the libraries, cannot be borrowed because they are always 'on loan'. No one knows to whom. One just knows that it is not to the readers. To my mind, such a fact is far more indicative than the lacking translations into German of Ibsen and Selma Lagerlöf.* It is this accumulation that makes the breakthrough of Gruppe Spur so uncontrolled and brutal. With the 'Bauhaus defeat' in Ulm, modern development in Germany was inhibited to the advantage of a political rearmament of the reactionary forces for which the USA and France have use in that country. Only England and Denmark are now left. Are they to go into the same casserole too?

When Grundtvig in his time came back from England, his great enthusiasm was expressed in a critique that is valid to this day. This critique has never been taken up again because Danes do not seem to understand that criticism is a necessary part of a sincere sympathy. The sympathy is there but the sincerity has gone. I wish to change this again precisely because my sympathy for the English is sincere and therefore they will have to accept that I am also sincere in my criticism of them, as this criticism is at the same time a criticism of my own country – and in that way of myself. My criticism is directed at the horrible English ideas about the setting up of what they call a 'eurocracy'. It is about time to get that tissue of lies rooted out. Perhaps this will not succeed. Perhaps it will go as in Ulm. Then the only thing I would have to say is that there is a choice, an alternative and thus a personal *responsibility*. No one will be able to squeeze in under the excuse that they did it from necessity. Untalented and lacking artistic critique is not a necessity. It is defeatism.

Can the opposition between art and work be weakened

Today the modern state apparatus is the same as the state's finance ministry. This apparatus can best be compared with the systems we have for the consumption of water and gas, with the difference that the system is double. One network branches out over society and sucks up the results of work and collects them in its container, which is the national bank. The other network redistributes the same quantity for the maintenance and advancement of social activity. So long as the money is in the container, no one asks where it comes from. Money does not smell. No one knows what it is created from. The result is that one activity can work for the other, and be thereby exploited by this other. If this happens because of the socialist theory of equivalence, then no one suffers need, whatever he is working on, and then is little to say about this, unless certain people are occupied just to keep them occupied, even though the same work could be carried out swifter and easier. If this happens then it can no longer be a matter of work. It is about entertainment, and this entertainment has to be evaluated according to whether it is boring or exciting.

This is the new problem that is today confronting the modern trade union movement, and where it is about to enter into a conflict which will perhaps be just as violent as the one that occurred around the very foundation of the trade union movement, but with the difference that it will not only become a struggle

208 The Natural Order and Other Texts

against society's external rulers but to a far higher degree an inner conflict. This will condition whether the trade union movement will in the future become the worst brake upon modern social development or the solid mainspring in the new construction.

How this problem is to be solved, the trade union movement's own people must discover, but this cannot happen unless the whole of the trade union movement's history, practice and possibilities of development are taken up in an intense discussion by the most intelligent part of the workers' movement.

Consequently, *Christian Christensen*, the greatest theoretician of the Danish skilled workers' movement, was the first to demand a reorganization that liberated it from *its trade* character, which he perceived as a relic of the craft period, and go in for the introduction of non-trade *industrial unions* on the American pattern. How far he was right, I will not discuss here, as I have not the competence. I can, however, mention one thing that is against the industrial union. When the Italian architect Nervi was about to cast his new constructions for the UNESCO building in Paris, the American builders pointed out that there were no carpenters in the United States who had sufficient experience to build the necessary cast-forms. However, this changes nothing about the fact that industrial mass production has no use for professional craft education. Thus if the highest trade professionalism, despite everything, still plays a fundamental role today, it is not least in the creative activity of working out *models and patterns* for industry. We have already indicated that *it is the creative process which, even in industry, is the value-creating factor.* This experience consequently shows us that today it is in the most despised part of manual work, the craftsmanly elite, that the highest exploitation takes place. At the same time, we have drawn attention to exploitation being above all the prohibition on the disposal of one's own surplus production.

Idleness is the root of art

The modern trade union movement has to face the fact that the United States will not under any circumstances be able to ease its current violent production crisis. This is a direct reason why that country is pressing for the opening of a European Common Market where it hopes to distribute some of its surplus output. The threatening spectre of unemployment will in the future become a reality of an even wider scope than that which began in America after the First World War because automation has reduced purely quantitative work to a phenomenon which, in the long term, will not have nearly so much significance as it had pre-war. The trade union movement can solve this question, but only in one way. This solution is above all conditioned by the working class beginning to look artistically at things. That is to say that it stops looking at unemployment as a curse and understands that the curse in modern society is work totally without quality. The more workers who are liberated from this work, the more artists we will have. Art is not a necessity, it is surplus or luxury. *No wealth is more precious than the valuable unemployed human being, if he can be placed in a creative production that increases the wealth of the country and the culture.* If the Scandinavian trade union movement were to begin today to prepare a development where the concept of relief work was erased from the programme and replaced by collective luxury work, then it would become a model for the whole world. This is dependent first and foremost upon to how great a degree the leaders of this movement have the understanding to draw the consequences of the special strengths in the Scandinavian workers' movement and to conquer the traditional dislike in Scandinavian culture towards collective luxury building.

If I were here to bring out something that I would call typically Scandinavian in the social perspective, then I would define it as the union of the popular and the celebratory, in the sense of the opposition between work and festivity. The current development within modern industrial society is going in quite the opposite direction towards a simultaneous mixture of work without quality and entertainment without value, so that everyone lugs around a shrieking pocket radio in the woods, on the beach, in the street, in the kitchen, in bed, on the cycle and in the car. I have stated a certain resistance to this fusion and this is connected with my feeling that Scandinavians are the only people who, like the Negroes in the United States, still really understand what a festivity is, and demand and understand what has to be offered by the individual on such an occasion. But I will not deny that I have also found people who are ashamed of this ability in us.

Social law decides the behaviour necessary for every individual to have the right to live in society. What he has to do and what he has no right to do. In a democratic society, this law is based on the concept of equality, which decides the equal rights and responsibilities of everyone before the law. Right in itself, developed for its own significance, can only be a prison of duties, the suppression of freedom. Therefore it is only the freedoms and the liberating element in life that can justify laws and rules. In itself freedom is unjust, and it is only that positive injustice called art and beauty which gives the system of rights any justification at all.

There are people who are boring and others who are interesting and amusing,

210 *The Natural Order and Other Texts*

and some are even downright exciting. A complete scale is found even in the most primitive and archaic community: stimulators who inspire, passives who look on and grumblers who annoy. Incredible numbers of people are to be found who cannot amuse themselves, but would nevertheless like to be amused. Few, perhaps, are able to liberate their inner energies without being influenced by an outside force. But there are people who just by their presence radiate an energy that seems to illuminate the surroundings. Such people are especially sought after by the community on festive occasions. They could be hunters, fishermen or whatever, and they often use some highly strung energy and are sought after so often that they neglect their practical work. If one values them as shamans, they will probably be helped. But today they are utilized and if they cannot manage existence then they are spat upon. This is the original and the natural state that even today shapes the group called artists.

We have deliberately avoid calling art a trade, for it is irrelevant what an artist makes. It depends upon how it is done. He who does it best regardless of what he does, is an artist in his area. [...] Every artist is king in his area, regardless of whether it is the underworld, industry or music. It must however be added that this perception of art is only typical in Germanic culture, and only covers the talented, not those of genius.

A peasant for a new time is standing in our paddock.* He is a boring fellow

In 1947 the Danish Social Democratic Party set up a committee to investigate the possibilities of an active and contextual cultural politics. In 1953 the programme for this was published in the form of the book *The Human Being in the Centre*, with an introduction by Hans Hedtoft. In a section called 'Cultural democracy', Julius Bomholt writes,* 'It must be recognized that it is often the loner who leads the way, not least in the cultural area. Therefore there must always be ample place for *the experiment*, not just in scientific areas, but in all fields of cultural life. The big institutions have the responsibility of making room for the experiment so that an authoritative stiffness from thinking in grooves and acting from habit must never come in. The free and perhaps now and again challenging experiment could blaze the trail for things that then become the property of all.

The big, trail-blazing talents are apparently relatively few. It is therefore a matter of them, regardless of the group of society from which they come, reaching positions that allow them to carry out work for which they have a talent. And then it is a matter of preserving the elite in the popular community, so that the elite performance is given its due. An elite can never in itself be enough...

The cultural ideal is not to get into a culture of passive enjoyment. The goal is this: that as wide circles as possible enter actively into cultural work – each person in *his* own field – so that this is not talk of cultural work *for* the people but *by* the people...

The whole of community life needs a thoroughgoing reorganization. Most communal buildings were built for general assemblies, informative meetings and dances. There is now a need for a community building for the parish or city quarter, the comfort of which is as high as the modern home, and where there is not only room for the discussions of the elders and the dances of the young. It is not enough to have a space for one-sided, intellectual activity and another for one-sided entertainment. A building is needed where people can meet in their leisure time when it suits them, and where they have the possibility of satisfying some of the hobbies they are taken up with, and where the entertainment has the character of a club.'

It would be wrong to maintain that since this has been discussed, nothing has been done in the outlined direction, which in many ways resembles what I myself had imagined in the foregoing pages. An artistic cultural centre like Louisiana could be said to be unique both in its kind and in its effectiveness, and yet it limps along.* Anyone can see that it is limping, and that it in reality was, on the whole, going in the wrong direction, so that we stand where we, where even the Folk High Schools, to which Julius Bomholt himself has been, today have to declare our bankruptcy.

It would be easy to indicate how indifferent Danish cultural institutions have been to artistic experiments in this period. To allow experimenting artists, who are today celebrated as the nation's heroes, go on unemployment benefit for many years is a strange way of preserving the elite in the popular community. Yet how altogether irrelevant this is in relation to it having being there and having introduced the very concept of experimental art into international arguments around the problem of art. All reproaches are irrelevant today, when it is a matter of finding the way to our own weaknesses and getting help for them. This can only be done by a dispassionate analysis of most current norms of action.

The most remarkable thing in 'the contribution to an active cultural policy' discussed here is that the concept of cultural policy has not meant civilized politics, and that culture is not identified with civilization. For a Scandinavian this is obvious, but it is precisely this separation that has brought the research within Scandinavia's human sciences into conflict with the rest of the world, where it is maintained that civilization and culture are and must be the same.

Civilization is a quite particular form of culture. It is a centralized city culture. If the representatives of the Danish working class recognize the opposition between culture and civilization, then they are recognizing thereby that agriculturalists are on a level with themselves and at the same time in a different situation. The Russian, American and Southern European agricultural policies are underdeveloped because they only reckon with civilization or urban culture as culture. If the Danish agricultural organizations today wish to get into the economic and political community with the rest of Europe, then they must know that this special Scandinavian perception of culture must thereby be relinquished.

How surprising it is that a flock of people who today ought to represent the most intelligent elite in European agriculture would sell their birthright, which even Marx and Engels discuss with respect, in such a way for a dish of spaghetti.

If one wishes to understand what has happened, then it is first necessary to understand the dynamic in the Nordic dialectic that would rather unite law and knowledge, unite rules of action with experience. It is this unity of wise customs that is called culture. But this unity must always stand in an opponent relationship to both art and renewal, and it was precisely this traditional opposition that Grundtvig wanted to mitigate with the help of the Folk High School method, and it is because this method was suppressed that the connection between culture and experimental renewal has not been established.

Today Nordic community life should have been so well-housed that the help we could offer the so-called 'underdeveloped countries' would have been to build something similar for them free of charge, but instead we are trying to buy into new markets according to the Marshall Plan. I have given myself so much inconvenience in order to demonstrate that, by renouncing any connection with the Nordic perception of culture, the Danish peasantry is first and foremost betraying itself, because I feel that it is my accursed duty to say so, not from any regard for the peasants, but because it is a question that in my opinion is of vital significance to the whole of humanity in relation to modern, technical development. The situation today has shown that the connection which exists between culture and experimental renewal in Scandinavia in Bomholt's conception is a shattered illusion, at any rate as far as Denmark is concerned. Culture is customs, and one does not customarily go and break one's own customs.

Topical additions

Art in the service of the object

In *The Natural Order*, I stressed that my triolectic arrangement demonstrated the necessity for the Latin culture to set up a dialectical opponent relationship between on the one side ethics and a fusion of aesthetics and science, and thus of subject–object, on the other. Nordic dynamism works in an opposition between the purely subjective or aesthetic and a fusion of ethics and science. It is this latter dynamic that has ruled the development of art since the end of the war, and has to an astonishing degree paralyzed French art.

In the last couple of years the French have gradually set up their dialectic in a new combination that suits them, a combination also reflected in their politics. I think I have demonstrated that such an arrangement is necessary for the renewal of dynamism in Southern Europe, and at the same time I have indicated that it is completely paralyzing and unusable in the North. If Scandinavia goes into the Common Market, then it will be precisely into the mechanism of this Southern Europe dynamism, which the French naturally wish to able to launch all over the world, so that they can turn the current which is going against them at the moment in the artistic area. That this has already happened in the USA, is shown by the new Latinized American theories and the peculiar stagnation that has come over American art life. It has been otherwise in Scandinavia. After having been afraid of what we ourselves had made before and during the war and having ignored ourselves a little since, in the last couple of years we have begun to find a way out and with such an explosive energy that a small country like Denmark has three art periodicals of conflicting characters going at the same time. Let us hope that such a colossal fermentation will not evaporate without us having reached a new stage in our artistic self-recognition. This will only be possible if we seek without prejudice to understand our strengths as well as our weaknesses in relation to other progressive tendencies.

In order to demonstrate the intense work being done on the basic problems in France, I would like to discuss a new published book by Robert Estivals, *L'Avant-Garde Culturelle Parisienne depuis 1945.*[*] In his study of *sincerity*, he has, without knowing it, arrived at a complementary relationship, which he does not, however, acknowledge could be perceived as complementary, but

214   *The Natural Order and Other Texts*

demands (like all Parisian avant-gardists) that it has to be solved in agreement with the Latin point of view. He says:

'Sincerity or the love of truth in art, as in science, forms part of the human consciousness's general dualism of subject–object and is used for both elements. For there seems to be exclusivity in a given situation. It is either sincerity about *the ego* or about *the object: the work. Everything seems to take place directly as if sincerity about the one leads to a complete or partial artificiality, according to the particular case, about the other.* Sincerity makes what it targets its goal and makes the rest into more or less indifferent means.'

Here is concentrated the whole problem about the centuries-old opposition between Southern and Northern European culture. If we maintain that the sincerity has to be in the action, in the movement, and seek our refinement there, then Latin culture on its side always seeks it in the thing, the work.

It is this strict demand for sincerity in the work, that is the key to understanding the construction of The Six, and also of the Catholic Church. However, it was the recognition of personal sincerity that brought Hammarskjöld to the top post in the UN. Here the choice stands. If one is insincere both personally and about one's work, but nevertheless wishes to attempt to enter a collaboration where a particular form of sincerity indicates the rules of the game, then one can only destroy the game for both parties. If, in order to be in a game, one gives up the rules by which one yields one's best, then one destroys oneself.

Estival's critique of the subjective-expressive art which has come forward since the war shows that Latin people can just as little understand the subtlety in subjective sincerity as we are able to comprehend the finesses of objective sincerity. When he sets up an opposition between the egocentric and the sociocentric cultural idea, he cannot abstract from the hierarchical system which in the Latin perception identifies society with a *centralized* construction. When he says that the egocentric artist who perceives himself as the goal, and must therefore perceive others as a means for himself to be great by elevating him above the others and becoming known and rich, and in this connection uses the painter Mathieu as an example, then he shows precisely how impossible it is for the French to understand what has happened in art in the last twenty years.

The French understand Nietzsche's Zarathustra, but they have never read Gustav Fröding's answer to Nietzsche,* and if they had they would not have understood it. The French understand the Germans, but they believe that Scandinavians are just a sort of naive and confused Germans. Sartre believes that he has understood existential choice, and yet he is of the opinion that *to* *behave* as if one is personally sincere is the same as really being so. He is forced to overlook this inexactitude in order to be able to unite anything at all existential with French philosophy and thought processes. This is the reason why that all his philosophy ebbs out into happy nonsense. Pascal's nose is sticking out.

To the Northerner, bragging self-promotion is a sign that one has not one's centre in oneself. If one has to stand on the heads of others to be great, then this is a sign that one feels small. The same is the case if one cannot be oneself unless one has the heads of others chopped off. We have not sufficiently prepared the rest of the world for this collective and decentralized socialism, this valuable and special character of community feeling, and it is, perhaps for this reason, overlooked, although Scandinavians have never allowed any insult against it. Let us hope that the political facts do not necessarily show that I am right.

Originality, fashion and style

What characterizes art and cultural life in Scandinavia is the opposition between the strict, inexorable demand for personal originality and at the same time a just as bone-hard, conventional feeling of style. These two demands stand in their opposition without any reconciling transition at all, and when such a transition has to be created, we become unsure, fumbling and ridiculous in the eyes of others. This form of transition is called fashion.

In Scandinavia there is an instinctive disgust for everything that can be perceived as fashion. In Paris it is just the opposite. In his definition of the avant-garde, Estivals demands as one of the conditions to be so recognized that it is generally acknowledged by society as such. Those who precede the avant-garde are precursors, scouts and freebooters. This is the reason why the French, with a good conscience, can describe the English founders of Impressionism, Constable and Turner, as precursors. Of course, such a description from a need to find the original point is meaningless, that is, for us.

That something original becomes *fashion* means that it becomes *method*, that there are certain fundamental processes that can be described, learned and discussed. It is only when an artistic experiment has reached this point that it begins to interest the French, indeed, that it has any existence at all for them, and it is at this point too that the phenomenon loses interest for Scandinavians. The French can only get interested in something original or meaningless, in whether one can enlarge it with one method or another when there is method in

216 *The Natural Order and Other Texts*

the madness. Northerners cannot value a method unless it is innate and stripped of madness. But at the same time we are not afraid of the happy insanity that the French call raging madness. Northerners stand completely paralyzed before the ability of the French to put system into a madness without giving a thought to the whole thing being idiotic. This is the reason why Paris is the centre of fashion. We find the whole of the French thought process, which is based upon the significance of fashion, in Descartes' *La methode*, which could just as well be called *The fashion*, its ideological elaboration.

To criticize fashions and methods and reduce them to their innate form has always been the Scandinavians' strength. As early as in medieval Paris, the Danish institution was famous for its solid activity in this area, whilst at the same time the Nordic group was regarded as the strongest supporter of reaction. That this perception was one-sided is because the original personalities in the Nordic constellation always fell outside *the normal parameters*. But they were nevertheless there. This always disturbs not only foreigners, but also Scandinavians themselves. It is astonishing to see that Georg Brandes, whilst maintaining that Scandinavians have *always* been half a century behind others, was *himself* not only a Danish but also a European pioneer for a long period. Either we have to come to terms with our special dialectic and learn to make ourselves conscious of and use in a fertile manner its *anti-methodical method*, or we have to subordinate ourselves to fashion. We are not able to do the latter except by dissimulation. It is precisely on this point we have to learn sincerity about ourselves. This sincerity consists in the recognition that we cannot do without Paris, but at the same time we cannot have anything at all to do with Paris except in certain passing situations. To acknowledge the significance that Paris has for us means that we are learning how the French treat the cultural problem from another point of view.

Something that struck me most forcibly when I first went to Paris was the French's strange love of the angled. I wondered how many edges they could get on a hand-basin, and it was the same everywhere. Contacting French intellectual life is like touching a hedgehog with all the spines out. When one comes from Scandinavian intellectual life where everything is about getting as smooth a surface as possible, then one understands nothing at all until one begins to comprehend that there is method in the madness and grasps why the French love the sharp-edged.

We cannot avoid seeing something artificial and mendacious in the sharp-edged way it is possible to control and make merry so effectively with public opinion. On the other hand, it is even more dangerous for Scandinavians to deny that the peaks and high points that really *have* existed in Nordic culture, but which have always been carefully broken off, have ever existed. That would be just as ridiculous as it would be to paste them on again and deny that they were ever broken off. For they would never get them to sit really firmly again, regardless of how much glue was used, and in Denmark a lot of glue is used.

I have now begun a quite different experiment. I am acknowledging the continued break with the smooth body and beginning to collect the broken-off peaks, the extreme, the rejected outer points in Scandinavian culture together, and then I will attempt to see the pattern they form in themselves. The result of this line of procedure has already been to form new and unexpected pictorial elements that cast quite a new light over Scandinavian cultural life. This is truly almost too exciting: like a jigsaw puzzle where one suddenly begins to see the pieces emerge here and there from the confusion, and if one can thus find new and surprising images, then one loses the desire to make them oneself. But perhaps I will have put my foot so well and truly in it that there will no longer be any artistic or creative significance in devoting my time to it. The top shoots of the Scandinavian elite must then continue to make do with only being able to develop in those countries where the development of top shoots is reckoned to be the only important method of cultural development, or, to put it more correctly, Scandinavians must make do with stressing continually that 'they came from here'. We did not have room for them, but we are nevertheless proud of them.

ASGER JORN

LUCK AND CHANCE
DAGGER AND GUITAR

> Why does my Don Juan mix
> Fine poison in his brush-strokes
> And in his daughter's beauty?
> Don Juan answered me:
> I paint thus, Donna Bianca
> Because it amuses me so to paint.
> *C.J.L. Almqvist**

Report no. 3 of the Scandinavian Institute of Comparative Vandalism, 1963

To Susanne

Why?
[Addition 1963]

I was once asked by a Frenchman, 'Why then have you begun to publish books in Danish when you have an international public?' I answered that I wrote because it interested me to write, but without any belief that I was offering anything important in that area. I therefore stay modestly in Silkeborg and if there is something in what I write, then it will probably seep out.

This was only a half-truth. In its development, any new idea will be connected to its point of origin, to the environment from which it has grown, but it will belong to the environment where it meets a resonance. It is a tradition that all significant Scandinavian ideas are only taken seriously the day they come back as a resonance from abroad. This has the effect that Scandinavian intellectual life is strangely homeless and is seen only in an indirect relationship to the environment from which it has grown, direct connection only being established to the international resonance.

It therefore so happens that Scandinavia receives its own impulses, which could have been directly developed from within, but were put out of mind until a later and far less advantageous stage, as something already recognized and utilized from abroad. This, in the main, seems to me to have been the case with all the artistic development around COBRA. But COBRA was just an intermezzo. We have not yet come to the most important thing and it is my conviction that this rests largely upon something new which began in Scandinavia after the great French Revolution, America's secession from England and the socialization of Eastern Europe, upon a particular appreciation of what in this period we in the North have regarded as the most important use for our freedom.

Through its conception of international law Scandinavia has played a central role within the UN. Today that organization is dead and powerless. At the same time, the popular shaping of the organization of Scandinavian private life celebrated great triumphs. This has been recognized and imitated everywhere. However, there are limits to how long one can maintain interest around this subject. Other important problems have arisen, above all about the areas of spiritual well-being and personal independence and enjoyment within the general way of life and social urbanization of the population. Here, I have demonstrated that the Nordic Folk High School concept has become the acid test as to whether we also have something to show and offer in this new complex of problems.

Therefore it is not because I believe that it will have any important

222 The Natural Order and Other Texts

instantaneous meaning that I have sent out my ideas in Danish. The silence about this particular book, which came out ten years ago, is sufficient proof of this. Why then reprint it? As a rule, a large edition is intended for a large circle of readers. However, it can also have the opposite purpose: by a wider distribution giving it better possibilities of reaching the individual for whom it was written and whom no one knows.* In a true democracy the many also have obligations towards the few.

Er irrt der Mensch so lange er strebt
Goethe

FOREWORD 1952

The extreme phenomenology of aesthetics and its personal, humane, social, natural and objective relativity is the subject of this little study. It is equipped neither with bibliography nor with references simply because there is nothing to refer to, as the grouping of the phenomena attempted here has no precedents, but represents something new, when regarded as a system.

A contrary reason is the situation that the knowledge from which this system of definitions is constructed is so elementary and so generally known that references to the details are not necessary to anyone who has occupied himself a little with aesthetics. The commentaries on the aesthetic perceptions of others briefly sketched in the book were in fact added after it was written and have changed nothing in the picture as the whole.

That a fleeting glance at Salmonsen's Encyclopaedia *is all I required to support me theoretically is not because I am an opponent of knowledge but in order to have present elementary knowledge or, one could even say, that knowledge left when one has forgotten all one has learned. This represents what an aesthetic artist has normally and abnormally come across in almost twenty years' activity in the aesthetic production of art.*

Within the natural sciences, all scientific results are worked out on the basis of experimental practice in the area under analysis. This has not hitherto been the case within aesthetics and this has given aesthetic research a distortion I am here attempting to correct.

Some years ago, the undersigned published Unknown Truisms about Art, *the posthumous manuscript of a lecture by the deceased painter Immanuel Ibsen.* * *That title would also be suitable to this current work, the direction of which was already indicated in my article in the catalogue to* The Line's *exhibition in the Copenhagen University Students' Union in 1939 and in the article 'Intimate banalities' in the art periodical* Helhesten, *no. 2.* * *That Dr. Sigurd Næsgaard's scientific rejection of the principle of psychological sublimation lies behind these showdowns with principles of formal beauty, to the advantage of the principle of beauty of character in art and theory, is a special pleasure for me to point out, even more so because I believe there have been have many extensive and sound consequences for me from this liberation.* *

This study is a return to a starting point after having covered a number of

224   The Natural Order and Other Texts

other and perhaps more deeply underlying artistic problems, especially in architectonics, in a series of articles in Danish, Swedish and Dutch magazines, all inspired by the Swedish architectural professor Erik Lundberg's new theory about 'The language of architecture'.*

These articles on architectonics were gradually infused with a growing interest in general elemental or primitive phenomena in the histories of art and religion, an interest which resulted in, amongst other things, some articles in the periodical Cobra (Revue internationale de l'art expérimentale) *and in a special study of the significance of animatism as a starting point for poetry and cultic development in the book* Golden Horn and Wheel of Fortune.*

As a study in the dramatic phenomenology of animism, which is identified with the kernel of aesthetics, the current work is thus a counterpart to the work on animatism, posed in an opponent relationship, drama versus poetry.

From this introduction as well as the study as a whole, it will appear that the points of views advanced here are by no means unknown. One could directly say that everyone has them, even if no one will acknowledge them. To advance them here, therefore, is not a question of knowledge but of audacity. Why hasn't one had this audacity before? It can only be explained as a question of historical maturation.

Is the fruit I am offering here now ripe? Has it reached the point where the core is capable of germination and giving birth to new possibilities? This cannot be said to be so at this moment, but it is also quite immaterial. One swallow does not make a summer, but it is a portent of summer regardless of whether it has itself come too early to take part.

It is said that man is an apprentice and that fear, suffering and danger are his teachers and therefore the day that danger no longer exists man will no longer learn. However, we learn best from our sufferings, and therefore one always has a tendency to judge the generation whose mistakes one experiences on one's own back with the most intense criticism. This is a natural movement. However, even if my work represents a reckoning with the inter-war generation's mistakes and weaknesses in particular, I hope I can avoid going to the other extreme. I hope I will be successful in stressing the narrow-mindedness of both the old men of our time, the rationalists, and their predecessors, the naturalists, as it comes out partly in their mutual contradictions and partly in their contradictory attitude to subjectivism, which is the starting point of this work, albeit established on a materialistic basis. My hope is to be able to explain these contradictory attitudes and thereby unite them and turn them to account in a system having the force of novelty, effectiveness and objective truth, even though it is about a not easily accessible area of human activity.

To learn is to struggle but to learn is more than to struggle. To struggle is to make mistakes and it is these that one must learn from. If one wants to learn as long as one lives, then one must struggle as long as one lives. 'Experience is the name every one gives to their mistakes', says Oscar Wilde, but this is quite incorrect. He who struggles and makes mistakes without forgetting anything and without learning anything is perhaps the ideal aesthetician, but he is also a complete idiot. It is precisely the intention of this book to demonstrate that idiots are never complete and that aesthetics are not absolute and ideal. This gives future generations the possibility of learning from our mistakes, to which category this study possibly belongs.

Silkeborg Sanatorium
May 1952

Werd ich zum Augenblicke sagen:
Verweile doch! Du bist so schön!
dann magst du mich in Fessln schlagen,
dann will ich gern zu Grunde gehn!
Dann mag die Totenglocke schalten,
dann bist du deines Dienstes frei,
die Uhr mag stehn, der Zeiger fallen,
er sei die Zeit für mich vorbei.

Goethe

The sublime or informal
FOREWORD 1963

Time has passed since I published this book privately and much has happened. It is perhaps difficult to understand this book without understanding its preconditions, without understanding the naivety with which I had thrown myself into working for that artistic tendency we called COBRA, which at that point lay a splintered ruin whilst Christian Dotremont and I, despairing and mutually distrustful in the extreme, lay side by side in the beds of Silkeborg Sanatorium, discussing what had happened. Neither of us dreamt that despite everything we had realized something unique. Many of our enemies maintain this today, so there must be something in it.

My naivety consisted of the belief in a sound artistic development able to vary the normal and healthy without making holes in the rules. This was explained in my 'Discours aux Pingouins' in the first number of the COBRA *magazine. I felt that I had read Franz Kafka's thoughts and when, on several occasions in Suresnes in 1950,* ★ *a similarity between my pictures and Kafka's world had been intimated, I began an article intended to show the morbidity which arose in Kafka's world because of the struggle against tuberculosis.* ★ *The article was not finished before I myself lay in the sanatorium. It was surely that same reaction that at that time made me bristle before the few pictures I saw of Wols and deny their validity. I have to say that at that time I had the same reaction to pictures by Wemaëre.* ★ *This was why I did not think he had anything to do with COBRA.*

Today I can see that my whole world had suddenly dissolved and that I had had to come to terms with myself in the wreckage. Luck and Chance *is a handbook on the relationship between ship and wreck.*

To come to terms with illness is probably the most difficult thing one can ask a person to do in Scandinavia, where health is the big dream, and without meaning anything at all derogatory by it, I can today say the big sickly dream. This is a stage surmounted. I discovered that what is unsuccessful has in certain cases greater artistic value than what is successful. It all depends upon what is unsuccessful and what is successful, on how much has been attempted and how much, in spite of everything, has been done. But it has taken me ten years before I have dared to issue this book publicly. If my own reactions are taken into account, then you will understand that I myself doubted whether I had the right to place my conclusions before people who had not been through the events which would have given them the maturity to understand and I did not want to demand of anyone that they ought to have

228   *The Natural Order and Other Texts*

been in extremis. *Today I am publishing this book because I feel that the dominion of the threat of death with which modern politics tyrannizes the world is in itself a sickness from which we all suffer and which marks all our thought processes from morning to evening. If the authorities can inflict humanity with such a sickness, then one can also allow oneself to explain publicly how sick people deal with illness, for then that is a form of health. Today, when literature and art are introduced in schools and kindergartens, although sympathetic insight into them demands the greatest maturity (I have myself taken part in this jest), there are no longer stages of inauguration. This is a fact that all must reckon with.*

It was my intention to find out what the concept called aesthetics meant, as I could not come to terms with the identification between what is called the aesthetic and what is called the beautiful. Far less could I fill out the concept of aesthetics with the concept of form. There must exist a third concept essentially different from the formal and the beautiful which must be the extreme, the extreme form of aesthetics, something that must resemble the ugly and dangerous far more than the lovely and harmonious. I was able to include this extreme element into the framework formed by aesthetics because I turned back to the original definition of the aesthetic discovered by Baumgarten, namely, sensory impressions.

I originally thought that this area was quite novel and uncultivated, that it was completely new and virgin territory. In the past few years, I have discovered that I am not the first to have been roaming in these areas, which have had various names. However, they appear to me to be like the Vikings' data about Vinland: not in an organic connection with the point of departure. The establishment of this connection seems to be possible only if the reports of the various explorers are gathered together.

The first time I had a suspicion that, in some way or other, I had a distorted attitude to the matter was on reading the art historian Werner Haftmann's characterization of me as a 'nocturnal' person, which I took to mean a dark painter.* This shocked me enormously, for my yearning for the light is perhaps the urge of which I am most conscious. However, do the light people of the South seek the dark? Because they are light, does their yearning give them a dark exterior, and are the people of the North dark people who look light because of our yearning for light, like shoots of potatoes in a cellar longing to be green? The thought was strange to me, but it struck me that there had been something about a nocturnal aesthetic in Kant and when I found it I suddenly discovered what this book is about.* It deals with the sublime, the yearning for the high, and then I also understood why I had been *speculating so much to discover what is meant by the high, what it is to raise oneself up.*

The sentence of Kant that had taken hold of me goes thus: 'Night is sublime, day is beautiful'. It is strange to see Kant setting up a contrast between two such aesthetic categories as night and day in this true dialectical manner. He also says that 'The sublime moves, the beautiful *charms. The sublime must always be great; the beautiful can also be small. The sublime must be simple; the beautiful can be adorned and ornamented, polished and embellished. A great height is just as sublime as a great depth.'*

That last statement is something that has disquieted me ever since Jens August Schade once confided in me that one can fall so deep that one begins to fall upwards. For the question is this: if the fall continues past zero then would the continued fall be a rise in relation to zero or to when one reaches the bottom and comes to a halt and then begins to drift upwards again? Is this new uplift closest to being considered a new fall from grace? Then a fall must be a question of from or to, if it is to have any meaning. If one has once fallen down to something, then one cannot fall down anymore, but the possibilities of falling from are endless. Therefore, in its pure essence, the fall seems always to be a falling from. However, as a fall is always in a relation to a centre to which it can be defined as fall, then a fall to earth is simply a question of gravity, whilst a fall away from the earth is the true fall out into the dark, but it is a fall which, judged from the earth's surface, has to be perceived as an elevation, a sublimation. It must be this self-elevating fall that is called Lucifer, the radiant or radiating fall, the falling from.*

A passive body influenced by an external force can only take one direction, and the least difficult is the straight line. The straight line or road is the road of adaptation or falling to. However, a body under its own power can wind along the strangest roads, if it is able to lift itself over the conditions of fixed movements. The true falling from cannot therefore be characterized as a movement in a straight line oriented in the opposite direction to the line of conformation. It has been characterized as an unpredictable movement, like a fly loosed from a bottle. This is the reason why nothing sublime can be straight.

The straight [rette] *way is the direct way, and there is every reason to call the direct way the ethical way if one agrees that the judicial system* [retsvæsen] *has to do with ethics, that the judicial system is a particular form of ethics. I cannot see that the concept of ethics can have any logical meaning whatever if this agreement is broken. When therefore Kant describes the sublime* [ophøjede] *and with it the elevating* [højnende] *as a particularly*

230   The Natural Order and Other Texts

radical form of aesthetics, then this has a direct relation to the wrong [urette].
*He says, 'The difference between the beautiful and the sublime quite obviously
depends upon the circumstance that the beautiful without any difficulty falls
under the schema of categories in which our capacity for recognition in the
aesthetic regard includes it. The 'sublime' behaves differently. It is formless
and unlimited.*

*Allowing this to act by itself causes both anguish and pleasure at the same
time. Our imagination, the task of which is to unite the parts of the given into
'one picture', into a completed perception, feels that it is barren before the
'sublime' object. In this impotence, our own insignificance and nonentity
becomes conscious as pure sensible being. But this is only possible because
we, in our reason, only possess the ability to comprehend eternally little, at
any rate, in ideas, and on a comparative scale. Through the impotence of our
imagination, supersensible (superior to our senses) nature comes to the
consciousness of our reason with pleasure. Whilst we, as pure sensible
beings, are lying in the dust, we feel as great as purely moral beings who have
focussed their actions upon endless tasks.'*

*Even though I cannot see what this pleasurable megalomania has to do
with morals, it is precisely what I have sought to define in my book. The
contrast to Kant is that I maintain the fundamental significance of interest to
all aesthetics. When Kant emphasizes that 'from concepts there is no
transition to feelings of pleasure or displeasure' then I admit this willingly,
whilst at the same time asserting that to a large degree there is a transition
from feelings of pleasure and displeasure to concepts, and that no new
concept is ever created which has not first been experienced as a symptomatic
demand provoked by feelings of pleasure and repugnance, then signalled as
a phenomenon through signs, and finally laid down as a concept. It can also
be quite rightly established that this movement is irreversible. You cannot
square the circle, but the circulation of the square explains itself, because the
square only exists as a function of the circle, whilst the circle does not exist
as a function of the square.*

I have pondered upon the question of the right [rette], *because in
Scandinavian usage this can only mean the straight, the correct or what is
before one, the front side, the right in contrast to the wrong side or obverse,
whilst the right* [rette] *side in all other European languages on the other hand
is to the right* [højre] *(German – recht, French – droite, Italian – destra), and
I would perhaps make linguists despair by maintaining that right* [højre] *is the
same as upwards or higher* [højere]. *No one will make me believe that a
Scandinavian does not identify, perhaps more or less unconsciously, that*

which is to the right with something that somehow represents or should represent something higher [højere]. *I can just as little be moved from the idea that these associations influence our political conceptions of what you can expect from right and left. That today this political preconception is more and more self-neutralizing is another matter, but it seems to me that popular left-oriented politics suffers incredibly from having symbolized the right* [højre] *wing as an elevated* [ophøjet] *and useless and thus aesthetic societal group. By this manoeuvre they have, so to speak, cut themselves off from an aesthetic or higher* [højere] *endeavour. It was this utilitarian inferiority complex which C.J.L. Almqvist and N.F.S. Grundtvig sought to forge weapons against.*

The 'picture' to which Kant refers, and by which one can compare and measure phenomena so that they become easy to grasp and beautiful, always gathers into a universal picture, a world picture. *When the earth was flat and the heavens arched over it with the sun and the stars in their tracks, this world picture was called religion. The new world picture of the Renaissance, with the earth revolving around the sun, came into conflict with religion, which has ever since been working away on its own, independent of the new world picture, on the basis of moral dimensions corresponding to the flat terrestrial disc. At the same time, moral and juridical evolution has replaced the principle of charity with the principle of justice, except where it is a matter of extraordinary achievements. It is here that Kant's teaching on the aesthetic essence of the sublime could lead to a deeper insight. Today, humanity is leaving the earth's surface and we are into a sublime new world which has become larger by a falling away on all sides. Many people try to shut this out and limit their own little world to Birkerød.* However, he who has a sense for the painful pleasures of the sublime is already thrown into a struggle with this informal new world in order to work out its unknown forms. This new artistic rearmament will, as usual, evoke a strong dramatic social response, as the tendencies towards dissolution have strengthened the demands on the old forms beyond all possible limits. It is possible that attempts will be made to classify the ideas set out in this book as belonging to this category. I would submit to such a judgement, if it could be proved that they are based on a lie, for truth can never be old-fashioned.*

The touching enthusiasm with which the critics have declared themselves unable to understand what I have written has perhaps soothed some of the unintelligent people, but has at the same time disquieted several independent thinkers, who have allowed their disappointment over this failure to be publicly voiced. In order to avoid the problems I have accumulated becoming

232   The Natural Order and Other Texts

the reason that the view is obstructed again and to make the task easy for those critics who do not in principle read the books they review, I here give a compressed account of my thesis:

When I assert that interest *is aesthetic and not ethical, this is because it is impossible with any logical justification to demand that anyone be funny, entertaining or* interesting. *As interest cannot thus be an actual duty, a necessity or an ethical requirement, then it can hardly be demanded of someone that they interest themselves in anything unless that interest is functionally justified. Apart from this, it is impossible to prevent anyone interesting himself in anything. The only thing that can be forbidden is to* show *one's interests to others.*

In order to repair this weakness, society had discovered a number of delusions that have to be believed, making it possible to draw up unfounded demands and duties in common. Materialism has revealed this swindle (or pictorial art) in modern society, and the delusion that the social organism could be made to function by allocating these duties fairly, quite without them having anything to do with interest, leads it to function on a basis of neutral indifference. In reality this just means that one has to make people believe that what interests them cannot *be of interest to them, and that other things which do not interest them have in reality their profound interest. This is called upbringing. Upbringing is cult, and cultic freedom consists of the right to cultivate one's personal interests. This cultic freedom is not to be found anywhere, and so the question is how many personal interests the individual has that cannot be completely satisfied collectively. The critical point comes when someone moves over from the duties associated with really necessary functions to satisfying his immediate, unnecessary interests. If these pointless interests are collectively imposed as a duty, as the Church attempted to do in the Middle Ages, then true interest can no longer be found, only forced attention. One can carry on a bitter struggle to liberate quite small and indifferent interests. It is the greatness of the scope of your interests which warrants the scope of the freedom and the struggle. But how can you measure the scope and capacity of an interest? You cannot affiliate yourself to it from the goal you have set yourself, if that is new and unknown. Neither can you judge it from the result unless you have already acted and realised it. The Latin superstition that the end justifies the means is no more absurd than the Protestant one that it is the result that does so, for neither ends, means nor results really have anything at all to do with each other. They are three complementary worlds in a common unity. It is humanity's fate to live and act in this paradox, and to make people believe that there is no such paradox is the task of the politicians. The trick is to get the better of it without going to pieces or, more correctly, is to go to pieces and grow together again in a better way than before. That is the difficult trick.*

The understanding of this common denominator of complementarity in European culture is astonishing clear in the French economist Raymond Aron's book on the industrial society,* where he says, 'In Max Weber's thought process, relativism was attached to the idea he entertained of the real, an idea the origin of which was a certain Neo-Kantian philosophy. For him the whole of reality was informal.' Weber's demonstration of the indissoluble connection between Protestantism and Northern European and North American capitalism shows quite irrefutably the lines of direction that decide not only our economics but also our politics and our culture. The contrast to the Southern European system is illuminating.

Sigurd Næsgaard's criticism of the traditional theory of sublimation, which identifies the sublime with the refined when they are really opposites, in the light of Kant's aesthetic category and Weber's economic principle thus turns out to be of fundamental significance to the liberation and flowering of artistic development in Denmark, with which he was so passionately preoccupied. The elements for a conscious formation of a specific artistic principle of general significance are beginning to come together.

Paris 1963

The status of the aesthetic problems of the present day

> One evening I sat Beauty on my knees – And I found her bitter –
> And I abused her.
> I armed myself against justice.
> I fled. O witches, O misery, O hatred, to you my treasure was
> entrusted!
> ... Misfortune was my god. I stretched myself out in the mud. I dried
> myself in the air of crime. And I played some fine tricks on
> madness.
> And the spring brought the idiot's frightening laughter.
> ... – oh! every vice, anger, luxury – magnificent, that luxury – above
> all, falsehood and sloth.
>
> *Arthur Rimbaud*

The two unsolved problems hindering further progress in the systemization of the scientific research of aesthetics today are the declining ability to give the topic *a serviceable definition* and the difficulty in finding *the clear and tenable distinction between the object of aesthetics and the object of art*, especially in the question of the essence of dance, music, poetry and pictorial art, that is to say, *the essence of the fine arts*. As far as these are concerned, an understanding has been generally reached that they are not identical with the aesthetic, but merely *represent an especially effective and rarely failing technique for the exposition of aesthetic effects*. Moreover, in certain circles there is also a gradually dawning feeling that *the fine arts themselves never represent pure beauty, but are above all arts*, and as such always more than beauty, with an effect going deeper and transmitting more than the purely aesthetic. This is something we touch upon here in the indication of the ethical character of art and which is manifested in more recent art by *the pictorial content being moved from the aesthetic over to the magical*, even though this word has to be understood in a new meaning as the expression of power.

As far as the problem of aesthetic definition is concerned, then the difficulty lies in being unable to limit the aesthetic area to *an easily comprehensible field of activity* with a clear distinction between the true *methodical* activity of aesthetics and *auxiliary investigations* into other disciplines, economics, sociology, politics, biology, psychology, technology, religion etc., from which benefit and experience can be derived. Furthermore, the blurred boundary between aesthetics and art also causes *even the most rigorous separation between aesthetics and the other philosophical areas* (ethics, logic) *to have no objective validity* and to be based merely upon sensory illusion uncovered more and more by each new experience.

236　The Natural Order and Other Texts

If, in an attempt at empirical aesthetics, we take the road of experience to find the aesthetic object in the articles and laws of beauty, we immediately come up against resistance from *subjective judgement,* which perceives *the human being as a primary existence in relation to his thoughts.* This judgement, the individual's judgement, takes its point of departure in the individual's reaction to the sensed object, a precondition and a point of departure which no one can deny.

The objective synthesis

If *the individual judgement* necessary to construct an aesthetic doctrine *is to be coordinated with the aesthetic judgements of other individuals,* then this can only happen by getting behind these judgements in order to *analyse the common preconditions reflected in the internal psycho-physiological similarities and the bio-sociological dependence of the individuals,* as is done, for example, in medical science, to discover *the common human subjectivity or the community of inter-humane interest* which is a bio-physiological, sociological and cultural fact.

The wider question then becomes whether this organic community of interest extends out over the human into the vegetable and animal kingdoms, whether *the whole biological world can be perceived as a collected interdependence, a fellowship of interest, an organic subjectivity* and mutual necessity, and historically as an evolutionary unity, or, in short, whether we can *make aesthetics relate to the natural sciences.*

However, to achieve a real *objective aesthetics* it is necessary to demonstrate *a causal unity between the forms of reaction of the organic and the inorganic worlds* which reaches from the macrocosmic aesthetics of *the universe* itself to the *atom's* microcosmic reactions of an aesthetic character. If this is not possible, then the results of both subjective and objective aesthetics are worthless and the establishment of a scientific aesthetics impossible.

The synthesis for which I am here the spokesman definitively breaks with the intermixing of aesthetics and art theory, a break which is based upon new experiences and arguments, the most weighty of which is perhaps the recognition, derived from the development of modern art, of the value of so-called primitive art and the consequent understanding that *aesthetic recognition and any acquaintanceship with the idea of beauty, the understanding even of the difference between the thing and its depiction, is quite meaningless for elemental artistic creation.* As, into the bargain, it is apparent that modern aesthetic education, as known from the art academies, is directly restrictive to creative ability in art, these facts demonstrate that *not only is the aesthetic knowledge of our time worthless but also directly damaging* and thus, in other words, false.

The extreme definition of aesthetics

This acknowledgment, which is shared by all aestheticians, has gradually made it generally appreciated that *aesthetics should not be understood as a phenomenon exclusively connected with the fine arts. On the contrary, it represents one of our forms of existential experience*, its subjective *point of departure in interest* having forced science to perceive the object of aesthetics as impenetrable by exact, scientific research, so that it has to be perceived as something 'which can be described and to a certain extent limited, but not defined and computed, remaining a demonstrable and communicable "unknown", which can throw its light over one of the problematic forms in which our being exposes itself, and thereby have an instructive significance for art and criticism'.*

That this instructive significance is only to the detriment of both art and criticism has really nothing to do with science nor obviously the critics, but it involves artistic activity and the artists' working conditions themselves in the most painful way. Because of this inconvenience it must, of course, be *the artists* themselves who, by theoretical activity, have to intervene and change course about this point.

What have I then been able to change in this hazy picture? Apparently something quite insignificant, as I have only tightened up this 'aesthetic definition' *from being 'something unknown and enigmatic' to mean 'the unknown' or everything unknown and enigmatic.* By this clarification of the aesthetic object, it takes on not only a subjective and *existential* but also an objective and *essential* significance, from its smallest detail to its greatest context. This makes possible the establishment of the following outline, of which we will only have occasion in the following text to deal with the first half and point c. III.

238   The Natural Order and Other Texts

Brief outline of the fields of activity in aesthetic research

Thesis: The aesthetic object is defined as *the unknown*, and aesthetics as the empirical science of the reactions of the known to the unknown or the unknown, unexpected or uncontrollable reactions of the known.

1. Objective aesthetics
then becomes the empirical science of the immediate reactions of substances to other substances and of the character of the substance's macrocosmic and microcosmic phenomena towards the borders with the non-existent, and thus the effects of chance.

2. The aesthetics of the natural sciences
then becomes the science of the reactions of biological organisms to unknown, unaccustomed or unexpected impulses and of their abilities to invoke such impulses biologically.

3. The aesthetics of the human sciences
becomes the empirical science of man's experiential and recognitive reactions to everything unknown, divided over the subjects:

a. Psycho-physiological aesthetics
The empirical science of man's spiritual and physical reactions to everything unknown: 1. destructive, 2. passively negligent as well as 3. actively absorbent reactions.

b. Sociological aesthetics
comprises the empirical science of the societal group's positive, negative and passive reaction to the occurrence of the unknown in societal life and society's ability to invoke unknown phenomena in all areas, political, economic, technical, artistic, scientific, ethical, philosophical, cultural, ideological, religious, etc.

c. The aesthetics of art scholarship
This comprises the empirical science of man's expansive reactions to unknown external and internal impulses, as *aesthetic art* is defined as our ability to invoke and satisfy unknown interests, phenomena, things, thoughts and ideas.

The aesthetics of art scholarship is divided into two groups, the aesthetics of direct experience and the aesthetics of indirect recognition, which can be grouped as follows:

c.I. The aesthetics of human artistic action
The empirical science of human reactions to what *cannot* be done; the interest in creating and enjoying unknown things, thoughts and pictures created by people. With connections to psycho-physiological and neurological aesthetics in general, this is divided into:

a. The aesthetics of productive experience
The empirical science of the process of human creative experience, which develops in a dialectical relationship of opposition and dependence to:

b. The aesthetics of receptive experience
The empirical science of the human ability to absorb aesthetic art experiences. Both are developed in connection with the artistic material which represents:

c.II. The aesthetics of the art-work or the artistic means
The empirical science of the character of the art object and its aesthetic effect upon the producer and consumer, comprising:

a. The aesthetic character of technique in general.

b. Aesthetic technique or *the fine arts* which form:
1. *Psychological sensory aesthetics*
The empirical science of immediate sensory effects (sound, pitch, light, colour, form, movement, etc.)
2. *The aesthetics of mental conception*
The empirical science of the aesthetic effect of visual formulation and conception. This leads to the opposite of the aesthetics of experience:

c.III. The aesthetics of recognition
The empirical science of human intellectual reactions to what is not *known*. This is divided into two contrasting activities:

240 The Natural Order and Other Texts

a. *The aesthetics of fantasy and speculation*

The empirical science of the human activity of idea and thought in the treatment of subjects neither understood nor known and the reactions of people to the results of such speculations and fantasies.

b. *The aesthetics of scientific research*

The empirical science of human interest in and attempts to gather exact knowledge about hitherto unknown phenomena which can be analyzed empirically, as well as the abilities and means to do this, and the significance of this activity for human art and aesthetics in general.

The aesthetic phenomenon – summing up and definition

'Disinterested pleasure'

Kant defined beauty as 'universal, disinterested and necessary pleasure', but as pleasure is really nothing other than a kind of interest, we have to reject this self-contradictory definition and assert that *aesthetics is the interest in the unknown, the effect of which can be unpleasant as well as pleasant, antipathetic as well as sympathetic. This brings out feelings of distaste or delight which give us the opportunity to judge the object of the experience as either ugly or beautiful*, a biological reaction called attraction and repulsion in the mineral world.

The essence of aesthetics is unconditional and immediate interest or spontaneous reaction, and the aesthetic object is that phenomenon which invokes this immediate interest, whilst the aesthetic subject is the field of immediate interest.

Known and unknown

> Beautiful are the things we see.
> More beautiful are the things we understand,
> but by far the most beautiful
> are surely those we do not comprehend.
> *Niels Steno*

Only the unknown or the apparently and partially unknown can possess this aesthetic property. What one already knows is effective only through its recognizability and corresponds to those deeper, regular interests which, on the strength of their vital significance and regulatory essence, we call ethical interests.

However, as soon as we become aware that the known and the unknown are relative phenomena, the question then becomes whether we can connect them with anything at all. We could say that *the objectively known is everything that acts as facts, as impressions in the context of sensory material, and can be directly or indirectly sensed*. But therefore it is not certain that we know it, and as in itself this is a matter of acquaintanceship or transmission, we must find another yardstick for the known and the unknown. What do these two concepts really mean? The latter is derived from the former as its opposite, but this does not take us very far, and we already appear to have excluded in advance any possibility of an empirical analysis of this subject, as science, as is well known, is based upon the study of the comprehensible, the known or the actual.

242 The Natural Order and Other Texts

We are not, however, giving up, even though we will have to reduce the area of aesthetic study to the border phenomena between the known from which we start and the unknown, to the study of the unknown reactions of the known and the effect of unknown phenomena on the known.

Aesthetics perceived as interest in the unknown

> Habe nun, ach! Philosophie,
> Juristerie und Medizin
> und leider auch Theologie
> durchaus studiert, mit heissem Bemühn.
> Da steh' ich nun, ich armer Tor!
> und bin so klug als wie zuvor.
>
> *Goethe*

Aesthetics as the law of change

But what have we really embarked on here? Simply that *the true point of departure of aesthetics is the law of change, allowing the unknown and the new to arise in the universe and create evolution, whereas the known is the static cycle or law of immutability, which we have perceived as the ethical principle of nature.* Here immediately we are in the elemental philosophical conflict between compatibilists and incompatibilists, empiricists and idealists. The latter was a school founded by Socrates, who came to the conviction that 'we only know that we know nothing', that everything is unknown and thus aesthetic. We also know about the opposite school of determinists, and aver simply that they are both correct, in the same way as the scientists who quarrelled about whether light was rays or waves, since the law of change exists on the strength of and because of the law of immutability, in the same way as the radiant character of light is conditioned by its wave system, and the aesthetic principle of nature is precisely its radiant essence, the material's 'ideality' or *éclat*.

We have thus transferred the world of the metaphysical concept over to matter, but can this work? Yes, it depends exclusively on whether it can form a system and if this system, which we regard as *primary*, connects naturally with *the secondary* spiritual or metaphysical system to form a unit.

Subject or area of interest

The elementary metaphysical concept is the subject, normally defined as 'the conscious ego', the observing, thinking, feeling, active individual, and thus the human object. But if we take into account how humanity originated, this definition is too narrow. When did the human embryo begin to be a subject? The question is meaningless. *Here we will use the concept of the subject as a designation for any exclusive or limited sphere of interest in matter*, any

244 *The Natural Order and Other Texts*

system of action, any individuality. But the limited phenomenon in matter is what is called the object. *Object and subject should thus only be two different ways of perceiving the same phenomena and two different sides of their essence.* Quite so!

This subjectivity of matter or classification of interest can be called the qualitative properties of the material, and 'the feeling, thinking and observing properties' are just the most consummate and differentiated means of existence of this subjectivity or sphere of interest, which here on earth has achieved the greatest perfection in humanity.

Objective subjectivity

Objective science is the science of how matter thinks, about the spirit of matter. Subjective science could be called the science of how material feels, of the materials's interests or the material's soul, its enthusiasms or eros, its body-forming principle. This science of the objective subjectivity of the material, which makes it corporeally identical with the spiritual and thus perceives the spiritual as a physical phenomenon, is obvious and easily understood if it is really made clear what an object or a body is. We can buy the materials in a human body at a chemist's shop, but we cannot unite them into a human body, yet the human body endures even when the materials of which it is formed are renewed. One is the same even though one is someone else. We can shape a lump of clay into a vase and a sudden movement will change it again to a lump of clay. We can lay out a rail-track and constantly change all the material. Even if there are completely new materials, it is still the same track, the same region of interest, the same context.

The bodily perception of the soul

We are, however, in no doubt that the living person exists as a latent possibility in the material we have bought. Thus the impotence we feel before a dead person whom we wish were alive is not caused by the soul forsaking the body. That it cannot do. But by the human soul having disintegrated, so that we are unable to put it together again.

Therefore, unlike the spiritualists, we perceive *the visionary faculty,* the highest achievement of the aesthetician, not in the form of a detachment of the soul from its bodily mortal frame, but *as a superior and intense radiation and receptive activity with its unavoidable centre in the physical ego.* From this it follows that we evaluate the proficiencies acquired by this clairvoyance according to their ability to serve our actions. With this, our opponent relationship to spiritualism in its traditional form appears to be clarified.

The subjective context of material

The word interest means what is between certain phenomena and thus the context. We have defined subjectivity as interest or context.

Every cell in the human body is an object and at the same time an area of interest, a subject or acting individual. Cells are again part of the areas of interest of the organs which in fellowship form a human ego, body or individual, together with his mental equipment.* The individual is a part of the ego of the family, the group, whose common interest is given its self-conscious expression in its codex of action or ethics. Together all human groups, classes, peoples, nations and races form a joint human object, humanity, which is thus not an idea but an actuality, a body, an ego or subject, which is, for example, the common object of medical science and the very basis of actuality for the whole of technique and culture, the joint human interest. I call this perception Nordic humanism.

246 *The Natural Order and Other Texts*

Michelangelo and Leonardo da Vinci
Insertion 1963

> What seems incredible in the future is never so in the past.
> *René Clair*

Today, new horizons are opening in science, technique and research and are breaking down the old world. The situation is reminiscent of the Renaissance. The new expansion of space alone is a far more radical upheaval than the discovery of America. On the one hand, there is enthusiasm about this development, yet, on the other, there is the simultaneous demand that life should carry on as it has always done, that one can pretend that nothing has happened, and that our traditional ideas of progress have continued validity. Art is judged on whether it subordinates itself to its architectonic surroundings and architecture or whether it subordinates itself to nature's harmony without any understanding that what we call nature does not exist and could just as well be called 'god'. This latter Neoplatonism appeared after the last world war in order to create order amongst the remnants of the *fin de siècle's* confused productive expansion, which had reached its limits. The division of Europe by the Reformation wars offered the possibility of two opposing developments, the informal conquest of unknown regions and the Counter-Reformation's bound Baroque. The latter dominated art until the struggle of Neo-Classicism and Neo-Gothicism in the Napoleonic era released the modern artistic development.

In his essay on 'Neo-Platonic movement and Michelangelo' Erwin Panofsky writes, 'It is significant that Leonardo da Vinci, Michelangelo's adversary both in life and art, professed a philosophy diametrically the opposite of Neoplatonism. With Leonardo, whose figures are as free from restraint as Michelangelo's figures are "inhibited", and whose *sfumato* principle reconciles plastic volume with space, the soul is not held in bondage by the body, but the body – or, to speak more precisely, the "quintessence" of its material elements – is held in bondage by the soul.'[*]

When a professor of architecture holds up this bound Prometheus, whose most heartfelt sculpture is *The Slave*, in order to cast the dome of St. Peter's upon the head of an 'unsuccessful' monumental art stretching from Joakim Skovgaard, over Larsen Stevns and Hansen Jacobsen to Asger Jorn, then this Counter-Reformationist art of equilibrium is in a good academic tradition. It is just impossible to tell how the pseudo-Romanesque pastiche architecture in Viborg Cathedral could harmonize with the end of the previous century. If Skovgaard and Hansen-Jacobsen had also worked on Grundtvig's Church then there would perhaps have been one single initial attempt that one could use in one's evaluation. Why did Thorvald Bindesbøll not get any architectonic projects? Before I started the Aarhus decorative project, I emphasized the difference in our perception of style to the architects. They were satisfied both before and after. So one cannot use that as an argument against the decoration afterwards. No, the truth is that this Scandinavian line in Denmark has been oppressed since the Vikings burned their stave churches. Long live St. Peter's Church and what belongs to it.*

248 *The Natural Order and Other Texts*

Aesthetics as meaninglessness and cynicism

> For a long time I boasted of possessing all possible landscapes, and found the celebrities of modern painting and poetry derisory.
>
> I loved absurd pictures, fanlights, stage scenery, mountebanks' backcloths, inn-signs, cheap prints; unfashionable literature, church Latin, badly spelt pornographic books, grandmothers' novels, fairytales, little books for children, old operas, silly refrains, naive rhythms.
>
> I dreamed of crusades, voyages of discovery never reported, unrecorded republics, suppressed religious wars, revolutions in manners, movements of races and of continents: I believed in all enchantments.
>
> *Arthur Rimbaud*

Secret interests

We are, however, going beyond human, even organic subjectivity and maintaining that *even the least atom with its rotating nuclear system, as well as the solar systems, must be perceived as spheres of interest, units of activity or subjects.* The study of the interests of these materials and peoples is not only complicated but dangerous, especially as far the latter are concerned. Not everyone is interested in having their interest clarified and this is undoubtedly the real reason that an objective and scientific basis for the so-called 'human sciences' has not yet been established and that there is still no interest in doing so. Yet we have apparently got to the stage that today artistic, philosophical, ethical and aesthetic development is simply demanding the renewal that can only be established by *the recognition and study of the objective subject.*

Subjective knowledge

> Who follows his own head must also stand on his own feet
> *Danish proverb*

We have stated that what is called objective knowledge is just the intellectual demonstration that a phenomenon exists in the world. But the word *know* has a more immediate sensory meaning, as when one says, I know myself. Here the word has the same meaning given to the Greek origin of the word aesthetics. *Subjective knowledge is thus a direct context, an acknowledgement of a phenomenon. For a subject, the absolute known, that which is within bounds, is thus a part of the context, the established, the determined, the law.*

The aesthetics of subjectivity

> Everything like is unalike.

However, we know that all phenomena, objects and spheres of interest are in constant change, are established, extended and dissolved, enter into other contexts, exchange, are condensed and exploded, that there are thus different *degrees of acquaintanceship*, right from the most airy and superficial to contextual, flowing and yet firm, compact, almost immobile and unbreakable connections, and that the aesthetic stage is thus the study of the superficial individual stages.

Universal rationalism

Aristotle, who in his metaphysics stressed the experience of this constant movement or change in matter by which it takes on new forms, maintained that it is the realization of an all-embracing reasonable plan that the divine spirit is following in the shaping of the cosmos through the development of nature, which is gradually and logically following the purposeful meaning of our existence, with which human reason can lead us into harmony. The movement in, for example, a plant's genesis is invoked by 'external' causes (Aristotle was the first person who dissociated himself absolutely from objective subjectivism), like the seed from the mother-plant. But the form that occurs as a plant is because of an intrinsic power in matter, and thus in the seed, of a preordained kind (inheritance?). The seed thus contains the coming plant in itself as a possibility which could come into being or reality, be activated, be unfurled and take on an actual form that is the true being. Every form is in this way developed by other forms, and all these forms ultimately point back to the first cause which is consequently the absolute divine idea.

The imbalance of matter

> He also makes new who destroys the old.

Even with due regard paid to Aristotle's doctrine of catharsis, this perception can only be a half-truth, and therefore wrong, especially when its further enlargement in connection with Christianity's belief in providence and the doctrine of immortality is borne in mind. On the other hand, Hume's liberation of the purely deterministic perception of the world offers no opportunity for the establishment of an opponent relationship between aesthetics and ethics, but forces, as we have noted, the establishment of the former as a side of the latter in 'the doctrine of pleasure'. His philosophy thereby becomes purely analytical without a perspective of development, or what we could call positivity, inclination forward or imbalance, and this absolute equilibrium automatically forces the denial of the actual existence of the objective context, which is only delineated in the dynamic of motion and not in what is stationary. Then even a realistic ethics becomes an impossibility.

We maintain the following:

No providence exists for people other than our own foresight, where ever we get that from, but we merely wish to maintain that it is always the present, existence, actuality or reality that manifests itself as the static and absolute, and that all development is and must be a break with the known, with laws, and takes place through the ceaseless dialectic between the establishment of law and lawbreaking, between ethics and aesthetics.

One-sided moral upbringing towards reason and justice, which inculcates an absolute disgust of all stupidity, injustice, lies, brutality and heedless, ugly self-assertion, to which orphanage children and future kings in particular are subjected, results in just as one-sided tendencies towards servility and desperation.

Aesthetics as injustice, disaster and crime

Law creates lawbreaking

> You walk over dead men... of your jewels Horror not least charming and Murder, amongst your dearest trinkets, there on your proud belly dances amorously.
>
> *Ch. Baudelaire*
> From 'Hymn to Beauty'*

On the other hand, it is health that changes the drama of life from being a perpetual tragedy to being a principle of development. *All renewal consists of casting oneself out into the unknown and thereby into almost certain annihilation, and even if it is the exception that proves the law or rule by renewing it, no successful renewal or introduction of the unknown can happen without the context and the order being destroyed,* crushed and dissolved to give way to new contexts. This revolutionary unrest, the unknown, incomprehensible and incompatibilistic element in existence, where the old is destroyed to give way to new, is the inevitable law of the universe and humanity. Incompatibilism is determined, and determinism acts only through this. The transcendent is immanent.

Lawbreaking creates law

> Diamonds are polished in diamond dust.
> *Taras Bulba**

If one loses this understanding of the dialectical context between law and lawbreaking necessary to establish this, then, instead of perceiving lawbreaking as a necessary ingredient, one must necessarily feel it as a disturbing, destructive, devilish element in existence, as something absolutely wicked, as nature's 'tragic principle'. *By denying this absolute ideality and independence of the aesthetic we are turning away from the abstract doctrine of suicide, which is its logical extreme point,* and like everyone with 'sound common sense' also turning from what it demonstrates: that all development would stop if 'sound common sense' came to rule.

252 *The Natural Order and Other Texts*

Unforeseen happenings

> Did you not see recently how eagerly the dove there over the treetops beat the air with its wings?
>
> He had seen his mate and the nest with the young: that was the reason for his quick flight.
>
> It appeared to him that it was under his own power that he moved his wings and took the shortest way. but it was love, his downy young and his beloved that awakened his soul, and this that thereafter moved his wings.
>
> Love is like the coachman who looks after the reins and controls us as the rider controls his horse. He obscures our soul and convinces us that we sit as chiefs or coachmen.
>
> *Swedenborg**

The circle of interest dominates the cycle of materials and life. But things can suddenly happen that quite change the picture. It can so happen that the dove suddenly leaves his track. As if drawn by a strange force within or without, it is thrown up against quite different experiences that attract and entice it. Apparently, we say expressly, there is nothing here for it to like, let alone love. On the contrary, there is something immediately loveless, something disquieting and unpleasant, something surprising, *the unknown*, and because this is new it is meaningless, irritating, unreasonable and worthless, but nevertheless a force, which, like the lighthouse or the lamp, could throw one off course, possibly even kill and annihilate, but which does, at any rate, enervate, interest, animate and obsess with an externally warm and inner cold excitement.

Why – why not?

> Misfortune often makes people pale, as hot water does lobsters.

Why this? Yes, the whole aesthetic problem consists of just this *why – why not?* If the question is answered, the enchantment is lifted, the unknown has become known, but the incomprehensible is often just dissolved by this intervention in an even greater sum of unknowns.

This is the essence of aesthetics. Is it of value but at the same time valueless, is there something harmonious in the paradoxical, something obvious in the unknown, in the insecurity and dissatisfaction? If one accepts that this is the case, then one accepts the obviousness and meaning of aesthetics, the actuality of the illusion. The need to separate illusion from reality results in concepts of god, but the need to make illusion reality and reshape reality according to our illusions is aesthetic activity or what one calls 'the fine arts'. The metaphysicians seek what is *in* this world, but not *of* this world. The aestheticians seek the precise opposite, what is *of* this world but not *in* it.

The legality of the illegal

> To do a great right, do a little wrong!
> *Shakespeare*

Aesthetics is the ceaseless hunt of the universe, nature and humanity to prove that nothing supernatural exists, for the truth of aesthetics is namely nothing other than the naturalness of the unnatural, the humanity of the inhuman, the health of the anomalous and sick, the clarity of the darkness, the good fortune of misfortune, the competence and power of the incompetent and powerless, the significance of the insignificant, the track of the trackless, the reality of the unreal, the rightness and the truth of the intolerable, of dislike, nastiness, faithlessness, lack of respect, disobedience, injustice, recklessness, cynicism, distrust, insincerity, falseness, immorality, irresponsibility, crime and lawlessness, the order and utility of the capricious, the ephemeral, the terrible, the awful, the doubtful, the uneven, the unusual and misplaced as well as the unusable, useless, inept, disordered and impractical, in short, all that is not interesting except in its immediate effect, *the new, the radical, the original and experimental, the fertility of the earthquake.*

254 *The Natural Order and Other Texts*

Aesthetics as repellent abnormality

> When the Indian teaching about evil perceives God as just as much the source of evil as of good, thus in a way placing the Devil in the Trinity, is this not Hegelianism?
>
> *Søren Kierkegaard*

The pleasure of distaste

This and nothing else is the immediate effect of the unknown in the known, the primary or extreme aesthetic effect, pure aesthetics. It is neither beautiful nor pleasant, but it is the raw material from which the beautiful is born, and, what is more, from which life itself is created.

You will perhaps say it is impossible for the repellent to be the precondition for the attractive, but let us just push these phenomena into the distance a little, into the future of the past, in the example of memory, so that we can more easily see their attractive sides. How truly *exciting and unforgettable, wonderful were those catastrophic events we experienced at that time, even though they were shocking, astonishing, terrible, upsetting, irritating, provocative, enervating and inspiring, and what a marvel it was that they strengthened us instead of crushing us and what a miracle* that they really took place, even though we had perhaps not experienced themselves ourselves but had read about them in the newspaper or in a novel. *It was sensational or, in short, aesthetic.*

Although we have thus pulled back from the phenomenon in order to perceive its meaning, we can nevertheless ascertain that this is the point that cannot be excluded – whether aesthetics should be made into a vital and independent function: *the procurement of the unknown.*

Dysmorphism and abnormality

> All sins are no more complicated than that they all would get their deathblow if one eradicated breach of confidence.
>
> *Nis Petersen**

On the occasion of the breakthrough of Expressionism in Denmark, a certain Professor Salomonsen undertook a very notorious and ridiculed analysis of this new aesthetic phenomenon and came to the conclusion that it was *a sort of 'dysformism' or an ugliness-seeking epidemic,* like the medieval self-tormentors, flagellants and other sick phenomena.* So the man was quite right, but he just did not understand that *the ugly is not ugly in itself, but is perceived* *so only because it is incomprehensible* and unknown and therefore meaningless, and that therefore any renewal at once appears ugly, because the ugly is nothing other than the abnormal, and the ugliness grows with the size of the abnormality. Only in the instant the meaningless has been comprehended, possessed, owned or understood, does it become beautiful.

Thus there is no way around it. If aesthetics is to have a meaning, it must be as the meaninglessness of existence, and if it is not to have meaning, then it thus becomes meaningless any way.

256 *The Natural Order and Other Texts*

Aesthetics as curiosity and wonder

> Zum Erstaunen bin ich da.
> *Goethe*

The interest of the new

When something is neither lovely, good nor logical, but nevertheless attracts us, then this interest can only be explained as purely immediate interest, curiosity, wonder or astonishment. Curiosity is thus nature's primary aesthetic factor.

'*The objects we meet for the first time immediately exercise a mental impression upon* us,' says the Russian painter *Kandinsky*, and in our need to collect rarities and rare experiences or strange and sensational articles, *curiosities*, we have the starting point of our aesthetic activity. This capacity and need is not associated only with humanity, even birds and insects can demonstrably develop such an aesthetic activity by the collection of strange stones, shells, pieces of metal etc. That even fish are immensely curious is known by everyone.

According to these observations, the capacity for wonderment is thus the basic element of aesthetic activity. No one shows wonder at the normal. But where does the abnormal come from? We are not the first who have banged our heads against this problem. However, we feel that it arises from within, as a part of the life process.

The need for the new and the desire for adventure
> Foreign food and forbidden fruit taste best.

That certain reactions are normal or known is to say that they have direct preconceptions or demonstrable grounds. Where these are lacking, we are before *unknown products of the known.* As we do not reckon with actual unknown powers, we must perceive these activities as their own object, a self-contradictory capacity in matter, as a sort of osmotic pressure in the spheres of interest, as enervating factors of tension, acting as an attraction towards the unknown. One could call this need for the expansion of capacity for development *the healthy sickness.* Rationalists call it, characteristically enough, '*horror vacui*', or fear of emptiness. The opposite description *deciderium ad vacuum*, longing for the unknown, the curiosity or aesthetic capacity of matter must be more correct.

Aesthetics as tension, surprise or shock

> The higher a species is
> the more uselessly it behaves.
> Hens do not write aphorisms.
> *Nis Petersen*

New and useful

The capacity for wonderment is thus a primary characteristic of the individual's or species's stage of evolution. The human being is the most curious, whimsical and changeable being in nature. This is the reason for our power.

In his history of Denmark, Professor Arup stresses that tattooing and the use of strange attachments are phenomena just as old as protective hide clothing.* We venture to assert that they are older and that even hide clothing was originally only used to appear sensational. An old, emaciated and frozen shaman one day just discovered that it was warmer to keep the bearskin on all the time. We believe that *any new development begins as something meaningless and worthless, from which the ability to create values is conditioned by the ability to occupy oneself with the valueless, and that this law is not just valid in the world of art but also in the biological sphere, and even overall, because nothing new can immediately be correct.*

But can we consequently make curiosity and the capacity for wonderment into the elemental phenomenon of aesthetics without further ado? It has to be said that it was not us who discovered this placing. Throughout the centuries and right up to Surrealism, surprise or shock has been perceived as a basic factor in the sphere of aesthetic experience.

Surprise and wonderment

> For him beauty was always the hidden.
> *G. Brandes on M. Goldschmidt**

Writing of unreasonable, pre-logical or irrational actuality, that border phenomenon between the existing and non-existent, *Descartes* says (although he exchanges pure *wonderment* with its sympathetic offshoot *admiration*) that 'admiration (wonderment), that is to say first and foremost *surprise, is the only thing that does not rest upon an organic process*, but exclusively on the state of the brain.'

That his latter statement about the activity of the brain alone is disproved by the fact that we are able to evoke the shock of surprise by purely physical

258 *The Natural Order and Other Texts*

means (with insulin shock, etc.), and that we have recognized the organic character of the brain and nervous system changes nothing in the condition *we have here, which is the essence of surprise itself: the break with the organic, that is, the anti-organic effect in matter.*

Aesthetics as opportunity or possibility

> Writing forewords is like remarking that one is in the process of falling in love. The soul searches restlessly. The puzzle is given up. Every event is a hint of explanation. Writing a foreword is like bending a branch to the side in the jasmine cabin and seeing her sitting there secretly: my love.
>
> - and how is he who writes this? he goes amongst people like a dupe in winter and a fool in summer, he is hello and goodbye in the same person, always happy and carefree, pleased with himself, a feckless gadabout, yes, an immoral person.
>
> *Søren Kierkegaard*

Luck in misfortune

Here we are at the very core of extreme aesthetics, its lack of preconditions, its groundlessness, its non-dialectical curtness towards nothingness, to what it is directed towards and seeks to overcome. This position as the negation of nothingness abolishes the normal dialectic of thesis, antithesis and synthesis. *It is the thesis that seeks the unknown antithesis, and the game is a merciless either – or, luck or misfortune, renewal or annihilation*, and we cannot therefore call aesthetic reactions true causal reactions, as we reject all theories of divine guidance, *being forced to perceive them as secretions, provocations, reactions of opportunity or possibility, as this is their immediate aspect, and this is precisely what we are trying to bring out.*

The paradox of aesthetic science

> There are some truths, at least, of a particular modesty and ticklishness of which one does not come into possession if not suddenly that one must *surprise* or abandon.
>
> *Fr. Nietzsche*

But how can one make science in this way? Let us explain our position. The disinterested research which is the mechanism of science is a result of human interest in its purest form, *interest in being interested.* We want to maintain this state, even though the result of the research influences our other interests and develops and renews them.

However self-contradictory this may seem, we could thus well interest ourselves in something that for us does not exist, in the unknown, but the real paradox lies in our interest consisting of *wanting to know the unknown.* When we have achieved this, the object of our research dissolves in our hands. This is what makes the establishment of the science of aesthetic experience so enormously difficult. *Acquaintanceship or experience kills and dissolves the unknown, the aesthetic object. From being interesting it becomes unimportant.* But this is an inner subjective process. Therefore if we are to work on the problem, we must find a method to keep the interest awake, to preserve our wonderment. However, as scientific truth is precisely the opposite of this, we can only approach it in short lightning visits that leave as few traces as possible, in order to keep the ability for experience awake and vitality intact in us. Life cannot be studied in a cadaver, nor experience in knowledge, nor fire in ashes.

Aesthetics as fanaticism and intolerance

> It is strange that people are so angry with the Jesuits. In a certain sense, everyone who is enthusiastic about an idea and wishes only its realization is to that extent a Jesuit.
>
> *Søren Kierkegaard*

Self-forgetfulness versus memory

Burnt children fear the fire, they say, but this is not so for foolish or forgetful children, for what is forgotten is also new. *One must thus have a short memory to continue to be a good aesthetician, whilst one must have a long and good memory to be a significant scientist,* as science is nothing other than experience, recollection or memory.

Aesthetic understanding is the completely intolerant will or control, the absolute talent. Scientific understanding is complete tolerance, disinterestedness, the all-forgiving lack of talent.

To contain enough of both these characteristics to establish an aesthetic science has not hitherto been vouchsafed anyone, and we would not assert that we have it. We would just like to point out that in any such explanation one has to evaluate whether *the passion of the idea* is sound and well, and that the necessary experience for this is not achieved through the experience of the art of others and imagined experiences, but only through *an intense and conscious experience of the aesthetic and artistic process during its creation, during the transformation of matter to a sphere of interest or art.* An aesthetic science must not only be true, it must also be interesting, not just useless ashes but firewood or artistic proficiency.

The need for non-critical experience

> Experience is the best teacher.

'Don't talk, artist – create!' they say, and even if it is from time to time necessary to open one's mouth to correct certain misunderstandings, there is something right about this. If only one could then get the artist, and incidentally also the viewer, to stop listening to what people who don't understand art say about it.

'He who will not listen, has to feel,' is another saying, and as feeling is aesthetics precisely, this explains something fundamental: that *the aesthetician will not be content with secondhand experiences, but will get into the hard school of the facts themselves. It is the task of aesthetics to confront people*

262 The Natural Order and Other Texts

constantly with themselves and their own experiences, to get them to feel and believe more in their own feelings and sensations than in the words of others. This Doubting Thomas attitude is neither an expression of lack of faith nor scepsis, but, on the contrary, of an expression of a need for experience without criticism that will realize the idea, the fantasy, the performance and the word in sensory perception. When the aesthetician reads a sign 'The ice is unsafe', then for him this is not just an invitation to see whether the sign is true, but also to see how unsafe ice feels. This is the precondition of aesthetics, development and progress: that one gets on thin ice.

Aesthetics as surplus of power or luxury

> The superfluous, a very necessary thing.
> *Voltaire*

The aggressivity of the desire for experience

Children and naive, forgetful and inexperienced people have their elemental aesthetic areas intact. They marvel easily and are without routine because of their ignorance. Consequently there is something childish in preserving one's aesthetic need: *one's capacity for wonderment, the longing for the new, for possibilities, for following one's impulses, whims, external causes and preambles, the invitations, temptations and provocations of others, the predilection for openings, introductions, beginnings and sketches, one's capacity for impulsive, immediate and unpremeditated action. It is called keeping oneself young.*

This initiatory capacity in children and young people with the great possibilities for development is a natural power for growth. It is an *aggression or conquest*, a reaching out beyond the static ego.

But one must not forget that children, idiots and naive people are also more limited and bigoted than experienced and developed people, because all organisms seek stability, limitation or morals. They therefore have to smash and destroy in order to develop, and as they neither understand nor know nor recognize anything other than their own world, they perceive many of the actions of developed people as meaningless, incomprehensible and unnecessary occupations, as games or secret black magic and wizardry, and will behave accordingly.

If one has absorbed or rejected all the normal skills and knowledge, but has nevertheless preserved one's 'childishness' or need for wonderment, then one will be drawn towards the unknown in human society and become *a conqueror, adventurer or researcher in the fabrications of the life of the imagination, the inventions of art life and the discoveries of science*, if one does not simply become an oppressor or exploiter of other people.

Surplus of interest

> When it comes to aesthetic value, I employ the following main distinction, 'Is it hunger or surplus that has been creative here?'
> *Fr. Nietzsche**

We have defined interest as context, and aesthetic interest as the unconnected

264 *The Natural Order and Other Texts*

or meaningless context, the accidental connection, the loose and fleeting interest. If we perceive this aesthetic state as a stage in a process of subjectivizing and concretion, then we come to think of the misty formations of globes in the universe, of clouds of pollen over rye fields, and of the whole of nature's innumerable and sumptuous brood. If this – *conception, superfluity, prodigality, munificence, surplus, the voluptuous, luxury, the generous* – is identical with the aesthetic principle, how fortunate it was that we noticed from the start the distinction between the aesthetic phenomenon and the treatment that is the lot of the fine arts in modern society, otherwise we would have risked charging the latter with senility.

> Hunger is also a sort of surplus.
> *A. J.*

Creative hunger
Addition 1963

The Marxist critique of the German philosophy of wretchedness has been misunderstood even by many so-called Marxists. Nietzsche never understood that it is only humanity's hunger that can make a surplus creative. Here also lies the misunderstanding by the Grundtvigians of Grundtvig's idea of spiritual awakening, which is the awakening of spiritual hunger and of dissatisfaction with the given conditions. This awakening was made platonic and anti-poetic and thus became conformation.

Hunger is a subjective surplus of the ability to appropriate something. If this is stronger than the vital surplus, the spectator arises, but no one can give without being able to take. A surplus can be a stupid and conventional ritual and diversion. The creative is based on dissatisfaction and hunger. One can be poor without longing, both spiritually and materially.

Aesthetics as absurdity or redundancy

> Man braucht nicht alles selbst gesehen noch erlebt zu haben; willst du aber dem anderen und seinen Darstellungen vertrauen, so denke, dass du nun mit dreien zu tun hast: mit dem Gegenstand und zwei Subjekten.
>
> *Goethe*

The theory of aesthetic luxury

Nevertheless, we find a certain support for this perception of the aesthetic object of art in the elucidations of the French aesthetician *Lalo*,[*] even if he has not elaborated a true theory of aesthetic luxury, which we, in contrast, are going to attempt.

Lalo defines luxury as a 'monetary outlay or an outlay measurable in money that exceeds the necessary, and which, if it necessarily has an effect on other people, never has any altruistic direction at all. It satisfies only a lower (in a moral and social sense) egotistical enjoyment.'

As we wish to objectivize the concept of luxury, even if we strike out that about money, the problem becomes more complicated. We have three factors:

1. The luxury product – the aesthetic, unknown or superfluous object.

2. The luxury producing subject, which produces and liberates itself from it.[*]

3. The subject receptive to luxury, which absorbs and acknowledges the product.

But, by its nature, the aesthetic product can be neither altruistic nor egotistic, morally or socially, even in the lower degree, but must simply be *an independent and thereby in itself impossible force, which does not immediately find a place in the context of necessity, a meaningless absurdity, pure, free action, and thus really matter's futile power of superfluity or luxury.* The study of objective aesthetics must first and foremost be the study of excess or irrational effects in context.

Objective luxury

> Nothing is so bad, that it is not good for something, and nothing is so good that it is not bad for someone.

The study of the presence of such reactions in the borderlands of atomic physics and universal physics, with the universal totality perceived as a context or subject, would of course demand specialist insight, but is perhaps already indicated in their latest results. At any rate, the possible presence of such new vibrations or irrational movements apparently gives the only logical explanation of the factual development that is happening and has happened in the manifoldness and internal distinction of matter.

Such vibrations are what we call accidents or *chance*, and, taken as an absolute and independent phenomenon, aesthetics is identical with pure chance or accident. But perceived as effect in an actual context, aesthetics is identical with the game, experiment or play, which is the effect of accident upon the ordered, something we call the meaning of aesthetics.

Aesthetics as accident or chance

> Wild and infinite impulse towards invisible splendours, intangible delights, with their maddening secrets for every vice and their dreadful gaiety for the throng.
>
> *Arthur Rimbaud*

The whims of nature

An accident is an event that occurs without demonstrable or calculable reason or purpose, or from causes that lie outside the immediately observed area and are not predetermined through insight or experience in those who experience it. The function of chance is normal and ordinary.

This experimental evolution of the manifoldness of the universe and nature is of such a kind that we could well say that *matter in all its regularity is an incurable gambler who never keeps strictly to anything in particular, even to the degree that nature is unable to produce anything unaesthetic or absolutely known at all.*

It is a strange fact that even amongst the most elementary crystal forms of the same material no two are ever exactly the same, and none of biology's plant or animal species are able to rear two beings absolutely the same. Just a small thing like the human fingerprint shows how consistent nature is in its function. Experimentation is taking place always and everywhere. Everything is original or personal in nature.

The aesthetic misunderstanding of the rationalists

> The mug always wins the first game. Fortune favours the foolish.

It is more than a strange chance that a rationalist like the architect *le Corbusier perceives humanity's ability to produce absolutely known or completely unaesthetic things (circles, balls, straight lines etc.) and to ignore aesthetic factors completely in the production of exactly uniform things to be the proof of humanity's superiority over nature.* In his time, Plato regarded the circle, which according to our definition has to be the most unaesthetic object thinkable (apart from a hospital ward), as the expression of complete beauty. Here the contrast between aesthetic perceptions stands out clearly and elementarily.

According to our perception, this elementary misunderstanding of the essence of aesthetics does not, however, refute the significant fact that, in contrast to nature, humanity is able to cultivate or abstract aesthetics in sheer worthless variation, in change without repercussions, in pure action. This is, however, a process in exactly the opposite direction.

Aesthetics as amusement or diversion

> In play no brotherhood counts,
> in war and love any trick does.
> Those who are lucky at cards
> are unlucky in love.

The play of the chances

Schiller defined aesthetics as play, from which it follows that *the aesthetician is the player.* In the game of chance for money we have also therefore the most typical parallel to nature's experiment. Everyone invests something, and hereby we have established the basis for aesthetics in human economics. By and large play is regulated, but in the individual fields of interests pure chance rules. Either one wins or one loses everything one has put in. It is all or nothing.

It was important to Dostoevsky, for religious reasons, to find a purely individualistic system in this game of chance, as is the case with the whole of individualistic theology. In our observations, we cannot, however, take account of anything other than the absolute *black and white, being or non-being, luck or disaster.*

Hereby we have in reality identified the extreme aesthetic with the struggle for life or nature's dramatic principle. *Aesthetics at its most extreme is the drama of consequences*, as drama has to be defined as the indissoluble conflict or the apparent incompatible opposite.

Utopia or pure mysticism

> Man's will is man's heaven.

We have defined the aesthetic as the absolute interesting and contemporaneous, as *the impossible.* Its opposite is *the indifferent*, which is nothing and cannot even establish an actual condition of opposition, and yet life is, as the Swedish poet *Karl Vennberg* has said,★ an unceasing choice between the indifferent and the impossible. But what we want to indicate here is that this choice does not hang floating in the air, but always starts with something, with the actual and the obvious, with existence's ethical synthesis of good and bad, of happiness and unhappiness. In the wheel-of-fortune principle of animatism described in my book *Golden Horn and Wheel of Fortune,* I have crystallized the basis on which the ecstatic or animating factor we are dealing with here is in a position to act. By themselves, both states are abstractions, since they naturally form an indestructible entity, but humanity has the ability to make this distinction.

270 *The Natural Order and Other Texts*

Humanity has the ability to play without playing for anything, to put money and interests aside and roll its dice, change its cards, to box and hit one another without any meaning or result at all or with just an inkling of a deeper effort, a context, in order to pass the time. In the world of nature and the universe, this absolute aesthetics or *pure amusement, change or diversion, which in the religious idiom is called eternity and blessedness*, has no place. It is humanity's utopian capacity and weakness, the aesthetic dream of the freedom of the future. Its creative connection with the existing is called utopia or the free arts.

Aesthetics as play or game

> ...a going out of our own nature, and an identification of ourselves with the beautiful, that exists in thought, action or person, not our own. A man, to be greatly good, must imagine intensely and comprehensively; he must put himself in the place of another and of many others; the pains and pleasures of his species must become his own. Imagination is the instrument by whose help one achieves goodness.
>
> *Percy B. Shelley*

Aesthetics is play

Let us just acknowledge that matter plays, that it even plays with humanity, and that this play, which is the apparent accident, is precisely that purposeless and uneconomic expansion of power which creates purposes, possibilities and meanings, the unlimited tendency that creates limitations. We find this tendency or chaotic principle of nature's manifoldness, this changeable and variable play, this playful disorder, everywhere. Regard the gnat swarm circling in the air in its humming dance, or the fishes playing in the water, or the cranes treading their complicated musical ballets, and the otter who amuses himself with making helter-skelters on slimy clay slopes alongside the water.

A quite astonishing perspective is opened up when French archaeologists report that, deep under the earth in the rumbling darkness of the primeval grottos, they have come across traces that show that bears had a helter-skelter on a steep clay slope down to a subterranean lake, where they ended in the cold water with a splash in order to experience the cold shudder that is the extremity of sensation or aesthetics. Bears must be marked aestheticians, for there are to be found photographs of wild bears in Sweden executing a quite peculiar and meaningless dance in the snow after having destroyed a quarry, a phenomenon that *Fabre* also observed in the world of insects.

The play of animals

On the whole it would be difficult to find a higher animal that does not play and joke in some way or other incomprehensible to us. Just watch the apes in the zoo or any pet, the dog, the cat, the horse, the pig, the cow. How inclined they are to jest and foolery. This play cannot just be perceived as a training or improvement for the struggle for life. For in itself it contains something that causes it to act as life, indeed, as perhaps its most intense and inspiring essence, as renewal. Could we call this aesthetics?

272 *The Natural Order and Other Texts*

Homo ludens
Addition 1963

There has been speculation about how humanity learned to walk on two legs, and attempts to give the phenomenon a practical explanation. Erik Nyholm's assertion that the first true human apes were singing apes whose developed jaws gave good place for the tongue sounds far more reasonable.* Song is an incitement to the dance, and this pleasant occupation distinguished humanity from the animals and gradually trained the dancing and singing apes to move lithely on their back legs. This is the creation report on *homo ludens*.

It is said that humanity wants to be taken in. This is a lie. Humanity wants to play. Play or be played with or to be played for. The opposition between play and earnest is false. Play seems to be the only thing anyone takes really seriously. This is denied because people can then, without hindrance, be played with without their knowledge.

Huizinga has brought out something on this subject in his *Homo Ludens*, of which I unfortunately was not aware when I wrote this book.

Aesthetics as intoxication or liberation

> If all days were holidays, then it would be beautiful to be alive.

The answer becomes a lot easier if we take up the Swedish architect *Erik Lundberg*'s definition of the aesthetic experience. He writes, 'Art offers riches and intensity in the sensations, a strong consciousness of living and being. All your essence, your organism, functions in a special way, in agreement with itself, as a unit. An uplifting of the mind that offers great and deep satisfaction, *that incites and extends our abilities in different ways. Perhaps above all there is in such experiences an extension of the senses, of the ability to understand more fully than otherwise, to embrace a bigger piece of 'reality'.'*

Could the essence of play be explained more distinctly or more completely? This identity between natural play and artistic aesthetics can hardly explained away, even more so when, purely linguistically, there exists that intermixing of the concepts of play and game, where they are utilized indiscriminately; play of colours, ball game, play football, play of weapons, play of strings, play the stock market, play the game, etc.

Freedom and intoxication

> From children and drunken folk shall one hear the truth.

The Swedish psychologist *Rolf Lagerborg* perceives the aesthetic experience as *the shudder of sensation*, '*le frisson*', a physical reaction comprising all forms of *transport or intoxication*, the elated, ecstatic, but fleeting or cursory flare of life, *rapture, love or infatuation*, as the fascinating element in all sport, play, drinking, bliss and idealism.

This musical sense of eternity is often perceived as a flight, far from reality and life, from the prosaic facts. This is, however, only the case where it is the unartistic or passive intoxication of opium, but is also true to a similar high degree for the 'down-to-earth' realist, who does not wish to change anything at all because he dare not believe in longing, hope and dream.

Bacchus, Dionysius, Liber and our Nordic *Frø* all personify this ancient principle of intoxication or natural aesthetics which is, indeed, *the divine origin of the concept of freedom itself.* But it is very significant to point out that these are above all symbols of fertility, work, love and libation, showing that *true freedom to consist of liberation into life, not of freeing oneself from life*, as is normally maintained in the modern presupposition of unproductive independence, where freedom means passivity.

Humanity's elemental freedom is subjective self-dependence or freedom of action, which is just the opposite of independence. Independence is aesthetic freedom – nothing less.

Aesthetics as celebration, variety or experiment

> Freedom is at its most profound in the human being, the need for freedom, the struggle for the independence of the self, the maintenance of the ego's subjectivity. Therefore we struggle. And if the ego's struggle is so strong that it follows us into dreams, it lives silently in the unconscious as a layer of inexplicable strength, to break out suddenly, to split itself into images fostered by our brain, materialized by our gaze, feasible to our senses.
>
> Hulda Lütken*

Joke and earnest

We began so solemnly and now we are ending in tomfoolery and games and gaiety. How can that be? Simply by pursuing the truth. But the truth is also that gaiety is the most serious and momentous thing in our existence. We feel that the fanatical missionary lay preachers are right in their criticism of the frivolity and futility of life. However, we draw just the opposite conclusion, that we do not want to eschew it, but seek it out, understand and utilize it.

One day some naive young people in Holland went to a functionalist architect. They said, 'We want to make a new town for ourselves. Will you draw it for us?' This he did, and when they saw the drawing their spokesman, who had travelled a little, said, 'It is a lovely town, but I was once in Berlin and there they have a street called the Friedrichsstrasse, with every possible entertainment. This is lacking here.' The architect did not understand what he meant, for he began to explain how prostitution and swindle and perversion and morbidity and decay were the background for these dazzling facades. He did not understand that the whole town should have been a Friedrichsstrasse, full of variety and celebration.

Work and sport

> The rose's thorns wound the heart.
> Then out runs the blood.
>
> C.J.L. Almqvist

One ought to say that red roses grow from sorrow and anger, but one says the opposite. Nothing demands greater strength and gravity than to take things lightly. If one does not understand this then one will never come to understand the essence of aesthetics and, what is worse, the very conditions of human life in nature.

Variety, celebration and amusement are the essence of aesthetics, and the

276   The Natural Order and Other Texts

human being finds the richest form of diversion in productive work. It is *a widespread* misunderstanding that work in modern machine industry is incompatible with beauty. *René Clair's* film *Vive la liberté*, in which a number of workers in a gramophone factory are treated like automatons, is typical of this perception. Finally the factory is modernized so that it can be maintained by a couple of men, pleasurable placed in armchairs, whilst all the other workers are given their leisure time, which they immediately utilize for – *work*, though with a greater chance of a useful effect than the fabrication of gramophones, as they begin to fish with lines in a nearby river – but, nevertheless!

Let us not here concentrate on the grotesque paradox that lies in the joyless entertainment industry, and in the lack of the aesthetic in work that is not free. It yields money and that says everything. On the other hand, there would probably be grounds to indicate that sport, which represents such an energy-consuming factor in our time, acts in many ways as a remote destroyer of human power, where the animating factor never achieves transformation into happiness or true satisfaction, into artistic expansion.

He who can unite the useful with the pleasant gets all the votes, it is said, but if these two elements could be united with *renewal*, then humanity's greatest problem really would be solved.

Conscious play or experiment

> He who never does ill, will never do well, and whoever suffers no evil, shall no good expect.

The unknown is facilitated into the existence of humanity first and foremost through humanity's own conscious and unconscious actions, through ourselves. Artistic and scientific play are not called games. but experiments, and it is through these experiments that renewal comes, both to nature and to humanity. In science, the conscious scientific method has come to be recognized everywhere as the most effective form of working, whilst artistic development still creeps up on people, because they turn their backs on it instead of seeking it face to face. Apart from certain technical experiments, no real foundation can be found for a conscious artistic experiment, not even for a consciousness of this experiment's independent and primary position. The demand for the immediate applicability and value of art still stands, with its critical censorship of quality as the official barrier to artistic renewal, so making this unnecessarily difficult.

Paranoiac or aesthetic criticism

> The ships were superficial. That they stayed on the surface was the source of their power, and for ships the greatest danger is going to the bottom. They were there and hollow and this hollowness was the secret and gestalt of their being. The deep slaved for them as long as they remained hollow. A wave of happiness lifted Charlie's heart with this thought. He laughed in the darkness.
>
> *Karen Blixen*

Empirical criticism, which seeks to establish scientific experience as the criterion of action, has, strangely enough, an aesthetic counterpart in the Spanish Surrealist Salvador Dali's theory about paranoiac-critical activity, controlled fanaticism or logical shock. When one looks at this artist's pictures, it is very clear that they in no way represent a renewal, but just a reshaping, reform or stationary change of existent phenomena, a variation upon a given theme. Let us therefore once and for all maintain the unavoidable fact that *real renewal, thematic or extreme aesthetics must reject any criticism and be pure and unbeautiful experiment, be itself.*

Aesthetics as superficial incompleteness

> I see that nature is only a display of kindness... Farewell,... ideals, errors...
>
> Reason is born in me. The world is good. I will bless life. I will love my brothers...
>
> I keep my place at the top of this angelic ladder of good sense.
>
> As for established happiness, domestic or not... no, I cannot. I am too dissipated, too weak. Life flowers in work: ...as for me, my life is not substantial enough, it flies away, floating beyond action, that dear focus of the world.
>
> *Arthur Rimbaud*

Aesthetics and evolutionary theory

We have attempted here in broad outline to specify a new aesthetic definition and demonstrate its antagonistic relationship to the earlier series of perceptions. We have defined the subject as the sphere of interest, with ethics as its exclusive principle and aesthetics its inclusive principle, and have attempted to demonstrate that this mechanism is a natural phenomenon, the condition for all differentiation and elaboration of matter. Here we could refer to Spencer's *demonstration* that *the tendency of natural evolution towards greater differentiation and greater unity is identical with the classical requirement upon aesthetics for the harmony of manifoldness.*

The requirement of classical *aesthetics* is thus in reality nothing other than the requirement for a natural evolution. Our deplorable task is to demonstrate the unfortunately unavoidable fact that no real evolution can immediately seem 'natural' or harmonious.

So it becomes our task to investigate how the harmonization of this disharmonious, changing and diverting phenomenon can take place and how it arises and is facilitated.

The relativity of height

> From bad habits come good laws.

Modern mathematical physics has created a new world picture, where concepts like up and down, forward and backward are not absolute, but relative in relation to centres. Today this perception demands that in our attitude to life we too critically revise our concepts and clarify for ourselves that both in social and cultural life, concepts of sublimation like 'higher endeavour', 'higher classes', and 'higher interests' are completely antiquated, because people have discovered that what is called lower in relation to these, could with equal correctness be called higher. When we today say 'up north and down south', we know that we could just as well say the opposite, and that of course one cannot build in one direction without at the same time building in the opposite direction. This pendulum movement of life is what the poet *Jens August Schade* is talking about when he says that *one can sink so deep that one begins to sink upwards*, that one must be able to go back to go forward. Aesthetic ability consists in precisely this, in mobility, the empathic, in being prepared to accept all eventualities. Some will call the aesthetic area the top, others perhaps the root, but in reality it is everywhere in the periphery of the sphere of interest, everywhere in the surface, and everywhere as a fermenting force or a vital salt in the depths, in the centre. Where it is smothered, everything becomes dead and clammy.

The aesthetics of banality

> He who sets parrot-like coloured images and expressions crudely against each other without fusion, and compares the noble with the coarse, the everyday with the high, will probably manage to be remembered, but will be laughed at as a makeweight.
>
> *Georg Brandes*

This activity of keeping the old young and tradition fresh is often forgotten when one talks of renewal, even though it is the precondition for true renewal. On the other hand, it is also perceived by many to be the only requisite. It is believed that one can continue to drive round in a closed circle of interest and stop the salt losing its savour.

Aesthetic criticism or the doctrine of exclusivity works like a tree dead in the centre and only alive in the bark, in extreme refinement. Then one shouts at 'critics who have so much ability that they can retrospectively conquer and give rebirth to the old expressions', as *Søren Kierkegaard* puts it, instead of simply maintaining a natural simplicity and unambiguity, an ability to sense the intimacy of the banalities in life. Apart from this, these so-called critics only destroy and never refresh what is destroyed by exclusive aesthetics limited by convention. This can only be done by the artist who experiences everything afresh, the popular artist, and when the point where this should be sought has been reached, then one believes that one can revert to the past instead of understanding that one is grasping what is central by its middle.

The sheen of memory

> A remembered vital state has already gone into eternity and has no temporal interest anymore.
>
> *Søren Kierkegaard*

There is a fundamental difference between the aesthetic need for the immediate, the authentic, the direct experience, and the belief in the reality of the dream of the past, the Elysian Golden Age without passions and disharmony. If one is not clear that in working with the past it becomes clad with contemporary problems, and that it is these and not the image that is the true actuality of the figure of the past, and that in the past we cannot see other than what has a relation to our own situation, then all this will result in is the deplorable aesthetic infiltration of Romanticism.

Of course, we are far from wanting to deny the great significance of the past, recollection, memory, as the reverberation of the experience. We will not deny the colossal significance of the past in our world of beauty, nor the necessity of keeping our history alive. We would just like to point out that if we do this, then the past is more than history: then it becomes context, the present. And we just wish to stress that it is not here that aesthetics begins, but it is here that it has to end, that here we are just at the beginning, and, indeed, that this has been our intention all along: to make a beginning, to write an introduction or a foreword.

Aesthetics as sensation and sensuality

> The stomach must accept what pleases the mouth.
> The seen depends upon the eyes that see.

Sensory objectivity

Knowing something means having felt, sensed, experienced, perceived or been united with this '*something*'. We therefore maintain that the definition of the aesthetic experience as *the knowledge of the unknown* is in all ways authentic, natural and logical. But what is this *something*?

What is the sensory object? It was originally believed that there was directly '*das Ding an sich*', or *the surrounding world in itself*, but gradually has come the recognition that not only the secondary sensory qualities like colour, taste, smell, sound, warmth etc., but also the primary sensory qualities like extent, form, movement, length etc. are subjectively conditioned qualities. However, as we do not perceive the subject as 'the conscious ego', as is generally the case, but simply as a sphere of interest or *a viewpoint in matter, and thus not as something outside this world but as something both of and in it. So we must also perceive sensory qualities as having objective validity, as subjectivity cannot mean pure imagination or 'non-being'*, which can be learned from the fact that those who are born blind cannot be given conceptions of colour. We perceive sensory qualities as existence or the world seen from a particular viewpoint, from which the collaboration of our senses then attempts to create as comprehensive and objective a picture as possible. *Consequently, we have to appropriate or subjectivize matter in the most comprehensive way in order to be able to recognize it as an object. This direct dedication is the aesthetic activity.*

Sensuality and sensibility. Sentiment and sensitive spheres of interest

We view and rework matter from different viewpoints, from innumerable viewpoints, and some of these can be grouped into that common viewpoint we can call the aesthetic. Our task is to indicate some characteristics of this grouping. We have defined *the viewpoint as the ego* and this is thus to say that *our ego is put together from several egos*, which again are bundles or groupings of subjectivity, and if we cast a glance at biology and sociology, we see that we are parts of bundles or groups not only as individuals, but that *even sides of our nature, our character, our mind, temperament, life blood or sentiment are connected with similar phenomena outside us.*

In this sentiment we have the puzzle of life or biology itself, as we are here confronted by a *sensitive sphere of interest that is not only able to facilitate and reproduce itself, but which produces, renews and develops itself, possessing an active will or a system of energy.*

The vitality or energy system of an organism is based upon *an antagonistic relationship between power and tension. This is what we call sensuality or sensibility,* its openness and closeness, its capacity for aesthetic or sensory extension, and its capacity for ethical or critical economy.

Aesthetics as free will, hope or passion

> Poetry turns all things to loveliness; it exalts the beauty of that which is most beautiful, and it adds beauty to that which is most deformed: it marries exultation and horror, grief and pleasure, eternity and change; it subdues to union under its light yoke all reconcilable things. ...its secret alchemy turns to potable gold the poisonous waters which flow from death through life; it strips the veil of familiarity from the world, and lays bare the naked and sleeping beauty which is the spirit of its forms.
>
> *Percy B. Shelley*

This tension or opposition between the need for expansion and resistance, between passion and inhibition, between will and ability, creates *reflexes, customs, urges and conduct, intention, resolution or what could be called the bound or organic will.*

Free will

Surplus sensuality of no particular use to the organism is thus identical to what is called free will, independent vitality, unrestrained passion, or the free aesthetic principle, desire. Sensibility, on the other hand, forms the subjective environment, the circle of interest with its critical reaction of *irritability, sensory tensions and vulnerability or sensitivity and testiness,* together with the capacity for pain and exclusivity, for closing-up or strain, for concentration, centralization, the static or ethical principle, which is the environment of the will.

The vitality of the will

> Laughter and tears belong in the same bag.

There is a fondness for calling this capacity for self-control and criticism the life of the will, but it is easy to see that this only forms its negative although necessary precondition, so to speak. For even if the absolutely unbiased sensitivity or acritical outpouring of sensual power only results in disembodied and impotent slackness, we must, however, assert that the antagonistic relationship often set up between desire and will is rubbish. It is desire that drives the work. Will is desire, but desire only becomes vital and powerful if it is organized, sensitized.

In a lack of concentration or 'dissipation', Emerson saw the elemental hindrance to the expansion of the heroic, to what we here will call the extreme

284 *The Natural Order and Other Texts*

aesthetic. How can that be? It is simply a question of vitality and possibilities. The instant an amoeba or bacillus possesses a surplus of energy in relation to the possibilities its structural make-up, its ethics, encompasses, then it becomes aggressive and begins a process of exclusion of an organic character. It splits. But if the capacity for concentration had not been present in what was excluded, then it would not have formed a new organism. *Free or unusable vitality is only purely aesthetic in the period before it begins to form the new organism, but if this is beyond its capacity then the surplus is transformed to loss.* Therefore the aesthetic is that which *is* before it really is, the unborn, the possibility, hope.

Passion and suffering – medicine and poison

Thus this facilitating process in the matter we call an organism *is conceived in a light and lascivious atmosphere as something luxurious and popular: thus it grows and gathers in passionate pain and is born in suffering and blood.* If one has a bent for compassion, one could say with Strindberg, that 'This is sad for the people', but the unshakable fact is that it is the unavoidable law of natural evolution, of society and personal development. *It is consequently exactly the same phenomenon that invokes desire and pain, pleasure and distaste, beautiful and ugly, good and bad. These antagonistic relationships of reactions are only conditioned by the organism's capacity in relation to the degree of influence.* What heals a smith can, as is often said, kill a tailor, and what in a particular quantity is poison, in a lesser quantity is medicine. If one possesses a love for humanity, one can try to ameliorate and utilize the effect of these facts. Indeed, one can even become an opponent of all evolution or simply deny its reality. But it can never wipe out the truth in Shakespeare's famous words, 'Out of this nettle, *danger*, we pluck this flower, *safety*.'*

Sensual 'decadence'

We know this phenomenon from communal life. When a form or framework of society begins to be too narrow to be able to utilize the powers it has produced, then detached and unusable energy begins to flow around in the body of that society, *an energy that has the character of pure sensuousness or nature.* The societal organism initially attempts to destroy this energy, but possibly cannot do so in relation to its own production. Over-production of energy grows and begins to explode and break down the structure of society like a pent-up rage, an anarchy, a nihilism, that at once seeks its own form, its nature, and seeks the abolition of its own state of *unnecessariness, detachment and anarchy.* This is the commencement stage of renewal.

If we are here getting into an area which belongs in a later chapter, then it is only to reckon with the current *theory of degeneration*, for which this stage is often mistaken, as the detached energies are perceived as a 'decadent' factor rather than it being understood that *it is precisely the detachment that creates renewal and that this detachment is conditioned by the framework being too narrow for the vital force, and thus discardable.* This stage can ostensibly have a stamp of depravation in its demand for a 'return to nature'. But for that environment of pastoral poetry and so-called 'depraved sensualism' we know from the luscious erotic art in post-Hellenic Egyptian and Sicilian cultural circles, in Provençal Gothic troubadour song, from the coquettish pastorals of the rococo, and in Baudelaire's *fin de siècle*, for them all and out into the future, the validity of Shelley's words stands: '*Had that corruption availed so as to extinguish in them the sensibility to pleasure, passion and natural scenery, which is imputed to them as an imperfection, the last triumph of evil would have been achieved.*' The peace of death would have mastered life's motion.

286 *The Natural Order and Other Texts*

Aesthetics as spirituality, sickness or neurosis

> ...a person to whom the sickness of his passions gives a strength to think and feel that a healthy person does not possess.
>
> *Søren Kierkegaard*

> Now and then health comes through sickness.

Nerve and brain

The nervous system is the coordinating or associating organ that forms the organism and facilitates contact with the surrounding world. It both keeps the internal rhythmic cycle or metabolism in motion and organizes the receptive and productive metabolic conditions with the surrounding world. *The nervous system is the sensory apparatus of the organism, and in this the brain has the special aesthetic function of reacting to unknown and remarkable sensory or sensational perceptions, whilst the routine sensory perceptions and organic sensations are looked after by the rest of the nervous system. The brain is a sensory apparatus that can collect and conserve unaccustomed impressions in what we call consciousness in the form of knowledge and experience, but the brain is more than a collector and reflector, it digests, coordinates and associates the impressions from our intellectual horizon to a range of ideas, an idea world, intellectual life, the intellect or the thoughts, and converts these ideas into action impulses* which are called conscious action, in contrast to reflexes or unconscious habitual actions. In the biological respect, the brain has received and developed all humanity's surplus aesthetic power, and this gives the human being its special position in nature.

Aesthetics and neurosis

Unusable energies and unconnected sensory perceptions create a state of sickness which act on the organism as a nervous suffering, a neurosis, both in the personality and in society. To create development would therefore be to provoke a neurosis and thereafter conquer it. This is the aesthetic activity, the creation of tension and relief, of obsession and thoughts of compulsion and liberation, of take-off or leap.

'It is my opinion that all aesthetic desire, for which the poets prepare us, has this character of "anticipatory desire" and that all true enjoyment of the work of the poets comes from being liberated from tensions in our psychic life,' says Sigmund Freud.

However, we maintain that this relaxation, this psycho-therapeutic or relaxing effect of art, is secondary in relation to its exciting, renewing and refreshing effect. Art can act as a surrogate for life, but this ersatz effect is not a 'sublimation to a higher plane'. Only as a true 'anticipatory desire', an inclination or an invitation to dance, does aesthetics fulfil its true mission. Only the day we have liberated ourselves from the perception of aesthetics as an averting measure, a diverting manoeuvre or a proxy function, and see it for what it is, a vital function in the human, social and natural context, will it be able to act for humanity in accordance with our wishes.

I am just a person with clay feet

> I look down at my feet: They are alive, my feet!
> They have conquered death!
> So life is stronger than death!
> My feet have risen from the dead!
>
> *Hulda Lütken*

The story goes that Achilles' divine mother Thetis washed him in the River Styx to free him from the mortal attributes she obviously possessed herself since she no longer exists, but the heel by which she had held him was not submerged. Because of this Achilles' heel, men are both mortal and immortal. We find the same parable in the story of the expulsion from Paradise.

This ancient image of perfect imperfection and the fragmentary essence of the independent illuminates the corruptibility of the transcendental, the weak point of the elements in their relationship to the unknown, just as it also shows the effect of the unknown upon men and their ideals, which we in this book would call the aesthetic effect, the Achilles' heel of matter and humanity, the unknown.

For the individualistic Hellenes, the death of the individual was a tragedy, and the death of institutions as well as ideas a catastrophe. For Plato, therefore, aesthetics was, as it is for so many Platonists, an abomination, later described more humanely by Christendom as original sin.

On more profound and intelligent consideration, however, the Achilles' heel loses the forbidding appearance it surely did not have originally. If the essence of nature and humanity is understood, then one discovers that the death of the single individual, indeed, his sickness unto death, is merely the condition that has to be created for the beginning of new life, and that the sentence 'One man's death, another man's bread' is just an expression of cultural continuity containing nothing at all repulsive. On the contrary it is an affirmation of life, if the individual is allowed to live out his time and carry on his life's work. From this bloody Achilles' heel flows not death but life, fertilization and renewal. When I am dead, another shall have my bread.

However, throughout the generations we have found it difficult to allow men to develop freely. Another Achilles story is told in the sagas. This is about the renowned and great artist Wayland Smith, the Nordic Hephaistos, who could shape the most beautiful jewellery in gold. King Nidud wished to utilize this ability, so he captured Wayland, crushed both his feet and placed him on an island to prevent him running away.

So Wayland fabricated ornaments for the king, but avenged himself first by

290   *The Natural Order and Other Texts*

killing the king's two sons when they came to visit, then by raping the king's daughter Bødvild. Then he turned himself into a bird with the help of a magic ring and flew to the king's house, where he expressed his scorn for the king in a song telling of his terrible revenge, which Bødvild had to confirm before he flew off.

With these examples, we wish only to point out the risk that is the essence of aesthetics, the danger of our treatment of the unknown. Let us state that aesthetics is a sickness in the universe, in nature and amongst men, not a decadence of age but a sickness of birth, a mortal risk, a sickness to life felt as an eternal longing, which must therefore never be eradicated, but always and unceasingly cured in the same way as we cure our thirst and our hunger. A children's disease, one could perhaps call it, but it is a children's disease which keeps us young as long as we have it, because it is called hope.

Where there is life, there is hope, they say, but it ought to be the opposite, for it is hope that creates life. Therefore aesthetics is the doctrine of eternal aspiration, the eternal process of creation.

About fifty years ago, Strindberg sat in Paris and found his inferno in the attempt to prove the unity of matter, convinced that the elements are not, as science was maintaining at that time, incompatible and indivisible terminal points, but that matter is a coherent fluid whole, a subject, and that everything that exists apprehends and in its innermost being knows everything else, is everything else, is really only the same thing in different states. Now every scientist in the world has to admit he was right, but that will give him no pleasure.*

Today we acknowledge Strindberg's perception, but here we nevertheless pose the opposite postulate: that there is a tendency in matter that functions towards exclusivity, exclusion, ignorance and incomprehensibility, towards the attraction to border regions, towards dissolution, towards fog-formation, and that precisely this dissolving activity is necessary for the sake of unity, that in its time the Tower of Babel really could not be completed because men knew each other all too well, with everyone doing and saying exactly the same thing. Therefore they were separated so that each could learn something the other could not and pronounce words that the other could not say or understand, so that when they got together and got to know each other again, then they could build the Tower of Babel.

We are interested neither in gold nor in the transmutation of base metals to gold. Therefore we will not create an inferno for ourselves by beginning with alchemy or attempting to prove our assertions scientifically. We just want to demonstrate something, to attempt to open a new perspective, for no one can demand that leaves and branches in bud should have the same form as in the grown plant. This is against the nature of growth. It is enough for us to plant a seed and see that is viable. For us art is more important than science, and if our work is able to open new perspectives for artistic activity and understanding, let this be a proof of the depth of renewal, though Hell is made hot for us. We ourselves could not think of doing this unnecessarily.

We will not, however, retreat for anything, will not put off these problems, as is usually done, but will take them in their natural order and look cheerfully to the future. Incidentally it is strange that when one begins to talk about the future it always ends in wicked threats. It is as if wickedness belongs to the future. Let us, therefore, as we are abandoning ourselves to this perspective, understand that the future we are talking of in such cases, is, in all its harshness and savagery, just the dragon stem of the present's ship and not the sea that we are navigating.*

There was once a man with great aesthetic abilities, a seer who could look into the future, and what he saw at the farthest extreme was terrible. The Deluge and Judgement Day approached, a Ragnarok was to break loose and destroy all,* the most terrible catastrophes, civil wars and disasters would wipe out humanity. The end of the world was nigh.

And he loved humanity and therefore thought in his heavy sorrow; 'They shall and must know the truth.' So he shut himself in his chamber and wrote and wrote this awful account born of the most frightful agony of soul. At last the work was finished and he went out into the street and stopped an acquaintance to say, 'You must listen to me. I have written down a frightful message. Judgement Day will soon come for us all, and now it must be made known to every person on the earth.'

His friend stared in surprise at him and answered, 'Judgement Day, but that was on Wednesday.' 'That is strange,' said the man. 'That day I was so immersed in describing the dreadful things I glimpse are coming that I noticed nothing at all. So I can just as well burn all I have written.'

'No,' answered his friend. 'You must not do that, for it is Judgement Day far more often than you suspect.'

To write is to hold Judgement Day over oneself.
Henrik Ibsen

Scientific and artistic aesthetics

> I have been enthusiastic about the natural sciences and still am. Yet it seems to me that I will not make them my main study. I have always been most interested in life on the strength of reason and freedom: to solve the puzzles of life has constantly been my wish.
>
> *Søren Kierkegaard*

The perception of the aesthetic element in existence we have just sketched is only valid, of course, if it can be united with the rest of the concept-world we have built up for the recognition of modern culture. We would therefore like to follow up in brief some of the consequences that our aesthetic perception has for our attitude to science, art, philosophy and culture.

The definition of science

Everything we know is a reworked result of direct sensations or physical contact with matter, of what we call experience. To experience is to sense. If this sensation has the character of a purely impersonal and observant absorption of sensory impressions, the gathering of knowledge through analytical experience, then this belongs to *the scientific activity, as we define science simply as what a subject knows at any given time.*

The scientific approach to the recognition of '*das Ding an sich*' is called *objective or disinterested knowledge,* and it is the task of pure science to order, broaden, extend and renew this knowledge, to obtain new knowledge, to make the unknown known. *The usual method of research to achieve scientific results is aloof discernment, observation,* because, as is well-known, the mote in a brother's eye can be seen more easily than the beam in one's own, as *one is blinded by the ego, the subject or personal interest.* Consequently there occurs in the scientific process a far-reaching *denial of personality, an exteriorization of interest or by-passing of ego, a self-effacement or lack of ego during observation.* This is the scientific method.

But, of course, such disinterested research presupposes in the researcher a deep-going interest in and an ability for this activity, a form of aesthetic temperament, otherwise he would not be able to start.

The scientific perception of art

> The public is a man who knows everything but can do nothing.

We have thus defined science as our knowledge, and the requirement for a definition of art which places the artistic activity in relation to the scientific activity now intrudes.

The French author *Zola* perceived *art as nature seen through a temperament*, and thus a form of knowledge, but *science is also nature seen through a temperament*. Seeing is a temperamental thing and absolute objectivity is an abstraction or an abstracting of a particular side of our relation to nature. Consequently we are here confronted with an identification of art and science, the scientific perception of art or Naturalism.

The technical definition of art

Art is a way of life.
*Johannes Holbek**

But what *do* we mean by the word art, when we introduce it here in our investigation? As a rule it can only mean the production of what are called 'good pictures', or be the expression of 'the fine arts' as a whole. Here, however, we would like to use the word in a far more comprehensive and existential sense, *the original sense,* which also still has validity *as the expression of ability on the whole:* the art of cooking, the art of smithing, the art of calculating, the art of war, etc. There is even talk of the art of horseplay,* so we are not even limiting the concept to the human world, but would maintain *that the concept of art in its original and widest sense describes what an organism can do, what it is capable of doing or is able to do, its ability, and thus the manifestation of subjectivity.*

Hereby we have determined the realistic, natural and ethical perception of art by means of ability, knowhow, knowledge.

The aesthetic definition of art

Die Kunst gibt nicht das sichtbare wieder, sondern macht sichtbar.
Paul Klee

Finally we have a third perception of art that maintains that *art is what one cannot do,* for, as Robert Storm Petersen says,* *If one could do it then it would not be art.* This aesthetically anti-artistic, unnatural or idealistic definition of art appears on closer inspection to be just as true and justified as the other two, for if there were no one at all who could do it, who could not even just think of being able to do it or have the possibility of doing it, then it would not even be aesthetic but simply nothing. *The aesthetic is the call or the artistic yearning.*

294   The Natural Order and Other Texts

Aesthetic art is, in its widest sense, what an organism or a circle of interest cannot do but wants to be able to do, does not do but wants to do, comes to do or at least could think of doing, the introduction of the unknown to the known. Aesthetic art is in its widest sense the subjective possibility of perfection: Das ich an sich.

As far as humanity is concerned, this represents the absolute ego, an abstraction or extraction of the same kind as the scientific, although in the opposite direction, an object-repudiating extension of the ego: an opposition, conscious of the future, to scientific experience or consciousness of the past. Here we have set up a triple opposition between the scientific, the artistic-ethical and the unartistic-aesthetic. We will attempt to perceive this opponent condition between what are normally called Naturalism, Realism and Idealism as a collaborative unity.

The aesthetic perception of art

> Even to this day all the world's rational grounds have not been successful in overcoming the deep sympathetic empathy in nature. Our body rises involuntarily at the sight of the noble pine. Before the leaping and falling beam of water our hand describes a wavy line. Our steps match the rhythm of the melody we hear. Sounds fill us and awaken feelings in the depths of our heart. The external world constantly finds an echo in our inner being, and the worn out soul of humanity always beats strongly under the impressions of the nature surrounding and shaping it.
>
> *H. Taine**

The opposition between art and science

From this perception, it is quite evident that art has to stand in a clear opponent relationship to science, even though this too represents a sort of ability, an anti-artistic or ego-less ability.

If science is the objective analysis of matter, then art is just the opposite, the subjective synthesis with matter. Nature reworked by an interest or a temperament? Das Ding für mich.

Artistic ability is perceived as the ability to intercede, the organic experience, the vital experience or *sympathetic insight*, the result of the knowledge achieved by, for example, eating and digesting a piece of bread, our subjective value-recognition, as opposed to science's chemical, physiological and social analysis of the bread's relationship to the human being, which does not even necessitate that a piece of bread has ever been tasted or that the need to do so has ever been felt.

In its method, this counter-scientific process of subjectivizing must be *anti-objective self-assertiveness*. For depth of sympathetic insight, a rule opposite to the one controlling objective analysis is valid. This can be expressed in the saying, 'A splinter in your own behind feels stronger than a sword-thrust in your brother's back.' Here is the extension of interest or the ego-sensation, which through magnanimity or fellow feeling creates understanding in accordance with the extent of the subjectivity.

Artistic aesthetics

> Du gleichst dem Geist, den du begreifst.
> *Goethe*

If objective research is the aesthetic area of *science*, then the sympathetic

296   *The Natural Order and Other Texts*

development of the feeling for the context of interest is the ethical area of *art*, according to the perception that *ethics is extended egoism or egoistic altruism*, the foundation for realistic morality. *Artistic aesthetics is the renunciation of this self-satisfied, controlled cycle of habits in favour of a self-forgetfulness, which, in opposition to the ego-less impersonal and self-effacing self-denial, is an acritical self-expansion and self-assertion extending the self or the ego to include others as well:* the development of association and solidarity, which is the only possible artistic and ethical basis of reality.

> Poetry that just reassures stands in no danger of going outside the limits of art. It is always occupied with antiquated ideas. Poetry that awakens (the dramatic – A.J.) is otherwise, it stands in a very serious danger of being so personally intrusive, so disquieting and aggressive that it stops making the impression of art.
>
> *Georg Brandes*

Thus we see that the conflicting perceptions of art are far from absolute in their mutual enmity, that, on the contrary, they advance and provoke each other as stages in a process of production, mutually enriching and fertilizing each other through the tension of the opposition liberated as dominance according to the changing demands of the development.

Idealism, realism and naturalism

> A man who wishes to mutilate himself is truly damned, is that not so? I believe that I am in hell, so there I am.
>
> *Arthur Rimbaud*

In the Middle Ages, the philosophical opposition was divided between *nominalism* which formed the starting point for modern or naturalistic science, and realism, which later split into the two oppositions *idealism and realism* (materialism). For practical reasons we have here replaced the word 'materialism' in this connection with the word realism, as they are often used indiscriminately, and we will *use the concept of dialectic materialism as the expression of the system that unites idealism, realism and naturalism in a connected mobile system with its point of departure in what we in daily speech call reality, the present or the state of the moment.* This last concept can only have an objective and current meaning, but when attached to an object it becomes the expression of its culmination, *its perfect stage as type.* In this way its future is identical with its possibilities, and its past identical with its accomplished experiences, so *the aesthetic stage becomes a subject's introductory stage and the empirical stage the final one.* This youthful or aesthetic stage is characterized by its *self-over-valuation*, where the stomach becomes full before the eyes, the interest and the will are greater than the ability, thereby creating *an overwrought state or active inferiority complex*, whilst the final stage is characterized by its *self-under-*evaluation, when the eyes tire before the stomach, interest is less than ability and creates *a blasé and passive feeling of* superiority, which thus is the real degenerative and moribund stage, even though in the course of life it is just as necessary and therefore just as valuable a stage as all the others. Thus we see that *the understanding and thereby the dedication, recognition and utilization of our aesthetic definition really presupposes the recognition of a completely new philosophical system, of which the aesthetic is just a detail.* But it would also be remarkable if something completely new was able to occur within the given frameworks.

298 *The Natural Order and Other Texts*

Aesthetics as drama, illusion or idealism

> True depression is like the vapours. It is only found in the highest circles.
>
> *Søren Kierkegaard*

*Epic, poetry and drama**

We have shown that the fine arts stretch over three outer points:

1. *Naturalism or the art of epic* memory, which we most characteristically find in novels, journalism and documentary pictorial representations (film etc.).

True naturalism is descriptive art. Through words, painting and sculpture, the human being is able to create objects which give humanity the illusion of other objects. This can be done so disappointingly that we believe that we are confronted by the things we are imagining. If this happens, we have an example of the purely metaphysical or idea, as the actual object is not sensed. Only the illusion is left. The medieval realists perceived this illusion as true reality. But from a materialistic perception, it is a misunderstanding to mix things and ideas.

2. *Realism or the art of poetic demonstration,* which unfurls itself strongest in dance, song and architecture, and gives the most authentic and immediate expression of the human existence.

3. *Idealism or the art of dramatic illusion,* which has its strongest expression in the theatre, which is a purely human conception or form of fantasy. As precisely the aesthetic is the subject of our attention, *the theatrical sensation* in its various phases and nuances becomes, as the extreme aesthetic-artistic manifestation, the main subject of our attention, though both music and pictorial art, which are the most elastic and comprehensive kinds of art, come into this area too.

Tragedy and comedy

> The best is the enemy of the good, and the good is the enemy of the best.

What is the dramatic? It is dualism or fissure, the conflict between what is and what would be. *Herbert Spencer* calls *tragedy* 'a generalization (or law) destroyed by a (new) fact'. One could also say like Kierkegaard that 'the tragic is really that an infinite spirit has been conjured into existence': the conflict between 'the law of the future and the duty of fidelity' in relation to the laws of the present, as *Georg Brandes* calls it. The strangest thing is, however, that it is exactly this same law and setting out of the problem that form the basis for *the comic principle*. The effect is just less and the conflict lighter. At a particular point, sensual pleasure gives off its fiery warmth in a consuming and destructive blaze. *Thus tragedy is really just a comedy that has become too big, that has grown out of all proportion.*

Gambler versus cynic
Insertion 1963

Behind the area of tragedy and comedy lies the endless field of the true gambler, where everything can be lost and won, where life and death are no longer the measure of good and bad, where the Viking dies with a joke on his lips, and where absurdity becomes a value.

The gambler's first step towards a sound social morality goes via cynicism, which at the very least is the science of how one protects one's own skin without regard for others, and is thus a sort of morality and reason. The cynic must therefore be placed higher on the stairway of morality than the gambler, the aesthetic artist. When Poul Henningsen fights artistic cynicism with the demand for quality, he forgets the most important thing in artistic creation, that something has to be staked, that something must be ventured. Without this wager, art is just traditional technique.

The perfect crime

> This is the supreme justice of the gods.
> To the border of crime they lead our steps.
> They let us commit it but do not forgive it.
> *Racine*

An action that breaks the law is called a crime. All drama is crime, and the perfect crime, the absolute drama, must be the tragedy, where not only the hero and the villain but also the actors and the public as well as the theatre vanish in annihilation, the absolute destruction, where no sacrifice, criminal, witnesses or testimony are left. This is absolute, pure aesthetics, the absolute suicide. But it is precisely the essence of drama that it can never be absolute, for then there is nothing. Someone must survive. The tragic is thus what one believes is legal, but which is shown to be a crime, or the opposite – what one believes to be a crime and is treated as a crime, but which then afterwards is shown to be legal – what one believes is reasonable, but which is revealed to be a meaninglessness and absurdity – and what one judges to be meaninglessly sick and absurd but which is revealed too late as reasonable, sound and normal.

300   *The Natural Order and Other Texts*

Suicide and judicial murder are the two extreme points of tragedy. It is thus the artistic extremity of aesthetics to invoke drama, conflict, war and destruction.

The English painter Whistler aptly called aesthetic art 'the noble art of making enemies'. *To create aesthetics is to sow enmity, unrest and competition, to create differential effects.* It is a lie when it is said that need makes the weak infamous and the strong sublime. The strong man is just the most infamous, whose aggression is so big that he conquers the opposition. *The infamous is just he who dies infamous.* If a man cuts open the stomach of another just for the sake of it, he is a criminal. The same action carried out by a surgeon, who thereby saves a patient's life, is a sound and sublime destruction. The soldier who cuts up his enemy's stomach is called a hero. There you are.

Experientia vaga

> Treason do never prosper. What's the reason?
> For if it prosper, none dare call it treason.*

Thus we have shown that drama is the extreme aesthetic phenomenon, and that it cannot be an independent and absolute phenomenon, as in that case it does not exist. Consequently drama must be an element in a process, if it has to be anything at all, a stage, and as we perceive aesthetics as a basic universal and existential phenomenon, one of existence's existential truths, our concepts should apply to everything in the vital drama of nature and society. The concept of *stage* cannot, however, here be taken as something irrevocable. The meaning of all our work is precisely to demonstrate the significance of constantly keeping the aesthetic stage intact and active.

The perception of the aesthetic as a stage in the life process is not a new discovery. In his time, *Spinoza* divided our knowledge into three kinds or stages, of which the first, which we call the aesthetic form of knowledge of everyday disconnected and dispersed observations, was *experientia vaga.* Carried over to active life, this corresponds to equally chance and *opportunistic tactics* and unprepared activity. But Spinoza's two other stages, *ratio*, regular, connected experience, and *scientia intuitiva,*★ also correspond to what we in active life or art have perceived as realism and naturalism. However, we cannot explore this problem here, but must turn back to the dramatic aesthetics of self-assertion and continue to reveal its mechanism, its ideality.

Sensory perceptions of the subject

> A property of reason is that it can make one mad.

How is this exploratory self-consciousness or self-knowledge achieved? *By the sensory perception of the ego or the interests.* This perception is of quite a different kind and disposition from the alert perception of the object. On the contrary, it is an unconscious or sleepy physical sensation, insight in itself, because the facts that are to be drawn out are *wishes and desire, the will, the apparently blind passion.* Of course, this aesthetic evaluation is also there in immediate sensory perception through direct contact with matter, but *the deeper ego-perspective occurs in the individual as wishes, dreams, fantasies or ideas, which are the gradual consciousness of one's own unreleased possibilities. Tied to feelings of dread about the elements that could threaten and hinder their realization, these form images* which are straightforwardly ascribable to our physique in the mental atmosphere as *imaginings.* These sheer illusions are certainly built up of matter from the actual and experienced world, but in their structure have nothing to do with it, as they are fantasies and *self-delusions: metaphysics.*

Illusion and imagination

> Between saying and doing is a long way.

Watch how a cat plays with a piece of paper as if it were a mouse or a dog chews on a stone as if it was a delicious meat-bone, or observe the dream reactions of animals during sleep, and you will see that this capacity for illusion is in no way a purely human phenomenon.

What gives humanity its unique position in relation to other natural phenomena is our specially developed *mental abilities,* which make us able to *capture, build up and work on notions and experiences in syntheses of active impulses: ideas, caprices, hypotheses, models and inventions, etc., human spirituality, ideality or superstition.*

All ideal or subjective thought is wishful thinking, invoked by capabilities or inner and organic sensory influences. The latent unsatisfied wish becomes a fixed idea or an ideal. Idealism is the common wish-world or daydreams of a societal group or humanity.

302 *The Natural Order and Other Texts*

Aesthetic, ethical and scientific truth*

> *Das Ding an sich,*
> *das Ding für mich*
> *und das Ich an sich.*

Subjective truth

What is truth? Now it is as if the foundation is slipping away from us. The pure idea must be the idea that one does not oneself believe in, and thus the pure *lie* in an objective sense, and the belief in pure illusion must be defined as pure *self-delusion* or superstition, and yet we maintain that here we are before *elemental subjective truth* – tell me what you are dreaming and I will tell you who you are. Indeed, we will go even further and maintain that *the ability to lie is not only the expression of the elemental truth about the ego, but that it is the basis on which we attain an oppositional relationship to objective truth,* experience, the knowledge of what has existed, even though the extension of our objective experience of things, for its part, extends and renews our idea-world with new material.

Objective truth

> The lie is valid until the truth comes to light.

Our wish, will or desire leads us on to new knowledge. No one knows more or gets to know more than he wishes to know, or sees more than he wishes to see. Even when one takes the existence of our greed for knowledge into consideration, this is an irrefutable fact which we run into everywhere – what a person does not wish to know, he doesn't know. Our ability to know is thus conditioned by our ability to wish, our scientific ability is a result of our aesthetic ability.

This does not mean that wish and knowledge are the same, on the contrary, they are two opposite poles, but you only reach the one if you take a run at it from the other, so *progress is conditioned by backward steps and the development of our consciousness of the future is conditioned by the development of our consciousness of the past.*

Natural truth

> Ur-Heilskraft ist Urtheilskraft.*

In order to understand the reality of these two opposite truths, it is necessary to make it clear that there is a third truth which is the starting point and basis of these two truths. This is the truth about objective subjectivity, *the actual existence of the experiencing and knowing subject in the present, the truth of sympathetic insight, the truth of naturalness or health.* This *truth of optimism* may appear to be just the confrontation of the two previous truths, the proper truth which occurs when everything irreconcilable in the two previous truths is eliminated. But even though this may be partly correct, it is nevertheless wrong, as this truth is quite independent of the other two and develops in relation to them in the triad that has been called *aesthetics, logic and ethics* and which we will call *the unity or cycle of beauty, truth and health.*

If, in spite of retaining these definitions, we cannot be said to be moving on a purely metaphysical plane, this is precisely because we have this third truth as a point of departure: *that we ourselves and above all what we do and think are a part of nature and can never get out of this affiliation,* which is why science must always continue to be nature seen through a temperament, however far one reaches in the direction of objective extraction, whilst aesthetics similarly must always continue to be the temperament's revolt against nature, however far even here one reaches in the direction of subjective extraction.

The truth of scepticism and guilelessness

> Fault and fall know all men.
> The most intelligent knows most.
> He who has to talk a lot, often lies.

Truth is what we believe in, but as science is scepticism, mistrust or disbelief and *doubt,* this in itself must be an empty if necessary truth. On the other hand, imagination or conception is again superstition, guilelessness or blind *despair,* and yet we perceive it as a necessary truth. An idea is a lie if one does not believe in it. To form hypotheses and ideas presupposes then the ability to lie or discover something that one does not immediately believe. From these apparent lies the scientist chooses the most *probable* and tests them, whilst the artist chooses the most exciting. Thus we see that *science lives on superstition and that the superstition does not decrease but grows with scientific development,* that freedom of belief is the precondition for scientific development and that the most enlightened people, if they are alive, must also be the most superstitious people in the world. Science develops in an uninterrupted sceptical combatting of superstition. The day that all superstition is conquered, science will stagnate.

304 The Natural Order and Other Texts

It is the same with art. The day that one only wants what one can do, or can do everything that one wishes, all artistic development will cease. Only through intolerance can we achieve greater tolerance, only by being able to do what cannot be done, by *introducing* and overcoming the ugly and the bad, will we achieve greater goodness and beauty. This is the inescapable dialectic of truth.

Artistic guilelessness resembles naivety as foolhardiness resembles foolishness. For the normal person it is literally impossible to distinguish between an artist and a psychopath. Both appear mad in the same way.

The witnesses for truth

> Aufrichtig zu sein kann ich versprechen, unparteiisch zu sein aber nicht.
>
> *Goethe*

Truth is eternal but not immutable. Therefore truth is not a pillow, 'a joy forever' which one need only obtain once. Truth is a process and only he who participates in this process is a witness for truth and can be trusted and be used as a guide and a model in human development. If what people struggled for at a particular historical moment was its highest truth, then that truth is still a part of the whole truth, even if today their standpoint is untrue and the witnesses for truth are not those people who still defend the same belief, say the same words and carry out the same actions, but those who with new truth are forced into the same situation that the demand for truth always forces mankind. History has millions and yet again millions of such witnesses for truth, whose abilities and range have been large or small but who have all been led to that subjective perfection, the sacrifice of life.

A witness for truth is above all a person who stands behind his words completely, who in his deeds will realize the truth, will burn for it and will sacrifice all, even life, will take on himself poverty, contempt, hunger and need, ridicule and laughter, prison, exile, indeed, the death sentence, without being shaken in his belief in it. But not even this fanaticism and enthusiasm is enough in order to talk of a witness for truth, or any criminal who believes in his right to break the law would be a witness for truth and it would only be necessary to provoke society to torture one to obtain a martyr's crown. *Martyrdom is no truth in itself. To hate, to defy and to go against the stream, to be an enemy of the people, has, like everything ideal, no value in itself, but only becomes truth if it contains its opposite in itself, the precondition that the words and deeds of the witness for truth have sprung from an all-encompassing love and dedication to mankind and that it has its goal in solving and removing the dangers that threaten humanity and of advancing human power, ability and value, zest for life and enjoyment of everything that nature offers in benefits, advantages and riches,* not by scorning this and destroying *oneself* in self-denial and *one's 'earthly' neighbour* in surfeit and passive consumption, but *in order to advance human health in the enjoyment of outputs and the outputs of enjoyment. Only social disassociation based upon and resulting in an even greater inwardness, unity and naturalness is of truth, as it transforms truth from an ideal to an archetypal truth,* as the painter Paul Klee called it.

This *naturalness and archetypal depth of truth is the third condition of truth,* for an ill-timed truth is not a truth, because it cannot be received. The ground is not prepared and the truth dies. This places the third criterion, knowledge and experience of his times, on the witness for truth. If his truth does not contain everything that the highest science of his times knows, indeed, if it does not contain room for an extension of this knowledge that explains and extends and can be united with it, then all is in vain, even if the first two preconditions are present. Instead of a witness for truth, we have only a deceiver and a seducer, a demagogue or aesthetician.

Nonetheless, just like error, seduction contains that pound of truth that makes them both indispensable. People want to be seduced, life wants to be seduced, nature wants to be seduced and can stand incessantly being tempted and seduced, incessantly being in error, indeed, cannot do without it.

A crime becomes transformed into an error the instant it brings with it the punishment which is that crime's natural consequence and consummation, whereas the unfinished crime, which is not punished, is revoked as a crime and becomes law or nature.

306   *The Natural Order and Other Texts*

Philosophy as the doctrine of human values

> The most beautiful children, they are mine, said the raven.
>
> This is in no way to say that someone who lives aesthetically does not develop. However, he develops from necessity, not from freedom. No metamorphosis occurs in him, no boundless movement.
>
> *Søren Kierkegaard*

Trustworthy truth

In science we have elaborated a rational system for the exploration of objective or analytical truth and could elaborate a just as rational system for the exploration of subjective or synthetic truth in aesthetics. However, this presupposes that ethics is elaborated as a corresponding system for the elaboration of *distinctive or critical truth*. This is only possible if one recognizes that *all criticism is and must be the evaluation of interest and nothing more, and ought always to formulate clearly this relationship between the actual and the desired against the background of desirability*. Criticism is the mark of the good and the good is what *is* and can maintain its existence, is what one believes. *Actual belief is being, is action, confidence, trust, realization, materialization*. This is the existential essence of the context or the sphere of interest. *For the cow. the cow is the good, and for humanity the human being is the good. Everything that exists is good because it feels itself to be good and can only exist on the basis of the attraction of this inner goodness, this coherence. If one cannot recognize that humanity is good, that nature and everything that exists is goodness itself, there being simply nothing that is not good, then goodness has no actuality, but is an hallucination, an idea, aesthetics.*

This is not to say that one ought to perceive either humanity in general or oneself or human society as *good enough*, but that one understands that *every endeavour beyond oneself must be based on self-consciousness and self-knowledge, that one must be oneself to be able to be more than oneself, that anyone who wants to be something other than themselves just annihilates everything*. With this we have moved the problem from the scientific into the philosophical area and will try to elaborate aesthetics in this perspective.

Artistic philosophy

The learned are not always the wisest.

We have shown that, through its spiritual development, humanity has been able to connect the action with the analysis of the action. Indeed, we have even been able to separate *pure action, the aesthetic activity, from pure analysis, the scientific activity – absolute acritical interest from absolute acritical lack of interest. We called their organic union and starting point human art* and, as a phenomenon of consciousness, we will call this union *human philosophy*.

The word philosophy is of Greek origin and means *love of wisdom*, which is the same as sagacity, *ratio* or reason. Of course, the aesthetician who wants to do what cannot be done is not very bright and neither is the scientist who is not interested in his own analytical results. If we then keep to good, sound and healthy reason, and there is no other criterion for sagacity than health – ethics, as we have called it, artistic consciousness, proficiency, mental or physical *strength* – and as love, as is well-known, is the most intense form of interest, transcendent interest or the genetic principle, that exists, it is natural to define *philosophy as the artistic consciousness or attitude to life of a person, a time, a society, a group, a people or humanity, as our knowledge of what is interesting and wise to us and as our interest in understanding our reactions to existence and the relationship of existence to us.*

The how of wisdom

The heart has some reasons, which are quite unknown to the head.
Pascal

In this way, philosophy comes into a contrary relationship with science in its *attempt to transform science to art, our knowledge to ability,* and similarly into a contrary relationship with aesthetics by criticizing its absolute and limitless interest. It also comes into opposition with itself because it lives off the development of science and aesthetics and can only function through an uninterrupted inner dialogue of self-contradictions or a dialectical monologue. But even though a special aesthetic philosophy, as well as a scientific one, could thereby be separated out with their basis questions of: *what and why – why not,* the elemental philosophical question for all activity and artistic efforts would still remain the burning *how.*

It is understandable that professional philosophers perceive the ability to meditate or philosophize not just as the central task of philosophy but as *the*

308   *The Natural Order and Other Texts*

aim in life of all humanity. If one had asked a jockey the same question, the answer would, of course, have been horse-racing.

But let us as artists state that *the criterion of wisdom is not science but value. If aesthetics is the doctrine of the value of the valueless and science the doctrine of the valuelessness of values, then philosophy is the doctrine of value itself* which also includes these two previously mentioned disciplines. A society or a person without a doctrine of value that can digest everything new is a plaything of fate. Our times are marked to a high degree by this weakness – by declining philosophical consciousness, declining recognition of value, declining sagacity.

Luck and Chance 309

On the value and inner contradiction of aesthetics

> Transformation hurts.
> Change delights.
> Refinement bores.*

The objectivity of value

We have defined philosophy as intellectual art and just as there is a general scientific perception of art, so is there also *a scientific perception of philosophy*. However, the boring thing about its empirical method is that it simply has to be a *passive* reeling-off of human conventionalism and nothing more. On the other hand, one has also *an aesthetic perception of philosophy which in its speculative wistful thinking is a just as passive* reeling-off of smart ideas, dreams and uninhibited visions. Thus everything indicates the advisability of defining *philosophy as the doctrine of people's actions and of identifying this with the doctrine of value, for we define the doctrine of value as the doctrine of the comprehensible or known, of what is obvious or necessary to a circle of interest.* Thus there can be no talk of an 'objective value' in the same sense as there is talk of numerical objectivity, as the scale of value is tied directly to each object as its subjectivity. The recognition of the mutual community or universal subjectivity of all matter, the truth of which modern science has had to admit to the old mystics, and the value of the universe or the cosmos, in which there are individual local circles of value, give us the starting point for the definition of value:

That which is necessary for and goes into the maintenance and state of a context as existence in the present, we can define as its artistic, actual or sound and healthy value, the value of the context or circle of interest for itself and in itself.

The value of experience or scientific value is the action that has continual validity. However, aesthetic value is the surplus that goes into a context without being immediately necessary or useable there.

The subjectivity of value

> Höchstes Glück der Erdenkinder sei nur die Persönlichkeit.
> *Goethe*

The value of the object as an element in a larger context could be called its *inclusion value*, its value as the seat of lesser areas of interest, its *incubation value* and its value as a precondition for *introduction value*, if we wish to try

310 The Natural Order and Other Texts

to create a distinction in the stages of value. Just as we can talk of *universal value*, we can also talk of *natural values* as elements in the cycle of nature, *biological values* as elements in the cycle of living *organisms, humanitarian values* as elements in the human context, *social value* as an element in social community as a whole or for the maintenance of special interest groups, and *personal value*. Whether these values are of an ethical and thus necessary nature or aesthetic and unnecessary, purely imaginary even, can be scientifically analysed. *The circle of interest is perceived as the subjective 'good', but that which attempts to break down and annihilate this has to be perceived by the interest group as 'the bad'. Thus nothing exists that, objectively for anything and everything and under all conditions, is good and valuable or bad and damaging, unless it is, on the one hand, absolutely everything, the world, matter on the whole or, on the other, nothing, the non-existent.* However, this does not stop certain interest groups widely attempting to give their interests the stamp of universality and incontestability by representing them as an expression of 'objective values'. Not even universal actual values can be so called, and the tolerance of modern science to this swindle has to be said to be reckless and even self-erasing.

Negation of value and absolute value

> It is the first step that is costly.
> But well begun is half done.

In its extreme character of acritical analysis, scientific research must necessarily reduce value, so in a certain way it could be said that scientific experience is *free*. This does not mean, however, that an objective philosophy is unjustifiable. On the contrary, passive and non-engaged philosophy is a sovereign and also necessary part of the comprehensive philosophical picture. The same is true of idealistic or aesthetic philosophy, which in its all-embracing acritical synthesis destroys the criterion of value by quite uneconomically perceiving everything into which human value forces us as *dearly-bought* experience. Their truth value is conditioned by their mutual dependence and union in the *economic* principle of the analytical synthesis or critical criterion of ethical insight.

But what significance do these philosophical observations have for our aesthetic understanding? They create a limitation of the aesthetic phenomenon which opens out a new perspective for our knowledge of the complicated mechanism of aesthetics.

The aesthetic doctrine of transformation

> Ein Teil von jener Kraft,
> die stets das Böse will und stets das Gute schafft.
> *Goethe*

From being a phenomenon, *the unknown*, we have developed the aesthetic into *an area that extends from the absolutely unknown to the absolutely known*, which describes the stages in the involvement of new phenomena in a circle of interest, as the absolute known has to be defined as the obvious and normal necessary condition for this. The advantage of this definition lies in now being able to achieve a greater depth and richness in our aesthetic understanding, as we can separate out stages or developmental oppositions in the aesthetic stage itself. We will also attempt a tripartition here.

Instead of the static doctrine of *the unity of manifoldness* of classical aesthetics, we have brought movement into the system by introducing novelty, *renewal*, as a third necessary factor, and by establishing an aesthetic line of development from *transformation over beautification to refinement*.

Anything new is immediately ugly because it is without unity and manifoldness and without active contact with its surroundings, being, on the contrary, a *process of detachment*. This is the *embryo stage redundantly going through the possibilities until it stops at concretion, birth*. In a similar way, the child goes through the development of the whole animal kingdom in this period. This, *the most interesting and hideous stage of all*, birth, creation, revolution, the transformation of the impossible to possibility, the introduction of the unknown and unusable into the known, is then succeeded by the stage of central aesthetic beauty, variation, *the stage of making sensible or manifold*, which goes in exactly the opposite direction to the first. In the child, this stage of being *a gradually growing sensory organ* lasts until going to school. They say that the child 'lives in the present' because it reacts with all its faculties to every sensory impression and throws itself acritically into everything that comes along, but *that the child develops is proof that it is not living in the present but, on the contrary, in the future. This is a misunderstanding running through all aesthetics, which makes the perception of the equilibrium between the aesthetic and the ethical, as for example in Kierkegaard, self-contradictory and meaningless. This wonderful development of the possibilities of the beautiful and lovely* has to give way to *a third stage*, which in its pure form is mankind's special phenomenon, aesthetic or imaginary unity, formal upbringing, *refinement*, which can, in all honesty, appear a bit boring and uninteresting, but is nevertheless that stage where *the character is formed*

312 The Natural Order and Other Texts

and the personality harmonized. This happens by *dealing with the unnecessary and unknown as if it were known and necessary and thus creating a formal or imaginary reality and ethics.* When this has been passed through, the child has become adult and can begin to transform itself to a true ethical personality, to *step out into life* as it is called and transform itself from some beautiful and imaginary 'good' to something truly good, unless, for other reasons, it continues its aesthetic life form out into this period too. *This division into three opponent stages is valid not only for the aesthetic development of the human personality, but for everything that is developed by mankind, society, technology, as well as the fine arts.* That the art academies have never had a renewing, let alone a beautifying or improving significance for artistic development, is no doubt because of their reversed position. They place the formal before the manifold and ignore renewal, and the result is stagnation.

Animism and the aesthetic attitude to life

> What in my innermost I want is to tear a hole in the reality around me and make contact with a world of light and harmony.
>
> *Ingmar Hedenius**

> Schon fast seit einem Jahrhundert wirken Humaniora nicht mehr auf das Gemüt dessen, der sie treibt, und es ist ein Glück, dass die Natur dazwischen getreten ist das Interesse an sich gezogen und uns von ihrer Seite den Weg zur Humanität geöffnet har.
>
> *Goethe*

Attitude to life and perception of the world

If *academic,* official and authorized aesthetics thus has no favourable results to show because of *its failing radicalism,* then, on the other hand, we have within the so-called *humanities or formal sciences,* which must really be perceived as *preliminary unconnected or constructed aesthetic stages in the scientific process,* a corresponding stagnation, but of an opposite cause and nature, as here there is a failure to comply with the organizational process that could transform these disciplines to natural sciences. There can be no doubt that this hesitation is because *the formation of our society and thereby our attitude to life remains at an inconsistent or aesthetic stage and hinders us from reaching an organic perception of the world.* We can only make progress or desperate tentative efforts.

The final aim of science, its perfection, is *an all-embracing objective consciousness or perception of the world* in which all our earlier limitations cease to exist, a form of consciousness in which secrets and mysteries are not to be found. But the growth of the proficiencies that are necessary to reach this perfection in our *knowledge* is conditioned by our *being,* our art and our attitude to life. Knowledge and being must be perfected into a unity, as it is through dedication and sympathetic insight that we approach perception. But in order for this goal to be achieved, our being must correspond to our *hope* and our wishes. *We must be able to do precisely what we want, and want what we can do, and have reached our subjective perfection in order to reach our culmination, the all-controlling ability, in order to achieve our perfect objectivity, an all-embracing knowledge, to become gods.*

314   The Natural Order and Other Texts

Animation, animism and religion

> In the end art should so dominate our lives, that we might say:
> There are no longer works of art, but *art* only. For art is then the way of life.
>
> *Herbert Read**

It is our surplus of interest that makes mysteries and secrets of external phenomena. The day we are not interested in anything other than what we *are*, no more problems and unsolved puzzles will exist. Some people seek to advance this completion by halting renewal, but everything has to reach its natural culmination. No one knows where this lies as far as humanity is concerned. *The human being's curiosity, thirst for knowledge and need for dedication appears to stop only at the limits of the universe, at absolute non-existence. The human being wants to know everything and be everything.* Will this will towards omnipotence, which has already driven us so far, end with us in the ditch, will we stop at an incapable dreaming, or will we one day rule the universe? No one can answer this question, and everyone takes their own standpoint.

Here we have come to the question of the position of aesthetics in the religious problem. *We have defined art as a way of life and aesthetic art as life renewal, the enlivening, animating, agitating, inspiring, aspirational, enthusiastic, fermenting, fascinating, fanaticizing, the explosive and rebellious, renewal or the unknown.* No one who has any knowledge of the religious problem can be in doubt that the factors we have been dealing with here are the same as those that form the basic themes of the religious complex of problems, even though they are here treated from another point of view.

The aesthetic concept of god

> The cat wants the fish, but won't get its paw wet.

Besides the temples for all the nature gods, the Greeks also built a temple to 'the unknown god', which we here have called the aesthetic principle of nature. Strangely enough, this is exactly where Christianity takes its point of departure.

But it was only at the Reformation, indeed, *really only by Søren Kierkegaard, that the purely animistic or spiritual, or what we would call the aesthetically paradoxical or absurd perception of religion, was set* out. We will not go outside our delineated task, but just indicate that this development in religious perception is clearly apparent when one compares the primitive agriculturists' perception of the *life-nourishing* bread as something holy, Catholicism's perception of the *priest-blessed* bread as divine, and then the

Reformed Church's emphasis that it is not the material but the word, *imagination*, fantasy, that is holy. That thousands and again thousands of people have fought, killed and have been killed for the development of this perception is completely incomprehensible, if one does not take the social background of the problem into account. We will later return to this problem. But, *as we have formulated the problem,* we cannot avoid pointing out that *neither the academy nor the university's scientific faculties can be perceived as the primary official authority for aesthetics. They are only sorting the fish that is brought to market, and serving it in melted butter, an immensely commendable but hardly renewing work. If aesthetics is to be perceived as the doctrine about and the treatment of the unknown, then the state church and the theological faculty are the highest aesthetic authorities in the country,* but since Peter's haul of fish, it has not, as is well-known, dared to dip the fishing-line. Without insulting anyone, it could perhaps be said that the Christian church is immensely content as far as fish and bread are concerned, and one has the impression that the conservation and protection of the word takes up their minds more than its use. After the salt has lost its strength, one goes over, as Paul Claudel says, to preserving with sugar, but thereby one has really denied one's own foundation. This question is sufficiently and clearly laid out in Søren Kierkegaard's writings.

Gods of sensation and supermen

Whosoever becomes a sheep, will be eaten by wolves.

The paralysing impotence of Christianity against the modern sensational and primitive forms of religion is, however, a highly disquieting sign. The modern *messiah, redeemer or saviour figure,* as delineated in popular supernatural gods or supermen like Jack Lightning or The Phantom and similar master criminals, super-beings or *lawless* heroes of the imagined struggle for justice, not to speak of that divine sensation, the hydrogen bomb, the reappearance of which is invoked by such heretical poets as Øverland,* shows that the petit bourgeois longing to place the responsibility elsewhere and become a passive sheep in the flock under an amoral or super-moral *leader's* leadership energetically and systematically saturates the folk mentality so consistently that one has the impression that journalism is little by little placing less weight upon distributing information than on animating with cartoon series for the cultivation of fascist religiosity. But if they represent a spiritual falling-back, then in itself this cannot be wrong. The fault lies with Christianity, the teaching of which has hitherto gone bankrupt when confronted with the new ethical and

316   *The Natural Order and Other Texts*

aesthetic problems that evolution has forced upon the modern human being, and which demand practical and spiritual solution.

Crime and fault

> Liars, thieves and vagabonds are the bitter salt of the earth.

This heroic cult of destruction, which, in the symbolic shape of the outsider and the superman or super-being, has released the self-sacrificing martyr cult and made them both into caricatures, forces a new and deeper insight into the essence of truth and the actions that witness to the character of truth, for we must not forget that *it is worse to be at fault than to commit crimes*, that the true fault lies in sins of omission, in saying no to life and personal responsibility.

'Ugly are the sins you have committed, but far worse groans the life unlived,' says Johannes V. Jensen,* and that life is there to be lived and lived by all, that it can only be lived by ourselves personally, is the full personal responsibility of every personality, every human being. Mercilessly, regardless and without compassion, this is the new, inexorable truth of today and tomorrow.

Aesthetics as action, coup de théâtre or effect

> I want to try to fasten my gaze upon myself and begin to act inwardly, as only thereby, just like the child by its first conscious action calling itself 'I', am I able, thus in a more profound sense to call myself 'I'.
>
> *Søren Kierkegaard*

> In choosing it depends not so much on choosing the correct thing, as on the energy, the earnestness and pathos, with which one chooses.
>
> *Søren Kierkegaard*

A conflict about words

After having briefly detailed our terminology in the various areas of intellectual life, we will now send our searchlight in a couple of sweeps over the biological and the cultural problems in order here too to draw in a cursory sketch the necessary consequences of our perception.

To most people, the previous passage will perhaps seem to have been just a conflict about words, and this could be quite correct. However, if it has been noticed what a prominent place this conflict about words has had throughout the times and with what bloody passion it has been waged, in order not only to master the word but above all its interpretation and meaning, then it will also have been understood that this word-conflict is a dispute about world-pictures, attitudes to life and perceptions of society, and as such the necessary precondition for understanding and actively entering into a new development. Language is the key to the understanding of the new, because it changes the context and the meaning of the old when new experiences come along. Words must therefore be constantly dislocated in their meaning.

Everywhere system and order is created, it is the one who is the strongest or the most superior at using orthography and what is placed in words that turns out to be right. It is left to the reader to judge whether our definitions possess the inner strength that can draw them in from the world of curiosities as an element in a universal perception.

318 *The Natural Order and Other Texts*

The action creates the idea

> And they sensed the sounding word and the airy thought.
>
> *Sophocles*

> *La pensée se fait dans la bouche.*
>
> *Tristan Tzara*

We have defined the aesthetic phenomenon as *effect without cause*, but natural science has demonstrated that any effect has its cause, its precondition, and that this cause is in its turn the effect of a previous cause. Thus by deduction we can trace back to the first cause discussed by Aristotle: the primary reason, meaning or idea that is the essence of the cause and the origin of all development. Along the way, we come logically to an idealistic world-view, and this perception of the primary position of the cause or meaning in a causal context leads us therefore naturally to the famous thesis: *In the beginning was the word.*

This thesis should not be perceived literally, for if we say that *it is the words that produce thoughts and ideas*, we have in fact said just the opposite, even though we feel we have said it correctly. The word in this first perception is identical with the idea or the meaning.

If we now go in the opposite direction and try to follow and enter into the development instead of analyzing it, then we come automatically to the opposite result, that *it is the effect, the meaningless, inane, absurd or free action, that in certain cases creates causes or is transformed to meaning and context*, that it is action which creates reaction, radicalism which creates conservatism, effect which creates influence. *Only when the effect collides with an opposition, as when two effects crash together, is it transformed into a cause.* This artistic or materialistic world view leads just as naturally back to Goethe's well-known thesis: *in the beginning was the action.*

Possibility creates meaning

> Life may well be understood backwards but it has to be lived forwards.
>
> *Søren Kierkegaard*

> There is never so little an eel, that it does not strive to become a whale.

We have hereby placed aesthetics foremost in the development or evolutionary context and maintain that *it is possibility that creates necessity and not vice versa.* We have in fact turned all of evolutionary theory hitherto on its head. If

Darwin perceives the aesthetic as the rudiment of necessity, then we, on the other hand, perceive *necessity as an extraction or organization of the surplus.* We maintain that the universe and nature evolve from within as an *ego* by an inner distinction. In contrast to Nietzsche, we maintain that *I is older than you.* The distinctions between I and you thus exist only as variants in a deeper lying ego called *we*, which is the theme on which the variations I and you are played. The novelty in our perception is that we maintain that it is variation or effect that creates the theme or the cause, which is in turn able to give birth to new variations, that *it is the discharge or expression which creates the impression or reflex.* The inherently obvious fact that *the action creates the meaning* or context leads naturally to the conclusion that there is no meaning behind things but only in the things themselves, that meaningless things are to be found, and that it is our ability to form new meaningless words and images which give birth to new thoughts and ideas, that expressions and gestures are not evoked by feelings, but are simply feelings we become conscious of through sensation. As early as Pascal it was demonstrated that religious action creates religious consciousness. Muscle movements create glandular secretions and thereby emotion or the body's collected continual reaction. It is the same with natural evolution as a whole.

320 *The Natural Order and Other Texts*

Features of the aesthetics of natural history

> The human being is neither an abortion nor a giant. The task of poetry is not to disturb or slander the human being. Our inborn human imperfection is in its order like the constant deformity of the petal of a plant. What we regard as a deformation is a form, and what seems the overturning of a law is the fulfilment of a law.
>
> *H. Taine*

Environment creates inheritance

What is called environment is just another expression for action or effect, whilst the inheritable is the expression of cause or context. Thus we maintain that the context is just one side of the essence of the environment, the side that reveals itself by an analytical backward look, the context and continuity of the established spheres of interest. Without any understanding of the present conflict between the biological standpoints of Morgan and Lysenko, our aesthetic theory compels us to set out this theory:

That pure heredity is an abstraction, that the biological system in a living individual can never appear as purely genetic, but that, because of nature's unceasing aesthetic mobility, in the nucleus of every individual there are always new purely individual dispositions which, however indistinct, meaningless or regardless, are not to be found in the mother individual and are not conditioned by external influences during growing up. That the family or species is a theme on which nature incessantly plays all the variations quantitatively, mathematically, geometrically and constructively possible. Thereby all the inwardly conditioned tendencies that can arise are consistently realized. That mutations are conditioned by possibilities and not by necessity or logic, and that individuality or personality is not a rarity but an inevitable general rule.

Foolhardiness creates wisdom

> Ich bin ein Teil des Teils, der anfangs alles war.
>
> *Goethe*

Is it not, however, a fact that matter and nature are not a chaos, but an ordered whole? No, that is a misunderstanding : *it is both a chaos and a whole*, and the wholeness is conditioned by the chaotic, the establishment of the dissolution.

A fool can ask more than ten wise men can answer, thus in one way a fool must be wiser than ten wise men, or at any rate be the precondition for wisdom, as all wisdom is an answer to foolish questions and is conditioned by such questions being posed: the greater the foolishness the greater the wisdom. This is immensely comforting to know, when one is working theoretically.

Just as the sense of sight invariably summarizes objects that lie close to each other into figures, units, bodies or objects according to the law of gestalt, so we too organize our knowledge in *forms* and units. Here we are only following a natural law. It is similarly so with our ability to *break apart* and dissolve this formal world, which is a necessary condition for extending it. We can set up the following law that is valid for nature as a whole, as well as every type, species or individual:

On the strength of its construction, every system, every sphere of interest, mental as well as physical, has an absolute limit of evolution, which it is unable under any circumstances to transgress in time or space except by dissolution in favour of the formation of a new and richer structure.

In contrast, because of the complexity of its structure, every sphere of interest demands an absolute minimum of matter, of spatial or temporal possibilities, without which its creation is impossible, and the disappearance of which marks the dissolution of the sphere of interest!

Ideality is possibility

These two laws limited by maximum and minimum possibility are valid not just in nature, but also in the world of humans. *Every machine, every form of society, every ideological system, every technique has its absolute limit of evolution, where it must be discarded to give place to a new system, in which the functions can achieve greater development.* On the other hand, it would have been impossible to invent the steam hammer in the Stone Age. Indeed, its very invention and utilization is conditioned by our continued ability to use a stone as a crushing tool, just as *the human being's existence is conditioned by the continued existence of the whole of plant and animal worlds down to the simplest virus and rhizopod, by the complicated existence of minerals, fluids and gases even.* When we therefore talk of discarding a form of evolution, this is only a partial truth, as *progress is not always an elimination of what went before, but rather an expansion of the central purpose through a cycle, where the evolution towards the perfect goes through a corresponding evolution towards greater imperfection.* Hereby we have in reality found the formula for the relativity of ideality and are able to give it its truth value in relation to concrete phenomena and spheres of interest, as we maintain that:

Ideality or the model exists in certain spheres of interest as latent possibilities not yet realized.

Thus we have seen that the ideal is something not outside but within the phenomena. But of what then does the subjective goal consist? It consists of *power*, of expansion, of the most unlimited control of matter. All organisms are striving towards this.

The process of sensation

It is said that one must learn to listen in order to be able to learn to command. *In nature it is just the opposite. Only by having the ability to control does this become serviceable.* The organism that at a given moment is able to negotiate the most varied and compounded interests controls these in a superficial sense or controls the surface of the material, being the *sensational or aesthetic* element in the context, as without effective resistance it is able to expand itself into something quite unusually significant. A process of fermentation creates a manifoldness of surfaces in matter and through this process of fermentation, the purified type evolves. From being a dominating and meaningless factor, it is transformed into an element in a new context. It is the transformation of infatuation to love.

We know this process of sensationalizing or fermenting from *the sensationalization and modernism* of cultural life. One just forgets that this stage – where a phenomenon, be it scientific like Darwinism and psychoanalysis or practical like new medicines and technical finesse or song, dance, etc., becomes a *pastime and occupation,* occupying all possible and impossible human beings and foaming up in a cloud of bubbling stuff and nonsense, fantasy and excitement, especially in a democratic society – is the touchstone of the value of the phenomenon, for *what is left where sensation has fallen back and is forgotten is what is called culture.* Its nature is conditioned by the kind of sensations. A cultural evolution will therefore be known by what it finds sensational. This is not a matter of *whether* lying goes on, but what the lying is about. *The task of aesthetics is to create rebellion.*

The human being is ideal

At a given moment the crust of the earth with all its chemical variants was precipitated in such a roaring and bubbling process, that, by a geological disintegration and dissolution of the surface, it gave place to plant and animal life, which in the Jurassic period expanded in all its unusual meaninglessness. We thus dare to maintain that:

True natural evolution, the inwardly conditioned biological process on Earth, has culminated. All biological beings, mankind included, have reached their natural perfection and as such cannot be improved, but only varied or form cancer tumours.

Any talk therefore of supermen or human racial improvement is rubbish. The nature and ability of humanity is unimprovable, even though it is not utilized to perfection.

On what do we base this statement? Simply *because humanity can now be seen to be able to interfere in and change the order and evolution of nature.* This would have been an impossibility as long as humanity was itself in nature's casting ladle.* One cannot create before one is created oneself, and humanity would not be able to know nature as an object unless nature as a whole had been shaped.

Features of the aesthetics of cultural history

> It is beautiful to see Adam and Eve in a paradise where they can have everything they point to, but it is however even finer to see a man acquire what he needs by his work.
>
> - thereby the human being is great, greater than all the other creations, in that he can care for himself,. It is beautiful to see a man have a surplus that he has himself acquired, but it is also beautiful to see a man make an even greater piece of art, to transform a little into much. This is the expression of the human being's perfection: that he can work. It is an even higher expression therefore: that he must do it.
>
> *Søren Kierkegaard*

Culture is imperfect

Throughout thousands of years, the human being has on the whole remained physically and spiritually unchanged. It is human community life, art, technique and culture that has evolved, not the human being as a biological incidence. The human being's changing of natural forms and natural sequences has evolved with incredible speed, and will result in nature, as it functioned before human intervention, being replaced by a new nature. Already today, the cry of 'back to nature' in the form of a return to the vegetative natural state is an absurdity, as this nature no longer exists and can never be recreated.

Natural value and human value are not the same, because the circles of interest of nature and the human being are not identical. Nature was not created for the sake of the human being, and *the human being is the first being that refuses to be created for nature's sake: the subjugation of nature to the human being's will is sought by imagination,* which has sprung from the belief that one can do *what* one will. This certainly also has the opposite effect of that intended, because one cannot do *as* one will. Because Mohammed wanted the mountain to come to him, he went to the mountain. To get nature to work for one, the human being reworks nature. To transform the earth into a paradise, he makes it into a hell at the same time. The diligence of the human being is because of laziness. This is quite obvious, as these two names stand over the same gate: when one is before it, it says *hell,* and when one has come through it and looks back, it says *paradise.* There is therefore no reason to take these signs seriously. There are too many of them. They are also called the impossible and the obvious, and with a touch of genius one has swapped the signs.

Natural and artificial

> In every Martha there is an aspiration to be a Maria.
> It is this aspiration that makes her a Martha.
>
> *Hulda Lütken*

As nature is the expression of what is, then the human being and everything that the human being does and can do must be natural or a form of nature. The human being cannot thus do anything at all that is unnatural. That he can do it, is simply to say that it is natural. But why does one talk of the artificial versus the natural, culture versus nature, when both technique and machines are nature? This is because certain actions can be unnatural or unhealthy *for the human being.*

In itself, objectively, a large juicy apple produced by culture is no better than the sour little wood apple. Indeed, for the apple tree it is perhaps even a less healthy degeneration. It is *for the human being* that the larger apple has an actual increase of value. *The human being thus utilizes the possibilities of variation in nature that lie outside its own sphere of interest and possibility.* A typical example of this is the many variants of roots and cabbages that have been extracted from the sea-kale.

The human being needs certain means of nourishment to live. This *need* varies according to climate and individuality. With a primitive agriculture, such as we know from the Stone Age and primitive peoples, the necessary food can be produced to cover the necessary need. However, in the cookery book we have thousands of recipes for food and drink that go beyond these demands of necessity, and *this aesthetic and unnecessary development can be traced back to primitive peoples.* So can even certain foods that have no nourishment value at all but only taste or animating value. We also find this condition in the question of clothes, buildings, everywhere. Why should the means of production utilized for the production of these obvious but biologically unnecessary goods not have arisen in the same way? *Did the brain of the human being not evolve through a purposeless expansion of mischievousness and pure viciousness until he one day he saw himself able to throw a stone and use a stick with purpose and in earnest?*

Nature and culture

This utilization of the tool is the point of departure for human art, culture and technique, and creates an opponent relationship between nature in and around

326   The Natural Order and Other Texts

us and our wider modes of action. *We come into conflict with the whole order of nature.*

Nature is a subject and has created and evolved itself from *within. Nature has no hands and cannot put anything together.* But the human being can. *In nature structure and function are identical.* However, on the strength of his ability to distinguish between *body* (the sphere of interest perceived as object or organ) and *soul* (the same sphere of interest perceived as subject, power or *function*), the human being is able to create *bodies that have their function external to them: in humanity,* and thus to create in themselves soulless bodies and make these into parts of the human organism, *not as absolute being* or what for the human being is the absolute known, *but as possession,* as something people *have* without being it themselves. The human being can fly without being a bird. *Human technique is thus something that is built up externally to the individual, mutually between people and between the human being and nature. Therefore all cultures and techniques are not personal but social phenomena, not a question of being but of having, a problem of property.*

The sociology of the aesthetics of European high culture

> For the sake of the rose one also waters the thorns.
> *Arab proverb*

The birds of the air have nests and the animals of the fields have holes, and both ants and bees have immensely complicated social formations, and all these are natural possessions. It is, on the whole, incredible how many parallels to human technique are to be found in the world of nature, but we have to let all this comprehensive problem around the art work and artistic technique be. Here we will content ourselves with dealing with the aesthetics of the way of life itself and even that only in its generalized features.

It is correct to speak of the communal body, for the human community really is a living organism, an ego, albeit a fissured and divided one, and can with full right be regarded a unit or circle of interest, a subject.

Aesthetic culture or civilization

> Der Künstler hat zur Natur ein zweifaches Verhältnis: er ist ihr Herr und ihr Sklave, insofern er mit irdischen Mitteln wirken muss um verstanden zu werden, ihr Herr aber, insofern er disse irdischen Mittel seinen höheren Intentionen unterwirft und ihnen dienstbar mach.
> *Goethe*

We have defined the aesthetic as the unusual and the unique, and, *in contrast to this, culture is tradition or custom, organized or social art, popular art.*

This definition of culture is, however, not valid for what is called *high culture, which is just an aesthetic traditionalism that is the experimental area of true culture.* High culture is a phenomenon that flares up and vanishes, whilst popular culture steadily develops by extracting the durable elements from the ruins of high culture. One is rarely aware of this *opponent relationship between high and popular culture*, because, as a rule, it is representatives of high culture who interest themselves theoretically in the question and precisely therefore perceive it as 'the high' instead of the superficial. We can thus thank high culture for the cultural picture being constantly broken down and by this having the possibility of renewal.

Culture is the cultivation of human values, and it is obvious that the human being will only become a real cultural being the day the whole earth is under a universal planned cultivation or administration of people. Anyone can see that this moment is approaching with violent speed. Even the fishes in the sea are

328 *The Natural Order and Other Texts*

close to being kept as pets.

However, the phenomenon of high culture as an aesthetic factor has to be the focus of our interest, because it is here that expansion and renewal occurs. European high culture is that phenomenon generally designated as *modern civilization*, and as such stands in a peculiar opponent relationship to true human culture.

Aggressive culture

> The course of civilization has been like that of Judas, and, like him, also seems to be driven towards suicide by an irresistible force.
>
> *Nis Petersen*

In our definition of organisms we made a distinction between the *reproductive* and the *aggressive* activity. What causes *certain races to stagnate upon a particular step of culture and not try to go further, remaining satisfied, harmonious and as if resting in themselves* until other races penetrate their area, and what is the reason why these *other races are unruly, discordant, curious and industrious?* That this is not for biological or racial reasons is well known, as all races can demonstrate the potentialities for the cultivation of the same abilities. That it is not because of nature and climate either is demonstrated by a comparison between the cultural developments of North American Indians and Europeans. Therefore it must be because of *the opportunities offered by the social and cultural structure of the various groups.* When an Indian chief wanted to show his power, he *destroyed* all his property. This form of the utilization of surplus power by simply destroying it, shows that the potentialities of exploitation in this given way of life were used to their fullest. *Life is productivity and forms of life are forms of production.* Probably no one would seriously deny this fact. The Western European production system has created modern technology and until recent years has been the most active and superior in the world. *The Western European has always shown himself to be the cruellest, falsest, most cunning, complacent, purposeless, greedy, and consequently also the most purposeful, humble, compassionate and self-sacrificing, in short 'the best'.* As, in the first place, this epoch in world history is past, and, in the second place, we ourselves belong to this cultural circle, we have every reason to use this phenomenon in dissolution, which has been called '*the European*', as an object of study for the phenomenon of the aesthetic society. '*Untergang des Abendlandes*' is not a future perspective, but a simple statement of what was happening to Spengler himself or Hitler. *Europe still exists but not as the best.*

The European aesthetician

No one is in any doubt that 'the European' is something other than the European in general. *The European person Spengler and all other 'Europeans' talk about, is quite precisely the European aristocrat*, just as *'European culture' in this connection is aesthetic high culture.*

The European aristocrat is the unproductive person in a material sense, and thus the aesthetic person, and where one talks of an aristocracy, the luxury class or the purposeless social class, it is a case of *the players*, the aggressors. In our society, this superficial and peripheral group is made a model or centre for the efforts of society, whilst *the power of production, the true vital force, is subjugated to this aggressive or destructive power of violence, these players.* Hereby an immensely fruitful tension and social disquiet is created. *The upper class has thus been the field of cultural experimentation for European society, and the aristocrat the experimenter.* This is this social group's greatest value, although its only social one. What has been the driving force in this social group's need for exclusivity and renewal? Principally it has been its fantasies or *idealism*, that made it able to squeeze the life force into forms that were actually quite *unachievable*, thereby making the effort *endless.*

Desire and comfort

Gold is good but cake is better.

One could say that *the European aristocracy has perceived luck as a holy duty and has made the movement towards the unknown, or evolution, into its profession or morality by perceiving the aesthetic craving not as a possibility but as a necessity, something a priori, static and inevitable or ethical, as bad luck was death to it.*

If the human being regards it necessary to fulfil all its *wishes*, then what it could regard as necessary is unlimited, for its ability to wish seems to be unlimited.

If the human being just regards it necessary to satisfy its needs, then what it can regard as unnecessary and as meaningless disturbance of its peace and quiet is incredible. *Thus it is aesthetic phenomena like dissatisfaction, envy, covetousness, the destructive urge and other idealisms that make people develop the good sides of their character.* In a biological sense, a human being does not need to stay alive after its children have been born and brought up.

However, aristocratic evolution has created new needs, this has happened simply by these being neglected in favour of wishes. 'If they cannot get their

330 The Natural Order and Other Texts

daily bread, let them eat cake', is the aristocrat's attitude to popular demands. When, however, the wild hunt for *cakes* created satiation and inertia, absolutely worthless values that replaced life values were found in *gold* and diamonds, and *when there is talk of value in Western Europe, then this means money, the pure, valueless dream* that justifies the insatiable hunger or absolute craving for evolution in the three stages of *sensory desire, craving for money and ambition.*

Money has no smell

> Money, violence and god's grace command respect, right and art.

Monetary value is an absolutely conventional or social illusion and the hunt for money is the hunt for an idea or an ideal. *In itself a currency note is quite without value. It is an absolute and pure possibility* conditioned only by people's *belief* in it. With this the perfect aesthetic goal is achieved. *But the hunt for money is the hunt to force new requirements on other people. The immense cultural value of the discovery of money* is that it only works for *added value.*

The development of this system took place through the Mesopotamian, Phoenician, Greek, Roman and Jewish cultural streams and marked the fate of these peoples. Only the Jews survived this process during their homeless wanderings on the strength of their contempt for *actual* values, and it was therefore figures like *Moses, Christ, Spinoza and Marx who,* in their attitude to things and to the duties and rights of ownership, *shaped epochs* in humanity's subjective struggle for freedom.

Debt and credit

> God is a millionaire!
> *Frank Buchmann*

In its innermost being, aesthetic evolution is a *credit system*, an uninterrupted *investment in the unknown*, in which there is to be found no demonstrable cover, only risk. This can, however, be profitable, because the belief in credit, deferred payment of debt, and the feeling of compromise compels renewed endeavour. *For centuries Europe has lived on credit and expected appropriation – for whom? For its future.*

If one is only one's own slave and is fighting for an uninterrupted liberation of oneself for oneself, then credit has ideality, but *if credit is compelled as a charity or help from without, then compliance is grudging and without ideality* and enthusiasm. This has always been the case with the broad masses of people in Europe and today it is the case for Europe as a whole. We have been well helped, as they say.

That this way of life *animated by a credit system* has had its ideological attitude to life shaped poetically in Christianity's teaching of guilt or deferred payment is so striking that no one can be a good Christian without knowing and valuing the practical investment economy. This is a question of what is officially regarded as most important in this teaching.

The bankruptcy of aristocratism

> He who takes gifts, makes himself a slave, and sells his freedom.

We do not produce to satisfy humanity's vital or reproductive needs, but to create surplus. However, *instead of talking about production surplus, it is now called surplus production, and from talk of free time we have today gone over to calling it unemployment.* This beautiful phenomenon has taken on a bitter taste, because idealism or possibilities are lacking. The same point has been reached as the North American Indians. One can only demonstrate one's surplus power and create new possibilities by destroying commodities or people. The possibilities of investment are used up and there is now use for new ideas, new perspectives, and these all point towards a change of the productive and ideological system from aristocratic production to productive democracy.

European aristocracy has had no race-refining or biologically improving value, despite this having been used as a pretext for the privileges enjoyed by this group. On the other hand, it has had a value as a driving force in the increase of production and the gradual union of humanity and inter-racial unity, even though in itself it has acted as a shock, a divisive restlessness and an unproductive exploiter. This is the self-contradictory condition of all action.

Conquest, exploitation and administration

> Peace is only best if one wants to do something.

This evolution has happened via *war, oppression, colonization and self-destruction* to the advantage of a new centre of violence. In this way high culture was shifted from Mesopotamia over Greece to Rome, which colonized the whole of Europe, and, with the Renaissance to the whole world. Just as we have divided the aesthetic process into three mutually conflicting movements, *transformation, beautification and refinement,* we can divide social acquisition into three corresponding stages: *conquest,* which is perceived by the aristocracy

332   The Natural Order and Other Texts

as the *aesthetic* stage, *exploitation*, which is perceived as the *ethical* stage, and *administration* or settlement, which is perceived as the resigned or *religious* stage, representing *a power shift between military aristocracy, trade aristocracy and intellectual aristocracy,* a trinity we often see symbolized in the sword, the scales and the book, but whose mutual conflicts have often been of a very dramatic nature. Of course, the aristocracy must also perceive its own existence as a necessity, and as this cannot be determined materially, then it must be done by maintaining the immobility of ideality. From this comes *aesthetic ethics.*

Perspectives of renewal

> Art only wishes war for the sake of peace.
> *Georg Brandes*

At a time when all the peoples of the earth, so to speak, know each other, these functions automatically lose their value, which lay only in their social, aggressive, domineering or aesthetic significance, and all the huge surplus of energy that modern technology has created is now streaming towards new tasks, *from the mutual rapprochement or infighting between human beings to a struggle to acquire nature and subjugate it. The productive or artistic human being thereby stands out as the dominant power factor, and the aesthetic or exciting factor, where the investment hazarded can be absorbed, goes over to science and the fine arts, whilst the democratic enrichment of living standards ends the fermentation in social tension.* Today this unknown perspective, which began with the democratic currents in the previous century, is what we are seeing expanding with an irresistible force. In prehistory, every man was buried with his weapon, because the group was not in peace with its neighbours. Today a war even between the Scandinavian countries is almost unthinkable and we are participating in the dramatic birth of united humanity with individual equal rights.* *This does not mean that the conflict of interests is becoming less. On the contrary, it is just becoming of another character.*

Aesthetics as radicalism, masculine aggression or seduction

> Oh, everywhere noise. And as one says of an exciting drink, it moves the blood, so in our times [always A.J.] everything, even the most insignificant affair, everything, even the most inane message, is just calculated to shake the senses or to touch the masses, the many, the public, the noise! And the human being, that sagacious head, that has been almost sleepless in order to find new, new means to increase the noise, to spread with greatest possible haste and according to the largest possible measure the row and the meaninglessness. Yes, contrariness is soon reached: the message is soon brought to the lowest level in the direction of significance, whilst at the same time the means of communication have about reached the highest level in the direction of rapid and all-flooding distribution. Consequently what is in so much hurry to get out, and, on the other hand, what has greater distribution than – rubbish? Oh, seek silence!
>
> *Søren Kierkegaard*

The dynamics of the state

The two principles *effect* and *cause*, aggression and reproduction, renewal or *aesthetics* and conservation or *ethics*, have been given their bourgeois expression in the social process by the opposition between *private initiative and the state*. We have demonstrated that these two concepts are neither absolute nor mutually independent but mutually invoke and abolish each other, that the state can never be a static or absolute *a priori*, and the private or meaningless by resistance is always conditioned by the context.

As is well known, the word idiot means private person, and this description harmonizes excellently with the consistently absurd and meaningless in the very character of aesthetic or private initiative. But if the expansion of this pleasant activity is reserved for certain tradespeople, one must then introduce the just as absurd belief in the absolute and eternal principle of the state, the immovable and inflexible regularity.

In our time, the understanding has been reached that nothing is immovable and that therefore the state as an absolute concept is just an abstraction. New ethical and aesthetic perspectives in social life have hereby been opened up. The perception of the state has become dynamic. The evolution of society is changing the social context incessantly, and what most indicates a development towards greater social stability is not the growing social initiative of the peasant and the worker – we have seen that before, for example, in the Middle Ages –

334   *The Natural Order and Other Texts*

but the growing equal rights and penetration into the administration of society of women.

When woman created man

> The first thought in women and the second in men are always the best.

It has turned out that much has evolved quite differently from our imaginings. If we examine biological evolution, then we will see that Eve comes before Adam. In primitive animal forms the male is just a little attachment to the female, a side-bone, a cutlet which, into the bargain, she eats after fertilization has occurred. If one looks further into evolution, then one gets the impression that *the male, who has the least genetic significance and who is the most superfluous* (something we also recognize in the law of the hunt), evolved into an aesthetic phenomenon for the entertainment, distraction and enjoyment of the female, until in the higher animals, the male develops his aggressive and destructive capabilities and becomes both attacker and defender, and thus, in short, the avant-garde of the evolution of life. *Consequently, on the strength of his lesser actual value, the male becomes the external and superficial power or ruler.* Therefore one will also see that the man's aesthetic or renewing abilities will therefore also be seen to be greater generally than those of the woman, whilst in return the woman has greater powers of conservation and harmonization or ethics than the man. In a purely aggressive race without culture, the man has to be the supreme ruler.

It is perhaps correct that women discovered agriculture, the foundation of humanity's constructive or cultural existence, but it is just as certain, at any rate, that where the man keeps to his earlier occupation with hunting and fishing, social development stagnates in a happy state where the men hang about idling and the women work diligently and with satisfaction.

On the strength of her genetic significance, the woman (apart from exceptions) is not and cannot be a luxury being. The man, on the other hand, (apart from some exceptions) can. It is therefore quite innocuous nonsense to perceive the woman as a luxury animal. But as far as the man is concerned, the situation is seriously different.

From killer to creator

> Woman has, all in all, an innate talent and a primitive gift of an absolute virtuosity for clarifying finiteness.
>
> – she understands this profoundly, she is therefore lovely, and, in essence, every woman is therefore is graceful, and no man is that. Therefore she is happy, happy as no man can or should be.
>
> - she is more perfect than the man, as the one who explains something is more than the one that hunts for an explanation. The woman explains finiteness. The man searches for infinity.
>
> *Søren Kierkegaard*

The man's transformation from killer to producer is in fact the most difficult process in human history and it is not finished yet. The difficulty lies above all in finding new perspectives for humanity's aesthetic or renewing abilities. The particular difficulty here lies in the idealistic or absolute belief in improvement or one-sided progress that halts opportunities for development.

However, as our task is not of a constructive but of an instructive kind, we will turn back to the European superman and see if we can also create a little variation and context in that picture.

336 *The Natural Order and Other Texts*

Faust • Don Juan • Ahasuerus • Hamlet★

> I have observed that the strange humming, plaintive sound with which a little projectile from a rifle penetrates the air is far more life-giving to the public than the fullest orchestral tones.
>
> Only in the projectile's *personality* do I find the explanation why its rough music makes an impression on the human race.
>
> *Johannes Holbek*

> What Holbek calls personality, I call *quality*.
>
> *A.J.*

Liberator, libertine and liberalist

In our aesthetic high culture, we have been able to distinguish between three different spheres of existence, which have furnished three different, apparently independent aesthetics, that mutually exclude each other, if they are not to be perceived as stages in the aesthetic process:★

1. *The aesthetics of idealistic conquest,* which we know especially from *German* philosophy, and which places the emphasis upon renewal, fantasy, the wish or the phenomenon of the idealization: *the aesthetics of liberation.*

2. *The aesthetics of varying appropriation,* which we know especially from *French* art and philosophy and which puts the emphasis upon manifold richness and initiation, the phenomenon of the introduction: *the aesthetics of beauty or the libertine.*

3. *The aesthetics of ennobling exploitation* which we know especially from the utilitarian *English* philosophy of pleasure where the emphasis is placed upon the formal problem of harmony: *the aesthetics of control or liberalism.*

German aesthetics

> Without war the world would stagnate in materialism.
>
> *Field-Marshall von Moltke*

This reference to the high culture of these three countries is not accidental. Throughout the centuries, Germany intellectually and materially has resembled a building site. *In spite of or rather because of their unique ability for conquest and renewal in technical, artistic and scientific respects, the Germans have never been able to conquer or appropriate, to use or maintain anything whatsoever.* Even the most refined and elegant German object has something raw, ugly, offensive and undigested about it. The Germans have been the most marked individualists in Europe, *independent and yet derivative.* The context has always been for them just an idea, capable only of realization by force from without. One might almost call *Germany the novelty centre or invention area of Europe.*

French aesthetics

> Je m'engage et puis je vois.
> *Napoleon Bonaparte*

In the same way one could call *France Europe's centre of beauty*, for no country has had the ability to get things going, to give shape to art and science, to make it look impressive, as this country. Yet *precisely their ability to capture and use everything makes France resemble a beautiful and immensely vigorous ruin, because they have lacked the ability to utilize, round off and complete* anything they have started (Panama and Suez). Frenchmen have been able to get even humanity's stupidities to look smart and elegant. They have a peculiar individualistic feeling of community. They love plans but would never think of following them. (*The ideal introduction area.*)

English aesthetics

> England expects every man to do his duty.
> *Admiral Nelson, at the bombardment of Copenhagen in 1807**

To a far higher degree, the English have understood how to criticize, discard, use and capture the essential. They have not asserted themselves with anything new or brilliant, but with *the noble and pure, the sympathetic or boring. If the Germans have been the greatest personalities and at the same time the most characterless and lacking in social attitude, then the English have been the strongest and most impersonal characters in European history.* It is almost as if they have no ideals or individuality, but only express themselves as club-people for whom the context is something absolute and obvious, something accidental – *aesthetic nonsense or sport* which best develops in meaninglessness. If the English are bored, they travel to France, and they do this all the time, just as the French seek renewal with the Germans, which happens extremely rarely. This distinction is, of course, not absolute. It merely makes clear where three amoral stages in the aesthetic process have developed in the richest and strongest manner. This was *the information area England.*

338   The Natural Order and Other Texts

Scandinavian poverty

> Je suis de race lointaine: mes pères était Scandinaves: ils se perçaient les côtes, buvaient leur sang. – Je me ferai des entailles partout le corps, je me tatouerai, je veux devenir hideux comme un Mongol: tu verras, je hurlerai dans les rues. Je veux devenir bien fou de rage.
>
> – Je l'écoute faisant de l'infamie une gloire, de la cruauté un charme.
>
> *Arthur Rimbaud**

But where does Danish and Scandinavian high culture stand in this context? Well, no European cultural history has seriously considered the existence of such a phenomenon except as an imitation. The Scandinavian countries are amongst the oldest and most intact cultures in the world and yet it is only in Sweden that there are tendencies towards a purely non-folk oriented cultural environment. *Our gift for admiration, which hinders us in choosing whilst letting others do it for us, is our most pronounced aesthetic characteristic. If one could call England Europe's centre of refinement, then one could call Scandinavia the dream centre of Europe*, if dreams can have such a thing. One of the first things that civilized history tells of the encounter with the Scandinavians is that they were such big gamblers that they not only gambled all their possessions away but also pledged themselves. Hamlet and Peer Gynt are typical of these peoples living in an unreal stage setting meant to represent Europe, but which at its most profound is just as much oriental as occidental. It is this cultural attitude that forms the basis of our study.

What Almqvist calls *the blessing of poverty* has been bestowed upon us in rich measure,* both materially and spiritually, whereas the curse of poverty, which in England became the grotesque opposite pole of refinement, human debasement, was to a great degree unknown. In no other place in the world do aestheticians plumb *the depths* in madness and poverty as often and as compellingly as here. We are brought up to it.

This delight in the dream has given Scandinavians the instinct that everything ideal is first and foremost imagination and this literally makes our cultural picture immune to the rule of aesthetic or classical high culture, which rests precisely upon the opposite principle that it is the ideal which shapes the imagination. This lack of classical tradition is the reason why Thorvaldsen was able to produce a sheer model illusion or *imitation*. In the North, we are not only at the cold frontier of civilization but of existence, truth and life themselves. *The naked field of the imagination.*

The tragic guilt

> The wild mind that has such a flight,
> that what it sees as bad soon becomes good.
> *Henrik Ibsen. Brand.*

That was the truth about that museum subject 'the European'. Crime is the juridical expression for what in psychology is called *guilt* or sense of indebtedness. *Evolution is a chain of crimes with liberation as a result. Hence the latent sense of guilt or debt that is also reflected in the economic area, unless one perceives meaninglessness and lack of responsibility as values of possibility.* The self-condemnatory element in the aesthetician's sufferings, torment, struggle and defeat, based upon his amoral wickedness, creates a crisis of conscience in him and the condemning society because the possibility endows the action with heroic pathos. *The aesthetician is at the same time guilty and not guilty.*

But we have gone beyond the tragic or heroic stage, and as Brandes remarks, 'The great characters put their honour in being guilty. This only means that the hero is too proud to move others (to encourage compassion and thereby absolution), not that he is too humble to be accused. But if the bridge is chopped off, if all the expedients for getting rid of guilt by putting them behind him, over the shoulder of fate, are not accessible, then the tragic hero has vanished.' This is interesting. *Only if one cowardly begs for grace or justification, does one become a hero.* If the aesthetician wants to be responsible for his lack of responsibility with the same dignity as the Viking or the French nobility as it was borne to the scaffold during the revolution, then heroism has vanished. Søren Kierkegaard remains in the heroic role, even though he whimpers, 'My choice is made, I divest myself of the hero's raiment and the pathos of tragedy, I am the humbled one, who feels his offence. I have one expression for what I suffer: *Guilt* – one expression for my offence: *Repentance* – one hope for my eye: *Forgiveness.*' Only a real hero who is on his way out speaks thus, hiding, like the American millionaire, his exclusivity under the grey suit of self-pity. Everything that Søren Kierkegaard and Nietzsche have written is simply aesthetics, aesthetics of genius. However, true aesthetics is a rare commodity.

340   *The Natural Order and Other Texts*

Aesthetics as inspiration, enthusiasm or spontaneity

> ...Reconnaissance, Amour, Dieu, Monarque...
>   Un homme reviendra peut-être, qui dans un seul ouvrage resumera ces quatre idées et alors notre siècle aura quelque terrible Rabelais, qui pressera la liberté comme Stendhal vient de froisser le cœur humain.
>
> *Balzac*

The artistic method of aesthetics

We have called the present work a study of the remotest or extreme phenomenon of aesthetics, and believe we have detailed it both in its independence and its essential connections.

We have not attempted to penetrate deeper into the world of beauty, but have followed its outermost limit, as in the task we set ourselves. It now seems natural if, to finish, we draw the conclusion that our perception must have for the fine arts that represent our professional interest. We will do this with a quotation from C.J.L. Almqvist:

Nothing unnatural can exist within nature. It must correspond to the general natural world hitherto presented to us and to some system or other, for otherwise it is not in nature and if it really confronts the eyes none can say: oh how untrue.

Answer in earnest for once: can art ever depict other than what can be found – namely in the human soul, in the draughtsman's soul? Is this not also a nature, a reality, a truth?

What? But by God, according to this rule, whence comes your judgement about the most idiotic irrationalities? What hinders the imagination from descent into ravings, Phoebus himself to febrile fantasy?

Take care! Perhaps after the apparent defence against irrationalities, the most dangerous still remain.

Paint, sing, write everything – only, only – *don't be boring!*

Now all the screws are loose, for if one sets oneself the goal of composing to the standard of not being boring – what rule decides such a thing? What one finds boring can please another. One is pleased with a bacchanal, another condemns that sort of thing and finds the admirable in a hymn, and not only when the genre itself is ruled by the same subjective, changeable and chance taste. What standard should the artist then have?

Have I ever said that in art one should work according to goals?

If a stroke of lightning thrills your soul, if a heaven (according to your way) dawns in it – then sing, paint or write, and you are an artist. Woe unto you otherwise. If you draw in the living features a happy stroke of lightning showed you, then this drawing is probably enjoyable – for you at the least. So you can be sure that the composition captivated at least one person.

But if you, however, sit down with resolution, despite the trouble and difficulties that it causes you (almost as if guided by a certain medicinal and expectant willingness) to compose a work that will give pleasure to, interest and refresh others – then be aware that this will please *no one*. What is vital – regardless of many a fault – has greatness within it, comes to life. What is limp and lifeless – whether or not it founders on some other good characteristic – lacks, at least, *the whole*.

Therefore obey the divine lightning, when it commands you – artist, do not speculate about whether it is reasonable, whether it is sublime, whether it is ..., be a fly caught in a spider's web, but draw – in the hour of your fortune – be glad and make glad.

But should everything then be judged according to pleasure, should enjoyment be made the core of the system and the purpose of things? In no way. But *for him who finds something admirable, enjoyment is surely there too*, a true and correct enjoyment as an inevitable consequence and fruit. By *its fruit can you thus know and measure your own work*.

Everything you put together under the rule of a heavenly fire certainly has *its own* true naturalness. If you venture to shape something outside this, be certain then that it, in a true artistic sense, will become unnatural, be it a copy of whatsoever reality there is in your vicinity, of whatsoever planks or cottage.

But – some would now say about me – how can you venture to do such a thing as to reject all theories, to hate systems, advise against all order? – and even worse, how can this be reconciled with morals, religion and all correctness, purity, virtue in fine art, when you deny the artist a standard, a goal, a mark – and just want him to be driven by an incomprehensible flame?

I hate no system that really is a system. – I have just said that the artist should not have his goal *before* him.

342   *The Natural Order and Other Texts*

The aesthetic artist and the laws of society

> Has existence become less beautiful by this observation? Not if one has an aristocracy to be joyful about, the significance of which is based on accident and accidentally based thereon. No, one has a kingdom of gods.
>
> *Søren Kierkegaard*

The social fate of aesthetics

Even though we take the fate that can overtake morals and virtue, religion and other good things lightly, we cannot, at any rate, permit ourselves to avoid detailing the fate that will overtake the enthusiastic aesthetician with sufficient courage to follow our bold programme.

We do not have space here to follow him in his struggle with matter and have to let the treatment of the aesthetics of technique and the art work wait until a later occasion, but, in continuation of the sociology of aesthetics, we would just like to investigate the reactions of the body of society to new or extreme aesthetic phenomena introduced by the human being, and thus perhaps indicate a freer position on the part of the aesthetician regarding the difficulties into which he has thrown himself.

Here it is not a matter of refined and aristocratic exclusivity feeling its right to kill, exploit and eradicate. On the contrary, we are interested in the working, artistic and creative human being occupied by this single thing, his harmonious, universally renewing and comprehensively valid art and, of course, the universal, indeed, cosmic human fellowship in artistic expression, even though the way the problem presents itself is at first the same, because the unknown has unknown intentions and effects.

We are even ignoring the struggle around the exploitation of aesthetic resources which is taking place in society today between, on the one side, the artists and the artistically conscious scientists and, on the other, the military, commercial and intellectual aristocracy, *for or against a democratic evolution.*

Heretic and criminal

> You are right – shot shall you be.

In his book on the golden mistletoe, *The Golden Bough,* Frazer describes how *primitive people often kill their medicine men when they demonstrate abnormal fortune in their healings, and thereby reveal that they have abnormal powers.* He relates that even in highly enlightened Rome, a case was brought against a farmer because his vegetables were always uncommonly well-grown, and despite the poor man being unable to point to other causes for his advance than rational working methods and well-kept tools, he was nevertheless condemned to death for his subversive activities. The story is also told that the discoverer of palm wine was killed because of his uncommon ability to invoke spirit or spirits, which did not, however, hinder his murderers from exploiting this inheritance to its fullest. *All such crimes are committed, not because of superstition but, on the contrary, because of scepticism* * *and sound common sense, in order to maintain peace and order, decency, the rules, custom and usage, bon ton and public rights and morals*, and this is in no way a thing of the past, but is and always will remain the primary social problem for aesthetics, because all renewal is crime against the rule, and as a consequence punishable.

Power and magic

Knowledge is power.

Crime or law-breaking is like a wound in the body, an irritation, that attracts all the interest because something has been committed that is not permitted. Every crime therefore is a miracle or wonder, be it just the theft of a chest of drawers.* If, however, the action is successful in showing that the impossible was possible *for someone*, then we have come outside the area of extreme aesthetics, *the unknown has become partially known, the powerless has become a power or a magical factor*, the aesthetic has been transformed into art in its primary meaning. We see that we are here using the word *magic* as a synonym for *art* or *power*, and the word *magician* for *the artist* in the meaning shoe*maker*, watch*maker* etc. and are ignoring that the word has gradually only been attached to makers of magic by thought, word and imagination.*

I want briefly to sketch this new presentation of the problem, even though it falls outside our demarcated task, also because much lack of clarity rules in this indistinct area.

Secret powers

Every advance is immoral until the majority is convinced.
*Bernard Shaw**

The *new, strange and unique* have these designations because it is the novelty that invokes our wonder on account of its rarity. We have hereby established the aesthetic state of *desire* and *anxiety* called neurosis. The *unique* power or

344 *The Natural Order and Other Texts*

sphere of interest acts in society, the sphere of interest wherein it isolates itself, as a *secret, a mystery* which can seem *threatening* and dangerous to others because it can act as a destructive or tyrannical monopoly. The aggression thus accumulated against this state within the state on the part of society is therefore just as healthy and natural as the body's reaction to bacteria or to the child at birth.

This is the reason why science's discoveries must always belong and be publicly accessible to the people – to humanity.

Models and admiration

> The barren ears of corns stand erect, whilst the full ones hang down.

But at the same time the unique achievement invites *imitation*, reproduction, which is the essence of art and culture, and takes on the character of *a model* and, through this, of *a forerunner*, if the initiative becomes of universal value. *Wonder has been subjectivized or critical and transformed to a play between disdain and admiration*, the comical and the heroic. A power that just rests upon imagination or that one believes is based on pure fantasy appears comical. Therefore in the discrepancy between their ability and their self-assuredness, all young people appear comical. Abominable is any power that directly and one-sidedly wishes to crush one's own sphere of interest, and tragic any power that acts in the same way and therefore has to be destroyed, but which under other circumstances could have been coordinated with our sphere of interest. The establishment of European high culture began with the establishment of secret, exclusive societies of mysteries which formed a privileged elite, a leadership or an established rule. The inevitability about democratic evolution lies in the elite only having reality as an avant-garde, as forerunners and pioneers and not as people of power. They are like the foreword to the book of life, and exclusive secrecy only has truth value if it is able to be transformed into one great secret, a universal human value.

Personality and character

> Es bildet ein Talent sich in der Stille,
> sich ein Charakter in dem Strom der Welt.
> *Goethe*

Static aesthetics has gone bankrupt in its attempts to find the absolutely admirable and the absolutely contemptible. It is profoundly symbolic that it was the parasitic plant, the golden mistletoe, that became the sign of the state within the state, the superman or master race in opposition to the masses. What has been said about the loner or the chosen one is undoubtedly correct, but *what makes the superman philosophy illusory is the condition that the masses, the indifferent multitude, do not exist at all*, are an abstraction, that everyone is a herd member as at the same time a loner or a personality.

Fate and character are synonymous, says Novalis, and Brandes adds that they, in their turn, are identical with morality. Here we have the point of departure for the superman theory. For the mistletoe, the tree is paramount and for the ruler the masses are: 'The you is older than the I' as Nietzsche said. But we maintain that fate and the ego or personality are synonyms because misfortune, as Jens August Schade has said, cannot strike he who does not carry misfortune within him, and that

I – personality, existence or expression is paramount.

You – the character, essence or impression that others have of the personality is secondary.

He – conduct is the footprint of the individual.

Individualism is not the essence of the one but of all. Character upbringing is the influence of others upon the individual, so that he adapts himself according to the social context, and character judgement is just an external evaluation of the drama of the course of life, an aesthetic evaluation of fortune and misfortune, not an evaluation of that inner accord with the action through all vicissitudes which lies beyond good and bad, which lies outside law and rights, humour and tragedy, outside the contemptible and the admirable, and which can only be expressed with words like vitality or *mood*. This is, as the Swedish poet Almqvist says, the primary criterion for all art and development, the inner strength. The social problem lies in the harmonization of the development of personality with the formation of character.

Heroism and monumentality

> Why life, why death?
> Why live, when we have to die?
> Why struggle when we know that the sword
> will be wrenched from our hand sometime?
> Wherefore these bonfires of torment and pain,
> this life of thousands of hours in slow suffering,
> this slow dying out in the suffering of death?
> *J.P. Jacobsen*

It is this difference that Johannes V. Jensen overlooks in his admiring homage

346 The Natural Order and Other Texts

to 'the superman' Knut Hamsun, when, in his book *Aesthetics and Evolution*, he compares that regrettable individual with the Nordic Vikings:

> Here Hamsun should be remembered, the great, admired model, who more than anyone else in his time tempted [one] onto the path of the author. From no one else have I received stronger impressions of Nordic revelation, sparkling Nordic genius.
>
> ...Association with him was association with the great Northerners, the exceptional menfolk of the sagas. Bjørnsson renewed the saga by placing the Nordic peasant in it again, Hamsun *was* the peasant, the saga itself, physically as well as mentally, a giant to look at and bubbling with wit and feeling, a finer instrument than any other so-called cultural personage has ever been able to show the equal.
>
> He had also the Northerners' great faults, but they were great weaknesses in a sumptuous style, as we know from Sigurd Jorsalfar, and most of the North's young history, *a magnanimity of a peculiarly self-destructive kind*, but we will not drag that in here. Instead one prefers to linger by the humour expressed, which connects the thought of Hamsun with memories from the Jomsvikings' Saga, the tough, long-haired fellows who were executed after the battle of Hjørungavåg, and who went to their death with a fine joke on their lips and an admonishment to the executioner not to get blood on their long, yellow hair. One *hastened* to put them to death, *one cut them short*, their wit was able to dishonour the victors for the rest of their lives, indeed, for all time...
>
> No other man have I loved like Hamsun, my most treasured experience is to have met him and to have been alive in about the same generation as him.
>
> Whilst this is being written, autumn 1921, millions of Russian peasants are breaking away from their burned fields and going to the towns in hungry groups, eating grass, dying in thousands under the open sky, after all humanity, the animal too, has been burned out of them with glowing irons, no help possible... What right has one to live, to write in comfort, when such things happen?
>
> Whilst this is being printed, December 1922, I read that the peasants are eating their thatched roofs in the Ukraine. Thus, what one saw a year ago was much exaggerated, they are not all close to death yet.*

What we find ridiculous here is not Johannes V. Jensen's cynicism, but his infatuated admiration for exclusive self-assertion.

Cynicism is, however, the only answer to the question about what right one has to live, to write in comfort, when such things happen. Was this question posed in this unideological way anywhere else than in Scandinavia on that occasion?

He certainly said, 'The human race does not renew itself from the top, but from the root – o, superman,' but in his contempt for the 'masses' he creates just a new form of superman theory, 'the democratic'. But here we find in the heir of Almqvist, Gustav Fröding, a powerful answer to the philosophy of admiration or of 'you' in his ironic commentary to Nietzsche's Zarathustra doctrine:

Thus spoke Zarathustra

One night Zarathustra went up the mountains with his disciples to look at the stars. And as they sat on the mountain looking up at the sky and peering down into the valley, where the forest grew alongside the slopes, Zarathustra bowed his head and fell into thought. Then he lifted his head again and said, 'How often have I not said these words to you: Avoid virtue and endeavour to do what is evil, for you know that virtue is the talk of restricted slaves, and that evil is good for he who is the lord of evil and not its servant?

How often have I not exhorted you to love and enrich yourselves, and not your nearest, for life is short, and he who does others' deeds and not his own, he shall be like a dry tree, and the dry tree can never be used for the production of that brew that leads to the superman?

But when did I tell you that you should bind people with bonds, in order to be free yourselves? That is the custom of slaves, when they come to power. Or when did I say to you that you should beat and trample on those who fight with you for elevation? That is a slave custom.

Look down over the forest, and see how many treetops are shooting up above the others. Will the high tree become higher if the lower trees are chopped down? Or lift your eyes up to the thousands, indeed, hundreds of thousands of stars, sparkling in space. Do you believe that the star Sirius will shine with a clearer gleam if the others are put out? That is the belief of small boys.

So beware of slave customs and small boys' beliefs when you allow the superman to grow within you. Who knows whether he who thinks himself greatest, is the greatest? And could not he who is still slow-growing, but has great growing strength, be already greater than those already fully grown, who had less strength in the beginning and have already fulfilled the goal of their growth?

So let each and every one grow and illuminate according to his kind and custom and not be low-minded. He who illuminates strongest and most of all, when all have achieved their fullness and culmination, from his seed and sparks shall the superman be produced.'

Thus spoke Zarathustra and his disciples were sore amazed.

As we have already indicated, the human type is incapable of producing biological changes other than variations and cancerous tumours, and as the

348 *The Natural Order and Other Texts*

special aristocratic place in the body of society no longer serves any expansive purpose, as we have also demonstrated, it must be in the area of art and technology that unique and superhuman performances have to find their release in future. It is here that the interest is gathering.

Who are they then who endeavour to offer their special achievements in the unknown and why? But above all how do they get the strength for it? Here too we must admit that appearances are deceptive.

The most beautiful, most admired tree in the forest, the greatest and the strongest, is always the unfruitful tree that uses all its strength for its own expansion. The aesthetic is similarly barren when it is sufficient unto itself. The tree is felled and thrown into the fire, if we do not wish to preserve it as an ornamental tree for the sake of its beauty. Beauty is a sickness that shows itself in an apparently unique healthiness.

Detritus and compensation

> He who is lame, dances the best, and he who is dumb, sings the best.

A Swede has very appropriately described this purely aesthetic vitality as phallus with condom. Whether one wishes to *be* or to *have* a model, this is the statuesque and dead essence of monumentality or the pure model. This leads to the conclusion that *the model is not sought because of its potency but because of its impotence, that the aesthetician is a detritus, a parasite, a* 'taugenicht',[*] *a hanger-on, a surplus person because of ineptitude and the lacking ability to act in the productive context,* his lacking ability to realize and perfect himself in 'the good', in community. We no longer kill the sick and the old. We can afford to let them live. But the personality, the soul, can be fit even though the character is weak, and if this is the case, then we are confronted with the true aesthetician, who in compensation tries to justify his existence through action. Instead of saying, like Paul, 'For the good that I would, I do not do: but the evil I would not, that I do,' he is simply saying that *what one does is called good and what one does not do is called evil, and as I cannot do what one does, I must do what one does not do,* or like Lautréamont, 'If I cannot be perfect in the good, then I will be so in the evil.' This is a far more honest attitude, for *what one would but cannot do, is never in itself good.* The renewer's options are thus reduced. He 'can do no other', as Luther said, so there is neither reason for admiration nor contempt for the crimes he brings about.

The half-truth of the concept of cause figures strongly in the evaluation of the aesthetic artist. He is not an artist *because* he is unhealthy. He is able to choose sheer imperfection, sheer infirmity. But he could never achieve the unique *without* his infirmity.

350 *The Natural Order and Other Texts*

Aesthetics as obsession, despair or desperation

> Every aesthetic view of life is despair, and ... everyone who lives aesthetically is in despair whether he knows it or not.
>
> So choose despair then, since despair is in itself a choice, for one can doubt without choosing to, but despair one cannot with choosing to do so. And when one despairs one chooses again, and what does one then choose? One chooses oneself, not in one's immediacy, not as this chance individual, one chooses oneself in one's eternal validity.
>
> *Søren Kierkegaard*

Mortgaged and bewitched

One becomes an aesthetician just by, like Faust, selling or mortgaging one's soul. It is rightly said *that beauty can kill.* Thus Semele died, they say, when she saw the delightful Jupiter. This, the seeing of a new possibility invisible to all others, and to a certain degree also to oneself, makes the aesthetician obsessed or bewitched. If it has become a part of his ego, he can no longer adjust himself to the world of realities he previously found whole and correct and which for others is obvious. *Their opposition to realizing the new becomes for him a fetter of stupidity, bone-headedness, narrow-mindedness, bigotry, philistinism, bureaucratism, pigheadedness and perfidy because he himself is bound to it.*

An earthquake has occurred in his innards, he has the fragment of the magic mirror in his eye, so that everything others find good and natural to him is a grotesque sham. He has been bewitched, getting ideas in his head. He has been struck by elves and in order not to bleed to death, everything must be realized, *immediately, now, here.** His decision sets dreadful things in motion. The monster surges out with its incomprehensible demands. He loves, takes and gives, tears down only to build up again. But the more he gives, the more he realizes his human affiliation, the more people shrink from him, the lonelier he becomes.

He grieves and says: I cannot have given enough. But the more he gives, the harder it becomes to accept. So finally there he stands, shouting desperately out into the vacuum. Whatever he did, it was wrong. His love spread sorrow and destruction, and his creative ability shattered and dissolved. Therefore people still gathered in interest around this idiotic creature in order to strike him down in natural and healthy self-defence, to chase him away or lock him up. A curse that does not allow him to love on earth rests upon the man. He cannot facilitate his strength, cannot transform, has not the necessary strengths.

'He who wants everything in a particular way and as it is – is this admirable? Or if he would have it otherwise, but is unable, has not the strength for it – is this then admirable? Could you ask for more?' says Almqvist.

One can be an opponent of the aesthetic life-view because one is an opponent of despair and suffering. One can fight both parts, yes, ban them, declaring the aesthetic to be insane, criminal, unhealthy and perverted, but one thing one cannot do, if one throws oneself into this just fight, regardless of which artistic excuses are made. One cannot avoid being highly unaesthetic, ugly even.

The mad dogs

This then is the aesthetician's lot. Plato suggested crowning them with laurels and guiding them to the borders of the country with orders never to come back and some are still trying to realize that programme. That's what the authorities are for.

The artistic aesthetician is the prophet, the seer who lacks the strength because *he lacks the people*. Thus it can be from time to time. But it can also be whole social groups which, like the German peasants under the leadership of Thomas Münster in the Reformation, rose in rebellion in order to realize the new. Then the adherents of the 'established order' say, like Martin Luther, 'Strike them down like mad dogs.'

> A dead dog once lay in a market-place. A group of people had gathered around it according the custom of crows. They always gather around corpses. One said of the animal: Ugh, how it stinks, and the third added some other terms of abuse. In short, everyone expressed their contempt and disgust at the dead dog's body. Then the prophet of the Christians, Jesus of Nazareth, came walking by. He regarded the dog for some time and said: The teeth are as white as pearls.

These words were the highest manifestations of sympathy that could be offered to C.J.L. Almqvist when he was struck down and hunted from Sweden.* For those who had felt his teeth in their back, it was perhaps a directly sublime gesture to set up this monument to a talented attacker. But we think that *even the aesthetic must be known by its fruit more than by its uniqueness*. This was the point of view asserted by Almqvist, one we have here taken up anew.

352 The Natural Order and Other Texts

The living statue

> To injury is added shame and to fortune honour.

There is a folk story that tells of a *wonderful statue that comes to life if a ring is put on its finger*. Thus it is with all thoughts, all attempts and all experiments: only through their continuance, when they form chains, do they come to life.

Ludvig Feilberg is undoubtedly correct that it is only the most extraordinary *physical* phenomena that can be observed at all in existence.* Indeed, that earthquake-like disturbance of the picture of natural development, which creates a synthesis and can not fall back into the old folds, is probably the only remarkable one to be found, whether it be an upheaval of nature, an upheaval of society, an upheaval in the individual's attitude to life or just in the perception of a simple little problem. In the *existential sphere*, where the artist is his own object of experimentation, or in the political arena, these upheavals are a question of life or death. These are the hard conditions of the evolution of life.

The incredible reality

> Who sees me as I am, does not see who I am.
> *Hulda Lütken*

Art is what we cannot do. Thus goes the aesthetic definition of art. Therefore the artist who tries to do what he cannot do, the most imperfect and incomplete artist, must also be the greatest aesthetician. This undeniably places the evaluation of art in a completely new light.

All those innumerable people who dreamt big dreams they never achieved, thereby become the nucleus of artistic renewal, even though they only take the first step, regardless of where this lapse leads them and how ever much they may regret it afterwards. ·

Is it not magnificent that nothing is meaningless, that no one is a number, that no action, however absurd and idiotic it be, lacks this immediate meaning in itself? Is there any paradox any more? Let us grasp events with the warmth of enthusiasm, because they are events whatever happens. We say with Rimbaud, 'Kill yourself or not. But stop bathing yourself in our world of unprotected mortal dread, and enjoying our rotting cadavers in advance. Stop letting that revolver shaft, which inevitably invites a kick up the arse, stick out of your back pocket. Do not mock the true suicide with that eternal hesitation.'

This is what our conscience and experience has taught us about the extreme frontier of aesthetics. We have said it, and each must think what they will.

The humanization of the inhuman

Therefore Ebbe Skammelsøn rides many paths so wild.*

The footprints lead and frighten on the road we have been roaming here. It was Fröding who took the inheritance up after Almqvist and carried it further, until his mind darkened in hopeless ruminations. When we decided to go further down the same road, it was in full consciousness of the risk and danger contained in this decision, and with the will to pay the price. *No price seems to us too great to reach the goal of the recognition of human divinity and the divinity of humanity*, and Almqvist's dialogue in *Luna's Drama*, which contains the quintessence of our standpoint, could hardly have been more burningly topical when it was written than it is today: Indeed, perhaps it will always be life's great problem, its great contrast:

What daring – I admit it – what daring in such serious times as ours to venture a poetry, and not just dare to contain it, but even to jot it down, indeed, to broadcast it. At a time when great political conflicts, plans and worries keep people busy in the interests of states to such a high degree.

To such a high degree that the most razor-sharp wisdom, level-headedness and exclusion of fantasy and poetry are apparently necessary in those setting the trend, so that no step to the side, no blunder, shall put in train disasters of a thousand kinds or give one's opponent an advantage or one's adherents a drubbing. In a word, how should one describe the whim of being a poet in the year 1835?' {Or the year 1952?}, {1963, etc.?}.*

However, the friendliness with which I have been received {?} has encouraged me. I know that in truth I have trodden a new, an extremely free path, and that kind of thing needs an excuse: even though, apart from its own nature, it can be excused on the strength of its novelty and great freedom alone.

A poetry where the verses do not go their symmetrical and fast way forward independently of the subject, but where these suit themselves to the content and the thing to the degree that without them they would not mean anything at all, but fall to earth, and become nil.

A garb created after nature to the degree that it only suits what it should and nothing else, cannot be taken out and shown off as a beautiful suit by itself, without a body – what can one say about such a garb – about such a poor, impoverished form?

But what does surprise me is that you in times that are so political, as you said in your first remark, do not find yourself occasioned to tread the light path of politics instead of just at this moment making poetry.

Look, sir, I profoundly and inwardly acknowledge the significance of politics, the significance of the reorganization of society in everything that needs help, and that is a great deal, and that there can only be a few feelings, a few thoughts, a few opinions, a few minutes left over for those who work in society to listen to poetry, that I find quite natural. But nevertheless note something:

Youthful hearts and warm senses, crystal-clear and sensitive ideas still guard this fire in the land just as before and just as numerously. They guard it in silence, in the holy silence of foresight. They have no voice in society. They listen instead to songs and they sing themselves.

I love them and I know that they love me. An invisible, secret but almighty sympathy moves between the hearts that beat like ours. In the memory of them is what verse and poetry will awaken in me, were I even the least of them all here in the world that ventured to love.

Venture, why do you say that? What is it to dare to love?

It is to be capable of dying, sir. But once more: were I the least amongst those that ventured that most dangerous thing on the earth – to love – I would venture it, however, endlessly, immortally: And those who are greater in delightfulness than me would just love me, because I am small. Were my hand the poorest of all those who raise themselves in order to tug a little feather from the wings of the great, beautiful subjects flying azurine over people's heads – I would lift up my hands, as happy as a child, and those who are stronger than me would not disdain the light, airy feathers that I was now and then successful in tugging down from the wings – they would love me – I know it – love me, just because my hands are so poor.

When the question turns upon noble people who in purity, strength and greatness exceed their times, then is it not so that we regard them with admiration as rising in development *upwards*? Their character grows, their hearts are purified to an even more transparent crystal. Their thoughts, their horizons and their words are almost no longer those of humans. We see them hardly touching the earth with their feet, but their countenances and heads have such a light radiance that we sink back. We kneel almost as if for super-earthly beings and we drop our eyes down towards matter in order not to be dazzled. They leave us in their greatness and we cannot follow them, we small ones. They do not take us with them, they hardly lead us: if they took us by the hand their handshake would just crush it. Such a vision of the ascension of personality, of expansion, of motion upwards, of the making divine of a human being is what is commonly shown in the history of the female saints. Nevertheless this is not the case in Luna's drama. On the contrary.

Here is a human being, who *by consequence of nature and misfortune already stands high*, who even at the beginning of the scenes stands at the top

– but who thereafter goes forward, goes more and more *down* to humanity, is reduced, gathered and diminished to an individual of ordinary limitations. In other words: *the humanization of a heroic character* is what I feel is reflected here.

Can M. Hugo solve the puzzle and tell me if it is good? – if it is noble? If it is noble enough on the earth to be a human and nothing more?

Homo sum, humani nihil a me alienum puto.*
Terence

Notes

xii   ★ The passage to which Schultzer refers was not included in the revised second edition. It states that the book was written, 'upon a conviction that its appearance would offer a chance to provoke or force a decisive reckoning with Kantian as well as objectivistic aesthetics and, as it is carried out not by a scientist but an artist, this could be perceived as a proof that such a reckoning is not a purely scientific matter, but is in itself provoked by an untenable situation in the question about... the artistic experiment...'

3   ★ *Golden Horn and Wheel of Fortune* was written around 1950 but only published privately in 1957.

  ★ Christian Dotremont (1922-79), Belgian Surrealist poet, was a co-founder with Jorn and others of the Cobra Movement (1948-51). The two men spent several months sharing a room in a Danish sanatorium whilst suffering from tuberculosis in the winter of 1951-52.

6   ★ Gustav Fröding (1860-1911), Swedish lyric poet, whose speculative poetry came more and under the influence of Nietzsche. He spent much of his last two decades in mental institutions.

10   ★ P.O. Runge (1777-1810), Romantic painter was born in Wolgast in northwest Germany, but attended the Danish Royal Academy as a student in 1799-1801. Jorn is thus wrong about his Danish origin and actually called him Carl Otto Runge in error.

12   ★ Werner Heisenberg, *Physic and Philosophy*, Harmondsworth, Penguin, 1989, 32. Jorn made his rather loose Danish translations from the 1962 English edition. The italics are Jorn's. Even a casual reading of this book will demonstrate just how much *The Natural Order* is a commentary upon it and how the language therein is mirrored by Jorn.

13   ★ Ole Rømer (1644-1710), Danish astronomer who discovered the speed of light. H.C. Ørsted (1778-1860), Danish physicist who discovered electro-magnetism.

  ★ John Dewey, *Reconstruction in Philosophy*, New York, Mentor, 1955, 14. Jorn quotes in English but adds the italics.

  ★ Thorstein Veblen (1857-1929), American economist and social scientist. Although of Norwegian stock, he was born an American citizen. *The Theory of the Leisure Class* dates from 1899.

  ★ This is probably a reference to the wartime speeches of Winston Churchill.

17   ★ Much of the two preceding paragraphs is a close paraphrase of Heisenberg, op. cit, 103ff. However, although the Heisenberg text in its English translation speaks of a 'quantum jump', I have chosen to use 'leap' as Jorn later equates the quantum leap with Kierkegaard's 'leap of faith'.

21   ★ Harald Høffding (1843-1931), eclectic Danish philosopher who maintained a humanistically based utilitarian moralism in his ethics.

  ★ This is the only time that Jorn mentions Egon Friedell, whose theoretical work betrays a certain cultural cynicism, and whose *Aufklärung und Revolution* (Hamburg,

358 The Natural Order and Other Texts

Deutscher Taschenbuch Verlag, 1961: in Jorn's SISV library) he must have read about this time.

★ In Nordic mythology Loke or Loki is the cunning, prankish and transgressive god, whilst Thor, þórr or Donar is the defender of gods and men. They often accompany each other on expeditions to the land of the giants.

22　★ All the Bohr quotations in this book are from Niels Bohr, *Atomfysik og menneskelige Erkendelse*, Copenhagen, Schultz, 1958, although Jorn occasionally paraphrases or makes minor mistakes in transcription. All the translations are my own.

23　★ Probably Heisenberg, op. cit., 78, in very loose paraphrase, despite Jorn's quotation marks.

26　★ Jens Peter Jacobsen (1847-75), Danish poet and novelist who influenced the young Rilke. Jorn is referring to a series of influential free poetic meditations. Jorn uses an excerpt from the poem *Arabesque to a Drawing of Michelangelo* as an epigraph in *Luck and Chance*.

29　★ Short sentence with *non sequitur* about Denmark's position vis-à-vis the two Great Powers omitted, following Jorn's own example in his German revision.

31　★ Fridtjof Nansen (1861-1930), Norwegian polar explorer, zoologist and philanthropist who was awarded the Nobel Peace Prize in 1922.

32　★ Henry Heerup (1907-93), Danish artist associated with Jorn in the Høst and Cobra Groups. Heerup attended the Danish Royal Academy of Fine Arts as a student 1927-32.

35　★ In the first edition of *Philosophy in a New Key*, Langer uses the triad sign-symptom-symbol. This is replaced by signal-symptom-symbol in later editions. However, Jorn's SISV library contains only the first edition, so the origin of 'signal' remains problematic, but in certain places Jorn uses 'significative' and in others 'signalistic', where (from reference to the appropriate diagram) he obviously means the latter. I have therefore standardized on the latter.

40　★ Where I have translated 'the symptomatic and the symbolic', Jorn has 'the significative and the symbolic'. A reference to the diagrams will reveal that he made a mistake.

44　★ For 'truth-beauty-health' Jorn uses the untranslatable alliteration '*sandhed-skønhed-sundhed*', a triad he used for the first time in the 1953 first edition of *Luck and Chance* and repeated with obvious delight many times after.

45　★ Instead of 'ideal', Jorn has 'idea' in his diagram. This apparent error is, however, useful to indicate the association between the two words that exists in Jorn's thinking.

62　★ Erik Lundberg, *Arkitekturens Formspråk*, Stockholm, Nordisk Rotogravur, 1945, a very influential book on Jorn's art theories of the forties.

77　★ Probably Heisenberg, op. cit., but I cannot identify it from Jorn's translation.

79　★ 'Focal point' is in Danish '*brændpunkt*', literally 'burning point', and hence distance would increase coldness.

85　★ These two sentences are a reference to an epigram by the Dano-Norwegian poet Johan Herman Wessel (1742-85): *At kærlighed er ikke had/ og smørrebrød er ikke mad,/ det er fortiden alt jeg ved/ om smørrebrød og kærlighed* [That love is not hate and open sandwiches are not food, this is all I know at the moment about love and open sandwiches].

86　★ Where the English Bible has 'mote' in Matthew 7:3, the Danish Bible has 'splinter' (*splint*).

87　★ Moral Rearmament was a religious movement founded in 1921, which became very

Notes *359*

anti-communist after World War II. Its supposed popularity in Scandinavia was regarded with dismay by Jorn, who often used it as a metaphor for religious intolerance.

88 ★ Almost certainly a reference to the prominence that Kierkegaard gave to 'the absurd'.

★ The confusion is more apparent in Danish (and German) where 'actuality' is '*realitet*' (*Realität*) and 'reality' is '*virkelighed*' (*Wirklichkeit*). The use of 'really' and 'in reality' later in this passage does not appear to be ironic.

★ Two passages of some 500 words have been omitted from this chapter. They are concerned with speculations upon Danish etymology which would be incomprehensible to those who have no Danish, and are, indeed, obscure to those who do.

89 ★ Danish *hvor* (where) also gives rise to the compounds *hvornår* (when), *hvordan* (how), *hvorfor* (why, wherefore), etc, which Jorn is including here (see following paragraph). Although German and Dutch have some similar compounds, only the Scandinavian group of European languages offers such a clear interrogative triolectic of *who, where* and its compounds, *what* to give yet another strand to Jorn's perception that triolectics is a particularly Scandinavian way of thinking.

96 ★ Niels Steno (1638-86), Danish anatomist, geologist and theologian, who formulated the basic principles of geology and crystallography. His Danish name was Niels Stensen, in Latin Nicolaus Steno (or Stenovius), but Jorn has used a not uncommon hybrid of the two.

★ Carl von Linné (in Latin, Linnæus) (1707-78), Swedish botanist responsible for the binomial nomenclature which gives each species a two-part Latin name.

★ The division of archaeological time into Stone, Bronze and Iron Ages was first made by the Danish archaeologist C.J. Thomsen (1788-1865).

★ 'introduction or *cause*' are in Danish the alliterative 'indledning' and '*anledning*'.

★ *The Sickness unto Death*, in the eponymous book written by Kierkegaard in 1849 under the pseudonym Anti-Climacus, was, roughly speaking, the denial of Christian belief, especially in an after-life.

103 ★ Schiller's slogan '*In tyrannos*' [against the tyrants] is more familiar in Denmark than in English speaking countries.

★ Nathan Söderblom (1866-1931), Swedish archbishop and religious historian, prominent in the ecumenical movement.

104 ★ The *futhark* is the runic alphabet.

105 ★ King Gustav Adolphus of Sweden was one of the leaders of the Protestant forces in the Thirty Years War (1618-48).

★ Johannes Scotus Erigena, John Scot the Irishman (c. 810-70). *De Divisione Naturae* was one of his texts. In the much edited German version of *The Natural Order* (*Gedanken eines Künstlers*, 302) Jorn infers that as Ireland was overrun by the Vikings, Erigena could well have come under Norse influence before he went to France in 847.

★ Thomas Aquinas was born near Aquino in south Italy and never travelled farther north than Paris, but Jorn finds his Nordic origins in Thomas's Lombard father and the Norman family of his mother. The Lombards (Langobards) were originally a Germanic tribe and the Normans were descendants of Vikings. Jorn often went to these sorts of lengths to establish a Scandinavian connection.

★ J. Jugnet, *La pensée de Thomas d'Aquin*, Paris, Éditions Bordas, Paris, 1949.

106 ★ In 1961-62 Europe had two free trading groupings, the European Common Market (France, Belgium, Germany, Holland, Luxembourg, Italy) and the European Free Trade

360 *The Natural Order and Other Texts*

Association (Austria, Britain, Denmark, Norway, Portugal, Sweden, Switzerland with Finland and Iceland as associates).

108 ★ N.F.S.Grundtvig (1783-1872), Danish priest and poet, established the basis for the Folk High School movement. Grundtvig was a prominent polemicist for a distinct Scandinavianism.

★ Jeppe Aakjær (1866-1930), Danish social realist author and poet. Martin Andersen Nexø (1869-1954), Danish social realist author and prominent Communist, best known for the novel *Pelle the Conqueror*: he was especially acclaimed in the Iron Curtain countries and spent the last three years of his life in Dresden, then in East Germany.

109 ★ 'the transport of forces'.This is one of Jorn's personal associations. In 1937, together with two other students, Jorn worked as an assistant on Léger's huge canvas *Le Transport des Forces* (4.90 x 8.70 m.), installed in the Palais de la Découverte in Paris. The word 'transport' is the same in Danish as in English and covers the same scale from rapture to the carrying of goods.

★ Paul Mouy, *Logique et Philosophie des Sciences*, Paris, Hachette, 1944. Jorn calls him Morny.

★ Tyge (Latin = Tycho) Brahe (1546-1601), Danish astronomer.

111 ★ Bertel Thorvaldsen (1768/70-1844), internationally renowned Danish Neo-Classical sculptor.

★ Julius Lange (1838-96), Danish art historian, known internationally for his exposition of the frontality law of symmetrical composition in antique sculpture.

119 ★ Sorø Academy, on Sjælland, has been a boarding school since 1580 (originally for 30 noble and 30 middle-class pupils). In 1840, Grundtvig petitioned the king to have it made into an 'Academy for Life', where the prevalent classical-clerical studies would be abandoned in favour of an education based upon the Danish language and Scandinavian values, and where the system of 'Chinese examinations' (competitive contests) would be abolished. The suggestion was not taken up. Today Sorø Academy is a sixth form college in the state system with 170 boarders and 180 day students.

120 ★ In 1960, 121 French intellectuals signed a manifesto protesting against their government's actions in the Algerian war of independence. Jorn's description of the outcome is over-stated.

121 ★ Christian Christensen (1882-1960), Danish syndicalist.

★ Hartvig Frisch (1893-1950), Danish philologist and Social Democrat politician, who published an influential book on European cultural history in 1928 which was re-issued in 1962.

122 ★ This section was prefaced by 8 short extracts from *Das Kapital*. I have managed to identify 5 of these from Jorn's Danish versions but because the others include the use of the first person singular, rare in that book, I wonder if Jorn took them from an anthology mistaking their origins. In any case, these are only a small selection of the passages in Marx upon which Jorn bases his critique. For those who wish to look up the identified passages, they can be found in the 1976 Penguin translation of *Capital* at p. 126, ll. 11-13; p. 149, ll. 10-13; p. 152, ll. 26-32; p.317, ll. 19-24; p. 711, ll. 1-6.

123 ★ Jorn was obviously unaware that Marx himself thought of *Das Kapital* as a 'work of art' (Letter to Engels, August 1865) rather than a scientific hypothesis. This may not have changed the trajectory of Jorn's critique, but would certainly have affected his desire to defend Marx's scientific approach.

127 ★ Potlatch was the ceremony of the Kwakiutl and other Indians of the American north-

west in which there is a public distribution of goods where the holder of the ceremony claims status on the basis of his ability to give. Jorn made occasional contributions to the Lettriste Internationale periodical *Potlatch* in 1954-56.

131 ★ Jorn actually has N-A-C-M-A-C-N here, which must be wrong. This is confirmed by the earlier French version (PHH 199), where the formula is as given here.

145 ★ Palle Lauring, (b. 1909), Danish historian and author.

147 ★ Poul Henningsen (1894-1967), Danish architect and author, designed the well-known PH-lamp (1925) and was involved in many polemics on art and design.

152 ★ Here Jorn is referring to selective breeding to create the best astronauts/cosmonauts. He elaborated this further in *Alpha and Omega*.

154 ★ Translated from Jorn's Danish version.

★ Jorn seems unaware of Milosz's history and ability as a member of the Polish 'creative elite'. Czesław Milosz (b. 1911), prominent Polish poet and novelist (translated *The Waste Land* into Polish). As cultural attaché at the Polish Embassy in Paris he defected to the West in May 1951, moving to the USA in 1960. He could thus hardly be described as a hardened state apparatchik. He did, however, become a member of several CIA-supported anti-Communist enterprises, but even there he did not always toe the line. He was awarded the Nobel Prize for Literature in 1980.

★ See the General Introduction for a description of this Jarry-inspired organization. The Grove Press published *The Evergreen Review*, which had a number on pataphysics in May-June 1960.

★ Four artists of Gruppe Spur were prosecuted in Munich in May 1962 and received short sentences for blasphemy and indecency, which were reduced to suspended sentences on appeal in November 1962. Jorn, who had taken an interest in the group since 1959, was active in supporting their defence both with his influence in the art world and economically.

155 ★ Translated from Jorn's Danish version.

★ The obliteration of Stalingrad was a great symbol for Jorn. After hearing tales of the Russian campaign from an Italian veteran, Jorn painted the huge picture (296 x 492 cm.) *Stalingrad, no man's land or The mad laughter of courage*, in 1956, making considerable adjustments to it in 1957-60, 1967 and 1972. It is now at Silkeborg Art Museum.

★ Konrad Adenauer was the first Chancellor of W. Germany 1949-63.

156 ★ A reference to a well-known lampoon of 1790 by P.A. Heiberg : 'Orders one hangs on idiots,/stars and sashes one gives only to the noble', etc., for which the poet was fined 150 rigsdaler for having 'grumbled about the government'.

158 ★ I strongly suspect that these two sentences describe what Jorn saw as the alternatives before the Situationniste Internationale (from which he had resigned in 1960) and his younger brother Jørgen Nash's Bauhaus Situationist (from which he distanced himself in 1962).

160 ★ Hal Koch (1904-1963), Danish theologian.

161 ★ Denmark once had a number of colonies and dependencies. Norway was ceded to Sweden in 1815 and became independent in 1907. Iceland declared independence during World War II. Tranquebar in India was sold in 1845 and some Gold Coast forts in 1850, all to Great Britain. The Danish West Indies were sold to USA in 1917. Sweden sold St. Barthélemy in the West Indies to France in 1878. Of the Scandinavian colonies etc., only Greenland and the Faeroes remain as autonomous parts of Denmark.

362 *The Natural Order and Other Texts*

★ The use of the neologism situcracy (and in other places situlogy and situmetry) suggests alignment with Situationniste Internationale theory. I do not find much in Jorn's thought of this period that matches the direction of contemporaneous SI thought.

★ 'not entangled'. Jorn here presumably means that, as he is not resident in Denmark, he has a broader view of the situation.

★ In 1962 Europe had two free trading groupings, the European Common Market (France, Belgium, Germany, Holland, Luxembourg, Italy) and the European Free Trade Association (Austria, Britain, Denmark, Norway, Portugal, Sweden, Switzerland with Finland as associate). Great Britain, followed by Denmark, attempted to join the European Common Market in 1961, and this was widely seen in Europe as reneging on their commitments to EFTA.

★ In 1807, during the Napoleonic Wars, the British, despite not being at war with Denmark, sequestrated most of the Danish fleet docked in Copenhagen. This still rankles with Danes today.

164 ★ Here Jorn is again referring to the Gruppe Spur affair in Munich in 1962.

★ Georg Brandes (1842-1927), atheist and anti-authoritarian Danish literary critic: a very influential personality in the European and Danish cultural life of his time.

167 ★ C.J.L. Almqvist (1793-1866), Swedish poet, dramatist and author. His pamphlet *The Importance of Swedish Poverty* (1838) has been described as 'a classic of national self-characterization' (*The Penguin Companion to Literature: Europe*).

168 ★ From J.P. Jacobsen's poem 'So stopped there the current of blood' from c. 1884.

170 ★ Jorn first attempted this definition in the 1953 edition of *Luck and Chance*, which, in its 1963 edition, is now the third part of this book.

171 ★ K.E. Løgstrup, *Kunst og Etik*, Copenhagen, Gyldendal, 1962.

★ *No*, a vaudeville of 1836 by J.L. Heiberg (1791-1860).

★ David Siqueiros was sentenced to four years imprisonment in 1960 for illegal political activities.

173 ★ Komintern: the Third Internationale (1919-1943), founded as a worldwide revolutionary organization (later became a tool for Soviet foreign policy). Kominform: Communist Information Bureau (1947-56), contact organization for collaboration between Communist Parties.

174 ★ 'an enemy of the people', a reference to Ibsen's play (called in one translation 'A Public Enemy') of 1882 about the various ambivalences of a small community when a principled but politically naive doctor blows the whistle on a pollution scandal which would require an enormous amount of money to correct. It ends with the statement that 'the strongest man in the world is he who stands most alone'.

177 ★ This is almost certainly Henry Moss, *The Birth of the Middle Ages 395-814*, London, Oxford University Press, which was re-issued as a paperback in 1963 (earlier editions 1935 & 1957).

★ Absalon (1128-1201), Danish archbishop and statesman, foster brother of Valdemar I the Great (reigned 1154-82). Absalon was a member of the powerful Hvide family, which supported the royal house in the so-called Valdemar Period (1154-1241). However, in 1282 Danish nobles, including the Lord High Constable Stig Andersson Hvide, attempted to curtail King Erik Klipping's autocratic power by making him sign a Royal Charter promising collaboration with his nobles. In 1286 nine constitutionalist nobles were banished for the murder of the King, and Hvide and his allies waged war against Denmark for two decades from a base in Norway.

Notes 363

★ 'Muslims and Germans'. By this anachronism Jorn presumably means the Levantine peoples (who later became Muslims) and the Germanic tribes.

178 ★ In 1960 Jorn had painted *Dead Drunk Danes* (now at the Louisiana Museum of Modern Art, Humlebæk), a title with obvious reference to Eisenhower's remarks. Ironically, this was the very painting which won the Guggenheim Prize which Jorn refused in late 1963 (after this book was published).

179 ★ Jorn is referring to the death of the Swedish UN Secretary-General in a mysterious air crash over Africa in 1961.

180 ★ This sloppy shift from 'art' to 'they' is one of the reasons I believe that this part of this book was written at speed and without revision.

★ Tøk, or þøkk in Old Norse, was a giantess, thought by some to be the god Loki in disguise, who would not weep at the death of the beautiful god Balder and thus prevented him returning from the underworld. The sentence here, couched in the language of the sagas, means Tøk is not weeping.

181 ★ 'a couple of noughts'. Jorn is probably referring to the French devaluation of 1959 when 1,000 old francs became 1 new franc.

183 ★ Carl-Henning Pedersen (b. 1913), Danish artist, associated with Jorn in several groups, including Cobra, in the period 1937-51.

186 ★ Jorn here, as in his introduction, is referring to the increasing use of the Folk High Schools as ordinary educational or training establishments, instead of following the original ideas of offering Danes education in social and cultural values without an apparatus of examination and competition.

190 ★ 'I know a lark's nest, I will not say where...' This song, with music by Carl Nielsen, is typical of those sung at assembly in Danish schools. Jorn's point is, however, that the words are by the poet Harald Bergstedt (1877–1965), a Nazi sympathizer during the war. Bergstedt's film *The Feast of St. George* had a nationalist theme, of the type from which Jorn wished to disassociate himself.

★ Finland war, The Germano-Finnish war of 1939-40 followed by the Russo-Finnish war of 1941-44. This caused great heart-searching amongst Communists in other Scandinavian countries.

★ Hans Kirk (1898-1962), Danish Social Realist author. Jorn is here being magnanimous as Kirk was one of the hard-line Party members who dismissed the art of Jorn and his colleagues as having no relevance to the Communist cause in 1948.

191 ★ 'Chessmann affair'. Caryl Chessmann (1921-60), American criminal executed in 1960 after trial for kidnapping 12 years earlier. His four books (1954-60) contributed to the contemporaneous debate about capital punishment.

197 ★ C. Wright Mills, *The Power Elite*, New York, Oxford University Press (Galaxy), 1959.

198 ★ Probably C. Wright Mills, op. cit., but I cannot recognize the passage from Jorn's translation, although it is certainly consistent with the thesis there, see pp. 13, 23, 324, int. al.

204 ★ The masculine bias in this chapter, as elsewhere, is Jorn's own.

206 ★ In 1953 Max Bill took over the *Technische Hochschule für Gestaltung* in Ulm in order to further what he claimed were Bauhaus ideals. After Jorn's offer of cooperation was refused, there ensued a long acrimonious exchange of letters. Jorn then formed the *Mouvement international pour un bauhaus imaginiste contre un bauhaus imaginaire* which lasted until it was incorporated into the *Situationniste Internationale* in 1957.

364 The Natural Order and Other Texts

★ Vilhelm Grønbech (1873-1948), Danish religious historian, whose liberal works on the special qualities of contrasting cultural forms were translated into German before World War II.

★ Selma Lagerlöf (1858-1940), Swedish author. Her first and best novel, *Gösta Berling's Saga*, lauds the life of the imagination and impulse over that of law and order.

210 ★ A line from *The Song of History* by Jeppe Aakjær (1866-1930).

★ *Mennesket i Centrum*, Copenhagen, Fremad Forlag, 1953. Hans Hedtoft was the then Danish Prime Minister, and Julius Bomholt, the then Education Minister. Both were Social Democrats.

211 ★ Louisiana, a museum for modern art at Humlebæk, north of Copenhagen, now one of the great modern art museums of the world.

213 ★ Robert Estivals, *L'Avant-Garde Culturelle Parisienne depuis 1945*, Édition Guy le Prat, Paris, 1963.

214 ★ Jorn includes this essay in irony in *Luck and Chance*, see p.347.

219 ★ From scene VI of Almqvist's play *Ramido Marinesco*.

222 ★ 'The individual' here is Kierkegaard's 'individual'. Kierkegaard writes that '"The individual" is the category through which, in a religious aspect, this age, this history, humanity must pass.' This and a long elaboration can be found in *Synspunktet for min Forfatter-Virksomhed* (Two 'Notes' concerning my Activity as an Author).

223 ★ Immanuel Ibsen (1887-1944). The lecture mentioned was published under the aegis of the Host Exhibition Group with a foreword by Jorn. (PHH 44).

★ *Helhesten* (The Horse of Hel) was a Danish art periodical issued in defiance of the occupying German authorities during World War II. It appeared in 9 numbers between 1941 and 1944. Vol. 1 no. 2 was dated 10.5.41.

★ Sigurd Næsgaard (1883-1956), Danish psychologist influential in the introduction of Freud's psycho-analysis to Denmark and in its effects on Danish art-life. Jorn and several of his artist colleagues were under analysis with him in the period 1938-1945.

224 ★ Jorn actually lists these as '*Dansk Kunsthåndværk, A5 Menighedsblad for unge arkitekter, Arkitekten (Meddelelser fra Akademisk Arkitektforening)* and the Swedish architectural journal *Byggmästeren (Organ for Stockholms Byggnadsförening, Svenska Arkitektföreningen)*, the Dutch architectural journal *Forum* and others.'

★ The *Cobra* magazine was the organ of the Cobra Group and appeared in 8 issues in 1949-1951: a further proof issue from 1951 was published in 1980. *Golden Horn and Wheel of Fortune* was not published (privately) until 1957. Jorn apparently follows the anthropological distinction between animism, a belief in intrinsic spirits, in, for example, trees or stones, and animatism, a belief in diffuse, impersonal spiritual power, but appears to equate the latter with the state of artistic creation, something he sees related to ideas of magic and shamanism.

227 ★ Suresnes was the location of the Maison des Danois, a house for Danish artists in Paris, where Jorn stayed in 1950-51.

★ This article was first published in 1988 in the Hofman Hansen bibliography. Jorn was the first person to translate Kafka's work from German into Danish, a couple of stories being published in *Helhesten* in 1941-42.

★ Pierre Wemaëre (b. 1913), French painter and tapestry designer. Fellow-student at Léger's academy and life-long friend of Jorn.

228 ★ Haftmann made this remark in the introduction to *Schweizer Suite*, a portfolio of 23 engravings from 1961.

★ Kant. In the subsequent paragraphs Jorn quotes from the early *Beobachtungen über das Gefühl des Schönen und Erhaben*, almost certainly from Kant, *Die drei Kritiken*, Stuttgart, Alfred Kröner, 1960. Where I can identify passages in Jorn's idiosyncratic translation I have used the John T. Goldthwait translation (Kant, *Observations on the Feeling of the Beautiful and Sublime*, Berkeley, University of California Press, 1991), slightly adjusted to follow Jorn's drift.

229 ★ Jens August Schade (1903-78), Danish lyric poet. Friend of Jorn from 1938 until his death.

231 ★ Birkerød, a middle-class suburb of Copenhagen.

233 ★ Raymond Aron, *Dix-huit leçons sur la société industrielle*, Paris, 1962.

237 ★ Jorn gives no source for the quotations in this chapter.

245 ★ Jorn's use of the masculine possessive pronoun here (and in similar passages) appears to be quite deliberate. The Danish nouns for 'ego', 'body', and 'individual' are neuter and Jorn flouts the rule that to be correct grammatically they require a possessive pronoun of the same case.

246 ★ Erwin Panofsky, *Studies in Iconology*, New York, Harper & Row, 1962. Jorn quotes this in the original English (with a couple of spelling mistakes).

247 ★ The whole of this paragraph is a riposte to a review of Jorn's ceramic relief in the State Sixth Form College in Aarhus in1959. Joakim Skovgaard (1856-1933), assisted by Niels Larsen Stevns (1864-1941) and others, covered the recently heavily (and clumsily) restored medieval Viborg Cathedral with over 2,500 square metres of frescos in a naive neo-Romanesque style (1901-06). Grundtvig's Church in Copenhagen (1921-40) was a radical reinterpretation of the Danish traditional step-gabled village church in cathedral dimensions. Niels Hansen Jacobsen (1861-1941) was a Symbolist sculptor responsible for several public projects. Thorvald Bindesbøll (1846-1908), architect, sculptor and ceramicist was a representative of that muscular Jugendstil which laid the foundation to much of the Danish design tradition. I take the final sentence of the paragraph to be ironical.

251 ★ Translation from Charles Baudelaire (trans. Carol Clark), *Selected Poems*, London, Penguin,1995.

★ Jorn presumably means *Taras Bulba*, the novella by Gogol, but I cannot find the passage in the Constance Garnett English translation (Nikolay Gogol, *Mirgorod*, London, Chatto & Windus, 1928).

252 ★ The Swedenborg Enquiry Centre in Beckenham cannot trace this quotation, so this must be seen as a doubtful attribution.

254 ★ Nis Petersen (1897-1943), Danish poet and novelist.

★ Carl Julius Salomonsen (1874-1924), Danish doctor & professor. His lecture and later book from 1919 was called *Infectious mental disorders in the past and now with special regard to the newest art directions.* He used the term 'dysmorphism' [*dysmorfisme*] to describe what he thought was poorly executed and ugly. Jorn uses both this term and a 'translation' or (unconscious?) anagram of it as 'dysformism' [*dysformisme*].

257 ★ Erik Arup (1876-1951), Danish historian, wrote *A History of Denmark* in 3 volumes (1925-55).

★ Meïr Aron Goldschmidt (1819-87), Danish author, was involved in the *Corsair*-affair, when Kierkegaard was mercilessly lampooned.

366 The Natural Order and Other Texts

263 ★ This is presumably a loose translation of aphorism 1009 from *Der Wille zur Macht*: '*Gesichtespunkte für meine Werte: ob aus der Fülle oder aus dem Verlangen?*'

265 ★ Charles Lalo wrote several books on aesthetics in the 1920s and 1930s. Graham Birtwistle, op. cit. (Bibliography), 66-67, 97, speculates that Jorn probably read *Eléments d'une Esthétique Musicale Scientifique* but I have as yet been unable to locate a copy of this. It is quite likely that a title combining 'scientific' with 'aesthetics' would have caught Jorn's attention.

★ Jorn has 'luxury-produced' (*luksuskroducede)* here, but this is probably a printer's error as 'luxury producing' (*luksusproducerende*) fits the bill better.

267 ★ In 1937, whilst a student at Léger's Academy, Jorn enlarged a child's drawing for le Corbusier's *Pavillon des temps nouveaux* at the Paris World Exhibition. Over the next decade, Jorn moved from admiration (expressed in an article in 1938) to strong opposition of le Corbusier's principles.

269 ★ Karl Vennberg (b.1910), Swedish lyric poet with socialist convictions and a strong opposition to fixed ideas and ideals.

272 ★ Erik Nyholm (1911-90), Danish ceramicist, one of Jorn's closest friends.

275 ★ Hulda Lütken (1896-1946), Danish poet and novelist.

★ 'Red roses grow from sorrow and anger', a paraphrase of the refrain from a poem *It bodes ill* (*Der bødes der for*) by J.P. Jacobsen (1847-85): 'There springs sorrow, springs anger from roses red.'

284 ★ Jorn quotes this inaccurately in English as 'Out of this needle *danger* wee pluck this flower *safety*.' (*Henry IV, pt. 1*, II, iii).

290 ★ Strindberg's hallucinatory diary/prose poem *Inferno* was published in 1897. It describes his state of mind when conducting pseudo-scientific experiments to prove his monist theories, as set out in his book *Anti-Barbarus*.

291 ★ The dragon stem is the prow of a Viking ship. See, for example, the famous Oseberg ship.

★ Ragnarok in Norse mythology is the final great battle where the gods and the giants destroy each other, and a new world comes into existence.

293 ★ Johannes Holbek (1873-1903), Danish Symbolist artist and writer. Jorn organized the first retrospective of his work in 1965.

★ Horseplay = *hundekunster* (lit. 'dog-arts'), usually translated as 'tomfoolery' or 'monkey tricks'.

★ Robert Storm Petersen (1882-1949), Danish Expressionist artist, book illustrator and popular satirical cartoonist, who also wrote penetrating texts upon art.

295 ★ All the quotations of Taine are translated from the Danish version used by Jorn (Taine's aesthetic theses were translated into Danish in 1867, 1868 & 1873).

298 ★ This division corresponds to the epic, lyric and lyric-epic (dramatic) Hegelian triad proposed by J.L. Heiberg ((1791-1860), Danish dramatist and author), in 1828 and endorsed and elaborated by Kierkegaard in his diary in 1836.

300 ★ This aphorism of Sir John Harrington was quoted in English without attribution.

★ Jorn has '*scientia intention*' here, but this is obviously an error.

302 ★ This section is an unacknowledged critique of Kierkegaard's perception of truth, particularly the much-discussed 'Subjectivity, inwardness, is truth' and the various passages on 'the witnesses for truth'.

Notes 367

309 ★ It may be that Jorn here was attempting a cross-language pun (*urt* = herb in Danish). If so, this is a very early example of what became quite common in his picture titles of the sixties.

309 ★ In Danish 'transformation, change, refinement' is another of Jorn's prized alliterative triads: '*forvandling, forandring, forædling*'.

313 ★ Ingmar Hedenius (1908-82), Swedish philosopher of the Uppsala school of atheistic or agnostic persuasions.

314 ★ Quoted in English.

315 ★ Arnulf Øverland (1889-1968), Norwegian poet and, after 1945, opponent of Modernism.

316 ★ Johannes V. Jensen (1873-1950), Danish poet, novelist and essayist, who was a big influence on Jorn.

323 ★ A reference to the Button Moulder's ladle in Ibsen's *Peer Gynt*.

332 ★ A popular perception of stereotypical antipathy between the Scandinavian countries is as persistent there as that of similar feelings between the regions of the United Kingdom.

336 ★ See Kierkegaard's 1835 diary entry: 'It is also interesting that Faust (who as the more mediate, it might be more correct to make into the third point of view) embodies both Don Juan and the Wandering Jew (despair). – / Nor should it be forgotten that Don Juan has to be grasped lyrically (therefore with music); the Wandering Jew epically, and Faust dramatically.' It is easy to see how this refers back to Jorn's definitions of realism, naturalism and idealism, but the transformation in this section into the German, the English, the French and, with the addition of Hamlet, Scandinavia seems to be sheer unexplained poetic correspondence. In the fourth book in this series of reports, *Thing and Polis*, Jorn uses the triad Ahasuerus, Hamlet, Don Quixote to represent 'the European triumvirate of fools'.

★ Jorn uses the same word, *stadier*, for what I have translated here as 'spheres of existence' and 'stages'. Here I am following Jorn's 'mentor' Kierkegaard who used the same word for his triad of aesthetics, ethics, religion for both stages and point-of-view and then wrote 'there are three spheres of existence, the aesthetic, the ethical, the religious' (*Concluding Scientific Postscript*, Ch. 4, sect II, § 2).

337 ★ This is a double anachronism. Nelson took part in the Battle of Copenhagen in 1801 (the famous 'I see no ships' incident), but was dead by the British Bombardment of Copenhagen in 1807. 'England expects...' was Nelson's rallying call at the battle of Trafalgar in 1805. Jorn originated the error in the title of a painting from 1949 (see Atkins, *Jorn in Scandinavia*, 67-68). In 1953 there was an exchange of newspaper articles and letters on whether this was a conscious anachronism between 'Amalie Nelson' (pseudonym for the anti-abstract art critic H.P. Rohde), the abstract painter Mogens Andersen and Jorn (see memorandum by Per Hofman Hansen in Silkeborg Art Museum archives).

338 ★ In Rimbaud's original, the final sentence comes first. Jorn often 'mangled' quotations by re-arranging sentences (see also a few of the Kierkegaard quotations).

★ Almqvist's pamphlet *The Importance of Swedish Poverty* (1838) has been described as 'a classic of national self-characterization' (*The Penguin Companion to Literature: Europe*).

343 ★ This is a untranslatable play on words: superstition is *overtro* (lit: excess of belief), scepticism is *undertro* (lack of belief).

368 *The Natural Order and Other Texts*

★ 'chest of drawers': in 1937 Jorn illustrated the book *Kommodetyven* (The Thief of the Chest-of-Drawers) by J.A.Schade with a set of collages, but the book was eventually published in 1939 with vignettes by Schade himself. Around 1948, Jorn attempted in vain to publish a French version including his illustrations.

★ This paragraph contains a series of word plays: *magt* (power), *magi* (magic), *magisk* (magical), *mager* (magician), *-mager* (-maker). The three base words *magt/magi/-mager* are all of different etymological origins.

★ This Bernard Shaw quotation is re-translated from Jorn's Danish version.

346 ★ This rather repetitious text by Johannes V. Jensen (see note to p. 316) has been cut by about 25%. Knut Hansum (1859-1950), Norwegian writer (Nobel Prize 1920), Nazi sympathizer during World War II (hence Jorn's adjective 'regrettable'). Bjørnstjerne Bjørnsson (1832-1910) Norwegian writer and poet (Nobel Prize 1903). Sigurd Jorsalfar (Sigurd the Crusader), Norwegian king 1103-1130. Jomsvikings' Saga, Icelandic, c. 1200.

348 ★ *'taugenicht'*, German: good-for-nothing.

349 ★ 'struck by elves'. In the medieval Danish ballad *Elveskud*, a knight riding to his wedding is accosted by the elf-king's daughter, who asks him to dance with her. He refuses all her offers of worldly goods to comply. She strikes him and he eventually bleeds to death.

350 ★ Almqvist fled Sweden in 1851 to avoid a charge of attempted murder by poisoning.

351 ★ Ludvig Feilberg (1849-1912), Danish philosopher, who postulated four qualitative grades of mental activity, the simple reaction, purposefulness and rationality, artistic sensibility, awareness of the divine.

352 ★ Refrain of a medieval Danish ballad about a man pursued by an evil fate.

★ All the fragments in {} are insertions by Jorn.

354 ★ 'I am a man, and reckon nothing human alien to me.' (*Heauton Timoroumenos*, 25). This was Karl Marx's favourite maxim (in the mid-1860s).